6123938

D1526241

Domestic DEVILS, Battlefield ANGELS

Domestic DEVILS, *Battlefield* ANGELS

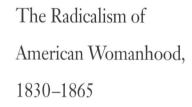

The Radicalism of
American Womanhood,
1830–1865

Barbara Cutter

NORTHERN ILLINOIS UNIVERSITY PRESS / *DeKalb*

Published by the Northern Illinois University Press, DeKalb, Illinois   60115
Manufactured in the United States using acid-free paper

Design by Julia Fauci

Library of Congress Cataloging-in-Publication Data
Cutter, Barbara.
Domestic devils, battlefield angels: the radicalism of American womanhood, 1830–1865 /
Barbara Cutter.
    p.   cm.
Includes bibliographical references and index.
ISBN 0-87580-318-1 (alk. paper)
1. Women—United States—History—19th century. 2. Women in public life—United States—
History—19th century. 3. Sex role—United States—History—19th century. 4. United States—
Social conditions—19th century. 5. United States—Moral conditions. I. Title.
HQ1418.C88 2003
305.4'0973'09034—dc21
2003052701

"Hooking a Victim": Lith. Serrell and Perkins, New York by Gas-Light, ca. 1850, Museum of the City of New York, Gift of Karl Schmidt, 37.361.423.

Engraving of Elizabeth Taylor Greenfield: Print Collection, Miriam and Ira Wallach Division of Art, Prints and Photographs, The New York Public Library, Astor, Lenox and Tilden Foundations.

Portrait of Charlotte L. Forten Grimké: Photographs and Prints Division, Schomburg Center for Research in Black Culture, The New York Public Library, Astor, Lenox and Tilden Foundations.

To my parents, John and Bernadine Cutter

Contents

Acknowledgments

Many people have helped me a great deal with this project over the years. Twenty years ago at Phillips Academy, Kathy Dalton and Tony Rotundo first got me interested in history. In more recent years, they have given me much friendly advice about graduate school and the history profession, and they have also read and provided very helpful comments on parts of this manuscript. I am indebted to Elizabeth Blackmar at Columbia, who worked with me closely when I applied to graduate school. At Rutgers University, my dissertation advisor, Alice Kessler-Harris, has been an excellent mentor and a critical reader in the best sense of the term. Jackson Lears's advice on the manuscript at various stages and his wry sense of humor were also indispensable. Mary Kelley, my outside reader, provided many insightful comments. Jim Livingston was always ready to give smart advice or to insult a hostile critic. Friends like Rosanne Curarrino, Ann Pfau, Nikki Shepardson, David Hyde, Elise Lemire, Sara Diamond, Christine Skwiot, Leslie Harris, and Katie Crawford discussed ideas and read and commented on various chapters.

The Rutgers University Graduate College at New Brunswick provided the majority of the financial support for this project, awarding me two years of fellowships and several more years of teaching assistantships, including two years in the University Writing Program. Kurt Spellmeyer, Richard Miller, and the rest of the Writing Program staff ran an exciting and innovative program. Their approach to writing transformed my teaching and vastly improved my writing.

I am greatly indebted to the staff at several archives and libraries, including the New York Historical Society, the New York Public Library, the Library of Congress, the Boston Public Library, the Massachusetts Historical Society, the Library Company of Philadelphia, the Peabody-Essex Museum, the Alexander Library at Rutgers University, and the Rod Library at the University of Northern Iowa. I particularly want to thank Joanne Chaison, Tom Knowles, Gigi Barnhill, Caroline Sloat, Marie Lamoureux, Laura Wasowicz, Dennis Laurie, and Sara Hagenbuch at the American Antiquarian Society for all their help with this project.

I would like to thank the history department at the University of Northern Iowa for a course reduction to give me time to finish up the project. I am also extremely grateful for the financial support for the project I have received at UNI, including a summer fellowship and a project grant from the Graduate College, and a summer fellowship through the College of Social and Behavioral Sciences. My colleagues also have been extremely supportive: Nora Jaffary read parts of the manuscript and provided important suggestions; a number of history department colleagues gave grant-writing advice and answered countless petty questions about book contracts and publishers' questionnaires. My editor at Northern Illinois University Press, Martin Johnson, also has been wonderful and has moved this manuscript along quickly and painlessly (for me anyway).

My parents, John and Bernadine Cutter, have provided me with endless support, including love, boundless faith in this project, and a cool place to write in the summer. Without them, I can safely say, this book would not have been written. My siblings, Lynn, John, and Susan; my sister-in-law Lynn Cutter; and my brother-in-law Dave Compton also have been supportive in a myriad of ways. My niece and nephew, Megan and Joshua Cutter, have inspired me by becoming budding historians themselves.

Of course, most of all my thanks go to my favorite colleague, my husband, Brian Roberts. It is impossible to list all the things I have to thank him for, but here are a few representative items: for knowing what my book is about as well as I do and sometimes better, for being such an insightful and honest critic, for cooking dinner while allowing me to continue in my own blissful culinary ignorance, for moving to Iowa, for naming the trees in our yard, and for never expecting me to be his "better half."

Domestic
DEVILS,
Battlefield
ANGELS

Introduction

Angels, Devils, and Redemptive Womanhood

*I*n December 1843, Polly Bodine, the daughter of "highly respectable" parents, allegedly beat and stabbed her sister-in-law and baby niece to death, then set them on fire to cover up the crime. According to her accusers she did so "with fiendish joy," "drunk with murderous longing."[1] Bodine's story is not unique; hers is only one of many mid-nineteenth-century accounts wherein apparently respectable white women are accused of committing horrific murders. The accused murderesses endlessly fascinated nineteenth-century Americans. Male and female spectators packed themselves into courtrooms to witness their trials. Printers published their life stories and accounts of the trials in newspapers, journals, and pamphlets; fiction writers turned their lives into novels, and a large audience of readers bought these accounts. Local citizens made pilgrimages to murder sites; in the Bodine case, they scavenged through the burnt remains of the victims' house, looking for relics of the crime. Where such female murderers did not exist, publishers invented them: pamphlets detailing the adventures of entirely fictitious middle-class murderesses far outnumbered those about actual middle-class women accused of murder.

This fascination was not limited to murderesses. It also extended to women—often, but not always, white or middle-class—who performed or were accused of performing a variety of public actions: "fallen women," as Americans described virtually all women who engaged in sexual activity outside marriage; female public lecturers; and female nurses, soldiers, and other Civil War workers. These were not the only kinds of women at the center of debates over the meaning of womanhood, but they were very prominent figures in such discussions. What did Americans think these very different groups of women had in common? What was simultaneously fascinating and troubling about the criminal behavior of some women and the benevolent activities of others? A look at the public and private discussions surrounding all four types of women reveals that their actions raised key questions about women's nature at a time when the meanings of womanhood, and of society in general, were in rapid transition. Debates about these women always centered on the question of what constituted proper womanhood; they were always investigations of whether the particular woman under scrutiny fell inside or outside the boundaries of propriety. These debates, then, are a unique window into the relationship between nineteenth-century ideals of proper womanhood and the lives of actual women. They are sites where Americans worked through the relationship between their gender ideology and female behavior. By revealing what Americans, male and female, believed about women, they shed light on the question of what it meant to be a woman in antebellum and Civil War–era America.

As historians have long pointed out, nineteenth-century Americans tended to divide women into two starkly opposite groups: good and evil, true and untrue, angels and devils. But *good* and *evil* are general and elusive terms. When antebellum Americans described a specific woman as good or true, they might well have been praising her for behavior that other Americans would consider sinful or untrue. For example, in the early 1840s, one Connecticut minister preached that a good woman was a Christian woman, and a Christian woman would not violate "the clearest commands of God . . . [that] women keep silence in the churches." In this sermon, the minister's specific goal was to condemn abolitionist public lecturer Abby Kelley as a "Jezebel" and a "servant of Satan" because instead of keeping silent she held public lectures on slavery. Kelley and her coworkers did not accept this assessment. In a letter to Kelley, Sarah Baker, the secretary of the Dorchester Female Anti-Slavery Society, asserted that virtuous women must speak out in public against slavery. As Baker put it, it was "a sin for woman to stay at home and remain silent" in a nation that tolerated slavery.[2] As this example illustrates, if Americans agreed that proper women must be virtuous, they did not agree on what specific behaviors virtuous women would or would not perform.

When antebellum Americans described the attributes of proper women, a few common themes did come up in virtually every discussion: proper women ought to be particularly moral, religious, and nurturing—that is, willing to sacrifice their own interests to care for and protect others. Still, agreement on these general tenets of proper womanhood did not prevent Americans from reaching opposite conclusions about the character of specific women. For example, virtually all antebellum writers agreed that one component of woman's special moral nature was her sexual purity. Proper women should not have sexual relations outside of marriage. George Foster, journalist and author of numerous urban exposés, and reformer Caroline Dall agreed on this point. According to Foster, "After a woman once enters a house of prostitution . . . [she] is transformed into a devil and there is no hope for her."[3] Yet, while Dall despised prostitution and believed that it degraded women's character, she saw the matter in a different light. She argued that in the ranks of prostitutes "there are women nobler and more disinterested than those who remain pure . . . women working for their kindred; a young girl of seventeen ruined to find bread for a crippled sister."[4] According to Dall, a prostitute who worked to earn money to care for her incapacitated sister might be nobler than a sexually pure woman who did nothing to help others, because the former was acting on her womanly duty to nurture others, while the latter ignored that obligation. In this account, motives are the key to women's character.

If gender ideology theoretically divided women into the rigid categories of good and evil, the moment Americans discussed specific women these apparently clear-cut boundaries began to collapse. Because one had to understand a woman's motives to determine whether she was proper, if a woman asserted that her motives were good, it was difficult for Americans to be certain she was improper. To judge a woman they would have to evaluate her sincerity. It was not enough to know, for example, that a woman worked as a prostitute; one also had to know whether she did so because it was the only way she could feed her family or because she was gratifying personal desires. It was not even enough to know that a woman had committed murder. Even then one had to examine a woman's motives. In 1851, Margaret Garrity, a nineteen-year-old Irish servant, stabbed a man to death in front of numerous witnesses, yet she was acquitted. Her lawyers argued and the jury apparently agreed that Garrity was a virtuous young woman with a "good character." According to her lawyers, the man she killed had seduced her under promise of marriage and then abandoned her when she became pregnant. As they stated it, such a man was even worse than a rapist, and essentially he got what he deserved: Garrity did not kill a man; she rid the world of a "fiend in human shape."[5] In such a case, involving an actual living woman rather than a fictional character or a woman already dead, the public found it extremely difficult to be sure she was immoral when a woman argued that her motives were good.

Yet the scholarship on American women's history and almost all popular and scholarly references to nineteenth-century American women suggest that ante-bellum Americans clearly divided and easily distinguished proper and improper women from one another, and that these distinctions served to confine and limit proper women's sphere of action.[6] The examples of women like Margaret Garrity, Abby Kelley, and Caroline Dall's noble prostitute suggest that we need to complicate this understanding of nineteenth-century American womanhood. Even as gender ideology taught Americans of that time that a woman must be either entirely good or absolutely evil, they knew well that actual women were far more complicated than such categories suggested. Those simple terms re-flected their need, even their desperation, to simplify women's complexities in order to distinguish women who were proper from those who were not. Yet these terms did not solve the problem: when Americans tried to distinguish good women from bad, they failed miserably, and that is why they kept return-ing to the issue.

THE IDEOLOGY OF REDEMPTIVE WOMANHOOD

Historians have written extensively on nineteenth-century gender ideology. They have alternately referred to it as the ideology of separate spheres, the cult of true womanhood, or the cult of domesticity. The first and most influential statement about true womanhood was Barbara Welter's article, "The Cult of True Womanhood." A true or proper woman, Welter argues, must be pious, pure, submissive, and domestic; conversely, a woman who did not possess these qualities would be "untrue."[7] Since Welter's article appeared, many historians have qualified or refined her argument, but almost all have accepted her asser-tion that gender ideology not only asserted that women ought to be pious and pure, but also controlled and limited women's actions. That is, the ideology ad-vised women to submit to male authority, and it also required them to focus their activities on the domestic sphere: their families and their home.

Because true womanhood was so confining, a number of historians have ar-gued that it excluded all but white middle-class women. They have argued that working women, African American or white, could not be true women because they worked for wages outside the home, and true womanhood required women's lives to be centered in the home, the domestic sphere. They also con-cluded that the few African American women who could stay home were still excluded, because racist beliefs would not allow whites to imagine that a black woman might be respectable. Scholars suggest that because working-class and African American women were excluded from the ideology, most of them re-jected it.[8] Some scholars note that black women sometimes tried to embrace the gender system, but assert that it was a white ideology and did not suit their needs. This exclusion from true womanhood supposedly left white working women and black women free to act in independent and assertive ways, unfettered by the ideology that constrained middle-class white women to be passive, submissive, and bound to a private sphere.[9]

Historians have understood the ideology of true womanhood as two ideas in tension with one another. As Lori Ginzberg summed up the field in 1990, historians argued that the ideology was "conservative" in that it "relegat[ed] women to a separate sphere" and "potentially radical" in that it gave women a "sense of solidarity from that experience" of living in their separate sphere. If the conservative part of the ideology encouraged women to remain in their sphere, the radical part encouraged women to develop a special women's identity and to begin to act together on their interests as women; thus, it tended to push them into public life and out of their proper sphere. Or as Julie Roy Jeffrey put it more recently, "Although seemingly conservative in its definition of woman's sphere as domestic and private," antebellum gender ideology "was capable of demanding behavior that took women beyond the boundaries of what the culture at large defined as womanly" and "pressed against gender boundaries." Historians' tendency to understand women as struggling between these conservative and radical implications of woman's sphere has become nuanced in recent years, yet the notion that nineteenth-century gender ideology was meant to control and limit women's actions remains a truism—perhaps *the* truism—of U.S. women's history. This notion, at least as a description for white middle-class women, continues to dominate U.S history textbooks, as well as scholarship in U.S. women's history.[10]

Yet scholarship on white middle-class women has begun to chip away at the notion that *any* group of antebellum women believed women must be passive, dependent and homebound.[11] For years, a number of scholars have argued that most antebellum domestic novels and histories had little use for passive and submissive heroines who moved only in the domestic sphere, and it is starting to become clear that the same is true for real-life white middle-class antebellum women.[12] This suggests that an ideal of passivity, submissiveness, and domesticity did not separate women by race and class in the antebellum era. But if the dominant gender ideology did not demand submissiveness and domesticity, then what was its nature?

I use the term *redemptive womanhood* to describe this gender ideology, rather than *true womanhood*, *separate spheres*, or *domesticity*, because the key to the properness of a woman was not her submission to male authority or her presence in a domestic sphere, but her ability to use her special moral, religious, and nurturing nature to redeem others. The concept of redemptive womanhood allows us to move beyond two problems embedded in the existing historiography of true womanhood. The first is the assumption that Americans shared a belief that women ought to submit to male authority and were confined to some well-defined and agreed-upon domestic sphere. The second is that the ideology of true womanhood only applied to white, middle-class women. Much evidence suggests that nineteenth-century women of all classes and races shared a belief that women had a particularly religious, moral, and nurturing nature and that this special nature gave women an obligation to promote morality and religion and to selflessly nurture others, both inside and outside of their families. This ideology of redemptive womanhood asserted that women were actively responsible for the moral and religious health of America and that only women could sustain the nation's virtue or redeem its sins.

This definition of redemptive womanhood builds on previous conceptions of antebellum gender ideology in its focus on values and motives. It takes Welter's emphasis on female piety and morality and focuses on the ways women's perceived moral superiority encouraged them, as Nancy Cott argues, to "rely on an authority beyond the world of men" and to take an extremely active role in public life. But it rejects the assertion that the ideology placed women in a particular behavioral or geographic sphere. This gender ideology defined men as much as it defined women. In labeling women as the nation's redeemers, it always implicitly or explicitly labeled men as nonredeemers or destroyers of the nation's moral and religious fiber. Redemptive womanhood for the first time demanded that women, as women, become active in the public sphere. Not only could they "rely on an authority beyond the world of men," but they were increasingly told that they must if they were to protect the nation from the immoral actions of men. The concept of redemptive womanhood, then, was activist by nature. The notion that they must fight sin wherever they found it could and did propel women into active public roles. From its genesis, the ideology of redemptive womanhood encouraged women to act in public, to ignore or defy male authority, and to engage in assertive, even militant, behavior, as long as they were involved in promoting religion or morality. It did not build fences around proper female activities; rather, it tore the fences down.

FROM REPUBLICAN MOTHERHOOD TO REDEMPTIVE WOMANHOOD

Redemptive womanhood had important roots in the earlier ideology of republican motherhood. In the aftermath of the American Revolution, historian Ruth Bloch has argued, virtue became more closely identified with women. Whereas classical republican thought had required a virtuous and independent male citizenry, the republicanism of the 1780s and 1790s identified the wife and mother as the keystone of republican virtue. It had become women's duty to quietly and privately instill virtue in their husbands and children, appealing to their emotions and convincing them to be virtuous, not through rational discussion but through love.[14]

Historians have generally assumed that the ideology of republican motherhood was the sole root of the nineteenth-century notion of true womanhood, that women's superior virtue and their exclusion from public life continued hand in hand into the antebellum era. I suggest, however, that redemptive womanhood embraced woman's superior virtue as articulated in republican motherhood, yet at the same time was a reaction against the exclusion of women from public life embedded in that earlier ideology. This reaction was triggered by the upheavals involved in America's transformation into a market society in the first part of the nineteenth century.[15]

By the 1830s, Americans were painfully aware of and quite disturbed by the dislocations their volatile market-oriented economy was producing. Such fears were widespread throughout the nation; they were by no means limited to a few urban areas. The market economy changed the countryside as well as towns and cities. For example, as Ted Steinberg has pointed out, the rise of textile mills in Lowell, Massachusetts, and other New England towns had a direct impact on the lives of rural New Englanders. These mills changed the water flow of the region's rivers, which decreased the fish supply, destroyed grazing land, and interfered with smaller mills and lumber businesses.[16] Americans did not understand and could not control the new economic boom-and-bust cycles. The rise of wage labor, urbanization, and new forms of transportation were quickly transforming family structure and, many feared, destroying it. Many of these fears manifested themselves in an intense preoccupation with moral reform, particularly, but not exclusively, in the North and the West. Reformers believed that vices like drunkenness, seduction, prostitution, and gambling had risen to new heights by the early 1830s. Because Americans believed that the fate of the nation was dependent on the virtue of its citizens, they linked such moral failings to the ruin of society itself.[17]

The rise of rampant public immorality indicated to Americans that private virtue instilled by wives and mothers in the home had not been sufficient to protect the nation's virtue. Men, it seemed, had rejected their moral training and embraced the self-interest of the market instead. Antebellum reformers attacked the disappearance of virtue from public life, arguing for its reinfusion, and hence woman's reinfusion, into politics. As Thomas Wentworth Higginson put it, "We need the feminine element in our public affairs to make us better."[18] The ideology of redemptive womanhood, then, was in part an argument in favor of woman's reentry into public life in the name of morality and religion. It allowed women to believe that as women they had a special duty to fight against sin and evil in society, because men either could not or would not. The more society glorified the independent, self-made man, the more the importance of the redemptive woman grew.[19]

The redemptive woman's belief system was the antithesis of modern market values. If the market encouraged self-interest, greed, and ruthless competition, the redemptive woman was to be selflessly nurturing and loving, a moral and religious woman devoid of selfish desires. She was always contrasted implicitly or explicitly with men. On countless occasions women heard in sermons and lectures or read in the press that they were "naturally more moral, more loving, more caring than men."[20] The ethical and religious system of antebellum America, then, was embodied in women and was in direct opposition to the nation's economic system, which was embodied in men.

If women embraced the values of the marketplace, Americans argued, they would lose their redemptive qualities, become like men, and eventually destroy the virtue of the entire nation. But this created a dilemma for which there was no easy solution. Although women must not hold market values, they could never be entirely disassociated from the market. As one historian pointed out, even inside their homes antebellum women participated in market relations. While such involvement may have been hidden by gender ideology, middle-class women also participated in the market economy in extremely public, quite visible ways. As Brian Roberts has revealed, for example, many Eastern men who sailed to California during the Gold Rush left wives, children, farms, and businesses behind. Their wives in the East, working as surrogate or "deputy husbands," commonly ran these businesses or farms, collected debts, managed accounts, and even financially supported their husbands for years while the men remained in California fruitlessly hunting for gold.[21]

If American wives had worked as deputy husbands when necessary since the colonial era, Roberts argues, this role gained new importance in antebellum America. As relations between employers and their employees grew more distant, it often became the wife's duty to conduct business if her husband was absent, indisposed, or dead. Thus, women were frequently duty bound to participate in the marketplace. As Amy Dru Stanley recently argued, "Even for the middle class, the idea is no longer tenable that the world of most women was remote from the market."[22] Women's entrance into public life was necessary, but always problematic. They would have to venture in the market, but they could never embrace its male values or they would lose their special redemptive nature. Antebellum Americans thus faced a complex situation when they attempted to understand women's relationship to the market. They could no longer define women as outside the market in a physical sense; if they tried, women constantly challenged that belief by their presence in places of business. Proper women would have to be in the market, but not of it.

Because they believed they were in the midst of a moral and religious crisis, a number of historians have noted, antebellum reformers tended to infuse virtually every activity and practice with moral and religious meaning, from dress and eating habits to slavery. One complaint appeared in the *New York Courier and Enquirer* in 1830: "men like Arthur Tappan are constantly employed in engrafting what they call religion upon every act and every incident in human affairs."[23] The proliferation of reform in the antebellum period was linked to the tendency of Americans in general to see daily life as a constant struggle between good and evil. The conflation of religion and morality and the transformation of all issues into moral and religious issues was characteristic of antebellum thinking. It was in this period that influential moral philosopher Francis Wayland divided virtue into two components, "piety (love of God) and morality (love of man)." Wayland went on to link these two components of virtue together inextricably, arguing that "the faithful performance of our duties to God is really the backbone of sound morality."[24] Antebellum newspaper articles and advice manuals were peppered with comments that reveal an unquestioned assumption that Christianity and morality were inseparable. As a piece in the African American newspaper, the *Colored American*, put it in 1838, "Christian ethics are the only true morality."[25]

As distinctions between moral and religious issues blurred, "the morally neutral ground between virtue and vice" disappeared in Christian perfectionist thought. Donald Meyer argues that these developments led to the creation of "an American moral idiom" that consisted of a "disposition to seek out the moral quality in every event and to express this seemingly ubiquitous element in terms of stark moral choices." Meyer also points out that the dominant moral theories of the antebellum era asserted that "ethical truth is knowable"; hence, to be moral one must "choose either to perform or to shirk one's duty." This kind of thinking encouraged radicalism and conflict because it "offered little room for ethical compromise." The most virtuous person was the one who did what was "right," regardless of popular opinion, laws, or any other obstacles.[26]

The conflation of religion and morality and the collapse of morally neutral ground had special implications for women in the antebellum era. Since the advent of the ideology of republican motherhood, Americans had identified women with virtue, and virtue had become synonymous with piety and morality.[27] In the antebellum era, as boundaries between morality and religion blurred and all issues became morally charged, woman's moral and religious duty could and did have serious political implications.

In 1830, many Americans' belief that women should not perform certain "male" activities was not part of the nineteenth-century ideology of redemptive womanhood, but part of an earlier gendered split between public and private in American society. This division began early in the eighteenth century and was transformed in the revolutionary era into the ideology of republican mother-hood, which made women the guardians of a private virtue they would instill in others inside the home. Mary Beth Norton argues that it was the change to a Lockean worldview, according to which family and state are entirely separate, that both created a split between public and private and excluded women from the public realm in the eighteenth century. Only in the nineteenth century would women "again be conceptualized as a part of the public."[28]

It was the ideology of redemptive womanhood that allowed women to reconceptualize themselves as public actors in antebellum America. For ante-bellum Americans, political issues were moral issues and moral issues were po-litical issues. Antebellum women's presence in the public worlds of reform, pol-itics, and business resonated with redemptive womanhood's emphasis on a spiritual rather than a geographical conception of woman's place. If, especially at the start of the antebellum era, many Americans still drew on older identifi-cations of women as private and men as public figures, when they tried to use particular geographical understandings of the woman's sphere to limit women's actions, they were largely unsuccessful. Definitions of women as private no longer made sense in an era of redemptive womanhood.

Even those who complained that women were stepping out of their sphere by speaking in public could not identify where exactly the boundaries of that sphere lay. For example, Massachusetts clergyman Jonathan Sterns warned women that if they lectured in public they would turn Americans into a "fierce race of barbarians." Yet in the same sermon he also told his parishioners that "the influence of woman is not limited to the domestic circle. *Society* is her em-pire, which she governs almost at will." He added that "the cause of benevo-lence is peculiarly indebted to the agency of woman," and "the true sphere of female usefulness will be constantly expanding."[29] Reverend Sterns, so con-vinced that public lecturing was outside woman's sphere, seemed unable to put any other limits on that sphere at all. For this reason, charges that women did not belong in politics were easily refuted. As one 1839 article in the *Liberator* put it, "Waiving the question altogether of the propriety of women having any thing to do with politics, is not the subject of slavery in fact a religious and moral question?"[30] If politics was inseparable from morality and religion, then it was woman's province.

The work of a few recent scholars suggests that this link between the moral, the religious, and the political had important concrete effects on women's participation in politics. As early as 1840, Elizabeth Varon has pointed out, the Whig party, in Virginia and nationally, actively encouraged women to participate in party events, even as public speakers. As more and more women participated in these events, Whigs claimed that American women were overwhelmingly pro-Whig. They used women's presence to argue that the Whigs were the moral party, the party without corruption. In response, the Democratic party began to recruit women as well. By 1844, the Democrats had also invited women to attend and even speak at party events.[31]

The idea of redemptive womanhood was the basis of the first argument women and men made in American history that justified women's direct participation in politics. This argument worked: Americans did become more accepting of women's involvement in political issues in the 1840s and 1850s. It was so powerful in part because, unlike their counterparts in the twentieth and twenty-first centuries, antebellum Americans did not believe it was possible to separate moral issues from political issues.

RACE, CLASS, AND GENDER IDEOLOGY

The general trend in American women's history in the last two decades has been to differentiate among women on the basis of race, ethnicity, and class. This approach started as a corrective to much of the women's history of the 1960s and 1970s, which focused largely on white, especially Northern white middle-class women as representative of women's experience in general. Since then there has been an explosion of work on the lives of African American, immigrant, and working-class women. This important scholarship has added new life to American women's history. It also has tended to stress the differences between white middle-class, native-born women and all other groups of women, arguing, for example, that white middle-class women were bound by the ideology of true womanhood, but African American and working-class women were not.

Class, race, and ethnicity were powerful structures in antebellum America, and they shaped women's lives in a variety of important ways. However, Northern African American, working-class, immigrant, and middle-class women all lived in the same society, and their lives had commonalities as well as differences. The current tendency to differentiate women by class and race neglects the beliefs and experiences American women shared across class and racial boundaries. The ideology of redemptive womanhood can help us make sense of the beliefs about womanhood that African American and white, working-class and middle-class women shared.

Even scholars who have highlighted the differences between working-class and middle-class women have sometimes suggested that both groups believed that women had a special moral and religious nature. For example, Alice Kessler-Harris argues that working women in the last half of the antebellum era were increasingly excluded from definitions of respectability, but she also notes that these women and their supporters continued to think of themselves as within the bounds of female respectability. In the period after the Civil War, she contends, Americans in general grew to believe that women could work and be virtuous, so long as the working conditions themselves promoted morality.[32] Mary Blewett also has stressed the importance of moral and religious womanhood to New England factory workers from the 1840s through at least 1860. Yet even as she argues that true womanhood was a middle-class ideology that working-class women could never entirely live up to, Blewett finds that both male and female New England factory workers in the antebellum era "saw women as essentially moral beings" and that the working woman in that region shared a special "moral duty as a woman" with her middle-class counterparts.[33] Such evidence suggests that working women throughout the antebellum era maintained a belief in redemptive womanhood, even if others questioned the respectability of their actions.

The historiography of true womanhood also has portrayed African American women as outside the ideology of true womanhood, either because they rejected the ideology as inappropriate to their lives or because the ideology was a white middle-class one, and even when black women embraced it, they could never fully become true women. Many scholars have argued that because black women needed to be active and assertive in order to resist the demands of slavery and racism, and because most of them needed to work outside their homes, it was easy for them to reject the domesticity, passivity, and submissive behavior true womanhood required.[34] Some have noted that many free Northern African Americans at least partially accepted the ideology of true womanhood; however, they have assumed that from the start true womanhood was a white ideology imposed on blacks and that Northern blacks embraced it in order to gain status and respectability in the white community. While allowing that this ideology in some ways worked to free black women from racist stereotypes of black women's sexuality, these historians, including Shirley Yee, James Horton, Dorothy Sterling, and Marilyn Richardson, have argued that as a white ideology true womanhood was ill suited for the lives of black women and that it imposed on the black community "white standards of inequality . . . in part symbolized by male dominance and female subordination."[35] The result of such reasoning, as Nell Painter recently pointed out in the case of Sojourner Truth, is that when African American female reformers seem too much like

ANGELS, DEVILS, AND REDEMPTIVE WOMANHOOD

white reformers, historians tend to neglect them or to lionize them as larger-than-life figures who were stronger and more independent than their white counterparts—as, of course, they should have been if they were unfettered by white middle-class notions of female submissiveness and domesticity.[36]

Part of my focus in this project is on African American women who by and large have been slighted by histories focusing on the development of separate spheres. If gender ideology did not demand submissiveness and domesticity, then it could suit the lives of African American women, and there is much evidence to suggest that the Northern free black community, at least, embraced a belief in women's redemptive nature and mission. For example, the Northern black community and some white abolitionists used stories about enslaved African American women who murdered their masters to protect themselves from rape or who killed their own children to save them from slavery to argue that black women too were responsible for the nation's virtue. Popular discussions of enslaved women who engaged in illicit sex also frequently occurred within slave narratives and other abolitionist literature. Such stories always asserted that the system of slavery forced virtuous black women to commit immoral acts, which degraded both the slave community and white slaveholding society.

Both African American and white women were at the center of controversy surrounding female public speakers and women's place in wartime. They engaged in the same kinds of debates and were subject to the same kinds of criticisms for their actions in the black and white communities. Black antislavery advocates, including Maria W. Stewart, Nancy Prince, Sojourner Truth, Frances Ellen Watkins Harper, and Mary Ann Shadd Cary; preachers, like Jarena Lee, Zilpha Elaw, and Julia Foote; and Civil War workers, such as Charlotte Forten and Susie King Taylor, were constantly engaged in struggles over the relationship between feminine propriety and women's public action.

To say that the Northern black and white communities shared a concept of redemptive womanhood is not to deny that many whites believed that black women were not virtuous. Most white Northern women saw little connection between themselves and free black women. This is why black women were seldom the focus of the mainstream press's obsession with murderesses. Apparently respectable white women who committed murder interested the press and the public because they believed that these women ought to be the most virtuous members of society. But if many whites excluded African American women from proper womanhood, blacks did not accept this judgment. The ideology of redemptive womanhood was not inherently white.[37] What James and Lois Horton have argued about the ideology of racial uplift in general applies also to the relationship of the free black community to redemptive womanhood. They explain that "some historians have taken" nineteenth-century black protesters' and reformers' stress on racial uplift "as an indication of their desire to assimilate into the white middle class, but racial elevation had value to blacks irrespective of white society. American values were not bounded by color, and the desire for liberty and equality was strongest among those to whom they were denied."[38] To assume that the Northern blacks' stress on moral and religious womanhood was an effort to "assimilate into the white middle class" is to assert that American values are created by and are the property of only white Americans. This denies agency and independent thought to African Americans who held these values.

African American women described themselves as redemptive women in public as early as, and sometimes earlier than, white women did. Many blacks and some whites argued that redemptive womanhood crossed racial boundaries and applied to all women in America. The black community asserted the moral and religious qualities of its women in the face of considerable white prejudice against such a view. The fact that many whites refused to consider African American women to be redemptive women does not negate the fact that free Northern African Americans believed that they were. They consistently asserted that black women were—or should be—moral and religious pillars of the community. For free Northern blacks, redemptive womanhood served as a key political argument against slavery and racism.[39]

REDEMPTIVE WOMANHOOD AND THE IMPENDING CRISIS

From the mid-1840s through the Civil War, an atmosphere of increasing conflict and crisis led Americans to fear that there were no peaceful solutions to the country's growing problems. Between the sectional conflict, which by 1846 had international implications in the form of the Mexican-American War, and the seemingly unpredictable and increasingly dramatic economic boom-and-bust cycles, Americans worried more and more that the country was headed for a major crisis.[40] By this time the ideology of redemptive womanhood had prepared Americans to understand this atmosphere of national crisis, these tensions engendered by a market-oriented economy as the product of male immorality, selfishness, and greed. It was this situation that led Americans to increasingly highlight woman's active role as moral regenerator of society, drawing heavily on existing images of female saviors and heroes and creating new ones.

The 1840s and 1850s saw an explosion of literature by and about woman that specifically focused on women's duty to family and society. Histories of women, such as Jesse Clement's *Noble Deeds of American Women* (1851), the domestic novel, and cheap pamphlet fiction detailing the exploits of female adventurers all became incredibly popular genres.[41] These literary explorations of woman's nature and actions both facilitated and were facilitated by the public actions of actual women in antebellum America. Literary heroines gave antebellum women a way to understand and justify their public actions, and publicly active women were models for authors. Histories and novels about heroic women encouraged ordinary women to believe that they could and should perform heroic actions as part of their duty to preserve the moral and religious health of the nation. This combination of women's public activism and the proliferation of literature about assertive and publicly active heroines created an atmosphere that made extremely assertive and publicly active redemptive women seem increasingly natural to Americans and encouraged even more women to enter public life.

If the antebellum period has often been characterized as the era of the Angel of the House, it was equally the era of the Angel of the Battlefield. Long before Clara Barton earned that nickname during the Civil War, American writers depicted women in fiction and history as angelic and aggressive battlefield heroines. One of these fictional accounts was Maturin Murray Ballou's *Fanny Campbell, the Female Pirate Captain.* Ballou, the son of a prominent New England minister, created this story of a woman who disguised herself as a man, enlisted as a sailor, and fought during the Revolutionary War, all in order to rescue her fiancé, an American soldier, from a Cuban prison. Ballou depicts Campbell as a heroic, virtuous, and respectable young woman. The popularity of this book spurred Ballou (under several pseudonyms) and other authors to write and publish many more such novels with heroic and angelic female pirates, warriors, or adventurers as protagonists. It also encouraged at least one real-life young woman nearly fifteen years later to, by her own account, leave home, disguise herself as a man, and enlist in the U.S. Army as a Civil War soldier.[42]

An increased acceptance of women's public action and even violence in the defense of righteousness was not a breakdown of antebellum gender ideology, but its culmination. The crisis of slavery and the Civil War gave women the opportunity to act as the Fanny Campbells, Joans of Arc, and Florence Nightingales they had been brought up to emulate. American women, especially in the North but also in the South, organized relief efforts, nursed soldiers, and even sometimes dressed as men and enlisted in the army during the Civil War because the ideology of redemptive womanhood had prepared them from birth to go to any lengths to defend the virtue of their nation.

"Drunk with Murderous Longing"

The Problem of the Respectable Murderess

CHAPTER
ONE

It has probably never fallen to the lot of man to record a list of more cruel, heart-rending, atrocious murders, than have been perpetrated by the subject of this narrative.

—*Narrative and Confessions of Lucretia P. Cannon*[1]

*T*n February 1778, Bathsheba Spooner, the well-educated daughter of a Massachusetts judge, paid three men to kill her husband, Joshua. The men were transients who had been staying at the Spooner residence and helping with farm work. They accosted Mr. Spooner one evening on his way home from a local tavern, beat him to death with a club, and threw him into a well. A few days later, one of the assailants, William Brooks, aroused the suspicions of the neighborhood: after a few drinks, Brooks began showing off a new watch that bore an uncanny resemblance to one owned by Joshua Spooner, and he was sporting a pair of silver shoe buckles monogrammed "J. S." He and the others were immediately arrested for Spooner's murder. The men immediately confessed and were tried, found guilty, and executed. Mrs. Spooner pleaded not guilty, asserting that she had not believed the men would actually kill her husband. She was tried separately, convicted of murder, and hanged soon afterward.[2]

Bathsheba Spooner was not typical of eighteenth-century murderesses in fact or in fiction. From the seventeenth century to the late 1820s, the female protagonists of published murder narratives had been representative of the kinds of women who were usually tried for murder in America. They were generally poor white, African American, or Native American women, and they were most often portrayed as killing their illegitimate infants. In fact, Spooner was the only accused murderess clearly identified as well-to-do or respectable in an eighteenth-century murder narrative.[3] By the 1830s, women like Spooner were still uncommon, but they gained immense importance in American popular culture. That is, while the well-to-do murderess remained extremely unusual in the United States, she became common in newspaper accounts, trial pamphlets, and even full-length biographies. In the same period, the number of published narratives of poor white, African American, and Native American murderesses declined precipitously.[4]

A closer look at Bathsheba Spooner's case may shed light on this transformation in popular literary, legal, and social treatment of female murderers. In 1778, at her trial, Spooner admitted that she had asked three men to kill her husband, but insisted that she had not believed they would go through with it. Her lawyers argued that the murder plot was so transparent that a woman like Mrs. Spooner, who was "admitted to have sense," could not possibly have conceived of it while in "the exercise of her reason," and that she could not have been rational when she solicited the men to murder her husband. Therefore, they contended, she was not responsible for the crime. If she had tired of her husband, they asserted, she could have left him and moved back to her father's house.[5]

At the time of her trial, Spooner's contemporaries did not suggest that her crime posed a special problem because she was a woman. Discussing her not as a murderess but as a murderer who happened to be a woman, they maintained that her mind was that of a "man disordered"; she was a "distracted person." They did not find the crime more shocking because she was a woman. When local ministers, the press, and the prosecutors dwelt on the horror of the crime, they focused on the fact that she was the spouse, rather than the wife, of the person she killed. She murdered her "professed friend"; she was "the near relation of him whose blood was shed."[6] This distinction may seem minor until one sees a mid-nineteenth-century account of the same event.

In 1844, young Massachusetts lawyer Peleg Chandler included a version of the Spooner trial in his two volume *American Criminal Trials*, a collection of "important" trial accounts, "abridged" and "divested of legal technicalities" for the "general reader." Chandler's depiction of Bathsheba Spooner was remarkably different from those that survive from the time of her trial. For Chandler, the key to Spooner's nature and her crime was gender. She was an unfeminine woman ruled by selfish passions: "Her temper was haughty and imperious, and the circumstances of her birth and early education were not favorable to that delicacy and refinement which constitute the greatest charm of her sex." He asserted that her immediate motive for the crime was that she "cherished a criminal regard for another person [one of the murderers], and in the blindness of passion, lost all self-control."[7] Chandler argued that Spooner's attempt to gratify her selfish passions destroyed her womanly character: "the effect of criminal indulgence on the female mind is the more remarkable, as we do not expect to find her a criminal at all. When woman oversteps the modesty of her position and breaks loose from the restraints of the laws—her whole character is changed—her affections are inverted—she is turned to stone."[8] Chandler's depiction of Bathsheba Spooner as a woman unsexed and even dehumanized by her selfish passions was not remarkable in the antebellum era; it had become the dominant way of understanding female criminality in America.

Antebellum Americans' fascination with apparently respectable female murderers was linked to the rise of a highly gendered, class-oriented, and racially inflected understanding of murder. Their new understanding of female murderers was tied to specific tensions created by the transition to a market-oriented society. Recent historians have illuminated a number of reasons for Americans' new fascination with murder in general in the antebellum era and have charted the rise of a popular culture of murder beginning in the 1830s. As Karen Halttunen has pointed out, Americans' understanding of murder in general shifted dramatically in the late eighteenth and early nineteenth centuries. No longer envisioning a murderer as a morally normal sinner, they began to understand the murderer as a "moral alien," an evil creature who lived outside the boundaries of human decency. Halttunen also has illuminated a gendered component in this popular culture of murder, connecting gender ideology to the treatment of female murderers. She has argued that "true womanhood" could protect white middle-class women from murder convictions by transferring the "feminine evil" to lower class or nonwhite women.[9] However, my evidence suggests that the impact of gender, race, and class on the popular culture of murder was more complex, that the true woman and the untrue woman could never be clearly separated from each other, not even by class or race. While their cases were seldom highly publicized, working-class, immigrant, and African American women did assert their status as true women when they were tried for murder. In addition, women accused of murder, whether they were convicted or acquitted, were never securely labeled as good or evil, regardless of their status; rather, the labels constantly oscillated back and forth between these categories.

Halttunen and Dawn Keetley have argued that popular accounts of female murderers illuminated tensions within domestic life. According to Halttunen, such stories reflected the "rough and contested" nature of the "transition from the traditional patriarchal family to the modern sentimental family." Keetley suggests that pamphlets about women who murdered their husbands played to "deep-seated fears about the contradictions of marriage," including the possibility that married women could "lust for freedom" from the male-controlled unions.[10] I would suggest that antebellum Americans' fascination with female murderers, particularly "respectable" ones, resonates beyond domestic life. The female murderer did not just destroy her family; she directly threatened society. The ideology of redemptive womanhood, itself a reaction to the rising importance of the market economy, asserted that women were more pious, moral, and nurturing than market-oriented men and that these qualities gave them a duty to protect the nation's virtue. But the proliferation of accounts of wealthy, refined, greedy, lustful, vengeful, and even irreligious female murderers suggests that Americans feared that even the nation's most respectable women were discarding their redemptive values and embracing the opposite qualities: immorality, impiety, and the relentless pursuit of self-interest. That is, like men they were embracing the desires unleashed by the market and were leaving the nation with no moral center.

In part, the transformation in attitudes toward female murderers between the seventeenth and early nineteenth centuries was the result of a major shift in American attitudes about human nature in general. For much of the seventeenth and eighteenth centuries, American religious thought stressed the doctrine of innate depravity. As long as colonists believed everyone was born depraved, tainted by original sin, any other explanation for murder was unnecessary. Until the last part of the eighteenth century, the popular literature of murder was composed almost exclusively of execution sermons. In these sermons ministers did not search for "what later generations would call 'motive.' Instead they explored the patterns of sinful conduct that paved the way to murder." Murder was merely the culmination of years of sinful practices during which the offender sank lower and lower, and farther and farther away from God, eventually becoming so depraved as to kill.[11]

To understand murder in this way was very simple. Esther Rodgers claimed in 1701 that the fundamental reason she murdered her baby was that she "had little or no thoughts of God or religion." Patience Boston traced her crime to the fact that as a child she "used to play on the Sabbath, tell Lies and do other Wickedness." On the day of his execution in 1686, James Morgan wrote that "the sin which lies most heavy upon my Conscience" is not murder but the fact that "I have despised the Word of God, and many a time refused to hear it preached." Explanations for the crimes of all offenders—men and women; African Americans, whites, and Native Americans; servants and masters—were much the same in this period. All had neglected God; all had been tempted and had succumbed to that temptation. In a world in which everyone was born a sinner and could be saved only through the grace of God, neglect of religion was the surest route to crime.[12]

In the eighteenth century, Enlightenment beliefs in progress and human perfectibility began to challenge the notion of innate depravity in both Europe and America. Writers and thinkers began to suggest that human nature was inherently benevolent rather than depraved and that individuals could choose between good and evil.[13] In the period after 1750, this belief slowly became the core of the dominant understanding of human nature in America.[14] For the first time colonists felt obliged to explain why a specific individual would do evil when she ought, by nature, be good. One result of this conceptual change was that by the mid-eighteenth century criminals began to explain their motives in criminal narratives, and increasingly these secular, individual motives became the centerpieces of the narratives. This attention to motives continued and grew stronger in the last quarter of the eighteenth century. By then criminal narratives almost always highlighted the secular aspects of crime. The sermonizing often shrank to little more than a paragraph on the last page.[15]

The decline of the doctrine of innate depravity transformed sin and crime from an inevitable evil into a problem that could be solved. The eighteenth-century discipline of moral philosophy arose in this flush of optimism; it offered to explain how the moral sense functioned.[16] If those with a properly developed moral sense would not commit crimes, the key to a better world was to learn how to properly train this moral sense. In the eighteenth century there were two strands of Enlightenment thought regarding this moral sense. One linked morality with reason; the other linked it with emotion. According to John Locke, perhaps the most influential philosopher in eighteenth-century America, moral truth could be "perfectly known and deduced by reason."[17] Lawyers, juries, ministers, and authors explored this connection between morality and reason in a number of fictional and nonfictional murder cases in the late eighteenth century.[18] When they believed that reason was the foundation of the moral sense, Americans did not expect women to be more virtuous than men. As one scholar puts it, in the colonial period Americans assumed that women were "more prone to excess of passion because their rational control was seen as weaker." If the moral sense was linked to reason, women, traditionally depicted as less rational than men, might even be less moral, as we can see from the example of Bathsheba Spooner.[19]

However, by the end of the eighteenth century, Americans increasingly linked the moral sense to the emotions, rather than reason, in their discussions of criminality. As influential Scottish philosopher Francis Hutcheson argued, "moral truth depended on an instinctual love of goodness for its own sake."[20] This connection between morality and emotion, historian Ruth Bloch has noted, helped pave the way for a "gendering of virtue" in American society. According to Bloch, the ideas of moral philosophy, American Protestantism, and literary sentimentalism all "opened the way" for a linkage between women, emotion, and virtue in the revolutionary era, but it was in the aftermath of the American Revolution that these connections solidified.[21] In that era, Americans identified women as the primary bearers and transmitters of virtue, heightening the connection between morality and emotion, which had long been associated with women. As Americans embraced the idea that women were especially virtuous—by which they generally meant moral and religious—and nurturing, as the primary transmitters of virtue, female criminality became a new problem.[22] But the new linkage of women and virtue did not suddenly overpower older ideas about women's nature. On the contrary, it took almost fifty years for Americans to turn these new ideas into a coherent set of beliefs, a way to understand woman's nature.[23]

The Case of Mary Cole and the Transition to a New Gender Ideology

The case of Mary Cole illustrates that the implications of the new gender ideology remained unclear for Americans of the early national period. In the spring of 1812, Mary Cole was tried in rural Sussex County, New Jersey, for the murder of her mother, Agnes Thuers. In December 1811, Thuers, who had been living with Cole and her husband, Cornelius, suddenly disappeared. Mary and Cornelius told their neighbors that Thuers had gone to live with her brother. A few months later, the Coles rented their farm to another family and moved out of the neighborhood. A month after they moved in, the new residents of the Cole farm noticed a foul smell in their house and upon investigation discovered a decaying body underneath the floorboards. Authorities identified that body as that of Agnes Thuers. They arrested the Coles and charged them with murder. Mary Cole was tried, convicted, and hanged for the crime; Cornelius was tried separately and sentenced to two years in prison for helping to conceal the murder.[24]

In Mary Cole's case, the notion that women are more virtuous and more nurturing than men played a key role. Yet no one, from Cole's lawyers to the trial's observers, seemed quite sure how to apply this idea to the case. Mary

Cole, the lawyers, the witnesses, and the press used parts of old and new gender ideologies to make a number of arguments during the trial, but no one was able to use these ideologies coherently. They shifted back and forth between new arguments about woman's moral, religious, and nurturing nature and older, nongendered understandings of the moral nature of criminals. An atmosphere of confusion surrounded Mary Cole's trial, but not because she, the lawyers, or the press were personally incapable of making clear arguments; their difficulties reflected Americans' shared confusion over the meaning of womanhood.

As Mary Cole described the murder, she stabbed and hacked her mother to death with a knife and an ax while her husband was asleep upstairs. She claimed that she had killed her mother in self-defense and also in a fit of rage brought on by a lifetime of abuse. Cole maintained that since she was a baby, her mother had consistently neglected and mistreated her. Cole had escaped from this miserable life when she married, but the persecution had begun anew when Thuers came to live with Mary and Cornelius. Thuers had tried to sabotage the marriage by telling Cornelius that Mary had been "false to his bed," and by insisting on sleeping with the couple even though she had a bed of her own. Once, while Mary was holding her two young children, Thuers had thrown a bellows at her, causing her to drop one of the babies. On another day, Thuers attacked her with a knife, and Mary finally fought back, stabbing her mother to death.[25]

At Cole's trial, her attorneys appealed both to old ideologies and to new ones to explain her motive. They argued that she had committed manslaughter rather than murder because her mother's behavior had enraged her. "The awful deed was begun in the intoxication of passion," they argued, "and finished before reason had time to resume its office." The lawyers then recounted several occasions in which juries had found a defendant guilty of manslaughter rather than murder, "because the accused had reasons for anger," and had killed in a moment of passion. In one such instance Mary Cole's lawyers compared her to a man who killed another in a rage because he had "rung" his nose, arguing that "it would doubtless appear to the jury that the offense given by the man who rung the other's nose could in no shape hold a parallel with the offense given the Prisoner by her mother."[26]

Cole's lawyers willingly admitted that her violent passion was the cause of her crime. They had an opportunity to play down that passion and focus on the crime as one of simple self-defense, but they chose not to do so. Rather, the defense tried to justify the murder, or at least mitigate the charge, by comparing Mary to a number of insulted men, and her passion to men's passion. Thus the lawyers simultaneously linked morality to emotion, and Cole's violence to a man's violence. This double assertion was problematic. The notion that one's moral sense was tied to the emotions was also associated with the new idea that women were particularly religious, moral, and nurturing. The lawyers, then, were making an argument that asserted that woman's nature was fundamentally different from man's at the very moment they attempted to justify Cole's crime by comparing it to the crime of a man.

The press portrayed Mary in a similar fashion: as a woman capable of both passionate rage and passionate love. They tried to reassure readers that Mary Cole was a virtuous wife and mother by describing how much she loved and nurtured her family; however, they seemed unable to reconcile Mary the good mother with Mary the matricide. Even Cole, as she is depicted in the two extant pamphlets about her crime and trial, seems to have been incapable of adopting one idiom over the other. Both pamphlets describe her concern for her child after her death sentence, and one includes a "farewell letter to her husband" that is a mixture of motherly tenderness and macabre imagery. She wrote to Cornelius: "Stay with your child, all things in the world notwithstanding . . . you must be father and mother both, and I fear its only friend; when it weeps, kiss it for me and rock it silent for me when I am in the cold and silent grave." If this seems to be written in the language of sentimental domesticity, in the very next line her tone shifts dramatically: "O Cornelius, above all things, don't forget to observe and obey the scriptures, which say, 'parents provoke not your children.' I send you here a lock of my hair, which I want you to keep so long as you live; and when you are tempted to go from your dear babe, first look on a part of its poor unfortunate mother; which will stand as a living monument of my wishes, when worms are devouring my flesh."[27]

In this letter Cole described herself as a gentle, tenderhearted wife and mother, yet she also invoked the specter of herself in two particularly threatening and frightening ways. First, in her reminder about the scripture "parents provoke not your children," she conjured up the image of herself killing her mother, in a not-so-veiled threat of what might happen to Cornelius if he did not care for their child. And second, she sent him a lock of her hair, a "living monument" to remind him of his duty to their son. This "live" bit of hair would simultaneously watch him and remind him of her worm-eaten corpse. This specter of a decaying ax murderess watching from beyond the grave hovers around the image of Mary the gentle mother. The fact that Mary Cole's lawyers and the press conceived of the strategy of describing her as capable of both passionate love and passionate rage reveals the persistence of pre–republican motherhood ideas of womanhood, as well as confusion over how to apply the tenets of the new gender ideology.[28] Twenty years later, the idea of a murderess who was both a loving, nurturing wife and mother and also a woman capable of killing her own mother in a violent passion would be almost unimaginable.

THE "RESPECTABLE" WHITE MURDERESS IN ANTEBELLUM AMERICA

It had been easy to convict Bathsheba Spooner and Mary Cole, but by the 1830s this was no longer true of "respectable" white women accused of murder. Americans were no longer inclined to believe that such a woman could be guilty of murder unless she showed herself to be utterly devoid of virtue. In an era in which Americans believed that, especially for women, "all aspects of manner and appearance were visible outward signs of inner moral qualities," all a woman on trial had to do was put on the trappings of virtue—a plain, modest dress; a serious, sorrowful look; perhaps a tear from time to time—to convince a jury she could not be a murderer.[29] Thus, as women's perceived moral complexity decreased and they were increasingly presented as entirely good or evil, it became more and more difficult for Americans to convict a woman of murder—even if she admitted killing someone—as long as she made a claim to respectability, however superficial.[30]

The rise of the sensational penny press in the 1830s dramatically changed the place of murder in American society. If Americans had flocked to local executions in the eighteenth century, in the 1830s their fascination with murder was magnified by the development of a national print culture. This commercialization of the press, this explosion of print, created an environment in which large numbers of men and women of all classes read criminal biographies, trial reports, novelistic accounts of crimes, and newspaper coverage of crimes and trials; many also attended criminal trials.[31] As murder trials in general became extremely popular in antebellum America, the murder trials of women received more attention than ever before.

Before 1840 in America, women were subjects of about 4 percent of the allegedly nonfiction published crime and trial pamphlets on murderers; from 1840 to 1860, this number jumped to around 12 percent, although the percentage of violent crimes committed by women had remained relatively stable.[32] All but two of the female murderers I have located from 1830 to 1860 who were subjects of published accounts, fictional or nonfictional, were white, and almost all were described as having come from respectable backgrounds.[33] Trials of well-to-do female murderers were the most sensational of all. These accused murderesses received more attention in proportion to their numbers than any other group in antebellum America, and this was a dramatically new development.

To understand the new focus on "respectable" white murderesses, one must take into consideration dramatic shifts in American conceptions of race and gender, as well as the massive economic changes of the early nineteenth century. In this period, whiteness and maleness became measures of status and full citizenship as states began to eliminate property requirements for voting. The transformation in ideas about the meaning of citizenship tended to encourage Americans to see various groups—African Americans, Native Americans, whites, men, and women—as made up of beings with distinct and incomparable natures.[34] In addition, the rise of a market-oriented society made female virtue even more important in the antebellum era than it had been in the early republic. If men had to embrace the values of the market—qualities like selfishness and greed—to be successful, then the duty to protect the virtue of the republic fell more and more to women.[35] Criminal narratives reflected this growing tendency to link internal character with race and gender. At about the turn of the nineteenth century, murder accounts began to treat male, female, black, Indian, and white defendants as discrete groups with distinct moral natures. By the 1830s, these ideologies of racial and gender difference were fully articulated. By then, published accounts of nonwhite murderers had virtually disappeared, while stories of white, well-to-do female murderers who committed horrific crimes of passion increased dramatically.

There was little room for individuality in antebellum descriptions of these passionate female murderers. Lawyers, reporters, and pamphleteers always established the murderess's appearance of respectability. They did this in two ways: by emphasizing her respectable family and background and by describing her respectable appearance and deportment. Such women were frequently said to have attended the most exclusive schools and to have come from "highly respectable," if not "ancient and noble," families. Their parents were "honest and industrious people," "highly religious and moral." And, of course, the women always looked virtuous and respectable.[36] The height of their status then magnified the depth of their fall.

These female murderers were depicted as, "polished and refined . . . lovely and gifted ornament[s]," who turned into, "loathsome, polluted and soul-stained outcast[s]." They became, not just "murderesses," but "unnatural creatures," "hyenas," "tigresses," and "fiends in human form," or as Karen Halttunen puts it, "moral aliens."[37] All shared the same fatal flaw. As "unnatural creatures" they had scorned their special duty as women to be moral, pious, and nurturing and to protect society from immorality and sin. Instead they had embraced the opposite qualities: immorality, infidelity, and the relentless pursuit of self-interest. Often their murderous careers began when this pursuit of self-interest—which usually took the form of passionate lust or greed—was thwarted in some way. The pursuit of self-interest was often specifically linked to a disregard for religion and morality. For example, Lucretia Chapman's lawyers asserted that she was "the daughter of a respectable citizen of Massachusetts, who helped fight the battles of our revolution. [She] has ever borne a reputation free from stain—a communicant of the altar of her God—the parent of five children, whom she had taught to worship that God." But to the prosecution, she was "utterly abandoned and lost to moral principle," a "fiend" ready to "make a bloody offering . . . to the altar of passion" because her "unholy passion" for her lover destroyed "all [her] moral and religious principles."[38]

According to the prosecutors at Emma Augusta Cunningham's New York murder trial, Cunningham, a respectable widow and mother, was consumed by "fiendish revenge" when Dr. Burdell, a dentist who boarded in her home, would not marry her. Her jealousy and hatred transformed her into a "greedy, lustful" being: a "woman in form, though a fiend in mind." Prosecutors also depicted Cunningham as an improper mother who had corrupted the morals of her children. For example, when witnesses testified to Cunningham's piety, commenting that they had heard her daughters singing the hymn "God moves in a mysterious way" the day after the murder, one prosecutor asserted that they must have really been singing, "Woman moves in a mysterious way." By presenting Cunningham as a woman who mocked religion and taught her children to do the same, the prosecution hoped to convince the jury that she was not a virtuous woman and that, therefore, she could commit murder.[39]

Accused murderess Polly Bodine allegedly cried out that she was "drunk with murderous longing" when she attacked her sister-in-law Emeline. Tellingly, she was said to have committed the act immediately after Emeline said her prayers. Lucretia Cannon too was overwhelmed by selfish passions. She supposedly poisoned her husband, the first in a long line of victims, because he interfered with "the gratification of her propensities . . . [for] she was very sensual in her pleasures." These passions, of course, destroyed her moral and religious sensibilities. She was untroubled by her crime, as she "was almost indifferent to any principle of justice, as well as to human suffering."[40] Other alleged murderesses apparently forged more intellectual links between selfish passions and infidelity. When the protagonist of one criminal biography, Ellen Irving, a virtuous young girl, was seduced and abandoned by a man who had promised to marry her, she allegedly "swore to revenge [herself] on all mankind for the crimes of one, to hate all, to disown [her] Maker, to believe death an eternal sleep, to spread the opinions of Voltaire and other infidel writers throughout the world."[41]

It is telling that the qualities of these "evil" women so closely resembled the qualities necessary in a successful market-oriented man. The problem with these women was not that they were passionate, but that they were overpowered by passions commonly identified as selfish, such as greed, lust, and revenge. The new market-oriented economy encouraged men to be self-interested and to disregard traditional ethical and religious values in the pursuit of wealth. If women joined in that pursuit, it was only a matter of time before the nation would collapse in decadence and corruption. The fear that women might succumb to the temptations of the marketplace, that they might embrace its promises of self-gratification, was the root of Americans' fascination with the apparently respectable murderess, for she was a horrific embodiment of all that went wrong when women embraced such desires. The fact that antebellum Americans often imagined respectable murderesses where none existed reveals just how deep this anxiety lay.

In 1854, Henrietta Robinson was tried for poisoning her neighbors, two Irish immigrants of a "lowly condition," with whom she had quarreled at a "grocery dance." Robinson refused to tell anyone her background or family history. Her own defense attorneys admitted that they "know nothing of [her] antecedents." At her trial, few people even knew what she looked like because she insisted on wearing a heavy veil in court. The judge finally ordered her to remove the veil, but still she managed to evade all attempts at identification. In response to his order, she "threw her veil partially over her bonnet, and sobbing, bent forward, burying her face entirely in her handkerchief. . . . Notwithstanding the determined order of the court, [she] effectually succeeded in concealing her face from view."[42] Throughout her trial, the press and lawyers speculated on Robinson's identity, but there was not a shred of evidence to support the dominant theory, the one both her lawyers and the judge accepted: that she had been rich, aristocratic, intelligent, and beautiful in her youth.

Shortly after the trial, New York lawyer and author David Wilson fleshed out this theory in a three-hundred-page biography of Robinson, which he published in 1855. He spent much of the book constructing an elaborate account of her early life, her charmed childhood, and her terrible fall from a position of wealth and high social standing. In Wilson's account, Robinson was the daughter of one of the "very first" families in Quebec, "influential from their wealth, and respected for their intelligence and integrity." Yet at the time of the crime, Robinson was living among Irish people of a "lowly condition" and frequenting "grocery dances." Although Robinson's physical appearance was a mystery, Wilson claimed that in her youth she had possessed "surpassing beauty . . . a complexion fairer than art could imitate, . . . teeth whiter than the snows of her native north," and "a mind of no ordinary strength and brilliancy."[43] How could such a woman sink so low as to commit murder? Because from childhood she was "the slave of passions she was unable to control." Already passionate and unstable when her father forbade her to marry her first lover and forced her into a loveless match with a wealthy old man, she began to engage in bizarre behavior and to show signs of insanity. Due to an illicit love affair, she worsened. In this state she allegedly poisoned her neighbors out of revenge for some slight insult.[44]

Americans wanted to believe that Robinson and others like her had fallen from the pinnacle of society. Apparently they needed no evidence to sustain such a belief. And Robinson, who refused to show her face or tell her own history may have known this. Although he had no evidence to support the claim, the presiding judge told the jurors that Robinson's situation was a "painful illustration . . . of the rapid decent which a woman makes to the lowest depths of degradation and vice, when she once consents to take leave of virtue and innocence." The same pattern can be found in many other trial transcripts and criminal biographies.[45] Such evidence suggests the flexibility of Americans' definition of respectable womanhood, which, in the case of murderesses, may have had more to do with courtroom behavior than class status.

Not only did lawyers and authors magnify the wealth, refinement, and beauty of actual women accused of murder, but the press created an entire set of imaginary murderesses who all shared these qualities. Most of the female subjects of antebellum murder narratives and published trial accounts never existed. In reality, the well-to-do white murderess was a very rare figure. After an extensive search, I found published trial accounts and criminal biographies from the period between 1827 and 1860 involving only fifteen actual women of this type.[46] Whether or not murderesses existed, all became the subjects of the same kinds of narratives. Stories about actual women tried for murder were influenced by accounts of fictional murderesses, just as descriptions of fictional murderesses were drawn in part from trial transcripts and published accounts of actual murder cases. For example, Lucretia Cannon was indicted for murder in Delaware in 1829 along with her son-in-law and his brother when human bones were discovered buried on their property. Cannon died in prison awaiting trial.[47] An 1841 pamphlet, *Narrative and Confessions of Lucretia P. Cannon*, described a woman and a career that Cannon scarcely would have recognized. Cannon was about sixty or seventy years old at the time of her arrest and had probably lived in the same Delaware county for her entire adult life. Yet in the pamphlet she was transformed into a beautiful young woman who killed her husband and child and them roamed through the eastern United States and Canada on a lengthy spree of violent crime. This story reappeared in a least two different forms, as *The Life and Confession of Sophia Hamilton* in 1845 and *Confession of Ann Walters, the Murderess*, in 1850. Each of these pamphlets is almost an exact copy of the first, with changes only in names, dates, and places, and with an occasional paragraph added or removed. Cannon was no more real in her incarnation in *Narrative and Confessions of Lucretia P. Cannon* than Sophia Hamilton and Ann Walters, women who may never have existed at all, were in the published accounts of their crimes.

If fact and fiction became blurred in antebellum trial accounts, criminal biographies, and novels, the existence of an actual defendant led to one significant difference from the otherwise similar treatment of fictional murderesses.[48] While fictional women were always found guilty, their actual counterparts were usually acquitted.[49] Regardless of the evidence against them, few real women who were subjects of published criminal biographies or trial accounts between 1830 and 1860 were convicted of murder. Even when jurors convicted such a woman, they were not always fully convinced of her guilt. Ten of the twelve jurors who convicted Elizabeth Van Valkenburgh of poisoning her husband in 1845 petitioned the governor of New York for clemency after her death sentence was passed. At the trial they found her guilty, yet in this petition they argued that she had not meant to kill her husband, only to make him sick in order to cure him of intemperance. Van Valkenburgh was hanged in spite of this plea. Even the judge in Henrietta Robinson's case reconsidered his position while Robinson awaited the death penalty for her crime, asking the governor of New York to commute the sentence to life imprisonment. This time the governor commuted the sentence. In the same period, nearly every man tried for murder for whom there is a published account was convicted and executed, if he did not kill himself first.[50]

The Trials of Polly Bodine and the Permeability of Gender Ideology

A paradox emerged: Americans' need to believe that women, particularly white middle-class women, were virtuous allowed women to claim status as virtuous women even as they engaged in extremely controversial and sometimes criminal behavior. The case of Polly Bodine is one famous example of this phenomenon. On 25 December 1843, Polly Bodine's sister-in-law Emeline Houseman and Emeline's young daughter Ann Eliza were found murdered and partially burned in their house in Staten Island. A number of valuables were missing, and theft appeared to be the obvious motive. About a week later, the police arrested Bodine, charging her with murder, in part because she was the last person known to have spent time with Emeline and the baby, and in part because some pawnbrokers identified her as the woman who had brought some of Emeline's belongings into their shops.[51]

Bodine, according to both her accusers and her defenders, came from a very respectable background. One lawyer told the court that hers was "the most respectable family on Staten Island." Her ancestors had been residents of the island since the early eighteenth century, and members of the family were prominent on the island's "Civil List," frequently serving as judges, members of the assembly, and county supervisors. Bodine's father was quite wealthy and owned substantial land. According to one reporter, he had recently earned $35,000 by selling some of this land to the Staten Island Granite Company.[52]

Polly was fairly well educated for a woman of the period; at one point she worked as a schoolteacher. But she also had some dark corners in her past. She had married Andrew Bodine when she was about fifteen and had lived with her husband for five years, during which time she bore two children, Albert and Eliza Ann. Her husband became "dissipated," they separated, and Polly and the two children moved in with her parents. According to some reports, Andrew died in prison while serving a sentence for bigamy, having married another woman after he and Polly separated. Polly continued to live with her parents in the small Staten Island village where she had grown up, except perhaps when she worked in Manhattan for some time in the millinery business and later as a teacher. When her son, Albert, was eleven, he became a clerk for a physician and pharmacist in Manhattan, George Waite. Polly visited her son in the city about every two weeks and eventually became sexually involved with Dr. Waite. At the time of her arrest in January 1844, she was more than eight months pregnant with his child. In prison, Bodine gave birth to a stillborn child. Despite this morally convoluted past, during her trial Bodine was consistently depicted as a member of respectable society.[53]

According to a number of observers, Bodine's case excited more popular interest than almost any other case in nineteenth-century New York. Soon after the crime visitors, "even women and children," flocked to the murder scene and scavenged through the burnt remains of the house for "relics" belonging to the dead woman or her child, including Emeline's half-charred bible and one of Ann Eliza's baby slippers. According to the newspapers, people discussed the case "with great vehemence in all the public places." And when the trial came, would-be spectators fought each other for seats in the courtroom. Of course, P. T. Barnum capitalized on the excitement by installing a wax figure of Polly Bodine in his New York City museum.[54]

Americans were fascinated by the question of whether Bodine, an apparently respectable woman, could have committed such a horrible crime.[55] The commentary surrounding her trials always focused on uncovering her true character in an effort to prove that she was or was not capable of murder. Accordingly, her trials and the popular furor surrounding them centered on debates about her character that were structured by conceptions of redemptive womanhood. Those who argued that Bodine was guilty always depicted her as immoral, implying that her bad character proved she had murdered her sister-in-law. One observer contended that Bodine had often been followed by "evil and bad report" and had taken advantage of her sister-in-law and brother, who had always "sheltered" her. Several others used her illegitimate child as evidence of her immorality; one paper even accused her of murdering the baby that was supposedly stillborn in prison. Another paper routinely referred to Bodine as an "inhuman fury." Others externalized her corruption, displaying pictures depicting her as "a gruesome old hag" although Polly was only thirty-four and apparently showed signs of having been "handsome" when she was younger. Barnum labeled his gruesome wax figure of Bodine "The Witch of Staten Island."[56] Bodine's supporters and her defense attorneys completely rejected accusations of her corruptness, calling them manifestations of "prejudice" and "popular excitement," yet they would not completely get rid of the charges. Instead they reversed them, portraying her as a respectable woman and mother wrongly accused and abused by the public and particularly by the female spectators in the courtroom.

According to all reports, "ladies" consistently described as "apparently respectable," "fashionably dressed," and members of "the upper ten thousand," made up the vast majority of the audience at Bodine's 1845 trial in Manhattan. From the beginning of that trial newspapers noted that women filled the courtroom, and apparently their numbers increased each day. The report that women filled the courtroom from the beginning yet their numbers were always rising suggests that the newspaper reporters were not simply recording what they saw, but were focusing on the women in court for a particular reason. This reason may be found in their descriptions of the female spectators. The press and virtually everyone except the prosecution described the women's behavior in the courtroom as disruptive, rude, cruel, or vulgar. Early in the trial, Bodine's defense attorneys asked that women be banned from the courtroom, both because lawyers would be discussing "delicate" issues and because the women had shown themselves to be "by far the most troublesome part of the audience." The judge denied the request but used it as an opportunity to chastise a number of women for getting up to stand by the door and stare at Bodine whenever she left the courtroom. Apparently one lecture was not enough. About a week later he repeated the same warning. The prosecution, on the other hand, consistently defended the female spectators; on several occasions they asserted that the women were actually better behaved than the men and that in general they conducted themselves very well. The prosecution seems to have recognized that making the female spectators evil would make Polly good.[57] In focusing on the supposedly vicious behavior of the female spectators, Bodine's lawyers, with the help of the press, were able to shift the positions of feminine good and evil in the courtroom so that Bodine would appear the innocent victim and the women who watched her on trial would become immoral.

Bodine's lawyers also recounted in detail the abuses she suffered at the hands of a number of immoral men. They described how on the day of her arrest, eight months pregnant, she was strip-searched "by the rude hands of men." They told of the "bitter animosity" the press and portions of the public directed at her because she had an illegitimate child, pointing out that "Man may . . . err—no matter to what extent and he can still go through society; but when an unfortunate woman, though made victim to his artifices errs, she is to be sacrificed." Her lawyers also asserted that the press had published false stories and pictures of Bodine that further prejudiced the public against her, humiliating her and making it impossible for her to get a fair trial. Even the name Polly, they argued, was a misrepresentation, a nickname given to her by reporters; they claimed that she had always been known as Mary to friends and family. The lawyers seem to have been engaged in a very conscious attempt to reposition Bodine as an abused victim. They must have known that at least their last claim was untrue. Polly appeared in Staten Island church records as "Polly Housman Bodine" as early as 1826. Even the judge in her Manhattan trial cast Bodine as the helpless victim of a vicious public. He told the jury that it was their duty to be a "barrier between" the accused and popular "prejudices, that seem to thirst for her blood."[58] If they convicted her, the defense lawyers and the judge implied, the jurors would reveal their own blood lust.

Bodine's trial history itself was evidence of the public's inability to determine whether she was good or corrupt. Her first trial, on Staten Island in 1844, ended in a hung jury. She was tried next in Manhattan in 1845 because the court could not find an impartial jury on Staten Island. After the jury attempted to return a verdict of manslaughter but was not allowed to do so, it convicted her of murder "with a recommendation to mercy," but a higher court reversed the sentence and ordered a new trial. The court attempted to try her again in Manhattan, but eventually gave up, unable to find twelve unbiased jurors there. The third trial took place in 1846 in Newburgh, New York, about sixty miles north of New York City. That jury acquitted Bodine. According to one of her lawyers, she was acquitted quickly because when the local people in Newburgh finally saw Bodine, they discovered that she was a well-dressed, attractive woman, not the "old hag" they had seen pictured in many papers. This convinced them the press had misrepresented her and that she must be innocent. In the end, it seems, she looked too respectable to be convicted.[59]

Yet even after Bodine was acquitted, her character remained a mystery; her contemporaries, as a whole, were never certain whether she was good or evil, innocent or guilty.[60] In fact, eight years later, the prosecutor at Henrietta Robinson's trial, apparently counting on continuing confusion over Bodine's innocence or guilt, cited the cases of Polly Bodine and Elsie Whipple as "instances where females have been guilty of the horrible crime of murder."[61] This remark also suggests something more. Both Elsie Whipple, in 1827, and Polly Bodine, in 1846, had been acquitted. The fact that Robinson's prosecutor could not recall even a single case in which a white woman of moderately high social standing was convicted of murder suggests the rarity of such convictions. In the antebellum era a woman who committed murder was routinely depicted as an "inhuman fury," a "woman-fiend" lost to "all moral and religious principles" and accused of "the most heinous crime ever recorded on the pages of history ancient or modern."[62] While fictional accounts of murderesses appeared to offer relatively easy resolutions in that the killers' depravity was obvious, pinpointing such a woman in real life was extremely difficult for people taught to believe that a woman's appearance was a window into her soul. As a result, juries seem to have been willing to overlook the most incriminating evidence if a female defendant acted convincingly enough the part of a proper woman.

RESPECTABILITY, CLASS, ETHNICITY, AND RACE

If women's ability to escape criminal prosecution was linked to their respectability and their virtue, then class, ethnicity, and race certainly complicated the situation. On the other hand, as we have seen in Henrietta Robinson's case, respectability did not require any real evidence regarding class status or ethnicity. Those who successfully claimed to be native-born, middle-class white women were by far the most common beneficiaries of the respectability defense, but they were not the only beneficiaries. While the crimes of white working-class, immigrant, African American, and Native American women were usually outside antebellum Americans' obsession with female murderers, occasionally the trials of such women generated public interest.[63]

In the beginning of August 1851, nineteen-year-old Margaret Garrity was living as a servant in a Newark, New Jersey, hotel. She had emigrated from Ireland about three years earlier and was engaged to be married to another Irish immigrant, Edward Drum. She had recently discovered that she was pregnant with his child. On August 4, a neighbor told her that Drum had married another woman the day before, and Margaret grabbed a carving knife from the hotel kitchen and went to confront her fiancé. When she found Drum out walking with his new wife, she stabbed him in the chest and ran away. He collapsed on the street and died within a few minutes. There was never a doubt that Margaret had killed him. Drum's wife had recognized her, and Margaret freely admitted that she had stabbed Drum.

In spite of the public's awareness of her guilt, they were on her side from the start. The *Newark Daily Advertiser* reported two days after the murder that

"There is everywhere . . . a strong popular feeling in her favor." The papers, Garrity's lawyers, a number of witnesses, and apparently the public and the jury all saw the case in the same light. They described her as an innocent, virtuous young woman whose character had always been good. According to a broadside describing the crime and trial, hers was a story of "Innocence Rewarded," a "Successful Triumph." She had loved Drum, he had promised to marry her, but then he had seduced and abandoned her. His act was so villainous—he was a "fiend in human shape"—that no one could blame the distraught young woman for killing him, especially considering that there was no legal way to punish his crime. As Garrity's attorney put it, "If a woman slays her ravisher in the protection of her brightest jewel, she is acquitted and the death of the man is considered a riddance for society. But there is a man far worse than the ravisher. . . . And what remedy has she [who is seduced]? Why, the law gives her . . . nothing. Gentlemen, in all attachment to the laws of my native state, I arraign the law. Make a new law, and one that will give a sufficient remedy."[64] The broadside's author showed even less hesitancy about condoning her crime. It asserted that the public would give Garrity "praise for what she's done." And apparently that is just what happened. Garrity was acquitted, and at the end of her trial she was greeted by a large, cheering crowd. There is also evidence to suggest that they never considered her permanently ruined. In the words of the broadside:

> She now is set at liberty,
> to act a worthy part,
> May she respected ever be,
> By every virtuous heart.[65]

Margaret Garrity was an unmarried, pregnant Irish servant who had murdered a man. Yet she was acquitted and lauded by the public. Garrity's social standing was lower than that of the majority of women who became the focus of published antebellum murder narratives, but she too successfully asserted her status as a respectable woman.

African American women were almost never the protagonists in antebellum published murder pamphlets, but in certain situations their crimes did generate other forms of popular literature, and occasionally their cases became the center of public controversy. These cases invariably involved enslaved women, and discussions of their crimes became debates over the institution of slavery. The discussions also relied on the same fundamental assumption: that enslaved African American women tried to live as respectable, redemptive women, but slavery thwarted their efforts and eventually drove them to murder. The 1855 case of Celia, a Missouri slave who beat her master to death, for example, was highly publicized and controversial. A team of Missouri lawyers argued that Celia was protecting herself from rape when she killed her master. They asserted unsuccessfully that laws allowing white women "to use deadly force to protect her honor" also applied to black slave women. That is, enslaved women were not simply property; they were women, and as women they had the same legal right to protect their honor as white women did. Melton McLaurin suggests that a large portion of the community was sympathetic toward Celia during her trial.[66] Although Celia was convicted, she and her lawyers had asserted that she was a redemptive woman who had the right to kill to protect her virtue, and at least some members of the community had accepted this argument. Even if the majority of the white community disagreed, the argument was available, and it was powerful enough to provoke the sympathy of a significant minority.

The most famous African American murderess of the antebellum era was the fugitive slave Margaret Garner, who killed her two-year-old daughter in 1856. In addition to receiving national press coverage at the time of the crime, her case generated poems, paintings, and at least three contemporaneous novels. It also inspired a more recent work: Toni Morrison's 1987 novel *Beloved*.[67] In January 1856, Garner had escaped from her Kentucky plantation home with her husband, her father-in-law, her mother-in-law, and her four young children. They crossed the frozen Ohio River and took shelter in Cincinnati, in the home of Margaret's aunt and uncle. Slave catchers soon found them, surrounded the cabin, and ordered the family to come out. At this point, according to her mother-in-law's testimony, Margaret cried out, "Mother, before my children shall be taken back to Kentucky, I will kill every one of them!" Margaret then picked up a carving knife and slashed the throat of her young daughter Mary, who quickly bled to death. She tried to kill the three other children, but only wounded them superficially before her aunt stopped her. According to the coroner, Margaret "voluntarily confessed" and informed him "that her determination was to have killed all the children and then destroy herself rather than return to slavery."[68]

Margaret Garner was never tried for murder. Instead, she and her family were tried as fugitive slaves and were taken back to Kentucky. The state of Ohio did attempt to extradite her from Kentucky to stand trial for murder in Ohio, but her master sold her south before she could be taken. She died two years later of typhoid fever on a Louisiana plantation.[69] Ohio abolitionists were a driving force behind the attempt to bring Garner back to Ohio. They wanted to bring her there to remove her from slavery and were certain that an Ohio jury would never convict her of a capital crime. Her lawyer believed that the worst punishment she would get was "a few years in the penitentiary." The local prosecutor agreed, speculating that it was "improbable that 'any jury, in admiring the heroic spirit of the mother,' would ever vote a guilty verdict on a first degree murder charge." The Republican governor of Ohio, Salmon P. Chase, later explained to a friend that he had hesitated to have Garner extradited at first because "I was unwilling to characterize the homicide as murder. I yielded, however, to my sympathies for the poor mother."[70] All these people characterized Garner as a loving mother who sacrificed her own child to protect the girl from the horrors of slavery. Even without a murder trial, Margaret Garner became *the* "tragic slave mother" in many published and unpublished accounts, a heroine who killed to protect her family, to save them from the moral and spiritual destruction of slavery. As abolitionist Henry C. Wright put it, "That heroic mother, in the deep, holy love of her maternal heart, cut the throat of one child and tried to kill her three others to save them from the lash and lust" of her master. One Cincinnati newspaper even suggested that its readers contribute money to a "monument honoring 'the heroic woman.'"[71]

The cases of Margaret Garner and Celia suggest that African American women asserted that they too were virtuous women, even in the most controversial situations. Redemptive womanhood, then, was not the sole property of the white middle class. Enslaved African American women, as well as their white and black abolitionist defenders, used the ideology of redemptive womanhood in an overtly political fashion: they transformed it into an argument for racial equality. That is, they asserted that enslaved women tried to live as redemptive women, to be virtuous and to protect others from sin and evil, but that slavery did not allow them to do so. In other words, they used African American women's claim to redemptive womanhood to put slavery itself on trial.

Americans in 1778 understood accused murderess Bathsheba Spooner as a person with a "disordered mind," but by 1844 Peleg Chandler envisioned her crime as utterly destructive to her womanhood. In 1778, it was easy to convict Spooner of murder and condemn her to death. By the antebellum era, it would have been extremely difficult to convict a well-educated, apparently respectable, white woman like Spooner of murder, especially when she did not commit the crime herself. It would have been even more difficult to execute her. It is likely that if Spooner had committed her crime fifty years later, her story would resemble Elsie Whipple's or Lucretia Chapman's: with no direct evidence linking her to the actual murder, she would have been acquitted, while the men who had killed her husband (like Whipple's alleged lover, Jesse Strang, and Chapman's alleged lover, Mina) would have been convicted and executed.

By the antebellum era, all explanations of female crime centered on the degree to which the accused criminal displayed the attributes of redemptive womanhood. Since women should by nature be more moral, religious, and nurturing than men, the question was whether an accused murderess had these qualities. In fiction and in nonfiction narratives of alleged murderesses already dead, like Chandler's account of Bathsheba Spooner, it might be easy to characterize a woman as corrupt. But in cases where it truly mattered, where a living woman was on trial for murder, the situation was much more complicated. All it took was the presence of an actual woman to destroy Americans' ability to confine women into two neat categories, the true and the untrue. Here was a problem from which their gender ideology allowed them no escape.

The development of a more rigid and strictly defined notion of woman's nature made it more difficult to convict women of murder. In this case, the impulse to label and define individuals led to a certain freedom from the very labels that were being imposed. The implications of this point go far beyond the issue of female murderers. They go to the heart of antebellum conceptions of womanhood, suggesting that the ideology of redemptive womanhood never defined or limited women's behavior; rather, it broke down such limits and was perhaps flexible enough for women of different class, ethnic, and racial backgrounds to shape to fit their own lives.

The "Fallen Woman" in Antebellum America

C H A P T E R

T W O

As an inducement to come up to this self-denying work,
let mothers, let females generally, think of the numerous
effects of licentiousness. . . . What will become of us, if this
monster is not arrested in its progress?

—*Friend of Virtue*, 1839[1]

*T*n 1830, Reverend John McDowall, a volunteer missionary fresh from Princeton Theological
Seminary, arrived in New York City bright eyed and
eager to fight sin. He quickly involved himself in a
number of urban reform movements. In 1831, a
newly formed women's moral reform group, the New
York Magdalen Society, hired him as an agent. The
same year, McDowall wrote the society's first annual
report, in which he asserted that there were at least
ten thousand prostitutes working in New York City.
According to his calculations, one in ten females (of
all ages) in New York City was a prostitute. This
claim angered and outraged many New Yorkers.[2]
The backlash against the report caused the Magdalen
Society to disband, yet McDowall's inflated claims
about prostitution established a pattern moral reformers would follow for the rest of the antebellum
era.[3] McDowall was the first of a generation of antebellum reformers and writers to assert that prostitution was rampant and growing rapidly in America's
burgeoning cities and that it would destroy the nation if left unchecked.[4]

Americans' discussions of "fallen women" and prostitutes shared much in common with their discussions of murderesses.[5] If antebellum depictions of women accused of murder revealed their fear that evil women lurked within the nascent middle class, hiding behind their apparent respectability, their accounts of fallen women and prostitutes exposed a similar concern. Both nonfictional and fictional accounts of prostitution frequently focused on "respectable" young women who were transformed by illicit sexual encounters into "depraved wantons," but who, at least for a time, retained their outward appearance of respectability. In isolation the female murderer was the more threatening figure, but the great threat prostitutes posed was their ubiquity. That is, although Americans were fairly certain that most women were not murderers, they worried that women's illicit sexual behavior was skyrocketing as society became more urban and anonymous.

Prostitution was, for antebellum Americans, "a lightning rod for all sorts of fantasies and anxieties." Historians have noted a sudden and dramatic rise in Americans' concerns about prostitution beginning in the late 1820s and 1830s and have linked this new concern with the rapid economic, social, and cultural changes of this era. Industrialization, urbanization, class formation, and new gender roles have been long cited as contributing factors in this new obsession with prostitution as *the* social evil. As Mary Ryan has pointed out, in the city of Utica, New York, increased concern with prostitution after 1830 was closely linked to the rise in the number of "unprotected sons and daughters" entering the city. Ryan notes that as often as not, these sons and daughters were members of the nascent middle class.[6] A number of scholars have noted the ubiquity of the respectable prostitute in antebellum fiction and nonfiction, yet they have not explored the reasons for this phenomenon. They continue to understand the antebellum fixation on the problem of fallen women and prostitutes as a manifestation of the desire of a white middle class to reform a supposedly immoral working class, which was becoming more visible in the nation's rapidly growing cities.[7] Lori Ginzberg, for example, has characterized antiprostitution reform as an effort to make working women embrace "middle-class respectability," and Christine Stansell calls the reform a middle-class "response to the growing social and sexual distance working-class women . . . were traveling from patriarchal regulation."[8]

Even if the majority of antebellum prostitutes were working-class women, when American writers and reformers discussed fallen women and prostitutes, they most often focused on white, rural, native-born young women from "respectable" families.[9] In addition to appearing in tracts, urban exposés, newspaper and journal articles, and biographies, these women could be found in nearly every sensational novel published in the 1840s and 1850s.[10] Virtuous rural women who had been seduced and abandoned or kidnapped and raped, then became prostitutes because they had no other way to support themselves, became a staple of antebellum potboilers. As Timothy Gilfoyle points out, writer Ned Buntline's fictional prostitute Isabella Meadows was representative of "the most common image of the prostitute" in the antebellum era. A young woman from the country, Isabella was "a soiled dove. Coming from a protected childhood and an affluent family," she was "tricked and seduced into commercial sex."[11]

A number of historians in addition to Gilfoyle have noted that antebellum Americans were fascinated by relatively high-status prostitutes. Lori Ginzberg has found evidence that reformers believed that "even middle-class girls became prostitutes." According to Christine Stansell, this "sentimentalist" image of the prostitute was so powerful by the 1850s that "poor girls knew enough about the politics of interpretation to invoke" it. Charles Loring Brace points out that "they usually relate . . . that they have been seduced . . . by the wiles of some heartless seducer. Often they describe themselves as belonging to some virtuous, respectable and even wealthy family."[12] Whether or not prostitutes were innocent young women from respectable families, that is what Americans both feared they were and expected them to be.

Americans' fascination with respectable prostitutes suggests that they feared that women in general were becoming less virtuous. Women needed to be the moral foundation of the nation, but now, it seemed, they were losing their sexual purity. As the transportation revolution, urbanization, and new forms of wage work made geographic mobility more common, massive social changes occurred in American society. One transformation was the breakdown of older patterns of community regulation of sexual behavior. Communities lost their ability to pressure a couple into marrying when an unmarried woman became pregnant, and suddenly, it seemed, large numbers of young women were being seduced and abandoned, then turning to prostitution to support themselves and their illegitimate children.

Americans responded to the threat they believed fallen women, prostitutes, and prostitution posed to the nation in two distinct ways. First, they attempted to fill the void left by the breakdown of community regulation of sexual mores by creating reform organizations and proposing new laws; second, they began to embrace a more assertive ideal of American womanhood. Americans grew increasingly convinced that to remain virtuous in this changed world women would need to become more assertive, to think and act independently so conniving and dishonest men would be unable to seduce them.

"DAUGHTERS OF THE WEALTHY, RESPECTABLE AND PIOUS CITIZENS"

From the very start of the antebellum era, reformers and journalists were obsessed with the idea that daughters of respectable citizens were becoming prostitutes. According to the 1831 Magdalen report, many prostitutes were "the daughters of the wealthy, respectable and pious citizens of our own and other states, seduced from their homes by the villains who infest the community, preying upon female innocence, and succeeding in their diabolical purpose, wither by promises of marriage; or after deceiving them into a brothel, by the commission of rape."[13] Most of the women whose stories McDowall recounted in *Magdalen Facts* a year later fit this pattern. One prostitute he described was the daughter of rich parents and a former student at Emma Willard's school. A school friend of her brother seduced her under promise of marriage, then abandoned her. Left deserted and penniless in New York City, she turned to prostitution. Another prostitute was a minister's daughter who had married a rich merchant. The merchant abandoned her for another woman and sold their house, leaving her homeless and penniless. She moved into a cellar with one of her former servants, began drinking, and soon turned to prostitution to support herself.[14]

Reformer, author, and public lecturer Caroline Dall described clergymen's and merchants' daughters as typical of the kind of women who became prostitutes. In her lectures on the subject, she referred to a number of such women, including "the daughter of a State Street [Boston] merchant" whom she had found "in the gutters of Toronto." When Dall wrote to the "wealthy" merchant, he acknowledged the woman was his daughter, but "refused to furnish her the bread that would have kept her from sin."[15]

In 1826, the Unitarian church in Boston decided that the city's poor were so numerous and ill-cared-for that they needed the services of a "city missionary." The church appointed the Reverend Joseph Tuckerman to the position. Charged to care for the poor of the city, Tuckerman wrote extensively of their plight in order to gain public support. Yet one of his gravest concerns about prostitution was its effects on the middle class. In an 1830 essay specifically criticizing women's low wages, Tuckerman warned that prostitution was a serious problem for all classes, but what seemed to disturb him the most was that it was spreading to the middle classes: "I would to God, indeed, that it were the children of the poor only, or that it were those of the rich alone, who are thus falling into the deepest depravity! But, in truth, the contagion spreads to not a few of all classes."[16] The fact that Tuckerman, a missionary whose work focused specifically on the urban poor, was so concerned with middle-class prostitution suggests the strength of Americans' tendency to see prostitution as a middle-class problem.

The most famous prostitute of the antebellum era fit neatly into this framework. In 1836, Helen Jewett was murdered in her room in a New York City brothel. Her case, and the trial of her accused murderer, Richard Robinson, became nationally famous events, generating numerous pamphlets and even full-length novels. As late as 1849—thirteen years after the event—the *National Police Gazette* revisited the story for its readers.[17] According to the most reliable reports, Jewett was born in Maine, apparently the daughter of a "mechanic." She was sent into service in a wealthy family, who had her educated with their own children. At some point, it seems she became a prostitute in Portland, Maine, and she later moved to New York City. But the story some reporters told about her past was different. In one account Jewett was the "daughter of a major general and had been seduced while at boarding school" and had fled to the city in shame. In this account, as in many narratives of accused murderesses, writers augmented their subject's socioeconomic status so that she was not just of "middling" status, but quite well-to-do. According to other writers, Jewett was "one of the most intelligent, beautiful and accomplished women to be found in her class of life," "full of intellect and refinement . . . with talents calculated for the highest sphere of life." Members of the press frequently categorized Jewett as a woman who had fallen from the very highest pinnacle of womanhood to the very lowest. In reality, Jewett was indeed well educated; she left a vast quantity of correspondence behind that allows no doubt of it.[18] Yet writers augmented her status and her beauty whenever possible, in order to magnify the depth of her descent.

This effort to augment a prostitute's status revealed Americans' fears that the most respectable young women in the nation could be and were becoming prostitutes. It was the innocent who were the most likely to fall, according to many accounts, because of their innocence and their ignorance of the trickery of male seducers. As Caroline Dall warned, "The Fairest and most innocent may be the first struck down." Women from respectable families, especially in the country, brought up in protected and sheltered environments and ignorant of the dangers of seduction were thought to be the easiest targets. In J. H. Ingraham's fictional account of Helen Jewett's life, he describes her before her "fall" as a young woman with "an innate love for purity, and [who] was modest and discrete." Yet because she was an isolated country girl, these qualities were not strengthened by "a refined education and the pure morals of society." Essentially, she was too naive, and she trusted in the goodness of the man who seduced her. As David Reynolds has pointed out, fictional accounts "almost invariably . . . portrayed [prostitutes] as products of male duplicity or social injustice."[19] After the men they loved and trusted had raped or seduced and abandoned them, prostitution seemed their only option.

According to journalist George Foster, the great tragedy of prostitution was that it destroyed the moral and religious nature of highly respectable and virtuous women: "The pure and gentle woman, capable of all high and holy duties and affections, as wife and mother—endowed by her creator with faculties fitting her, if properly directed, for the guardian angel and the consoler of man—goes, in utter recklessness of herself and all the world, to add one more to that frightful phalanx of female depravity which is the terror and curse of an enfeebled and depraved civilization."[20] Prostitution was so terrifying because it could destroy the best of American women. As author George Thompson put it in *The Countess; or, Memoirs of Women of Leisure:* "Woman may be purer than it is a possibility for a man to equal. . . . But when her ruin is consummated . . . she falls forever from the high pinnacle on which nature and heaven ordained her to stand, and if she continues on in the downward path . . . she can attain a depth of miserable existence to which it were an utter impossibility for man in his most infamous transactions or crimes, to reach."[21]

Foster and Thompson asserted that prostitutes and other sorts of ruined women could not be redeemed. They believed that because women were naturally purer than men, if they acted against this nature they destroyed it utterly, becoming worse than the most depraved men. Just as women's duty as redeemers made them responsible for the nation's virtue, women who were not properly redemptive actively destroyed the nation's moral fiber. Foster, Thompson, and many other writers portrayed the fallen woman and prostitute as a woman who was consumed with a desire to destroy all virtue; she wanted to "bring others to the same level, to find companions in her pleasures, and to this end she spreads wide her net to catch the thoughtless with the tempting bait of her own charms." As one fictional prostitute asked, "What are men to me, but as victims to pluck, or food for my insane and fierce appetites?" The fallen woman, "used every art to tempt and seduce and ruin young men . . . and hundreds were slain by her." As David Brion Davis puts it, nineteenth-century novelists asserted that the criminal woman "was a breeder of contagious evil."[22] She was an evil woman who corrupted those around her rather than a redemptive woman who saved them. Because Americans believed so strongly in redemptive womanhood, female depravity was always a grave threat to the republic and a powerful symbol of societal decay.

Antebellum Americans developed detailed narratives of women's fall from respectability into depravity. The first step, of course, was from a single illicit sexual affair to prostitution. According to contemporary accounts, when women became prostitutes, they first seemed to enjoy an improvement in economic and social status. They lived in luxury in fashionable brothels that were frequented by wealthy men who lavished gifts upon them and treated them as

fine ladies. But, of course, this did not last. Each month and every year in prostitution corrupted women further. This depravity showed in their looks and
their manners, and so they were repeatedly cast out of one class of brothel and
into a lower one.[23] Minister Joseph Tuckerman traced the history of the prostitute from her start as an attractive, ladylike woman in the "highest class of prof-
ligates" through her descent "step by step into the poor, filthy residences,
where the lowest of her sex, with scarcely garments to cover them, the
wretched victims of loathsome disease, are daily deadening more and more the
little sensibility which remains to them, by intemperance, profaneness and riot;
. . . lost to virtue, to shame, and to all that is human."[24] In only a few years, the
refined and respectable-seeming "high-class" prostitutes who lived in opulent
mansions were transformed into beings one could no longer identify as female
or even human. Now their homes were in the street or in the worst slum hov-
els. A number of historians have pointed out that this was probably not the reality of prostitutes' lives, but it was the dominant way the antebellum public
understood their lives.

Journalist George Foster and others linked the prostitute's moral decline not
only to class decline, but also, ultimately, to racial amalgamation. Foster asserted that prostitutes frequently began their careers in elegant "first class"
brothels, but soon came down "the ladder of infamy" and were reduced to the
lowest of streetwalkers, "in search of sailors, loafers, greenhorns, negroes, anything or anybody, to decoy into their filthy dens." This decline of the prostitute, Foster asserted, turned "the pure and gentle woman" into one of "that
frightful phalanx of female depravity which is the terror and curse of an enfeebled and depraved civilization."[25] John McDowall recounted the experiences of
a surgeon's daughter who was seduced and abandoned and eventually "sank to
the lowest class of courtezans, mingling with negroes."[26] Sporting papers, like
The Flash, in New York, made precisely the same argument, if in more gruesome detail: "A woman of respectable connexions in this city fell from purity
some years since. . . . She followed through the different grades of vice, from
guilt and shame to infamy and despair—from gilded luxury to squalid poverty,
until at length she was compelled to herd with the most miserable of the dissolute blacks in the suburbs." The woman's sister sent a man to search for her
and try to redeem her, but by the time he found her, in a house where "blacks
and other inmates . . . were rioting in beastly intoxication," she lay dead in another room, "a bloated corpse, surrounded by filth, and yet more horrible, rats
had devoured nearly one side of her cheek." In this account, steeped in racist
ideology, the writer suggested that prostitution had pushed a formerly respectable white woman below the level of most African Americans: her acts
had nullified her claim to whiteness, and even to humanity. This prostitute was

portrayed as living like a beast and as dying like one among other such creatures who did not mourn or even notice her death.[27]

William Sanger, in his mammoth *History of Prostitution*, mapped out in greater detail a similar path of moral, class, and racial decline that all prostitutes supposedly followed. Sanger described prostitutes and houses of prostitution in terms of "classes," or "grades," from the first class down to the fifth. The inhabitants of first-class houses of prostitution he depicted as largely young, pretty, well-educated, and refined natives of New England or the mid-Atlantic states who passed as respectable women when they ventured outside their brothels. In his discussion of the second grade of prostitutes, Sanger noted that many of these women started out in first-class houses, "but left them when their charms began to fade." He asserted that the "longer continuance in the habits of prostitution, and the association with a less aristocratic class of visitor, has diminished the refinement of the women and imparted to them coarser manners." He depicted these second-grade establishments as "tawdry" and cheap imitations of first-class brothels. While Sanger acknowledged that all prostitutes did not start on the first tier—that a great number of immigrant women, for example, started on the second level—he always maintained that "the natural tendency of prostitution is to depress . . . its followers." Sanger categorized the fourth grade of prostitutes as largely the "refuse of the other classes" and the fifth grade, "the outcasts of the outcasts," as "so disgustingly hideous that all feminine characteristics are blotted out." These women, who had fallen "far below humanity," he maintained, "are experiencing the degradation to which every prostitute . . . is rapidly tending."[28] In this formulation, a woman's immoral behavior directly led to a decline in her socioeconomic status, her racial status, and even her claim to humanity.

This conflation of virtue, socioeconomic status, race, and even humanity, particularly in the case of women, who were thought to be especially virtuous, has made it easy for historians to overlook the middle-class prostitute and other middle-class female figures of vice and immorality. For antebellum Americans, prostitution transformed respectable young merchants' daughters into "gay and thoughtless creatures . . . luxuriously reclining on velvet sofas" in fashionable high-class brothels, and later into "drunkards in the kennels of five points" who had fallen "far below humanity."[29] The notion that nineteenth-century American middle-class women were virtuous and moral is perhaps now so embedded in American culture that we read the word *prostitute* and assume the author must be referring to a woman outside the white middle class. What may be most surprising about antebellum Americans' attitudes toward prostitutes is that when they looked at impoverished prostitutes in places like Five Points, the New York City slum district, they saw formerly innocent and virtuous daughters of well-to-do and highly respectable families.

A LADY "WHOM I NEVER SHOULD HAVE SUSPECTED"

The fact that the innocent victim of seduction and the depraved streetwalker of the slums were the same woman at different stages of development made it difficult for Americans to distinguish one from the other. Because they could not clearly differentiate the innocent victim from the depraved prostitute, they feared that prostitutes were indistinguishable from respectable women. If many prostitutes started out as respectable women, it seemed plausible that they could pass as the virtuous women they once were, particularly early in their careers when they supposedly lived lives of luxury in first-class brothels. Public debate over prostitution reveals that Americans were preoccupied with this problem. In the American imagination, prostitutes passed for respectable women all the time. According to Marilynn Hill, "contemporaries mistook many prostitutes and managers of brothels for boarding house keepers." Timothy Gilfoyle notes that "visual images depicted streetwalkers . . . as attractive young women in elegant gowns and bonnets, surrounded by gentlemen of substance." While Gilfoyle regards this as a "nonthreatening" image of prostitutes, I contend it was extremely threatening because it suggested that prostitutes were undetectable and could not be distinguished from proper women.[30] So surprised was George Templeton Strong when he first saw brothel keeper "Madam" Rosina Townsend that he wrote in his diary that she seemed to be "an old lady, dressed in black with a very good-natured, mild countenance whom I should never have suspected of being such a character as she is." Joseph Tuckerman complained that Boston brothel keepers "walk our streets in the dress of ladies." Not only could prostitutes be mistaken for respectable women, but houses of prostitution could be hidden in "respectable neighborhoods, disguised under the mask of boarding houses, dressmakers, milliners and shops of various kinds."[31]

Prostitutes' success at feigning respectability could have serious consequences. Scottish minister Ralph Wardlaw warned his American audience to beware of "secret or sly harlots" who were especially dangerous because they "corrupt and seduce innocence, and which, assuming appearances most honorable, paralyzes authority, sets it perpetually at defiance, and spreads with impunity the most frightful contagion." Tuckerman asserted that poor girls were tricked into entering houses of prostitution, thinking that the madams were "ladies," and the brothels regular boarding houses.[32] Antebellum accounts of prostitution were filled with stories of this sort. One fictional prostitute decided, after her seducer abandoned her, to dress as a respectable woman and go out walking to look for a man to support her. "She dressed with . . . simplicity" because "she understood that it was the triumph of art to conceal art." Soon

she met an honest man, seduced him, and tricked him into thinking he had ruined her, and he agreed to marry her. Fictional prostitute Ellen Grant achieved
revenge against her seducer with the help of several prostitute friends in a similar fashion. They disguised their brothel as the home of a wealthy family and
lured the seducer, a doctor, there on the pretense of caring for a sick daughter.
The doctor was so convinced that the young women in the house were wealthy
heiresses, he tried to marry one of them.[33] According to these accounts, any respectable-looking woman walking down the street, even the most elegant,
might well be a secret prostitute.

Americans believed that one reason prostitutes were so elusive, so hard to de-
tect, was their access to abortion. The abortionist facilitated the concealment of
the depravity of all women. As one reformer wrote, abortionist "Madame Restell
shows your spouse how she may commit as many adulteries as there are hours in
the year without the possibility of detection." The abortionist encouraged not
just depravity, but secret depravity that might remain concealed for a lifetime.
The acts of the abortionist, then, appeared to allow any woman to engage in
prostitution or adultery without facing consequences. Mid-nineteenth-century
opponents of abortion were convinced that society's most respectable women—
well-to-do married women—were having the majority of the abortions.[34]

The abortionist was thought to conceal both her own depravity and that of her
customers. Like a prostitute, she could pretend to be a respectable lady, setting
herself up as a legitimate female physician. Then any woman, any wife or mother,
sister or daughter, might one day slink off to her without her male friends or relatives ever knowing. And, they feared, many women did. Abortionists were so
threatening both because they helped women conceal illicit sexual behavior and
because they themselves hid behind the guise of apparent respectability.

Ann Lohman, alias Madame Restell, was almost certainly the most famous
abortionist in antebellum America. A resident of New York City, she was arrested on several occasions and was tried three times in the 1840s for performing abortions. However, she was convicted only once, and then was sentenced
to only a year in prison. This was not because juries were sympathetic to abortionists, but because performing an abortion before quickening, when the
mother first felt the fetus move, was not a felony in New York until 1869.[35]
The press was nearly unanimous in its condemnation of Madame Restell and
Madame Costello, New York City's other prominent female abortionist, during
the 1840s, the decade during which abortionists were first singled out as em-
bodiments of pure evil and total depravity.[36]

Yet Madame Restell could not be distinguished from the most pious of
women, even at her own trial. A pamphlet noted her arrival at her 1841 court
appearance: "The accused was attired in the most elegant manner, in a black

satin walking dress, white satin bonnet, of the cottage pattern, and a very elegant white veil of Brussels lace. In her hand she carried a parcel of printed papers, which made some persons mistake her for the lady Presidentess of the
Tract Society."[37] George Lippard similarly described the female abortionist as
undetectable yet absolutely evil in his account of "Madame Resimer," a thinly
veiled fictional rendering of Restell: "Lofty mansions lined the street, but their
wealthy occupants little knew the real character of the woman (woman!—fiend
would be a better name) who tenanted the gloomy house. . . . [She was] the
very instrument of the very vilest crime known in the annals of Hell."[38] Americans were obsessed with the notion that prostitutes and adulteresses lived secretly within respectable society and that secret abortionists allowed them to
continue to do so by ending their unwanted pregnancies. The apparently respectable yet undetectable fallen woman and abortionist, like the undetectable
murderess, existed because Americans could not believe that a woman who possessed any sign of virtue could, in reality, be an embodiment of pure evil.

THE COUNTRY AND THE CITY

If writers and reformers were fascinated by a prostitute's respectable background, they were just as interested in her rural origins and in the role of the
city in her fall. Antebellum Americans' fixation on prostitution was linked to
specific social and cultural changes involved in urbanization. Historians have
noted that the new geographic mobility associated with the growth of cities and
urban employment seemed to break down older sexual mores, but their descriptions of this breakdown are very general and do not address the ways in
which specific sexual mores ceased to function.[39] Here I look at traditional
community sexual policing patterns and consider how the values and traditions
these reflected helped shape Americans' fears about prostitution and their responses to changes in sexual behavior.

As Laurel Thatcher Ulrich points out, in late-eighteenth-century America,
the married women in a town were responsible for upholding the community's
sexual mores. In the same time period, "premarital pregnancy was common
throughout New England . . . and . . . had been so for at least a generation." To
uphold the community's sexual values, it was the married women's duty to find
out if an unmarried woman was pregnant. Once they determined she was pregnant, they urged her to reveal the father's name, and then, with the community's support, they pressured the couple into marrying.[40]

It appears that the system of community policing Ulrich delineates began to
break down as urban centers became larger and more important in the early
nineteenth century. If young men were no longer economically bound to their

farm communities, they might not succumb to the social pressure to marry, but might leave town instead. This resonates with Ulrich's finding that the small number of men who did not marry their pregnant lovers in eighteenth-century Hallowell, Maine, tended to be transient sailors and lumbermen.[41] The number of transients in the American population skyrocketed with the urbanization of the early nineteenth century. The growth of cities increased men's options even before the United States was industrialized to any degree. As a result of a transatlantic shipping boom, jobs, and therefore geographic mobility, expanded tremendously for men in the Eastern seaboard cities beginning in the 1790s. As the industrialization of the 1820s and 1830s created jobs for both men and women in large towns and cities, geographic mobility became much more common, and according to both fictional and nonfictional accounts of prostitution, the men invariably took advantage of this newfound freedom to avoid marriage. Such stories often began with seduction under promise of marriage, then subsequent abandonment by the man, who fled to a city to avoid marriage. Sometimes the seducer took the woman to the city with him, promising to marry her there, but, of course, he never did.

These stories asserted that young women were being exposed to the dangerous consequences of urbanization even in their parents' homes in the country. In *Magdalen Facts*, for example, John McDowall recounted the story of a young woman who was living at home with her parents when her brother brought a school friend to visit. This friend had no ties to the local community, so he felt free to seduce the young woman, promising to marry her, because he could leave town if she became pregnant. When she told him she was pregnant, he took her to New York City, saying he would marry her there. Instead, he deserted her and left her among strangers and with no means of support. Too ashamed to ask her parents for help, she stayed in the city and turned to prostitution.[42]

The Reverend Joseph Tuckerman was fearful that large numbers of virtuous women from the country were being corrupted in the city of Boston. As he put it, young women who came to the city "with all the truth and artlessness of a virtuous country life, are seduced, despoiled, destroyed, by profligate and base young men, who yet call themselves *gentlemen!*" The subtitle of J. H. Ingraham's famous novel about prostitute Helen Jewett is *The Dangers of the Town*. According to Ingraham, Jewett's naïveté was her downfall. Having grown up in the secluded countryside, she was simply too trusting and believed her seducer's promises of marriage.[43]

From a present-day standpoint the women in such stories seem almost ridiculous in their gullibility—or disingenuous in their protestations of innocence. How did all these women allow themselves to be seduced under promise of marriage? If they were so virtuous, why were they willing to participate in premarital sex? Did they truly believe they would be married, or did they cynically craft these stories to garner sympathy from reformers? We can never know each woman's motive for telling her story as she did, but there are important historical questions here that can be addressed. Why did these women and other Americans who wrote about them tell this particular story about their sexual fall, and what is it about our understanding of nineteenth-century American history that makes it very difficult for us to take that story seriously? I suggest that our disbelief stems from our unspoken assumption that a virtuous woman in the nineteenth century was necessarily chaste before marriage. But as Ulrich points out, premarital sex was quite common in late-eighteenth-century rural America. When an unmarried young woman in a small New England village had sexual relations with an unmarried man, she could reasonably assume that if she became pregnant he would marry her. In this era, a woman could afford to be seduced under promise of marriage and still expect to keep her reputation intact. There need not even be a specific promise to marry. In the diary of midwife Martha Ballard and in the public records of Hallowell, the fact that a man had had sexual relations with a woman and that she had become pregnant was evidence enough of a promise of marriage.[44]

Reformers' and other writers' words about seduction under promise of marriage reveal their shock and confusion over the breakdown of older community policing patterns.[45] Antiprostitution reformers suggested in their writings that the traditional sexual mores that had functioned well enough in the late eighteenth and early nineteenth centuries were by 1830 liable to turn a whole generation of American young women into prostitutes. It was easy for men to seduce and abandon young women in part because "virtuous" women *did* commonly have sex before marriage at the beginning of the nineteenth century. The nineteenth century's emphasis on premarital chastity was a new one; it represented a change in sexual values resulting from the breakdown in the community's ability to compel men to marry their pregnant lovers.

THE "PREYED-UPON INNOCENT" AND THE "VICE-RIDDEN JADE"

The belief that virtuous women were becoming the sexual prey of men and had few ways of protecting themselves ran through antebellum discussions of prostitutes and led to some extremely sympathetic portrayals of fallen women not only in reform literature, but throughout the public press.[46] Yet historians of prostitution have generally argued that antebellum Americans, particularly those of the middle class, condemned women harshly and completely for any sexual indiscretion; they have tended to assume that, with the exception of certain moral reformers, middle-class Americans generally considered prostitutes unredeemable. According to Timothy Gilfoyle, fiction and nonfiction writers "all assume that once a woman 'falls' it is forever." Marilynn Hill argues that the notion that fallen women were unredeemable helped Americans to "uphold contemporary notions that women must be either mother-angels or whore-devils." She asserts that, in Judith Walkowitz's words, this categorization of women as angels or devils "helped to . . . establish a demarcation between the respectable and 'dangerous' classes of society." David Brion Davis points out that by the 1840s in American fiction, "if a girl had natural warmth and passion, even a single sexual experience made her capable of any crime . . . once a girl's soul had been 'murdered' she had no chance for recovery." While Christine Stansell notes that "antebellum . . . culture generated two opposing images of the prostitute"—the "preyed-upon innocent" and the "vice-ridden jade"—she too highlights the importance of the image of the depraved and unredeemable prostitute over that of the "innocent victim" in American thought, especially after 1850. Rodney Hessinger points out in his recent study of the Philadelphia Magdalen Society that writers "fitfully veered between the two images of the prostitute, [but] neither proved fully satisfying." Still, like Stansell he argues that by 1850 reformers tended to understand prostitutes more as "vicious women" and less as innocent "victims of seduction."[47]

Literary critics suggest, however, that the idea that a prostitute could be redeemed was quite common in antebellum writings. As David Reynolds points out, even in sensational fiction, which "reveled in titillating descriptions of debauchery and seduction," writers debated the notion that prostitutes were unredeemable.[48] Even as they told tales of women transformed into devils, writers often asserted that it did not have to be so, that even the worst of women might be reformed.

If a number of writers asserted that prostitutes could never be redeemed, others argued that they could regain their virtue. For every novel or urban exposé, like George Foster's *New York by Gas-light*, that asserted that fallen women could not be redeemed, another argued the reverse. For example, the protagonist of Osgood Bradbury's 1853 sensational novel, *Ellen Grant; or, Fashionable Life in New York* is a "virtuous country girl, much respected and beloved by a large circle of acquaintance. Her parents were pious members of the Methodist church." When Ellen is in her teens, the local Methodist minister tells her he loves her and promises to marry her. He seduces her, then runs off when he finds she is pregnant. Ellen has the baby, who dies shortly after birth, and soon after that her parents die. Ellen then leaves for the city, where she supports herself as a prostitute. Seduction has turned this pious and virtuous young woman into a depraved "wanton" who "mortally hated religion in all its forms" and is consumed with desire for revenge, not just on her seducer, but also on the world that abandoned her after her "fall": "She thought the world would forever despise her, and she resolved to despise and hate the world." Eventually, she stabs her seducer to death and dies soon after of yellow fever.[49]

If Ellen Grant has become utterly corrupt by the end of the novel, the author makes it clear that the women of Ellen's village were partially responsible for her decision to become a prostitute because they blamed her for seducing the minister: "If she had received as much [sympathy] as he did, it might have saved her from a life of prostitution."[50] As evil as Ellen has become, Bradbury asserts that she might have been redeemed if anyone had treated her kindly. The author explicitly states that even the most depraved and fiendish of prostitutes could have been reformed at the right time:

> There are periods in the life of such women when they might be reformed with the proper means and appliances. There is always hope for a man, and why should there not be for a woman? Public opinion is very wrong upon this subject, and does the female nature injustice. Why should a woman, when she has fallen from that virtue her sex so highly prizes, and justly too, be treated with such scorn and contempt, when a man equally guilty and often more so, passes as a respectable member of society? No good reason can be given.[51]

Like George Thompson and virtually all other antebellum writers, Bradbury considered virtue a particularly feminine quality. Yet, in opposition to some, he reasoned that if virtue was more important to women, it ought to be at least as easy to reform women as to reform men.

The author of a novel about fictional prostitute Cecilia Mayo also asserts that fallen women can be redeemed fairly easily. The protagonist proclaims: "At times I would have returned to an honest life, had there been any one to take me by the hand; but alas! there was none, and I was compelled to associate with those, more base and miserable than I can describe." On more than one occasion Mayo writes to her parents, begging them to forgive her and promising that if they take her back she will "sacredly tread the paths of virtue and honesty," but they refuse.[52] Mayo, like Ellen Grant, wants to be virtuous; she is capable of being redeemed. It is society's refusal to allow them to be redeemed that destroys these two women in the end.

If a fallen woman could be redeemed at a certain point in her career, Americans needed to know exactly when a woman transformed from an innocent victim into a fiend. How depraved could a woman become before she was unredeemable? This line was never clear. Antebellum Americans debated incessantly over which fallen women could be redeemed and at what point in their careers. Their confusion suggests that the two common understandings of prostitutes and fallen women—as "preyed-upon innocents" and as "vice-ridden jades"—could not be separated. These terms were commonly used to describe the same woman at different points in her sexual career. Even in the 1850s, the innocent fallen woman always remained closely linked to her depraved sister. As with the murderess, if a fallen woman possessed any claim to virtue, Americans found it extremely difficult to imagine that she was depraved. Some writers went to almost any length to ignore the facts of a woman's life in order to avoid believing that a woman who seemed virtuous was a "vice-ridden jade."

Sarah Josepha Hale encountered exactly this difficulty when writing her massive biography of women in history, *Woman's Record.* Hale, the editor of *Godey's Lady's Book* and certainly no radical, included a piece on the author George Sand in her book. She reported that Sand had left her husband and moved in with a lover, and later had left him also, put on male attire, and proceeded to "indulge in a life of license, such as we shrink from even in man." Yet Hale also described Sand as a "genius" who was cursed by the fact that she did not have proper "moral and Christian training" and argued that her recent works evinced a "feminine purity of tone." Hale hoped this was a sign that Sand would "henceforth . . . employ her wonderful genius on the side of virtue and true progress." Thus Hale described Sand, even after she had long been living a "life of license," as capable of redemption. Reformer and author Lydia Maria Child shared the same kind of confusion about George Sand in a letter to a friend: "I can never believe that George Sand is as debased and impure as many represent her to be. . . . I deem it impossible for . . . a woman [of impure soul] to write books that breathe such pure aspirations as many of hers do."[53]

Mary Boykin Chesnut, like Hale and Child, believed that a woman who wrote of noble and pious sentiments must be good. In January 1864, a friend told Chesnut that George Eliot, a writer she admired greatly, was a "fallen woman." Chesnut, distressed by the news, wrote that her "idol was shattered, [her] day star fled." Two months later, rereading some of Eliot's novels, Chesnut decided that her friend must have confused Eliot with one of the other "literary ladies." "I cannot believe that the woman who wrote that book [*Adam Bede*] is a "fallen woman." Six months later, obviously still disturbed, Chesnut read Eliot's *Romola* yet again, then reiterated her point, "No, No! It is all Lamar's wrong hearing of English scandal! She writes such beautiful things of love and duty, of faith and charity and purity. They even say she is an atheist. . . . It cannot be true."[54] Chesnut could not believe that a woman who seemed so pure and pious could be fallen. She could not accept the information that Eliot was living with a man out of wedlock, so no matter what she heard about it, she refused to believe it was true.

"NOBLE VESSELS MAY BE BUILT FROM THE TIMBERS OF A WRECK"

Sand and Eliot were, of course, internationally famous writers. Hale, Child, and Chesnut were also writers and thus would have been particularly predisposed to admire Sand and Eliot for their work. But their unwillingness to see a fallen woman as an unredeemable fiend extended to ordinary women as well. Lydia Maria Child, for example, was living in New York City in 1843 when young Amelia Norman stabbed her alleged seducer, Henry Ballard, on the front steps of the Astor House hotel, in full view of a number of bystanders. Norman could not deny committing the act, but she and her lawyers argued that she was driven to it by the vile behavior of Ballard, who had seduced and abandoned her.[55] When Norman was charged with and tried for attempted murder, Child immediately took up her cause, and even sat by her side throughout the trial. Margaret Fuller later applauded Child's "noble" defense of Norman; she included a description of the case in her *Woman in the Nineteenth Century*.[56] Norman's case is another revealing example of the continuing tension between the images of the "preyed-upon innocent" and the "vice-ridden jade," and of Americans' inability to clearly separate the two, for Child and Fuller were not alone in supporting Norman. New Yorkers followed the case closely, and by the time of her trial it appeared that the public had largely taken her side.

According to contemporary accounts, Norman was the daughter of a "respectable citizen" and had grown up in Sparta, a rural area in the northwestern corner of New Jersey. She had been brought to New York around 1835, when she was either thirteen or fifteen years old, by a local woman from Sparta, and she worked as a dressmaker in the city. In 1841, Norman met and was allegedly seduced by Henry Ballard. She claimed that he had promised to marry her but had eventually abandoned her, pregnant. After making several attempts to see Ballard and being rebuffed and insulted, she finally waylaid him in front of the hotel and stabbed him. Although he was seriously wounded, he did not die, and Norman was tried in early 1844 for attempted murder.[57]

Immediately after the crime, the New York press appeared unsure of how to deal with Norman. They vacillated between depicting her as an innocent victim of an evil seducer and portraying her as a depraved seductress. The day after the crime, the *New York Herald* asserted that Ballard had seduced Norman, explaining the crime in these terms: "The vengeance of a woman upon her despoiler cannot be checked, when jealousy and desertion goad her to its accomplishment." The next day, the *Herald* changed its story, now arguing that Ballard had not seduced her; rather, "In the pardonable excesses of youth, Mr. Ballard became acquainted with this female, whose position in society placed her at the command of any one whose purse could satisfy her demands." The

New York Daily Tribune, on the other hand, initially referred to Norman as a "harlot" and suggested that she was intoxicated at the time of the attack. Two days later, the paper acknowledged that Ballard might have seduced Norman and that she might not be a harlot; however, the paper still maintained that it "cannot deem it [seduction] a justification of an attempt to murder."[58] The authors of these early accounts of the crime were ambivalent about Norman's character, but by the start of the trial two months later, the press, the majority of the public, and seemingly all of New York except for Ballard's lawyers had taken Norman's side.

At the time of the trial, Norman may have been a prostitute. According to one recent historian, many New Yorkers believed that she was.[59] Certainly all knew that she had engaged in illicit sexual activity: she asserted that Ballard had seduced her, and she was the unmarried mother of a thirteen-month old-child at the time of the trial. Even so, the public apparently considered her the innocent victim and Ballard the criminal. The papers noted that every day "the courtroom was crowded almost to suffocation" and that a "strong feeling is present in favor of the prisoner." The reporters themselves seemed to concur in this sentiment. They invariably described Norman sympathetically as "very neatly dressed," young, attractive, and always surrounded by respectable-looking women. They also seemed to take great satisfaction in recounting the behavior of courtroom spectators who took an active role in supporting Norman.[60]

From the start of the trial, the spectators made their hatred of Ballard painfully clear. On the first day, when the prosecutor exhibited the knife with which Norman stabbed Ballard, the spectators applauded. Time after time they broke into applause when they approved of something the defense attorneys said. When one lawyer accused Ballard of being "too ashamed to publicly show himself in this court" and said that he tried to "skulk behind the stove pipe" in the courtroom, it took "all the officers and criers of the court" to "quell" the "great applause."[61] As Ballard left the courtroom, the crowd threatened to hit him with canes and umbrellas.[62] Even after the court recorder warned the spectators that they had too frequently interrupted the proceedings with "applause or displays of disapprobation," they continued to do so, clapping and stomping their feet, for example, when one defense attorney suggested Ballard should move to Texas because no respectable person in New York was willing to associate with him any longer.[63]

The defense argued that Norman had been a virtuous young woman until Ballard seduced her, and that she had loved him and believed they would be married. After he tired of her and refused to see her, she, the mother of his child, devastated over the loss of her honor, became temporarily insane and stabbed him. The prosecutors denied that Ballard had ever seduced Norman;

they asserted that she was a "vile prostitute" and had been before she met Ballard. Their goal seemed to be to frighten the jury into convicting Norman by invoking the specter of a city overrun by murderous prostitutes. According to Ballard's lawyers, in New York City "there were 12,000 public women who lived by prostitution who would be licensed to commit murder by the acquittal of the accused."[64]

The jury, like the audience in the courtroom, obviously considered Norman the victim of an evil seducer regardless of her sexual indiscretions and her violent actions; they acquitted her after only eight minutes of deliberation. According to Lydia Maria Child, the jury "felt little anxiety to protect Ballard, by sending his victim to Sing-Sing, that he might feel safe to prowl about after other daughters and sisters of honest families." While some New Yorkers were disturbed by Norman's acquittal, the main consequence of the case was, as Marilynn Hill has suggested, that it became a "focal point in the debate . . . [over] tougher laws against seduction and adultery."[65]

The Norman trial hardly focused on the attempted murder; it always centered on the problem of seduction. When occasional letters to the editor suggested that seduction did not justify murder, the papers replied in a manner much like the *Tribune*: "the deliberate, plotting, impenitent seducer is a wolf, who may be shot down any how and where by . . . any sufferer from his fiendish depredations."[66] Even as Lydia Maria Child claimed that her "compassion for the prisoner's wrongs has never for a moment blinded me to the guilt of revenge," she asserted that "legislators may rest assured that the law will yield like a rope of sand before the influence of humane sentiment in cases of this kind, until the laws are better regulated."[67] The broken promise was the heart of the problem. As long as male seducers refused to honor their promises of marriage with legal impunity, one could only expect their victims to try to destroy them.

Amelia Norman had had at least one illicit sexual relationship, and many believed she was a prostitute. She had borne an illegitimate child and had tried to murder a man. But not only was she acquitted, the public never agreed that she was permanently ruined. The mainstream press commended Lydia Maria Child for offering Norman a home with her family at the trial's end so she might have an opportunity to live a respectable life. And when Norman reportedly told Child, "I don't know as it is worth while to try to make anything of me. I am nothing but a wreck," Child responded, "Nay Amelia, . . . noble vessels may be built from the timbers of a wreck."[68]

Acquittals of women who killed or tried to kill their alleged seducers continued to occur in the 1850s.[69] Such cases reveal that female violence, while problematic, was not incompatible with virtue for antebellum Americans—they could understand and even condone it if the right motive was present. Still, such violence was an extreme and disturbing response to the problem of seduction, and the reformist and mainstream press looked for other ways to protect women from the problem of male seducers. The response that has received the most attention from scholars is the call for antiseduction laws, but these laws turned out to be extremely difficult to enforce where they were passed.[70] When forcing men to honor verbal promises of marriage seemed to be a losing battle, reformers and writers shifted to another approach: teaching women not to believe men's promises, but to steel themselves against lying seducers. In this way critics of prostitution began to articulate a more independent and assertive vision of womanhood.

New Women for a New Era

By the 1840s, narratives of fallen women revealed a growing sense that a new ideal of woman as more active and even cunning was required for women to survive in the impersonal, dangerous, and urban modern world. As society changed quickly in the course of only a single generation, Americans feared that women raised with values suited to a more stable rural society could not function in the modern urbanized world. According to popular narratives of prostitution, a woman with an innocent and trusting nature was the perfect victim for a devious seducer. Reformers, journalists, and novelists who discussed the problem of prostitution began to suggest that American women needed new qualities to remain virtuous in such a dangerous and constantly changing society. They needed to learn how to rely on themselves rather than having to depend on others to protect their virtue.

If young women's ignorance, innocence, dependence, and helplessness made them easy prey for seducers, Americans began to question the desirability of those qualities. One of the primary arguments moral reformers made was that young woman needed to be educated about the dangers of seducers; they needed the knowledge to avoid those who preyed on female ignorance. One young woman wrote that the reformist periodical *Advocate of Moral Reform* had saved her from a would-be seducer by alerting her to "the dangers to which she was exposed, and of which she would otherwise never have dreamed."[71]

This new focus on an innocent woman's need for sexual knowledge and her need to be able to defend herself from male seducers encouraged Americans to begin to see female dependency as a potential problem rather than a virtue. Some Americans asserted that moral reformers encouraged vice by exposing women to sexual topics, and reformers and writers responded by detailing the perils of female ignorance. When minister Hubbard Winslow preached in the late 1830s that women "must act only under [a man's] *legitimate guidance*" and that to him "she must be strictly subordinate in moral effort," the moral reform journal *Friend of Virtue* immediately attacked these "degrading ideas," arguing that they "weaken and unsettle the foundations of virtuous character in both sexes," in part because "they make woman an easier prey to the profligate and licentious man." It was necessary for women to publicly discuss prostitution; in the words of the constitution of the Cambridge, Massachusetts, Female Moral Reform Society, they should be "diffusing light in regard to the existence of this sin, . . . pointing out the numberless lures and arts practised by the unprincipled destroyer, to seduce and ruin the unsuspecting."[72]

In an 1844 article in the *New York Daily Tribune*, a reporter told of a young woman with an "unblemished character" named Mary who had recently come from the country to live with "a respectable family" in the city. Mary was running an errand around three o'clock in the afternoon and lost her way. Finally, as it was growing dark after she had walked for several hours, she asked a man who looked like a "respectable citizen" if he could tell her the way home. He said he would walk her home, but instead he tricked her into a brothel to have a drink of water. He drugged her and would have raped her if she had not seen powder in her water glass and fought him. She escaped only by stabbing him with his own knife, breaking down the door, and fleeing down the street.[73] In such a world no woman who left her house alone, no matter how virtuous, could afford to be dependent on anyone else.

Discussion and knowledge of the dangers of prostitution were not enough. Reformers asserted that women must actively fight against prostitution because if they did not this "soul-destroying" sin would only be committed more often. A woman must actively "lead her unsuspecting sisters to the path of safety and . . . raise from the degradation those who are already fallen," if for no other reason than because men would not. Someone must fight prostitution to protect innocent women from falling into it unawares and to save those who had already fallen. According to female moral reformers, men tended to "shirk from the performance of their own duty" and left it for women to perform.[74]

Even as female reformers responded to the charges of some men that moral reform was "men's duty," it seems likely that American women were never convinced that moral reform was the province of men. After all, the policing of sexual behavior had traditionally been the duty of women. As women's traditional ways of protecting the community's sexual mores became less effective, antebellum female reformers worked to fulfill the same duty with a new institution: the moral reform society. Upholding sexual mores had been and remained a woman's duty. In the eighteenth century, men's role was to give moral or more formal legal support to the married women who enforced sexual mores when this was necessary to ensure that couples married if the woman was pregnant. Men seemed to be shirking this duty by the 1830s. Female reformers could no longer count on the support of men in the community, or on the courts, to help them enforce sexual mores.

When Margaret Fuller discussed prostitution in *Woman in the Nineteenth Century*, she argued that men were responsible for the creation of "at least nine thousand out of the ten [prostitutes] through the vanity systematically flattered, or the promises treacherously broken." She conceived of prostitution reform as women's mission of redemption because men generally were content with the present situation. Fuller addressed her remarks on prostitution to women rather than men, asserting that men simply would not listen to such appeals; they had been raised to think prostitution was an "inevitable" byproduct of civilization. Fuller advised women that in addition to working to redeem current prostitutes, they should fight against the evil in three ways: they should avoid vanity, stop rejoicing in their "conquest" of men, and cultivate a love of truth and excellence. Essentially, Fuller advised women to stop focusing on pleasing and attracting men; instead they should more fully develop their own souls and learn to be "self-dependent."[75] For Fuller, then, it was women's dependence on men and their focus on male approval that made them easy prey for seducers. Only when women became fully developed, independent souls would they be able to protect themselves against such men.

Caroline Dall, always more focused on material conditions, argued that all women must be allowed and prepared to be financially independent if prostitution was to be ended. So long as women had to depend on men to support them, prostitution would continue. Husbands and fathers might die or become dissolute; they might refuse to support their families. If women could not earn enough in an honest trade, Dall argued, they would become prostitutes for the most selfless of motives: to care for their families.[76]

Boston publisher M. Aurelius illustrated the necessity of a new vision of an independent and extremely assertive woman in two parallel fictional autobiographies. Aurelius published (and probably wrote) the 1843 and 1844 autobiographies of two fictitious women, Cecilia Mayo and Emma Cole. One of these women becomes a prostitute; the other narrowly escapes that fate. The protagonist of *Life and Sufferings of Cecilia Mayo* is a wealthy young woman from New York who is seduced by a rich young rake and then thrown out of her house when her parents discover she is pregnant. Her seducer promises to marry her but, of course, reneges, and eventually she leaves him to avoid his habitual drunken beatings. She then forms a liaison with a sea captain who promises to marry her but does not; instead, the captain plots to poison her when he tires of her company. A shipwreck intervenes, Indians in a canoe rescue Mayo, and she tries to travel home on foot. Another group of Indians captures her during the journey. They decide someone in the tribe should marry her, and several men argue over whom it should be. After three Indians are killed fighting over her, the tribe decides to kill Mayo to avoid more conflict. They hit her on the head and leave her to die, but the blow has only stunned her, and she struggles along after regaining consciousness until a poor frontier family finds her and nurses her back to health. After she recovers, she eventually finds her way to Buffalo. She writes to her father two times after this, begging for forgiveness and promising to live a life of virtue, but he refuses to acknowledge her. She engages in prostitution to support herself, unable to earn a living in any other manner. She does not have enough to eat, cannot pay her rent, and soon becomes ill and dies, supposedly having written her autobiography on her deathbed.[77]

In this story, Mayo is constantly at the mercy of evil or, at best, cold-hearted men. From the moment she leaves her father's house, she is passed from man to man, dependent on those who are interested only in abusing her. In her naïveté, Mayo had trusted the man she loved, and that is where her problems began. She does not want to work as a prostitute, but her father refuses to take her back under his protection, and prostitution is the only way she can get "protection" or support from other men. She always evinces a strong desire to leave her life of vice: "I would have returned to an honest life, had there been any one to take me by the hand; but alas! there was none, and I was compelled to associate with those, more base and miserable than I can describe."[78]

If Mayo's story exposed the problems of female dependence, linking them directly to prostitution, a pamphlet Aurelius published the following year explored the alternatives to this ruinous dependence. In addition to its title, Aurelius's *The Life and Sufferings of Miss Emma Cole* shared several striking similarities with the account of Cecilia Mayo. Its protagonist, like Mayo, encounters a rich would-be seducer at a young age, but she does not believe his false promises, and she spurns him. The young man then tries to destroy her reputation by hiding stolen silver in her trunk. Cole, an orphan, is banished from the family of her guardian and forced to fend for herself. She finds work as a servant in three households. One treats her well but leaves town, the other goes bankrupt and pays her no wages, and the third turns out to be a house of prostitution. Not knowing she is in a brothel, Cole is sent to talk to a young man. He tries to rape her, but she defends herself with his knife, stabs him, and escapes from the house. Although she has not killed her attacker, she initially believes that she has. To get away from the scene of the crime, she decides to disguise herself as a man and enlist in a ship's company as a cook. Cole remains a sailor for a few years. She writes that she is unwilling to return to life as a woman until she has sufficient money to live in a respectable place so she will be able to avoid becoming the sexual prey of men. One day Cole happens to save from drowning a small girl who falls off a wharf, and the girl's parents take

Cole in and adopt her. A few weeks later, she reveals to them that she is a woman. They educate her as a young lady, and in a few years she marries an honorable and wealthy man and lives happily with him thereafter. She supposedly wrote her narrative after thirty-three years of marriage to show the youth of the nation that virtue is rewarded and vice punished.[79]

Both subjects of these accounts are young women exposed to seducers and subsequently abandoned by their parents or guardians and forced to fend for themselves in the world. If Emma Cole had trusted and relied upon men as Cecilia Mayo had, she too would have ended up a prostitute. But Cole does not trust the false promises of her would-be seducer, and she goes to every extreme to protect her virtue. When she finds that she might even have to kill a man to do so, she is reluctant but willing to attack the man. Dressing as a man and going to sea to escape the brothel keeper is also part of her effort to maintain her virtue.

Cole retains her feminine virtue even while dressed as a man. When pirates capture her and her crewmates, they offer them the choice of joining the pirates or dying. When she alone chooses death, the pirates come to respect her; instead of killing her, they treat her better than the crew members who have joined them. As Cole puts it, "The principle of virtue and humanity, which actuated me, seemed to have its benign effects, even on their flinty and murderous hearts."[80] No matter what situation Cole finds herself in, she always takes responsibility for herself, even managing to use her redemptive influence on pirates, the most depraved of men. Mayo, on the other hand, allows herself, even against her better judgment, to be pushed in or out of vice by the men in her life.

The stories of Mayo and Cole are set in a world in which women cannot depend on family or community to protect them, a world in which women will easily come to ruin if they do not become accountable for themselves. In such a place, a woman might have go to incredible lengths, as Emma Cole does, to protect her virtue and remain a redemptive woman. In the world of Cecilia Mayo and Emma Cole, a woman has two choices. When thrust into a modern, urban, violent, and greedy world, she can remain in a submissive and dependent role and allow herself to be led by violent, passionate, and greedy men—to live like them and be destroyed by them. Or she can remain independent of men and keep herself virtuous, refusing to have any part in the gratification of their base passions. Ironically, to maintain the character of a virtuous redemptive woman, Emma Cole has to resort to violence and dress as a man, while Cecilia Mayo, much more traditionally feminine in her actions, helpless and unable to support herself in the world outside the home, loses her redemptive character because of her inability to protect herself and her virtue.

Fictional comparisons of passive victims, like Mayo, to more assertive women who are able to protect their virtue, like Cole, became extremely common during and after the mid-1840s. For example, E. D. E. N. South-worth's best-selling novel *The Hidden Hand* includes such a pairing. In one part of the novel, the heroine, Capitola Le Noir, befriends Clara, a young woman of about the same age, who is being held captive by her uncle, who is Clara's legal guardian and is about to force Clara to marry her evil cousin. The contrast between Capitola and Clara is telling. Clara can think of no other way to avoid a forced marriage than to attempt suicide with a penknife. When she tells Capitola of her trouble, Capitola exclaims, "Oh how I wish it was only me in your place." What passive and obedient Clara sees as a hopeless situation, Capitola can easily solve; for her it is a "rare frolic." The two young women switch clothes, and Capitola takes Clara's place. When Capitola arrives at the church, she loudly refuses to be married and enlists all the bystanders in her favor. Capitola simply will not allow herself to be forced into marriage. She easily extricates herself from a situation that had led Clara to contemplate suicide. The message here is clear. A woman cannot rely on a man, even her guardian, to protect her virtue. The only way a woman can be safe is to be independent, to protect herself from male deception and trickery.[81]

Americans' fear that young women from respectable country families were engaging in illicit sexual behavior encouraged them to articulate and accept an image of a more independent and assertive proper woman, particularly by the 1840s and 1850s. If naïveté, dependence, and weakness were now likely to lead women into seduction and eventually prostitution, then women needed knowledge, independence, and strength to protect themselves, other women, and society from the danger.

At the same time that Americans created images of powerful and evil women—murderesses, prostitutes, and abortionists—who destroyed respectable society from within, they also invented similarly powerful figures of good women who protected society from such threats. And some of these "good" women, like Amelia Norman, attempted to commit murder and engaged in illicit sexual activity, making it impossible for Americans to be sure if a given woman accused of prostitution or murder was evil if she claimed to be respectable. A growing sense that family and community could no longer protect women made many Americans believe that women needed to learn to protect themselves more aggressively. Antebellum accounts of prostitution focused on this need for aggressive, independent, and virtuous women to fight against sexual immorality, in their own lives and in their communities. In this context, female independence, self-assertion, and even violence were not necessarily problems. Women's motives became the key to understanding whether their actions were proper or improper. By the last half of the antebellum era, Americans routinely depicted the most virtuous women, in both fiction and nonfiction, as extremely independent, assertive, and even capable of violence.

Redemptive Womanhood and
African Americans in the Antebellum North

CHAPTER

THREE

O, ye daughters of Africa, awake! awake! arise! no longer
sleep, nor slumber, but distinguish yourselves. Show forth
to the world that ye are endowed with noble and
exalted faculties.

—Maria W. Stewart, October 1831[1]

On 17 November 1838, the African American weekly newspaper the *Colored American* printed a special issue. The editors announced they were devoting "a large space" of that week's paper to "statements, observations, and remarks on female character, influence and eloquence." They explained that they had two motives for this focus on women: first, they were "anxious that woman . . . should fill the *whole* of her important and truly elevated sphere," and second, they believed that "colored females, from education, are more especially deficient in fulfilling their appropriate duties, and in redeeming the character and carrying forward the interests of their oppressed and injured people." African American women must not be "merely silent friends of education and virtue, or prudence and industry, but their active patrons and efficient agents." The editors then explained to female readers why they must become more active in their community:

If ever any class of any community, in any age or country, was called upon to act definitely and efficiently, their part—to study carefully their duty, and show themselves worthy the position in which God has placed them, and Christianity conceded them, colored females are called on to do so. We ask our mothers, wives, sisters and daughters to read carefully the following selections, and practice the narrated virtues. Such a course will tell loudly on our present interests, and influence, mightily, our future posterity.[2]

This editorial was a serious challenge: it told African American women that they more than any other group in human history were "called upon to act" in support of their community, that the future of all African Americans depended upon their actions. If female readers were unsure exactly what actions they should take, specific articles outlining their duties followed. One article focused on women's "moral influence" over their husbands. Another highlighted the importance of women's acts of charity and benevolence. A third celebrated "woman's eloquence," noting that while women could not "plead at the bar, or preach in the pulpit, or thunder in the Senate House," they should be trained in conversation so they could educate their families, "friends and acquaintances," in the importance of virtue and religion.[3]

In this series of articles, *Colored American* told African American women that they were—or ought to be—redemptive women and that they needed to act more directly on their duty to promote morality and religion in their families and their community because the future of the African American community depended on it. *Colored American* tied the concept of redemptive womanhood specifically to the experiences of African Americans in the antebellum North. The newspaper asserted that it was especially important for African American women to behave as redemptive women because their community was weakened and constantly threatened by racism. The editors acknowledged that not all free African American women seemed to live up to the standards of redemptive womanhood, but explained that this was the result of institutional racism, specifically the lack of a decent educational system for black women. Another editorial reiterated the point a year later: "We expect our females to be educated and refined; to possess all the attributes which constitute the lady, yet we fail to provide the means whereby they can acquire an education."[4] The newspaper was directly responding to the common racist argument that by nature African American women were not respectable and virtuous. The editors asserted that white women generally received the training and education required to live up to their duties as virtuous women, but black women often did not. Both whites and African Americans tied proper womanhood to female education, but antebellum blacks highlighted the importance of female education even more because they lacked access to decent schools.

REDEMPTIVE WOMANHOOD AND AFRICAN AMERICANS   67

According to the vast majority of historians of nineteenth-century American women, the dominant gender ideology of the time—true womanhood, separate spheres, or domesticity—was a white, middle-class ideology. African American women allegedly took one of two approaches to this dominant ideology. Some tried to live up to it, but they were always unsuccessful because many African American women had to work outside the home for wages even after marriage, which supposedly contradicted the notion that woman's sphere was the home. Even if an African American woman was wealthy enough to avoid paid labor, she would still be excluded from the ideology by white racism, which asserted that a black woman simply was not a true woman. Many African American women, knowing that true womanhood was a white ideology that excluded them, supposedly rejected the ideology. This rejection left them free to enter public life unfettered by fears that they were leaving their proper sphere.[5] Yet much evidence suggests that individual African American writers, as well as the Northern black press in the antebellum era, consistently embraced the dominant gender ideology. Some scholars have noticed this, but most have treated the phenomenon as a form of false consciousness; that is, they have asserted that some educated African Americans tried to live up to "white" gender ideology that did not suit their needs, but white racism did not allow this to happen.[6]

Racism in the antebellum North was an extremely serious and widespread problem, and the Northern black community was well aware of this. It was, along with slavery, the primary concern and focus of virtually all antebellum black newspapers. Yet the fact that many, if not most, Northern whites in the 1830s did not consider African American women to be respectable, redemptive women does not mean that blacks were excluded from mainstream gender ideology. First, antebellum Americans argued over whether women's wage labor was appropriate and what types of jobs were consistent with female respectability; they never agreed that a respectable woman could not work for wages outside the home. Antebellum gender ideology did not confine women to specific locations or behaviors. And second, if racist whites assumed African American women lacked a redemptive nature, African Americans did not accept this assessment of themselves. As literary critic Lora Romero put it, "no one group owns domesticity." Romero contends that Northern African American women "depended on the concept of female influence to put black women at the forefront of abolitionist and antiracist causes." They understood the dominant gender ideology as their ideology.[7] Antebellum gender ideology did not belong to whites; whites could assert that African Americans were excluded from the ideology, but African Americans could and did maintain that they were included. When African Americans positioned black women as redemptive women, they made an argument against slavery and racial prejudice, as well as one about woman's moral and religious nature.

The notion that black women were less virtuous and more sexual than white women was common in the antebellum era. This belief was part of a more general popular argument that blacks were inferior to, less civilized than, and more animalistic than whites.[8] To depict African American women as redemptive women was to undermine notions of black inferiority. By doing so, the black community challenged the racist stereotype that black women were not virtuous. As Frankie Hutton points out, the antebellum black press was "diligent in helping to counter negative images of black women" as part of its antiracist argument.[9] Because for Americans in general at this time the nation's virtue was linked to the virtue of its women, to assert that black women were virtuous was to assert that blacks in general were virtuous. The ideology made as much sense for African Americans as for whites—if not more sense.

The antebellum free black community and black and white abolitionists consistently applied the tenets of redemptive womanhood to free and enslaved African American women. The Northern black press, from its inception in 1827, focused on redemptive womanhood as an ideology particularly relevant to black women. African American Maria W. Stewart was the first American woman to justify her public speaking through the ideology of redemptive womanhood. The first female antislavery society ever formed in the United States was also founded by "females of color," in Salem, Massachusetts, in 1832.[10] Black abolitionists were able to construct a defense of their antislavery activities through their understanding of redemptive womanhood, just as white abolitionists did a few years later. This is not to argue that redemptive womanhood started out as a "black" ideology, but calling it a "white" one makes little sense.

Northern African Americans and whites did not always use the ideology of redemptive womanhood in precisely the same ways. In the African American community, redemptive womanhood was almost inextricably bound up with antislavery and antiracist arguments. White Americans might use the concept of redemptive womanhood as an antislavery, antiracist argument, or they might use it to justify slavery and racism by asserting that African American women could not be redemptive women. The gender ideology itself was not inherently racist or antiracist; rather, it was a flexible and broad concept that different groups of Americans could shape to suit their own social and political concerns.

"Women of Refinement"

African American speakers, writers, and newspapers editors in the antebellum era consistently asserted the respectability, the ladyhood of black women, often making the explicit point that in so doing they undermined racial stereotypes of African Americans. When lecturer Maria Stewart asserted that black women should have a public voice because "women of refinement in all ages . . . have had a voice in moral, religious and political subjects," she was making an argument for black women's status as refined women, as well as for women's right to speak in public. Stewart understood redemptive womanhood as a key part of racial uplift for African Americans, arguing that black women would have to act as redemptive women to improve the condition of their people. She noted that whites in America promoted the "political moral and religious development" of their children, and it was the duty of blacks to do the same for their own children. She appealed specifically to black mothers, who, she claimed, were responsible for the souls of these children and must give them "a thirst for knowledge, the love of virtue . . . and the cultivation of a pure heart." She argued that by acting as redemptive women, white women were uplifting their own race. Black women had to do the same if African Americans were ever to be truly free: "O, ye daughters of Africa, awake! . . . no longer sleep, nor slumber, but . . . show forth to the world that ye are endowed with noble and exalted faculties." "Never," she contended, "will the chains of slavery and ignorance burst, till we become united as one, and cultivate among ourselves the pure principles of piety, morality and virtue." Stewart believed that women, both black and white, were more moral and religious than men and that they shared a special duty to uplift their race, battle against sin, and redeem the nation.[11]

Stewart, like the editors of the *Colored American*, expressed anxiety that African American women were not quite redemptive enough. Stewart's charge to African American women to "no longer sleep, nor slumber" suggests that she believed too many black women were not living up to their duties as redemptive women. But this in no way suggests that African American women were unsuited for redemptive womanhood: they simply needed to wake up and show whites that they were "endowed with noble and exalted faculties." The problem, then, was not black women, but the lack of a decent educational system for African Americans. As "Matilda" put it in an 1827 letter to another black newspaper, *Freedom's Journal*, while African American women did not have the same "advantages" that white women possessed, it was vital that they work hard to educate themselves: "The influence [women] have over the male sex demands, that our minds should be instructed and improved with the principles of education and religion, in order that this influence should be properly directed."[12]

An examination of early black newspapers suggests that African Americans in the antebellum era were fully aware of the power of redemptive womanhood as a critique of racism and consistently used it as such. The first African American–run newspaper in the North was *Freedom's Journal*, published in New York

City from 1827–1829, and it was followed by *The Rights of All*, which lasted less than a year. These and other African American papers, including the 1837 *Weekly Advocate*, which was soon renamed *Colored American*; Frederick Douglass's *North Star*, begun in 1847 and renamed *Frederick Douglass' Paper* in 1851; and the two major black Canadian newspapers, *Voice of the Fugitive*, founded in 1851, and the *Provincial Freeman*, begun in 1853, shared a set of common goals.[13] They all worked for "the moral, religious, civil and literary improvement of our injured race," "hastening that glorious period when our unfortunate race shall no longer be the victims of galling slavery or cruel prejudice." They called for the "improvement" and "protection" of free Northern African Americans, as well as the abolition of slavery in the South. Frederick Douglass, for example, wrote of his newspaper's work on behalf of African Americans, calling his publication "the grand instrumentality for their improvement and elevation."[14] These newspapers were solidly antislavery and antiracist. They were also filled with comments on women's special moral, religious, and nurturing nature and the set of duties that come with such a nature. They linked these descriptions of redemptive African American women specifically to the newspapers' broader efforts to combat slavery and racism.

African American newspaper editors and letter writers routinely and actively encouraged black women to become more involved in redemptive activities as part of a larger effort to combat white racist attitudes. When they argued that some African American women were not moral, religious, or nurturing enough, they were not suggesting that black women had to learn to live up to a white ideology; they were criticizing the structural racism of the North, especially the education system. They asserted that all women needed training and education to understand and perform their duties as redemptive women, but white women had access to an education that was denied to African Americans. They used the notion of redemptive womanhood to criticize the racist society that afforded African American women fewer educational opportunities than whites.[15]

Even as they suggested that not all African American women were sufficiently redemptive, black newspapers and certain other publications, including white abolitionist papers, made a concerted effort to focus on African American women, both individuals and groups, whom they considered models of redemptive womanhood. The author of an 1836 article introducing some of Sarah Forten's poems first referred to Forten as a "colored female," then remarked, "I ought to have said young lady, even at the risk of exciting a sneer in certain doughfaces; for her whole deportment bears testimony to the fact that she is truly such." The Reverend Dr. James W. C. Pennington, in his preface to the *Essays of Ann Plato*, described Plato as a "colored lady . . . of pleasing piety and modest worth." He noted that he did not usually use the word *colored* to de-

scribe people, but he had done so in this case as a refutation of "that stupid theory, that nature has done nothing but fit us for slaves."[16]

By the time he started his first newspaper, the *North Star*, in 1847, Frederick
Douglass was adept at identifying and shaping the powerful racial and gender
ideologies of the antebellum period to make political arguments about African
American rights and women's rights. In his papers, articles on women's duties,
rights, and nature proliferated. While many of the articles referred to women in
general, Douglass was also careful to provide specific examples of virtuous
African American women. For example, Douglass titled his obituary of Katy Ferguson "A True Woman" and pointed out that Ferguson, who was born a slave,
was a "worthy and Christian woman" who "probably established the first Sabbath
School" in New York City and who, in the course of her life, had cared for forty-
eight orphaned or abandoned children. The paper reprinted an account of a con-
cert of sacred music at an African American church in Washington that said that
the black female singers had performed with "modesty, propriety and grace,
which would have reflected credit on the most cultivated ladies in America."[17]

Contributors to the paper also seemed to take great delight in describing the
successes of the African American singer Elizabeth Taylor Greenfield, who was
also known as "The Black Swan." Greenfield had been born a slave in Mississippi. Her owner, a Philadelphia Quaker woman, brought her north at a young
age and freed her. With the encouragement of her former owner and other
white friends, Greenfield began her singing career, and by the early 1850s she
had become nationally known. *Frederick Douglass' Paper* consistently used
Greenfield as an example of the refinement and respectability of black women.
One 1851 article in the paper pointed out that the audience for one of her concerts was filled with "wealthy, refined and influential" people and that Greenfield was a "noble" and highly trained opera singer who performed her pieces
so well as to "charm and delight the most refined audience." Such pieces invariably asserted that Greenfield was equal or superior to the most popular white
female singers of the day, Jenny Lind and Abby Hutchinson. The articles also
highlighted her racial background: one noted that her complexion was "dark
brown" and her features "African," and another applauded her for publicly ad-
mitting that she was "a black woman." In case the implicit argument against
slavery was not yet clear to the reader, the articles hammered home the point.
One noted that the talented Greenfield was a member "of that race held in
slavery . . . to be bought, sold and hunted like wild beasts."[18] By stressing
Greenfield's talent, refinement, and race, the articles quite self-consciously used
her to refute arguments of African American inferiority.

Editor Mary Ann Shadd Cary made similar arguments in the *Provincial Freeman*. She included essays and poetry of Frances Ellen Watkins Harper in the

journal, along with a letter explaining that Harper, a "gifted" African American
woman, had to struggle for her "high intellectual culture" and was accomplish-
ing "great good in the advocacy of the rights of her fellow creatures." Like
Frederick Douglass' Paper, the *Provincial Freeman* followed the career of Elizabeth Greenfield, "The Black Swan," using her accomplishments as an antislavery argument. In one column, the paper's Philadelphia correspondent described
the success of Greenfield's concerts in Baltimore, Maryland, and noted that
"the Baltimore Press . . . Pro-Slavery, as they are—manifested towards her,
however, quite a respectful attitude, and not a few gentlemen and ladies 'conquered their prejudices,' and made 'calls' upon the gifted vocalist." The author
suggested that prejudice against African Americans could not hold up when
whites, even proslavery whites, were confronted with such powerful evidence of
black refinement and talent. As the author had it, "Doubtless, mountains of
prejudice . . . would soon be removed" if large numbers of African Americans
would follow Greenfield's example, if they would "cultivate their talents" and
pursue "improvement of intellect."[19]

In addition to Greenfield, "The Black Swan," there was also Mrs. Webb, the
"Black Siddons," whose nickname was a reference to the renowned British actress Sarah Siddons. The *Provincial Freeman* praised Mrs. Webb for her dramatic readings in front of public audiences in the Middle Atlantic and New
England states. The *Freeman* described Webb as "extremely graceful and pre-
possessing," "delicate," and highly talented, and asserted that her public debut
in Philadelphia was one of the best ever. Such comments on the refinement and
talent of African American female actors and singers were commonplace in the
antebellum black press and explicitly or implicitly reinforced the idea that
African American women were capable of respectability.[20]

Black writers did not limit their descriptions of women to African American
women. Black papers also included articles on the accomplishments of publicly
active white women, such as antislavery lecturers Angelina and Sarah Grimké,
Abby Kelley, and Lucy Stone; English nurse Florence Nightingale; and physician Elizabeth Blackwell. Many of the frequent articles on "woman's mission"
and "woman's nature" referred specifically to African American women, but
others, often reprints from popular white-run newspapers, did not mention
race. On the one hand, the black press stressed the accomplishments, respectability, and moral decency of African American women. On the other
hand, it stressed the ideology of redemptive womanhood in a general way, asserting that black and white women shared a nature and a mission distinct from
those of men, and providing examples of both white and black women who
worked to redeem the nation. In this way, black newspapers suggested that gender ideology crossed racial boundaries.[21] By using white women's accomplish-

ments and ideals as evidence of what African American women believed and should do, they suggested that black and white women had much in common.

Stressing the commonalities between white and black women was another way African Americans bolstered antiracist arguments. This was Sarah Forten's specific point in linking black and white women together in the famous poem she wrote for the Anti-Slavery Convention of American Women: "We are thy sisters, God has truly said / That of one blood, the nations he has made / . . . Our skins may differ, but from thee we claim / A sister's privilege and a sister's name."[22] By comparing African American women to white women, Forten was asserting that redemptive womanhood transcended racial boundaries.

In addition to linking moral black women with moral white women, writers often compared moral black women with immoral white women to assert that redemptive womanhood was not a white ideology: a woman from any racial background might be good or evil. This was a major theme in African American author Harriet E. Wilson's autobiographical novel *Our Nig*. In 1859, Wilson published this fictionalized account of her childhood as an orphan living with a white family in New England. Like other Northern black writers in the antebellum era, Wilson paired Northern racism with Southern slavery, suggesting that they were the two major problems facing the antebellum black community. And like other authors who focused on African American women, Wilson relied heavily on the ideology of redemptive womanhood to make her argument against both Northern racism and Southern slavery. Wilson's novel is the story of an African American girl who tried to live a respectable, pious life yet was constantly thwarted in her efforts by her racist and notably unredemptive white female employer.

Harriet Wilson probably was born free in New Hampshire and spent her entire life in New England. As Henry Louis Gates Jr. suggests, the protagonist of the novel is a thinly veiled fictional version of Wilson herself.[23] *Our Nig* is the story of Frado, the daughter of a white woman and a black man. Sometime after Frado's father dies, Frado's mother abandons the six-year-old child. She leaves her with a white family, the Bellmonts, supposedly for one day, but never returns. Most of the novel describes Frado's life in the Bellmont home, where she is overworked, beaten, and psychologically abused by Mrs. Bellmont and one of the daughters, Mary, and intermittently protected by Mr. Bellmont, his son Jack, and some other family members. Finally, Frado reaches adulthood, leaves the Bellmont home, goes to work, marries, and has a child. Her husband periodically abandons her and finally dies of yellow fever in New Orleans, leaving her to struggle to support herself and her child.

In the novel, Wilson consistently positions Frado as a decent, respectable girl, and later woman, who values religion and education and tries to "elevat[e] herself" despite her racist mistress's attempts to degrade her. In addition to administering frequent brutal beatings, Mrs. Bellmont tries to keep Frado as ignorant as possible. She argues that Frado should not be sent to school because "people of color . . . were incapable of elevation." She does not allow Frado to go to church with her, telling her, "Religion was not meant for niggers." When she finds Frado reading the Bible, she is furious. She takes the Bible away and tries to convince Mr. Bellmont to make Frado stop reading it. When she sees Frado pray, she says it will "do no good for her to attempt prayer; prayer was for whites, not for blacks. If she minded her mistress . . . it was all that was required of her." The novel characterizes Mrs. Bellmont as a completely unredemptive woman. She is unloving and feels no sympathy for Frado; she attempts to degrade Frado and destroy her virtue. By telling Frado that she doesn't need to worry about religion, that she only needs to worry about obeying her mistress, Mrs. Bellmont is essentially telling Frado she has no soul. Her job is to obey and to have no will of her own. Although Frado is not a slave, Mrs. Bellmont seems to think Frado's skin color entitles her to treat Frado like a slave. But Mrs. Bellmont, the author is careful to stress, is immoral in her interactions with whites as well as blacks, and even toward her own children. She tries to force one of her daughters into a loveless marriage because the suitor is wealthy. She lies and hides letters in an effort to destroy her son Jack's marriage because she is furious that his wife is poor. Mrs. Bellmont's racist treatment of Frado is consistent with her bad character in general. She is, according to one character, a "she-devil."[24]

As much as her mistress thwarts her, Frado, on the other hand, works hard to be a respectable, redemptive woman. When she finally leaves the Bellmont home, she first goes to work as a straw-bonnet maker. She finds a white woman to teach her the trade, and this woman also furthers her literary education. As Wilson describes it, while they "read aloud, . . . Frado experienced a new impulse. She felt herself capable of elevation; she felt that this book information supplied an undefined dissatisfaction she had long felt, but could not express. Every leisure moment was carefully applied to self-improvement, and a devout and Christian exterior invited confidence from the villagers."[25] Once Frado is free from her oppressive mistress, once she has access to the kind of knowledge Mrs. Bellmont tried to keep from her, Frado immediately becomes more "elevated." And because she acts like a redemptive woman: respectable, devout, and Christian, her neighbors recognize her as such. By depicting Mrs. Bellmont as a "she-devil" and Frado as a virtuous woman, Wilson asserts that race is not the determinant of proper womanhood. White women might be bad and African American women might be good.

According to literary critic Lora Romero, *Our Nig* has the plot of a typical domestic novel: the "orphaned girl in search of self-dependence." Yet, Romero warns, this is not evidence that Wilson adopted a "white" ideology in her book.

"Since Wilson . . . apparently addressed her novel to other free blacks, she did not need sentimental conventions to appease a skeptical white audience." There is no reason to think that she incorporated an ideology alien to her own belief system in the novel. The book, then, suggests that Wilson, a free Northern black woman, was embedded in the dominant gender ideology of her period. She, like other black and white American women, shaped redemptive womanhood to fit the circumstances of her own life. Just as white domestic novelists, such as Catherine Maria Sedgwick, used the genre to assault patriarchy, Wilson used it to argue against racism.[26]

Enslaved Women, the Literature of Slavery, and Redemptive Womanhood

Enslaved women, obviously, had a dramatically different relationship to the ideology of redemptive womanhood from that of free African American women, yet much evidence from slave narratives and other abolitionist literature suggests that women who escaped or were freed from slavery, as well as their white and black abolitionist supporters, considered the ideology of redemptive womanhood relevant to enslaved women. They too used the ideology of redemptive womanhood as one of their central and most powerful arguments against slavery.

Historians have tended to assume that enslaved and formerly enslaved women, even more than African Americans who had always been free, existed completely outside the dominant gender ideology of their time. In part this can be linked to the racial stereotypes nineteenth-century Americans promulgated. Many whites in the antebellum era, including a number of abolitionists, embraced belief in a variety of so-called natural racial differences even as they rejected slavery. Specifically, they often described African American women as stronger and more passionate and aggressive than white women. On the basis of these nineteenth-century descriptions of slaves and ex-slaves, historians have suggested that enslaved women were in fact stronger, more passionate, and more aggressive than white women. As Nell Painter has argued, the connections between historical and contemporary depictions of Sojourner Truth, the most famous African American woman of the nineteenth century, reveal the limitations of this sort of thinking.

Sojourner Truth was born a slave in upstate New York and was freed in 1827 as a result of New York's gradual emancipation law, when she was about thirty years old. By 1843, she was traveling through the northeastern United States as an itinerant preacher. She almost immediately fell in with a biracial, but mostly white, group of Northern reformers, and she decided to spend a winter at the

Northampton Association, a Massachusetts utopian community, where she remained for three years until the society dissolved. From this point on, Truth was involved in both the antislavery and the women's rights movements. As Nell Painter points out in her biography of Truth, white middle-class reformers in the mid-nineteenth century preferred to see Truth as a "natural and uncorrupted . . . exotic." For them, and consequently for Americans even today, she is a "symbol" that means "Strong Black Woman." Painter argues that Frances Gage and Harriet Beecher Stowe's incredibly popular writings on Truth are "inventions" that reflect this sensibility.[27]

White women's rights activist and abolitionist Frances Gage created the famous "A'n't I a Woman?" version of the speech Truth delivered at a 1851 woman's rights meeting in Akron, Ohio. Gage's account, written in 1863, twelve years after the actual event, described the 1851 meeting as an affair in which timid white women were bullied into silence by male ministers, who essentially took over their convention and gave lecture after lecture on male superiority. According to Gage, Sojourner Truth, the lone black woman at the meeting, was the only woman strong enough to stand up to the hostile male audience and argue for women's equality, and she did so with her famous "A'n't I a Woman?" speech. Painter points out that the events in this 1863 story are entirely inconsistent with contemporary accounts of the meeting. According to 1851 newspaper reports, Truth was merely one of many women who spoke in favor of women's rights. Hostile men never took over the convention; white female participants had no fear of public speaking; Truth did not have to come to their rescue. Gage's lack of interest in accuracy is also revealed in her depiction of Truth's speech patterns. Gage rendered Truth's speech in a version of Southern black dialect. Truth, who was born and raised among the Dutch in upstate New York, had a Dutch accent and spoke like the "unlettered white people" of New York, according to a former owner's daughter. As Painter suggests, Gage created a version of Truth she thought would appeal to white readers: the strong, authentic black woman. Gage's article also reveals that the symbol of the strong black woman was constructed against the implicit or explicit foil of the weak white woman imprisoned by her own gender ideology. To make her version of Truth so heroic, Gage had to stereotype not just Truth, but also the white reformers at the convention. Harriet Beecher Stowe wrote about meeting with Sojourner Truth in an article called "The Libyan Sibyl." She created a Truth who spoke in yet another mock Southern dialect and wore a "madras handkerchief," something that Truth, who dressed like "a respectable middle-class matron," did not wear.[28]

Painter also argues that while most (though not all) white reformers saw Truth as a powerful, naive exotic, Truth made a concerted effort to present herself as a "gentlewoman in possession of the determining requirement of ladyhood, 'unimpeachable moral character.'"[29] Even Sojourner Truth, the most powerful symbol of the strong black woman and unhindered by the oppressive gender ideology that allegedly crippled middle-class white women, asserted her claim to redemptive womanhood. Like antebellum white female reformers, Truth did not need to stand outside the dominant gender ideology to be a publicly active reformer.

While few enslaved women had lives as well documented as Truth's, those who did leave written records behind confirmed that they also could and did embrace the ideology of redemptive womanhood. Harriet Jacobs escaped from slavery in North Carolina in 1842 when she was about twenty-nine years old. She spent the 1840s and 1850s living and working in the North. In the 1850s she composed the story of her life in slavery, and finally, with the backing of famous white abolitionist Lydia Maria Child, she found a publisher. In 1861, she published her narrative, *Incidents in the Life of a Slave Girl*, under the pseudonym Linda Brent. Virtually all scholars who have studied *Incidents* have noted its central focus on motherhood, domesticity, and ideals of proper womanhood. One of the central issues of the book is Jacobs's long struggles with her immoral master, Mr. Flint, who tried to bully her into becoming his mistress. Jacobs rejected his sexual advances. She fell in love with a free black man and asked permission to marry him, but Flint refused to allow it. Finally, after Jacobs feared she could no longer fend off Flint, she began a consensual sexual relationship with Mr. Sands, a local white man of high social standing. Flint was outraged when he discovered she was pregnant with Sands's child, but he stopped his sexual harassment of Jacobs. Harriet spent some time in her narrative explaining her decision to engage in that illicit sexual relationship, which produced two children. She was ashamed of having children outside marriage; she believed it was immoral. She had tried to "keep [herself] pure," but the "demon Slavery . . . proved too strong." This opinion was reinforced by her grandmother, the moral center of the novel, who would have "rather seen [her] dead" than pregnant out of wedlock. Jacobs argued that the fundamental problem lay with slavery: "The condition of a slave confuses all principles of morality and, in fact, renders the practice of them impossible."[30]

Literary critics have paid a great deal of attention to Jacobs's portrayal of her sexual relationship with Mr. Sands. Hazel Carby, Jean Fagan Yellin, and a number of other scholars, building on the critics' work, have read *Incidents in the Life of a Slave Girl* as a challenge to the ideology of true womanhood that exposed its "inherent contradictions and inapplicability to her life." These scholars, like so many historians of African American women, have pointed out that slave owners and the system of slavery in general tended to prevent enslaved women from acting as proper, virtuous women. But they have also assumed that if enslaved women were not allowed to fulfill their duties as proper women, they could not or would not subscribe to the dominant gender ideology. Carby and Yellin argue that by actively resisting her master and by having children outside of marriage in a consensual relationship, Harriet Jacobs challenged the applicability of true womanhood to her life. Carby in particular asserts that Jacobs's statement that "the condition of a slave confuses all principles of morality and, in fact, renders the practice of them impossible" was an "alternative discourse of womanhood," a challenge to true womanhood's system of morality.[31] Yet, by asserting that slavery makes morality impossible, Jacobs used the moral standards of redemptive womanhood to condemn slavery.

Carby also suggested that Jacobs did not feel readers had a right to judge her because the "material conditions of a slave woman's life were different from theirs." Yet Jacobs did explicitly invite at least one white Northern woman to do exactly that. In a letter to her friend Amy Post referring specifically to her life as a slave, Jacobs wrote, "I have placed myself before you to be judged as a woman whether I deserve your pity or contempt."[32] At the same time Jacobs explained that slavery made it extremely difficult for slave women to live up to the standards of redemptive womanhood, she expected to be judged *as a woman*, not just as a slave woman, for her actions.

Jacobs and many other abolitionists frequently used notions of redemptive womanhood to show the horrors of slavery, largely by focusing on brokenhearted mothers whose children were torn away from them or the sexual immorality that slavery produced in both blacks and whites. They asserted that enslaved women tried to act as redemptive women but that they were frequently thwarted in their efforts to do so. By showing black slave mothers to be just as loving as white mothers, and black slave women at least trying to be just as virtuous, these works countered racist claims that African American women simply were not capable of such exalted sentiments.

Slavery was so horrible for Jacobs precisely because it did not allow her to live as a moral, pious, and nurturing woman, no matter how hard she tried. While action and resistance were not incompatible with redemptive womanhood, sexual impurity certainly was a problem. Jacobs challenged the applicability of redemptive womanhood to herself, not in order to challenge the gender ideology, but to challenge slavery, which denied her the opportunity to be a moral, pious, and nurturing woman. As Donald Gibson points out, Jacobs's book reveals an "implicit belief . . . that domestic values prevail by nature and *should* prevail politically over marketplace values." This is the key to women's redemptive duty: to promote morality and piety, to protect family and the nation from the amorality and greed generated by a market-oriented economy.[33] Jacobs made some sophisticated arguments, but they were not unique; African American and white women and men had been making similar points for some time.

above—"The Staten Island Tragedy." Artist's rendition of Polly Bodine as she might have looked murdering Emeline and the baby. Reprinted from *National Police Gazette.* 27 December 1845. (Courtesy of the American Antiquarian Society)

left—Henrietta Robinson: "The Veiled Murderess Unveiled," as depicted in a sensational pamphlet of her trial. Robinson, in contrast to Bodine, seems too beautiful to be evil. Reprinted from *Life and Confession of Mrs. Henrietta Robinson, the Veiled Murderess* (1855). (Courtesy of the American Antiquarian Society)

above—"Hooking a Victim." These prostitutes are deemed threatening because they are
successful at masquerading as "respectable"
women. 1850 Lithograph. (Courtesy of the
Museum of the City of New York)

left—"The Female Abortionist." Like other
female criminals, the female abortionist was
threatening because she hid her "fiendish"
nature beneath an apparently respectable
exterior. *National Police Gazette*, 13 March
1847. (Courtesy of the American Antiquarian Society)

left—Elizabeth Taylor Greenfield: "The Black Swan," whose respectable appearance, as well as her refinement and talent, could remove "mountains of prejudice." (Courtesy of The New York Public Library)

below—Frances Ellen Watkins Harper: African American poet, abolitionist, and public lecturer. Harper reinforced her argument that African American women were refined and virtuous with her representations of herself. Reprinted from *Women of Distinction* (1893). (Courtesy of the American Antiquarian Society)

"Ye May Session of Ye Woman's Rights Convention—Ye Orator of Ye Day Denouncing Ye Lords of Creation." These women's rights activists look suspiciously like the fiendish murderesses of pamphlet literature. Note the similarities of their features to those of Polly Bodine. Reprinted from *Harper's Weekly*, 11 June 1859. (Courtesy of the American Antiquarian Society)

below—Abby Kelley Foster: public lecturer, abolitionist, and accused "servant of Satan in the garb of an angel of light." White reformers like Foster also recognized the power of somber, plain, respectable clothing to convince their audience that they were not outside their sphere. Lithograph from daguerreotype, 1846. (Courtesy of the American Antiquarian Society)

FANNY CAMPBELL,
THE FEMALE PIRATE CAPTAIN.

Portrait of the Female Pirate.

BY LIEUTENANT MURRAY.

BOSTON:
UNITED STATES PUBLISHING COMPANY. F. GLEASON, 1 1-2 Tremont Row, Boston
S. FRENCH, 293 Broadway, New York.   A. WINCH, 15 Arcade, Philadelphia.
W. BENNET, No. 1 North St. Baltimore.   D. JUNE, 274 Main St. Buffalo.
STRATTON & BARNARD, 121 Main Street, Cincinnati.
1846.

Amelia Sherwood: "Unparalleled Heroism of Amelia. She rushes between the combatants in their quarrel about the Gold." As she performs her feat of heroism, the angelic Amelia is bathed in light from above (heaven). Reprinted from *Amelia Sherwood* (1850). (Courtesy of the American Antiquarian Society)

left—"Fanny Campbell, the Female Pirate Captain": an inspiration to future female soldiers. Fanny dresses as a man, engages in piracy, and still retains her "womanly" virtue. Reprinted from *Fanny Campbell* (1846). (Courtesy of the American Antiquarian Society)

left—Charlotte Forten Grimké: teacher, author, abolitionist, and self-described "daughter of the regiment" of the 1st South Carolina Colored Volunteers. (Courtesy of The New York Public Library)

below—"Kady Brownell in Army Costume." Not-so-gentle Kady tried to bayonet a wounded Confederate soldier. In this picture, Brownell embodies the threat of the female soldier, which images like that of Annie Etheridge were meant to defuse. Reprinted from *Women of the War* (1866). (Courtesy of the American Antiquarian Society)

above—Clara Barton: "The Angel of the Battle-field." Barton was always adroit at managing the tensions between respectable womanhood and public activism, in her appearance as well as her writings. Daguerreotype, circa 1850–1852. (Courtesy of the American Antiquarian Society)

left—Seal of the U.S. Sanitary Commission. On this seal, a literal angel hovers above the battlefield. Reprinted from Charles J. Stillé, *The History of the United States Sanitary Commission* (1866).

Annie Etheridge: "Gentle Annie" leads her troops into battle. This portrayal of Etheridge as gentle and angelic helps defuse the threat of the female solider. Reprinted from *Woman's Work in the Civil War* (1867). (Courtesy of the American Antiquarian Society)

Jacobs was not challenging dominant concepts of morality in *Incidents*; she was critiquing slavery. Scholars have, of course, noted that Jacobs attacked the institution of slavery, but most have assumed that she also rejected the dominant gender ideology of her time or, in a more nuanced version, that she altered that "white" ideology to suit her own situation and to convince white readers of the horrors of slavery. As P. Gabrielle Foreman and Sandra Gunning put it, Jacobs "delicately transplants true womanhood" onto slave women; she "appropriates the domestic discourse of maternity in order to reform it for the use of black women."[34] While these scholars are right to point out that Jacobs used the dominant gender ideology in her antislavery argument, they still suggest that gender ideology was white in that it had to be transplanted or appropriated by Jacobs, that she—and other African American women—would not have had unmediated access to the gender ideology.[35]

These assumptions are rooted in scholars' continued reliance upon Barbara Welter's definition of true womanhood. If historians and literary critics define a proper woman as "pure, pious, submissive and domestic," then clearly enslaved women could not fit into such a definition. Nor could most middle-class white women. This is precisely the point Nell Painter makes about Sojourner Truth's image: the stereotype of the strong black woman was dependent on the stereotype of the passive and submissive, weak white woman. Yet neither image represented the reality of these women's lives and belief systems. If, however, proper womanhood is defined in terms of woman's redemptive nature and her duty to redeem others, all women might have access to the ideology. On the basis of the vast amount of evidence in the black press that African Americans embraced the ideology of redemptive womanhood, we can conclude that Jacobs would not have had to appropriate it. Black women, like all other American women, had long been shaping that flexible ideology to fit their own lives.

If scholars have suggested that Jacobs took on a "white" ideology to appeal to white readers, Lora Romero points out that the same cannot be said of Northerner Harriet Wilson, who directed *Our Nig* toward the free black community.[36] Romero's point also applies to a recently published autobiographical novel, *A Bondswoman's Narrative*, written by ex-slave Hannah Crafts. Crafts's handwritten manuscript was, according to Henry Louis Gates Jr., "unedited, unaffected, unglossed, unaided by even the most well-intentioned or unobtrusive editorial hand." Gates bought the manuscript of this unpublished novel at auction in 2001; he then had it authenticated and published. He discovered that the manuscript was written in the late 1850s and was able to confirm a number of details of the author's life. It is still unclear whether the name Hannah Crafts is a pseudonym, but, according to Gates, "we know the central and defining facts about her life: that she was female, mulatto, a slave of John Hill Wheeler's, an autodidact, and a keen observer of the dynamics of slave life."[37]

Hannah Crafts was born a slave in Virginia and escaped to the North in the late 1850s. She probably settled in New Jersey and wrote *The Bondwoman's Narrative* there. Her portrayal of slavery and racism has much in common with those of Harriet Jacobs and Harriet Wilson. Like Jacobs and Wilson, Crafts strove to lead a pious, moral life and was frequently thwarted by her masters and mistresses in this effort. As Crafts describes it, her owners cared nothing for inculcating religious or moral values in their slaves. As a child on a Virginia plantation, she had "no training, no cultivation," and she was free from all "moral culture," although she had always had "an instinctive desire for knowledge." One day while secretly trying to teach herself to read, she met a kind old white woman who brought her home and taught her reading and religion and "cultivated my moral nature." From then on Hannah resolved to "do my duty, and be kind in the sure and certain hope of eternal reward." The result of this, Hannah tells her readers, was that "the rude and boisterous became gentle and obliging, and how ready ~~they~~ all were to serve and obey me, not because I exacted the service of obedience, but because their own loving natures prompted them to reciprocate my love."[38] Thus Hannah portrays herself as a woman who tried her best to be religious, moral, and nurturing—a redemptive woman. By describing the effects her efforts had on other slaves on her plantation, she suggests that she succeeded. She asserts that others almost automatically obeyed her because she brought out their better natures. She made them better: she redeemed them.

Sexuality and marriage in the slave community was a central theme for Crafts, just as it was for Harriet Jacobs. Crafts was not sexually assaulted when she was a slave, but the specter of sexual slavery permeates the book, both in Crafts's account of her own life and in the stories she tells of other enslaved women. Crafts's first brush with such danger occurred when she ran away with her mistress. Her master had recently married this beautiful, refined, and compassionate woman, whom Crafts had grown to love. But the new mistress had recently found out, much to her surprise, that she was actually a slave. The mistress had been brought up as white and continued to pass for white, and the man who had discovered her secret threatened to tell her husband she was a slave. The mistress confided in Crafts, and the two of them decided to run away. Eventually they were caught and thrown in prison.

In prison, Crafts was told the story of a slave named Ellen and her white friend, Mrs. Wright. Ellen, a beautiful fifteen-year-old slave girl, a young woman "of delicate sensibilities and fine perfections," had found out that her master had sold her to a slave trader who was "purchasing beautiful girls for the New Orleans market." Knowing that this would be "a life of misery ten times more horrible than a death of torture," she fled to Mrs. Wright, who helped her escape, but Ellen was soon captured and sent south. The aptly named Mrs. Wright was also arrested, for kidnapping, and was thrown into prison. There she soon succumbed to "mental hallucination," but she remained lucid long enough to tell Crafts this tale.[39]

Immediately after relating this story, Crafts returns to her own narrative. Her master, it turned out, had killed himself upon finding that his wife was a slave, and Hannah and her mistress now belonged to a Mr. Trappe. Trappe decided to sell the mistress to a Mr. Saddler, who dealt exclusively in the sexual slave trade. When the mistress heard this, she was so horrified that she suddenly "ruptured a blood-vessel" and fell to the floor, dead.[40] Trappe then tried to convince Saddler to buy Hannah Crafts instead, telling him she was a good woman, virtuous and religious. Saddler was disturbed by this information and launched into a monologue on the difficulties of dealing with virtuous slave women:

> Bah: I hardly think that religion will do her much good, or make her more subservient to the wishes of my employers. On the whole I should prefer that she wasn't religious, ~~but I suppose that they can drive it out of her~~ because religion is so apt to make people stubborn; it gives them such notions of duty, and that one thing is right and another thing wrong; it sets them up so, you'll even hear them telling that all mankind are made up of one blood, and equal in the sight of God. . . . Give me a handsome young wench, pleasant and good-tempered, willing to conform herself to circumstances, and anxious to please, without any notions of virtue, religion, or anything of that sort. Such are by far the most marketable.[41]

Virtue and religion undermined slavery. It made female slaves stubborn and less marketable; it taught them equality and duty to God. Slavery, then, was incompatible with ideals of redemptive womanhood, and as Harriet Jacobs did in *Incidents*, Crafts clearly used gender ideology to condemn slavery, and particularly the sexual violence that slavery promoted.

When Saddler agreed to buy Crafts, she was very upset at first, but then she reasoned, "I thought that though my perishable body was at their disposal, my soul was beyond their reach. They could never quench my immortality, shake my abiding faith and confidence in God."[42] Her mistress had chosen to die rather than be sold as a sexual slave, but Crafts argued that if she were raped, if she were forced into prostitution, it would not be her choice, so these things would not undermine her virtue. Rather, it would undermine the virtue of those who forced her to do such things. Drawing on the logic of redemptive womanhood, Crafts considered her motives, rather than her actions, to be the key to her nature.

Crafts narrowly avoided being sold in the New Orleans market when she and Saddler had a wagon accident in which Saddler was killed. His heirs sold her to a Mrs. Wheeler, a woman who revealed her bad character in their first conversations. Upon deciding to purchase Crafts, Mrs. Wheeler reminded Hannah of what her fate might have been, casually remarking, "of course you prefer the service of a lady to that of a gentleman, in which probably you would be compelled to sacrifise [*sic*] honor and virtue." Such an offhand comment suggests that Mrs. Wheeler considered this an insignificant sacrifice for a slave woman. She, like Saddler, cared for obedience rather than virtue in her female slaves. As she told a friend, "I never trouble myself about the principles of my girls; so they are obedient is all I require."[43]

Initially Crafts lived with the Wheelers in Washington, D.C., then she went with them when they returned to their North Carolina plantation, where her stay with them grew more and more unpleasant. One of the other slaves there was jealous of Crafts's status with Mrs. Wheeler and spread rumors about her. In particular, she accused Crafts of spreading the story of a mortifying incident in which Mrs. Wheeler had used a new whitening face powder that turned her face black and as a result had been mistaken for a "colored person" in Washington, D.C., society. Ignoring Crafts's protests of innocence, Mrs. Wheeler decreed that Crafts would no longer be her personal maid; she would go to the fields and pick cotton with the "brutalized creatures." In addition, Crafts would be forced to marry one of these "creatures." This was when Crafts finally decided to run away. As she put it, "I should probably have resigned myself" to being whipped or sold, "but when she sought to force me into a compulsory union with a man whom I could only hate and despise it seemed that rebellion would be a virtue, that duty to myself and my God actually required it." Crafts did escape, and at the novel's end she is living in her own small "cottage" in the North. She had managed to find her mother, whom she had never known in slavery, was happily married to a Methodist preacher, and was running a school for "colored children."[44]

Crafts made her antislavery argument by undermining the concept of race itself. She described Mrs. Wheeler's experience of using whitening powder and being mistaken for a "colored woman," and she told the story of her kind and gentle first mistress who was, by mid-nineteenth-century standards, black, but had spent almost her entire life thinking that she was white. Such examples suggest just how fluid and arbitrary definitions of race could be. And when Crafts described the degraded lives of slaves, she was always careful to point out that degradation was not a natural quality of African Americans; it was caused by slavery. For example, when she called field hands "brutalized creatures," she was careful to explain that their state was the direct result of a lack of "moral cultivation" and education.

Crafts's argument against racism and slavery also was inseparable from her understanding of gender ideology. One of the primary ways in which she undermined the idea of racial difference was by asserting that enslaved African American women believed in the ideology of redemptive womanhood and did their best to live up to those beliefs, but that in many cases their white mistresses did not. Time after time in her novel, female slaves—Hannah, her mistress who turned out to be a slave, the girl Ellen—tried to live up to their own high moral and religious standards, and time after time slavery, often embodied by white mistresses, attempted to thwart their efforts. While slavery did not threaten the white women in the novel with rape, the threat to black women had a direct impact on the moral natures and lives of white women. White women who, like Mrs. Wheeler, learned to look the other way, or even to condone sexual violence against slave women, lost their claim to redemptive womanhood. White women who, like Mrs. Wright, tried to protect slave women from rape kept their virtue but lost everything else. Crafts described a completely different world in the free North, however. There, for the first time she could form a family and live the moral and pious life of which she had always dreamed.

This argument—that enslaved women understood themselves as redemptive women, but that slavery undermined redemptive womanhood in both the slave and Southern white communities and frequently destroyed enslaved and Southern white women who tried to live up to its standards—was typical in abolitionist literature. In 1837, an article in the *Colored American* asserted that, in addition to turning slave women into "concubines," the slave system transformed "female amiableness . . . into fury by habits of despotic sway."[45] The fact that *Uncle Tom's Cabin* was such a controversial and popular book in the 1850s shows just how powerful the construction of slave women as redemptive women could be. Harriet Beecher Stowe relied heavily on racial stereotypes in her portrayal of Sojourner Truth as the "Libyan Sibyl," as well as in her depiction of many of the African American characters, particularly dark-skinned ones, in *Uncle Tom's Cabin*. Yet this does not erase her argument in *Uncle Tom's Cabin* that both African American and white women ought to— and can, given the proper circumstances—be moral, religious, and nurturing figures. As Myra Jehlen, Jeanne Boydston, Mary Kelley, and Anne Margolis point out, *Uncle Tom's Cabin* pits domesticity against slavery. Slavery was wrong because it destroyed the ability of slaves to have lasting marriages and families; it made it extremely difficult for slave women to act as redemptive women, no matter how hard they tried.[46]

Stowe explicitly argues that enslaved women followed the tenets of redemptive womanhood as much as they could, unless, of course, the depravity of slavery had already destroyed their redemptive nature. At one point in the novel, Eliza, a virtuous and loving slave mother, discovers that her young son, Harry, has just been sold and will be taken away from her. That night she flees with Harry, and in the course of her escape, as she is closely pursued by slave catchers, she runs across the Ohio River, jumping from one ice floe to another. Just across the river, she stops at Senator Bird's house. Stowe closely links Eliza to Mrs. Bird, the senator's wife, who has recently lost a child of her own to illness. Mrs. Bird gives Eliza clothing for Harry that had belonged to her own boy before he died because she identifies with Eliza as a loving and grieving mother like herself. A neighbor of the Birds describes Eliza as a "poor crittur! . . . [who] was hunted down, jest for havin' natural feelin's, and doin' what no kind o' mother could help a-doin'!" Stowe also points out that even a slave woman whose redemptive qualities seem to have been destroyed by slavery can be redeemed in freedom. Cassie, a slave who for years has been the mistress of her depraved master, Simon Legree, is almost insane with rage at Legree by the time she escapes and would have murdered him if Uncle Tom had not convinced her otherwise. Yet in freedom, under the influence of the virtuous Eliza, who turns out to be her daughter who had been sold from her years before, she transforms into an entirely different person, becoming a "devout and tender Christian."[47]

Stowe's portrayal of Eliza Harris as a pious, moral, and heroic mother was not lost on African American reformer and author Frances Ellen Watkins (later Watkins Harper), who included a poem titled "Eliza Harris" in her 1854 collection of poetry. Watkins, like Stowe, emphasizes Eliza's virtue, bravery, and the loving nature that inspired her go to incredible lengths to save her child. The Grimké sisters also address slave women's attempts to act as redemptive women in their testimony in Theodore Weld's *American Slavery as It Is*. Sarah and Angelina both focus on the sexual assault of virtuous slave women by their masters or other white men. Sarah Grimké, for example, narrates an account of a young slave woman whose master ordered her to be publicly whipped in the workhouse for refusing to retract her statement of an unpleasant truth. She writes, "Her delicate mind shrunk from the shocking exposure of her person to the eyes of brutal and licentious men; so she declared to me that death would be preferable." The woman ran away to avoid the whipping and was caught and, Grimké hints, raped by slave catchers. She escaped from them and was found a few days later dying of a fever. Thus, as Sarah Grimké describes it, slavery was responsible for the brutalization and murder of a virtuous young woman whose only crime had been a refusal to lie.[48]

THE BLACK PRESS AND AFRICAN AMERICAN WOMEN'S CHANGING ROLES
IN THE ANTEBELLUM ERA

By the 1830s, the black press embraced redemptive womanhood in that it consistently asserted that women had a special duty to redeem their community and the nation. But between its start in 1827 and the Civil War, it changed its understanding of women's roles significantly. As the antebellum era progressed, the papers became increasingly accepting of the most controversial forms of women's public activism—such as petitioning and public lecturing—in the name of a just cause. In the late 1820s and 1830s, the papers frequently expressed fear that such actions were too extreme for women to perform, even if their motives were proper. However, these expressions almost disappeared from the black press by the late 1840s and 1850s.

In 1827, two African American men in New York City, Samuel Cornish and John Russwurm, founded *Freedom's Journal*, the first black newspaper in the nation.[49] Both men were well-educated, prominent members of New York's free black community. Cornish was trained as a Presbyterian minister and Russwurm was the first African American graduate of Bowdoin College in Maine. In article after article, the editors affirmed that woman were more moral, religious, and nurturing than men, that they were the redeemers of the community. In one piece in *Freedom's Journal* entitled "Thoughts," the author effused, "With the holy name of woman, I associate every soft, tender and delicate affection. . . . Oh! There is something in contemplating the character of woman, that raises the soul far above the vulgar level of society." Another writer announced, "The female sex is greatly superior to the male in mildness, patient benevolence, affection and attachment."[50]

From the start, *Freedom's Journal* encouraged female readers to use their special womanly influence to convince their neighbors of the evils of slavery. One article, "What Does Your Sugar Cost?" suggested that it was women's responsibility to encourage other women to boycott sugar produced by slaves because the price of that sugar was the "blood of slaves." But at the same time the paper warned its female readers they must not go far in their public activism. In May 1827, the paper celebrated reformer Frances Wright for her philanthropy, announcing that she had established a community in Tennessee, Nashoba, to give "asylum to slaves." The next year, after Wright began lecturing in public throughout the nation, the paper changed its tone, complaining that she "ought to get into pantaloons immediately, she is a disgrace to the fairer part of creation." A couple months later the paper presented a more general version of the same argument in an article titled "Woman." According to this piece, "The modest virgin, the prudent wife, or the careful matron, are much more service-able in life than petticoated philosophers, blustering heroines or visage queens. . . . They are confined within the narrow limits of domestic assiduity and when they stray beyond them, they move out of their proper sphere; and conse-quently without grace."[51] These statements reveal both an embrace of women's duty to redeem others and anxiety that women were becoming too publicly ac-tive. This was the key tension in debates over roles for both white and black women in the late 1820s and the 1830s.[52]

Between 1830 and 1836, African American newspapers were virtually nonex-istent. The next black newspaper that lasted longer than a few months was New York City's *Weekly Advocate*, which was begun in 1837. The *Advocate* was ini-tially edited by Phillip Bell, but after two months of publication the paper changed its name to the *Colored American* and added Samuel Cornish to the ed-itorial staff. If the African American papers of the 1820s had mentioned women's special duties to society, such references were markedly more frequent in the *Weekly Advocate* and the *Colored American*. The first issue of the *Weekly Advocate* informed its readers that "female influence is powerful and may be ex-erted either for good or evil. . . . In any enterprise for the improvement of our people—either moral or mental, our hands would be palsied without woman's influence." Specifically, the success of the newspaper itself—a paper whose goal was to end slavery and racism—was dependent on African American women. While its editors disapproved of female lecturers, the paper consistently ap-plauded women for using their special "female influence" to help the African American community. One address published in the *Colored American* pointed out that a few years before there had only been "two or three [African America] female societies," in New York. Now, the speaker noted proudly, there were "more than a dozen."[53] The *Colored American's* special November 1838 issue on woman's influence also focused specifically on women's duty to protect and im-prove the black community.[54] Although these newspapers stressed the need for female activism more consistently than *Freedom's Journal* had, the same tensions over female lecturers surfaced again and again. The paper's stress on the need for women's participation in reform exacerbated these tensions by condoning women's antislavery work while condemning female abolitionist lecturers, and by celebrating "woman's eloquence" while noting that women could and should not "plead at the bar, or preach in the pulpit, or thunder in the Senate House."[55]

By the late 1840s and 1850s, women's relationship to the black press had changed again in two important ways.[56] First, women became directly involved in publishing and editing these newspapers. Second, the newspapers more fre-quently included positive accounts of female public lecturers, women's rights activists, women's rights conventions, and women workers in their pages. The papers refuted or completely rejected the argument that women's well-intentioned reform activities could somehow lead them out of their proper sphere. The most well-known black paper in the 1840s and 1850s was the *North Star* (later renamed *Frederick Douglass' Paper*), founded in 1847 by Frederick Douglass, a former slave, author, and avid advocate for women's rights. In 1848, Douglass's friend Julia Griffiths, an Englishwoman, came to Rochester, New York, to help him run and edit his already struggling newspaper. Griffiths took over the financial side of the paper and some of the editorial duties. According to Douglass, as well as historians, she was instrumental in shaping some of the content and in saving the *North Star* financially in the late 1840s.[57]

Articles in the *North Star* and *Frederick Douglass' Paper* often asserted that women's special nature justified her involvement in benevolent and political activities. Women were "the source of tender sensibilities and moral affections." They were "ministering angels," and as such they had a special duty to actively protect their communities.[58] The writers argued that "female influence serves to refine and temper" men, that women's "benevolence, virtue and constancy" make them vital to reform efforts." While many articles, like those in the black newspapers of the 1820s and 1830s, focused on women's reform efforts, others made very explicit references to politics. Frederick Douglass himself attended the 1848 Seneca Falls women's rights convention. In his defense of that convention in the *North Star*, he commented, "In respect to political rights, we hold woman to be justly entitled to all we claim for man." The *North Star* also made a point of defending specific female lecturers who were attacked in the press for being outside their sphere. When the *United States Gazette* suggested that antislavery lecturer Abby Kelley could not "broil a steak or knit stockings," the *North Star* took the paper to task for suggesting that a woman who gave "evidence of superior mental cultivation" could not have domestic skills.[59] The paper's consistent and highly positive coverage of women's rights conventions; female antislavery, temperance, and other reform societies; and women in the professions also worked to justify women's involvement in a variety of public and political activities.[60]

Women played a central role in both of the major Canadian black newspapers of the antebellum era.[61] When Henry Bibb founded the *Voice of the Fugitive* in 1851, he did it with a great deal of help from his wife, Mary Bibb, a free-born African American woman from Rhode Island. The Bibbs had met in Boston in 1848 and moved to Sandwich, Canada West, in 1850 because Henry, a former slave, feared for his freedom after the passage of the fugitive slave law. Mary Bibb had taught school in Boston, and soon after her arrival in Canada she started teaching again while Henry founded the paper. Despite her teaching career, Mary played a major role in the paper. She handled some of the paper's correspondence from the beginning of its publication, and when her husband traveled for an extended period in 1851, she ran the paper in his absence. Even when he was present, Mary continued to "influenc[e] the editorial direction" of the paper. According to editor C. Peter Ripley, the *Voice of the Fugitive*'s "polished style" suggests that Mary "had a good deal to do with the publication's style and content," since Henry had little education and his writing style lacked such polish.[62]

Samuel Ringgold Ward, another African American who emigrated to Canada in the early 1850s, had been a newspaper publisher in the United States. Ward was the son of fugitives who had escaped from slavery when he was three years old. Ward had spent virtually his entire life in the North, mostly in New York. He was educated and worked as a schoolteacher and an antislavery lecturer, and while living in New York he founded at least two antislavery newspapers. He moved to Canada to escape possible prosecution for his role in assisting a fugitive slave. Shortly after he arrived, Ward founded the *Provincial Freeman* in Windsor, Canada West, in 1853, with the help another African American, author and schoolteacher Mary Ann Shadd.[63] Shadd, a well-educated free black woman from Delaware, had come to Canada in 1851 with her father and brother to help fugitive slaves. In 1854, the paper moved to Toronto and became a regular weekly publication. At first, Ward was the nominal editor, but he soon left for England to solicit money for the fugitive slaves in Canada, and Shadd (who married Thomas Cary in 1856) assumed the role of the paper's official editor until 1857.[64]

The *Provincial Freeman* consistently supported women's rights in a variety of contexts. It included articles on women's political and legal rights and working conditions, new careers for women, and of course women's duty to the participate in reform causes.[65] The paper reprinted Harriet Beecher Stowe's "Appeal to the Women of the Free States of American on the Present Crisis in Our Country"; Lucy Stone and Henry Blackwell's protest of marriage laws, which they delivered at their wedding; and selections from the proceedings of women's rights conventions in the United States. The *Provincial Freeman* closely followed the actions of New York State Assembly's Committee on Women's Rights in 1854. It frequently focused on married women's property rights and other legal inequalities in marriage. It reported on women who were successfully engaging in formerly male occupations, including female legislative reporters, scientists, doctors, clerks, bookkeepers, and even horse tamers. It also ridiculed restrictive notions of woman's proper sphere with articles such as Jane Swisshelm's "Man's Sphere," which suggested the absurdity of claims that women's new occupations "unsexed" them, by turning the argument on its head. Swisshelm wrote that modern men unsexed themselves by performing "feminine" occupations: men "have condescended to petty shop-keeping, to the vending of laces, and ribbons and doll's heads. Fancy the sinewy arm, and strong hand of a man deploying webbs [*sic*] of gauzy texture before the eyes of lady customers." Jane Swisshelm, a Pennsylvania-born white woman, was a well-known abolitionist and women's rights activist with a reform newspaper of her own, the *Pittsburgh Saturday Visiter* [*sic*], which she founded in 1848.[66]

In the early 1830s, Maria Stewart had taken such charges much more seriously and clearly felt that she was on the defensive when she justified public lecturing. She faced so much opposition that she abandoned her lecturing career in 1833. The African American press of the 1830s also took these charged very seriously. Newspapers included long and earnest articles on the nature of woman's sphere and frequently debated what acts would or would not unsex a woman. Stewart and white lecturers Angelina and Sarah Grimké spent a great deal of time and energy defending themselves against the charge that women's public activism corrupted their special nature. But in her article, Swisshelm treated the notion that women's rights and new careers would destroy woman's special nature as ridiculous. The articles Cary included in the *Provincial Freeman* suggest a similar transformation. These articles praised women for taking a role in public life as reformers, lecturers, and paid workers, and they linked these new rights and occupations with woman's special nature and duties. For example, one article suggested that a female horse tamer had succeeded in taming difficult horses where men had failed because of her "intuitive knowledge of the points of a horse" and her understanding of the horse's "morale." That is, she used womanly influence and "gentleness" to teach the horse, rather than resorting to the violent techniques on which male trainers relied.[67]

Like Maria Stewart and Samuel Cornish, Mary Ann Shadd Cary embraced redemptive womanhood; however, unlike them, she did not feel she had to seriously argue against the belief that women's public activism corrupted their special nature and unsexed them. The fact that Cary could mockingly dismiss this argument suggests she considered marginal an argument that had not been marginal in the 1830s. This shift in argument style suggests that African Americans had grown more accepting of women's presence in public life by the 1850s. And, of course, women's increasing participation in the publication of black and white newspapers was evidence of this trend.[68] The more extensive, positive, and confident coverage of female lecturers and women's rights activists in the black press by the late 1840s and early 1850s was part of a larger pattern.

Public Women

Lecturing and the Logic of Redemptive Womanhood

C H A P T E R

F O U R

The mere departure of woman from the duties of the domestic circle, far from being a reproach to her, is a virtue of the highest order, when it is done from a purity of motive, by appropriate means, and toward a virtuous purpose.

—John Quincy Adams[1]

*T*n 1838, Lydia Maria Child observed that "the sound part of the community" was never entirely sure whether abolitionist and public lecturer Angelina Grimké was properly named or if she really should be called "Devil-ina."[2] We might expect accused murderesses, prostitutes, and Quaker-garbed female antislavery lecturers to have little in common; however, in the antebellum era the three types of women were at the center of the same types of public controversies. The fundamental question Americans asked of these women was whether or not they were proper women—whether they were angels or devils. Only after knowing this could Americans judge their actions. Yet, as Child's comment indicates, "the sound part of the community" could never definitively answer the question.

The actions of female reformers, African American and white, particularly public lecturers, sparked a tremendous amount of controversy in the 1830s and

1840s. The vociferous antebellum debates on woman's sphere were in many ways a direct response to the phenomenon of publicly speaking women and Americans' uncertainty about whether such women were angels or devils, redeemers or destroyers. Virtually every printed work that addressed the topic of woman's sphere or role in society after 1836 alluded to or directly invoked female public speaking as an issue to be reconciled with proper womanhood.[3]

Antebellum Americans, North and South, strongly approved of women's participation in benevolent causes; however, many of them were troubled when women spoke in public in front of mixed-sex audiences, particularly at the start of the antebellum era.[4] The fact that written sources often referred to female lecturers as speaking to "promiscuous" audiences is telling. Critics of the lecturers called them unwomanly, often likened them to prostitutes, and frequently asserted that they were outside their "proper sphere."[5] These critics argued that public lecturing undermined women's purity and piety; therefore, according to the logic of redemptive womanhood, it undermined the moral fiber of the nation.

Despite all these criticisms, Americans in the 1830s were never certain whether public lecturing was inside or outside women's proper sphere. From the moment female reformers began their lecturing careers, they asserted that lecturing was well within women's proper sphere because pure and noble motives justified their actions. As Sarah Baker, a member of a female antislavery society put it, "The crisis *has* come when it would be a sin for woman to stay at home & remain silent." Baker insisted that a religious and moral woman had no choice but to speak out in public against the sinful institution of slavery.[6] As a Massachusetts congressman, John Quincy Adams defended women's right to submit antislavery petitions to the government in those very terms, arguing that the key to a woman's virtue was not that she remained in "the domestic circle," but that she acted "from a purity of motive, by appropriate means, and toward a virtuous purpose." Adams argued that women's political activism was justified by their selfless motivations and the virtuousness of their goal: the abolition of slavery.[7]

Many historians have pointed out that women flocked to reform movements in the antebellum era precisely because men and women of the time embraced the idea that women were more moral and religious than men and that they therefore had a special duty to protect and sustain the nation's moral and religious health. Scholars have argued that this belief system allowed antebellum Northern female reformers to assert that women's moral and religious duty justified their entrance into public life and to contend that they were behaving as proper women when they engaged in public reform activities. Yet the existing historiography of separate spheres, true womanhood, or domesticity has also

assumed that, at least in part, the ideology of women's moral and religious superiority was imposed on women by men in order to control women and confine them to the home. Scholars frequently have noted an apparent contradiction between the ideology's emphasis on women's moral duties and their
confinement to a separate sphere. They sometimes have labeled the contradiction ironic, but the definition of antebellum gender ideology they have generally accepted posits just such a contradiction between an emphasis on women's
moral and religious activism on one hand, and an attempt to confine women to
a domestic sphere on the other. Historians have often distinguished between
the vast majority of female reformers, who accepted woman's sphere and were
careful not to venture outside of it in their reform activities, and the few feminists who rejected the ideology and therefore began to undermine it.[8] This understanding of gender ideology has tended to make publicly active female reformers, particularly lecturers, into exceptional women who broke out of their
separate sphere and thus paved the way for other women to do the same, leading to the eventual destruction of the ideology of separate spheres.

A number of scholars have directly and indirectly been poking an increasing
number of holes in the separate spheres thesis, generally by arguing that the
women they study did not subscribe to an ideology that confined them to a domestic sphere. For years, scholars have argued that separate spheres did not apply to working-class white women or African American women. Elizabeth
Varon recently suggested that the model did not fit the lives of well-to-do antebellum white women in Virginia either. Carolyn Lawes, in her study of women
in antebellum Worcester, Massachusetts, found that white middle-class women
there did not believe they belonged in a private separate sphere. According to
Lawes, "if separate spheres existed anywhere, it was in the major urban centers,
not small urban centers."[9] One begins to wonder what group of women did
subscribe to the ideology. Yet, as Lawes notes, the "paradigm of separate
spheres" remains "pervasive" in scholarship to this day. Despite new scholarship suggesting that antebellum gender ideology was not, even in part, an attempt to confine any group of American women to a domestic sphere, it remains the primary way in which historians in all fields understand
nineteenth-century American women. According to Lawes, the separate
spheres paradigm has allowed historians to "assume that women stood on the
sidelines of what truly mattered in nineteenth-century America: politics, economics, and the power the two conveyed." It "therefore permits scholars to
continue to disregard women in their analyses of the vigorous antebellum political system."[10] Our dominant understanding of separate spheres posits that
women must have been marginal to politics and economics in nineteenth-
century America even though more and more scholarship suggests that they

were central to both. The problem, then, is not simply that the paradigm is outdated, but that it suggests that women do not belong at the center of the historical narrative of nineteenth-century America.

As the nation's moral center, antebellum women were central figures in the American historical narrative; they were key figures in reform, politics, and many other fields. An examination of female lecturers reveals that antebellum gender ideology encouraged women to become more involved in public life. When women became public lecturers, they were not contesting or undermining gender ideology, because the dominant ideology did not embody an attempt to confine them within a separate sphere. Redemptive womanhood was an ideology that women as well as men molded and developed, an ideology that women used and shaped to justify their lecturing and to thwart older, eighteenth-century notions of women's private nature.

The historiography of antebellum gender ideology, as Nell Painter points out, also has tended to marginalize African American female reformers. It neglects those who seem too much like white reformers and lionizes those who seem least like middle-class white women, describing them as "exotic" and "earthy" figures, larger-than-life, stronger and more independent than their white counterparts.[11] Yet, as Painter suggests, there is much evidence that white and black female lecturers shared a great deal in common. From its inception, the ideology of redemptive womanhood was shared across racial boundaries.[12] Northern African Americans and whites justified and criticized women's reform and public lecturing efforts in remarkably similar ways. This suggests that the ideology of redemptive womanhood was a powerful force in both communities that actively encouraged both African American and white women to move into public as female reformers and lecturers in the antebellum period.[13]

But if antebellum gender ideology did not confine women to a separate sphere, why then did antebellum Americans seem to write and speak so much about woman's sphere? As Amanda Vickery suggests in the case of nineteenth-century England, "one might . . . argue that the stress on the proper female sphere in Victorian discourse signaled a growing concern that more women were seen to be active *outside* the home rather than proof that they were so confined." That is, the constant debate over woman's sphere was not evidence that women were confined to a separate sphere; rather, it may have been an anxious commentary on the rapid expansion of women's opportunities in antebellum America.[14]

FEMALE PREACHING AND ANTEBELLUM FEMALE LECTURING

The antebellum female lecturers were not the first American women to speak in public, but they were they first group to do so because they were women. Women who spoke in public in the early national era did so in spite of their womanhood. At least eighty black and white women were "prominent" preachers in America before 1845. Some of them were "immense[ly] popular, . . . preaching to audiences of hundreds and even thousands." Invariably, these women asserted that they had become preachers reluctantly, and only when God called them. Many of them published spiritual autobiographies in which they detailed God's call and their spiritual struggle, which often lasted years until they finally began preaching. This struggle always revolved around the propriety of women preaching in public.[15] They told of ministers, church members, and family members who tried to stop them from preaching, and they wrote of their own fears of overstepping the boundaries of feminine propriety. But in the end, all decided that they must preach regardless of public feeling against them, believing it was far more important to obey God's will than man's.

African American female preacher Jarena Lee, in her 1836 narrative, explained that one day she heard a voice that told her: "Go preach the Gospel!" At first, she thought this was a trick of Satan, but after much prayer she became certain it was a call from God. However, her minister told her their faith did not allow female preachers, so she gave up any thought of preaching for eight years until the torment of disobeying God's will was great enough for her to overcome her fear of popular disapproval. Countering claims that it was "heterodox or improper for a woman to preach," she appealed to biblical example, asking her readers: "Did not Mary *first* preach the risen Saviour?"[16] Another black woman, Zilpha Elaw, was told by her pious dying sister that "an angel came to her, and bade her tell Zilpha that she must preach the gospel." Like Lee, Elaw ignored her call to preach for several years, until she became seriously ill and had a vision of God. Yet even then she waited another fifteen months until she felt moved by God "as it were involuntarily" to speak at a camp meeting. After this she became an itinerant preacher.[17] Salome Lincoln, a white woman, began her career as an itinerant preacher in 1827, about four years after she felt she had received a call from God. Initially, she believed that it was wrong for women to preach in public, and she tried to avoid the call, exclaiming, "Lord I pray thee, have me excused!" Eventually for her also, the ever increasing torment of disobeying God's will convinced her to preach.[18] These women, who all began preaching in the 1820s, argued that they had a duty to preach in public regardless of popular disapproval. Yet they always preached because they were called; they never argued that as women they had a right or duty to preach.

Female public speakers in the early national era tended to emphasize their exceptional nature, their distance from other women; this suggests that many

Americans were troubled by the idea that a woman would preach or speak in public. It also suggests that the notion that women belonged in a private sphere was not a product of the antebellum era. As Linda Kerber recently stressed, the concept of coverture, the legal covering of the child by the parent, the servant by the master, or the wife by the husband, meant that those who were legally covered—children, servants, wives—would have no direct political voice in the state: their father, master, or husband would speak for them. Women's exclusion from politics was reinforced after the Revolution, Kerber contends, as coverture was eliminated from parent-child and master-servant relations yet still applied to marriage. As she puts it, "the assumption that women owed their primary civic obligation to their husbands" remained the ideological root of women's exclusion from political participation after the Revolution.[19]

Yet revolutionary-era women did not accept their exclusion from politics. Instead, they developed the ideology of republican motherhood "as a way of deflecting male criticism that the women who 'meddled' in political ideas necessarily desexed herself." The republican mother asserted that she must be well versed in politics to properly educate her children and, perhaps, her husband. Republican motherhood did maintain that there were certain limitations on women's political activity; it assumed that a woman "fulfilled her civic obligations through her service to her family," not through direct participation in public politics.[20] Whatever its limits, Kerber points out, republican motherhood was not an ideology imposed on women by men. Women were actively involved in crafting the ideology, and they used it to expand their involvement in politics even though it justified only indirect involvement. Like republican motherhood, the antebellum gender ideology of redemptive womanhood was not imposed on female victims by male oppressors; it was no plot to confine them to a private sphere.[21] Women were some of the earliest proponents of redemptive womanhood, which, like republican motherhood, stressed female morality, piety, and nurture, but unlike republican motherhood, challenged the exclusion of women from direct participation in the nation's political life. As the new ideology spread, female lecturers proliferated.

Secular female lecturers were uncommon in the United States before the late 1820s. But then, "beginning in the 1830s, solo voices became a chorus."[22] The first female public lecturers of the antebellum era were reformers who justified their controversial public lecturing in the name of their religious and moral duty as women. Like female preachers, they spoke of being called by God, but, in a conflation of the religious and the moral, they were called to lecture, not to preach. Maria W. Stewart, Sarah and Angelina Grimké, and Abby Kelley, all reformers and public speakers in the 1830s, claimed to have received a call from God before they ventured to give lectures.[23] At one lecture in 1833,

Stewart, a thirty-year-old African American widow from Connecticut, told her audience that she had never wanted to speak in public and had only done so because God had called her to do so:

> The Spirit of God came before me, and I spoke before many. When going home, reflecting in what I had said, I felt ashamed, and knew not where I should hide myself. A something said within my breast "Press forward, I will be with thee." And my heart made this reply, Lord if thou wilt be with me, then I will speak for thee so long as I live. . . . I believe it is the divine influence of the Holy Spirit operating upon my heart that could possibly induce me to make the feeble and unworthy efforts that I have. . . . I believe that for wise and holy purposes . . . he hath unloosed my tongue and put his word into my mouth.

After her first speech, Stewart did not want to continue lecturing, yet she decided that she must, since soon she "must give an account at the awful bar of God."[24]

For Sarah and Angelina Grimké, a call from God was the impetus for every major change in their lives up to their entrance into antislavery work. The sisters came from a wealthy slave-owning South Carolina family. Both left the South and became Quakers in response to a religious call. In the summer of 1836, Angelina announced that God had called her to antislavery work and had told her to write an appeal against slavery to the women of the South. She completed the book, and soon afterward she accepted an invitation to lecture on slavery to women in the North. Sarah asserted that she had felt called to preach years earlier, although she had not acted on it at the time. When Angelina announced her intention to lecture, Sarah again felt called, this time to accompany her sister and support her efforts. Their mother had begged Sarah to travel with Angelina, and Sarah later explained, "It was like a voice from the Lord . . . and I instantly resolved to do so."[25] The belief that they had responded to a call from God sustained the Grimkés in the face of the immense opposition they faced after they began speaking in front of "promiscuous" audiences. As Sarah wrote to their friend and fellow abolitionist Henry C. Wright: "the Lord knows that we did not come to forward our own interests but in simple obedience His commands and I do not believe we are responsible for the consequences of doing the will of God. I do most fully believe [Angelina] has been called to the work of preaching the gospel."[26]

Abby Kelley, a white Massachusetts abolitionist who began lecturing against slavery in 1839, believed her calling as a public speaker was revealed to her one morning as she read a passage from the Bible. When she shut the book, she immediately told her mother, "My way is clear now; a new light has broken upon me." She believed she had received a "divine call . . . to go forth and lecture." Even so, Kelley hesitated, afraid that she might have been mistaken about the call. As she put it in a letter to her friend Anne Weston, "I wait the bidding of my Heavenly Father, praying that I may not mistake my own will and fancy for the voice of his unerring spirit in the soul."[27] These lecturers drew on a long tradition of female preaching to justify their public lectures, but at the same time, they transformed the arguments female preachers had used. They secularized older justifications of female preaching and applied them to lecturing in general. In addition, they argued that public speaking should not be limited only to women who had been called by God; they expanded their argument to include all women, believing that women could and should speak out in public on moral and religious issues because they were women, not despite that fact. Their argument supporting female lecturers in general supported the older notion of the religious call with a new conception of women's moral and religious duty as redemptive women.

Maria Stewart lectured in Boston between 1831 and 1833, four years before Angelina and Sarah Grimké, the next female abolitionists to speak in public. As more than one historian has noted, Stewart's speeches "heralded the arguments" the Grimkés would rely on. Indeed, they included the themes that virtually every publicly speaking female reformer would invoke in the antebellum period.[28] As female preachers had done before, Stewart appealed to her religious duty, but also, in the language of redemptive womanhood, she began to meld women's religious and moral duty together. She argued that in a broad sense all women were called by their special role as the religious and moral foundation of the nation to save it from sin and evil. Thus, she justified public action not just for exceptional women who had received a special message from God, but for all women, because all were called to act in the name of morality and religion.

Countering the argument that the Bible forbids women to speak publicly, Stewart was critical of contemporary interpretations of Paul's letters to the Corinthians: "Did St. Paul but know of our wrongs and deprivations I presume he would make no objections to our pleading in public for our rights. . . . Women of refinement in all ages, more or less, have had a voice in moral, religious and political subjects." Stewart's confidence in her ability to predict how Paul would have reacted to current social conditions is striking. Her lack of deference to religious authorities, her assertion that women have an absolute right to have a public voice, suggests that the ideology of redemptive womanhood contained from the start an argument against men's authority over women. Stewart, like Sarah Grimké and nearly every other publicly speaking female reformer after her, developed new interpretations of Paul's words to justify her actions. She linked her public speaking not only to her religious duty, but also to women's roles in history. All women, black and white, she argued, had a right to be involved in "moral, religious and political subjects" because they were women.[29] Since this was the case, no man had the right or the authority to stop women from involving themselves in such subjects.

In private letters and reminiscences, the Grimké sisters and Abby Kelley also wrote of having received a call from God, but they did not use their call as a public justification for women's lecturing in the 1830s and 1840s. In their public writings and speeches, they focused on the right of women in general to lecture. In this fashion, they too expanded that right on the grounds that all women, as "moral," "responsible and immortal" beings, had a duty to promote morality and religion in society. Because these duties were part of their sphere, whatever they might do to perform them was legitimate.[30] In her 1837 resolution at a female antislavery convention, Angelina Grimké described these general duties of women:

> That as certain rights and duties are common to all moral beings, the time has come for woman to move in that sphere which Providence has assigned her, and no longer remain satisfied in the circumscribed limits with which corrupt custom and a perverted application of Scripture have encircled her; therefore it is the duty of woman, and the province of woman, to plead the cause of the oppressed in our land, and do all that she can by her voice, and her pen, and her purse, and the influence of her example, to overthrow the horrible system of American slavery.[31]

As moral beings, then, women shared every moral duty that belonged to men. Since slavery was immoral, they had a duty to end it. Thus, any action that would tend to overthrow slavery was appropriate for women to perform. Kelley made virtually the same point in an 1840 article in the *Liberator* titled "The Woman Question." She asserted that "God has bestowed upon *women* the same moral powers he has bestowed upon *men*." Hence, she reasoned, women must have the same moral duties as men, including the duty to speak out against slavery.[32]

The example of these early female lecturers inspired other women to believe that they had a right and a duty to be at the center of public reform activities. By the late 1830s, women asserted less often that they participated in reform because of a unique call from God, and more frequently that they did so as the result of a call from their conscience. In 1837, responding directly to attacks on the Grimké sisters for their public lectures, the Boston Female Anti-Slavery Society contended that "the sphere and duties of woman it rests with each woman for herself to determine and that to do this they are aided by revelation, which it rests with each one for herself to interpret."[33] The assumption that all women would be aided by revelation was a significant expansion from the focus on an exceptional call from God. In a similar vein, a New Hampshire woman wrote to the *Liberator* in 1840: "I became convinced that if I would ever enter the kingdom of Heaven *myself*, I must read the Bible *for myself*, and make *my own* comments. . . . I *shall* speak in religious meetings, *whenever* and *wherever* the spirit of God leads the way. . . . I know not how soon I shall be driven from all religious meetings, and I care not. My object is to do my duty."[34] While this woman's letter referred to personal contact with God, that contact would not take the form of a sudden, unexpected divine call or even an expected revelation. She had already decided that God would want her—as he would want any woman—to speak in religious meetings. The role of God's spirit would not be to call the correspondent to take on some exceptional duty, but to let her know when to exercise her ordinary womanly duty to speak out. This conflation of a religious calling with women's moral duty expanded women's justification for public action. Now any woman could justify all forms of public activism in the name of her moral and religious duty to the nation.

If female abolitionists secularized the religious calling, applying it to lecturing rather than preaching, they also infused their reform efforts with religion by linking God's call to their abolition work. When they defended their actions, they stressed women's right in general to speak in public as morally accountable beings. Individual women might receive a unique call from God, but all women were called by duty to go to any extreme in order to fight sin and immorality. The notion of redemptive womanhood, that women are the moral and religious foundation of the nation, for the first time in the history of the nation allowed women *as women* to justify their entrance into public debate.

Female reformers were not the only group to embrace this expanded vision of women's moral and religious duty to society in the 1830s. Even conservative men, such as ministers who constantly criticized women for leaving their proper sphere, vociferously promoted women's moral and religious public activism. As Lydia Maria Child explained, evangelical sects actively encouraged women to understand themselves as the nation's redeemers. In an 1841 article, "Speaking in the Church," Child argued that evangelical sects were "the first agitators of the woman question." Evangelical ministers, she wrote, had been telling women for years that they had a unique and "prodigious influence" over society and that this special influence required them to leave "hearth and nursery" and to move into the realm of public religious activism. Ministers had encouraged women to form tract societies and prayer groups and to perform missionary work. But as women had become more publicly active, many of the same evangelical ministers who had encouraged them began to grow uncomfortable with women's new independence. They did not like the "unexpected directions" women's activism was taking; the situation was now out of their control. Child pointedly told them, "You have set in motion machinery that you cannot stop."[35] Child's article suggests the pervasiveness of Americans' belief in redemptive womanhood by 1841: even those who complained that women were out of their proper sphere embraced the ideology. It also suggests that Americans' belief in redemptive womanhood tended to push women into increasingly independent and public roles. As recent scholarship indicates, women did indeed become more active in reform and politics in the 1840s and 1850s, and as they did so, Americans in general became more accepting of their presence in public life.[36]

"IT WOULD BE A SIN FOR WOMAN TO STAY AT HOME AND REMAIN SILENT"

From the beginning of the 1830s, white and African American female reformers and their supporters routinely justified women's lecturing and other reform activities in two ways. First, they described the grave moral and religious crises the nation faced; and second, they referred to the ideology of redemptive womanhood to assert that women must play a central role in addressing and overcoming those crises. Many reformers, especially, but not exclusively, abolitionists, believed that they were fighting a holy war, a crusade against sin. The writer of an 1838 letter from the Dorchester Female Anti-Slavery Society to its sister society in Lynn, Massachusetts, conceived women's duty to the antislavery cause in exactly this light: "The crisis *has* come when it would be a sin for woman to stay at home and remain silent. It is necessary and important that woman should consult with woman and that they should bear their united public testimony against the brutalizing system of slavery. . . . The great crisis which will shake our nation to its centre we believe is verging on. The day of tremendous conflict is at hand."[37] The author of this letter turned the private, stay-at-home woman, instead of the publicly speaking woman, into the sinner by appealing to women's religious and moral duty to combat sin. Redemptive womanhood, for these female abolitionists, required active participation in a holy war against slavery. Maria Stewart understood herself as a Christian soldier "enlisted in holy warfare," willing and expecting "to be the hated of all man and persecuted even unto death, for righteousness and the truth's sake."

Reformers did not apply these arguments only to antislavery activism; they used them to justify women's participation in a variety of reform movements. Women's rights advocate Ernestine Rose told her audience, "We must remember that we have a crusade before us, far holier and more righteous than led warriors to Palestine. . . . Like the knight of old, we must enlist in this holy cause with a disinterested devotion, energy and determination never to turn back until we have conquered." Lucy Stone, in an 1850 speech to a Massachusetts female moral reform society, told her listeners that they were warriors "stand[ing] upon life's broad battle-fields."[38] Seeing antislavery and other reforms as holy wars, reformers depicted the United States as a nation in the throes of a religious and moral crisis. The severity of the crisis, reformers argued, made women's activism necessary, and made criticism of women's public lecturing immoral in itself.

In her support of female lecturing, Maria Stewart consistently contended that women have a unique moral and religious nature. On one occasion, for example, she asserted that throughout history women have had a special closeness to God.[39] In 1832, William Lloyd Garrison, the white editor of the antislavery newspaper the *Liberator*, encouraged black abolitionist Sarah M. Douglass to be more publicly active in the movement, telling her, "You cannot not be ignorant of the victorious influence you possess over the minds of men. You cannot, if you would, be passive; you must pull down or build up, either corrupt or preserve the morals of the age."[40] Garrison too believed that women were responsible for preserving the nation's morals.

In 1836, white abolitionist Lucy Wright, the secretary of an Ohio female antislavery society, justified women's participation in the antislavery movement on the grounds that "we are called upon as christian [*sic*] females, to engage in other benevolent enterprises of the day."[41] In the same year, African American James Forten Jr. gave a speech to the white and African American women of the Philadelphia Female Anti-Slavery Society in which he justified women's right to petition and to engage in antislavery work in terms similar to those Stewart had used. In his address, Forten told the women, "I rejoice to see you engaged in this mighty cause; it befits you; it is your province." In response to critics' claims "that the females have no right to interfere with the question of slavery, or petition for its overthrow; that they had better be at home attending to their domestic affairs," Forten asked, "but from whom does this attack upon your rights come? . . . Invariably from men alienated by avarice and self-importance from that courtesy and respect which is due to your sex . . . men . . . like the Representative from Virginia, Mr. Wise, who, lost to all shame, openly declared you to be devils incarnate." Since these critics were not "respectable men," as Forten had it, they were no judges of proper female behavior. Instead, he told his audience, "Yours is the cause of Truth, and must prevail over error; it is the cause of sympathy, and therefore it calls aloud for the aid of woman. . . . Never was there a contest commenced on more hallowed principles." By conflating women with morality and their male critics with immorality, Forten argued that women should feel free to ignore all male critics.[42] The next year, Forten's sister Sarah asserted in a poem for the *Liberator* that abolitionism was well within woman's "appropriate sphere" because it was a work of mercy, "and nought should drive her from the mercy seat, til mercy's work be finished."[43]

In 1839, a Hartford, Connecticut, newspaper printed an essay by an anonymous African American woman in which the writer inquired of the women of Connecticut: had they "signed the petitions in behalf of the dumb [slaves], and entreated *all* the women in town to do the same?" If women did not sign these petitions, she wrote, she would "blush with shame to acknowledge myself a woman, if women's souls have become . . . so blighted, so shrunk to nonentity, as to neglect this labor of humanity." Writing to an audience made up of both white and black women, this author positioned herself as a redemptive woman, one who was capable of instructing white as well as African American women in their duties.[44] In 1842, the predominantly white but biracial Boston Female Anti-Slavery Society highlighted women's special moral and religious mission in its annual report, reprinting the following statement of women's duties to society: "What, let me ask, is woman's work? It is to be a minister of Christian love. It is to sympathize with human misery. It is to breathe sympathy into man's heart. It is to keep alive in society some feeling of human brotherhood. This is her mission on earth."[45]

Articles in the *North Star* and *Frederick Douglass' Paper*, publications edited by African American abolitionist and women's rights activist Frederick Douglass, often asserted that women's special nature justified their involvement in benevolent and political activities. The paper argued that "female influence serves to refine and temper" men and that women's "benevolence, virtue and constancy" made them vital to reform efforts. While many articles focused on women's reform efforts, others made explicit references to politics. The *North Star* defended the 1848 Seneca Falls women's rights convention, asserting that "in respect to political rights," women were "justly entitled to all we claim for men."[46]

Time after time, African American and white reformers asserted that women must play a central role in reform and politics because of women's redemptive nature. If women were not permitted to act in this vital role, the consequences would be dire. Well-known woman's rights supporter Thomas Wentworth Higginson argued that the decline of civilization would result if women were kept in a constrained and limited sphere: "Whether the future of the world is to be bright or dark—whether it shall be painted with the hues of heaven or Hell, depends upon the sphere which we now give to woman."[47] Whether women wanted the responsibility or not, these reformers believed the moral and religious fate of the nation was women's to determine.

JEZEBELS AMONG US

Debates over the nature of woman's sphere most commonly arose directly out of instances in which women were supposed to have transgressed its boundaries. The controversy surrounding Angelina and Sarah Grimké's 1837 New England antislavery lecture tour sparked the antebellum era's most famous debate over woman's sphere. In the spring of 1837, the American Anti-Slavery Society invited the Grimké sisters to travel to New England and give a series of antislavery lectures to women in Boston and surrounding towns. The sisters arrived on 28 May and immediately began their work. Soon they were attracting larger and larger crowds, and although the talks had been "arranged for women," men too began to attend. The sisters spoke to "their 'first, large mixed audience,'" on 21 June 1837.[48] The Massachusetts clergy of the Orthodox Congregationalist church, the most powerful denomination in the region, lost no time in responding to the sisters' actions: they released a pastoral letter on 27 June in which they strongly condemned female lecturing, asserting that the Grimké sisters and all women like them "threaten the female character with wide-spread and permanent injury." Arguing that a woman's appropriate influence was "unobtrusive and private" "as becomes the modesty of her sex," they criticized the "unnatural" female lecturer who "assumes the place and tone of man as a public reformer." If other women emulated such behavior, it would soon lead to the "degeneracy and ruin" of society.[49]

The pastoral letter marked the beginning of the Massachusetts clergy's long and public battle over the propriety of female lecturing. The ministers also preached to their individual congregations on the evils of female lecturing. At least four of them had these sermons published. Minister Hubbard Winslow turned his set of sermons on women into a book. In it, he based much of his argument on the premise that women are more "Christian and pious" than men. He hoped to show how the "false education and habits" of women had led them out of their appropriate sphere. If unchecked, such behavior would result in "the downfall of states and nations."[50] Jonathan Sterns, a like-minded minister, told the women of his congregation that, if they became public speakers, they would irreparably damage the social order: "Yours it is to decide, under God, whether we shall be a nation of refined and high minded Christians, or whether, rejecting the civilities of life, and throwing off the restraints of morality and piety, we shall become a fierce race of barbarians, before whom neither order, nor honor, nor chastity can stand."[51] Sterns and Winslow linked women's public speaking with absolute chaos and the destruction of morality in American society. In a number of similar sermons, the Massachusetts Congregationalist clergy told women that they would be either the redeemers or the destroyers of the nation, depending on whether they properly performed their womanly duties.

The controversy over the Grimké sisters was not merely local, it was played out in newspapers throughout the country, including the African American press. The *Colored American*, published from 1837 to 1841 in New York City, embraced many of the Congregationalist clergy's criticisms of the Grimké sisters. The *Colored American* consistently opposed female lecturing despite its ardent defense of abolitionism. On 22 September 1837, the paper reprinted an essay critical of Sarah Grimké's defense of lecturing. The essay expressed sympathy with the antislavery cause, but its author feared that, by arguing that the Bible supported female lecturing, Grimké "had furnished a weapon to the . . . infidel." This anonymous author asserted that the Bible established the man's supremacy over the woman. If women challenged that authority, they would "weaken her influence, and impair her usefulness." The next week, the paper printed a letter from a reader who asserted that "the appropriate sphere for a female to use her influence over man, is the domestic fireside." This author also wrote disparagingly of the woman who had "the desire to appear before the world as a writer or speaker." Another letter asserted that women who were members of mixed-sex organizations should not be allowed to vote in those societies because "Government is, and was from the Beginning, vested by their common Creator in the man." The *Colored American* prefaced this letter with a statement that it completely concurred the author's views.[52]

If initial attacks on female lecturers did not depict them as fiends and prostitutes, they quickly devolved into such. Early condemnations stressed the original "good feelings and benevolent motives" of most female speakers but contended that such women had been misguided by "bad teachers." Then, as publicly speaking women ignored ministers' advice to throw off their "bad teaching," ministers began to describe them as evil and "unnatural" creatures. They argued that even if the speakers' original motives were good, they had destroyed their character by taking on masculine roles.[53]

One common way of maligning the character of female lecturers was to identify them with Frances ("Fanny") Wright, a Scottish female reformer and religious freethinker who had settled in the United States in the mid-1820s. Wright began her career as a public speaker in 1828 and spoke to large, mixed-sex audiences throughout the United States. Fanny Wright's name cropped up constantly in attacks on women who spoke in public in the antebellum period. Lori Ginzberg has noted that the charge of "Fanny Wrightism" was invoked any time a feminist made an attack on religion. The epithet made it difficult for antebellum women to question religion in any way, because of the close linkage being made between "irreligion and sexual and domestic instability." Since women's presumed greater religiosity was linked to their greater morality, Americans would expect an irreligious woman to be immoral. But whereas Wright had "unsexed" herself in the late 1820s with her public expressions of irreligion rather than simply by speaking in front of mixed audiences, those two actions were merged into one by the late 1830s. Harkening back to public reaction against Fanny Wright, Parsons Cooke asked his congregation in 1837, "Now what was it in this case that constituted the outrage upon the feelings of the community? . . . [Fanny Wright's] unblushing licentiousness . . . no doubt aggravated the horror which we had of the whole affair. But after all, the main shock to the good sense of the world was caused by the fact that she was a *woman*—a woman standing forth as a public lecturer."[54] The name of Fanny Wright was not only employed to frighten women from questioning religion, but because it transformed the meaning of Wright, the epithet was also used to discourage them from speaking in public in front of men and women for any cause.

Reformer Amos Farnsworth wrote to abolitionist Anne W. Weston that Grafton, Massachusetts, minister Dudley Phelps had told him that women who lecture "will land on Fanny Wrightism and that such is the fate of all women who venture out of their sphere." Samuel Cornish, editor of the *Colored American*, warned African American women of the dangers of Fanny Wrightism in an editorial titled "Ladies Beware." In this commentary on female public speaking, he noted that "Fanny Wright's first steps toward skepticism were her masculine assumptions. Male speculations and male experiments addled her brain, and male achievements engrossed her soul."[55] According to Cornish, Cooke, and Phelps, Wright's primary sin was her public speaking rather than her infidelity. Speaking in public masculinized her and led to all her other evils.

"Fanny Wrightism" was only one of many slurs used to discredit these outspoken female abolitionists. All such attacks focused on women's character, charging that the speakers were the opposite of redemptive women. According to *History of Woman Suffrage*, "Abby Kelley was . . . the most persecuted of all the women who labored throughout the antislavery struggle. [She faced] scorn, ridicule, violence, and mobs accompanying her, [and] suffer[ed] all kinds of persecutions." On various occasions, Kelley was called an infidel, a monster, a prostitute, even "half witch and half devil." "Unsexing herself with impunity," she was like "women in corrupt and profligate cities who were among the most vicious and abandoned of the human race."[56]

Soon after Abby Kelley began her lecturing career, she was invited to speak in Washington, Connecticut. Her first four lectures there were well attended. She left town for other engagements, then returned a few weeks later. In her absence, a minister had preached a sermon against Kelley that dramatically altered the local attitude toward her. In his sermon he accused Kelley of being a modern-day version of Jezebel:

Another Jezebel had arisen making high pretensions to philanthropy and Christianity, and with fascinations exceeding even those of her scriptural prototype, was arising to entice and destroy this church. He added: . . . "Do any of you ask for evidence of her vile character? It needs no other evidence than the fact that in the face of the clearest commands of God, 'let your women keep silence in the churches, for it is not permitted unto them to speak.' She comes here with brazen face, a servant of Satan in the garb of an angel of light, and tramples this commandment under her feet."[57]

By arguing that publicly speaking women were by nature irreligious, regardless of their professed piety, ministers tapped into the linkage that Ginzberg has noted was being made between women's religious infidelity and all immoral behavior. Ministers asserted that the most seemingly pious woman, one who professed religion, was in reality a "servant of Satan" if she spoke in public. Such criticisms followed Kelley wherever she spoke. In Cranston, Rhode Island, Kelley was accused of "corrupting the minds of the youth, enticing them from the path of rectitude; . . . and so perverting their understandings . . . as to lead them to disregard all religion." In upstate New York in 1843, she and her companions were "sometimes called a 'traveling seraglio.'" Kelley wrote that she was generally "hated and condemned," that her name was "the loathing of the people," and that she had "suffered all manner of obloquy." When she visited her sisters in East Hampton, she wrote to her future husband, "the people . . . almost start at the sight of so ungodly a being as myself." They did not care "to come so near a monster."[58]

Kelley's name, like Frances Wright's, was invoked to destroy the character of any woman who associated with her or spoke in public. One abolitionist wrote that he and his associates were "vilified" as "freelovers, infidels, and last and mightiest, Abby Kelleyites," and complained that "solemn-faced ladies asked why we associated with such a vile woman, and why she had left her pretended husband Stephen Foster and whether it was seven or nine she had at various times cohabited with." Kelley's friend Paulina Wright wrote in 1843 that she was very lonely because "there is scarcely a woman in the city that will speak to me" because she associated with Kelley. When African American newspaper editor Mary Ann Shadd arrived in 1855 at the eleventh Colored National Convention in Philadelphia, the delegates conducted an extended and heated debate over whether she should be allowed to participate in the proceedings. While "there was much opposition manifested," the convention finally agreed to let her participate, leading one disgruntled member to ask, "if we would admit Abby Kelley also."[59]

Attendance at one of Kelley's Sunday lectures was one of the main charges against Rhoda Bement, who in 1844 was tried by the Presbyterian Session of Seneca Falls, New York, for "disorderly and unchristian conduct." All the charges against Bement were related to Kelley's lectures and Bement's conflicts with her pastor regarding these meetings. Much of Bement's church trial was taken up with ascertaining her role in the meetings Kelley held in Seneca Falls, as well as the character of Kelley and the meetings. Specifically, this testimony consisted of numerous attempts to show that Kelley's lectures were irreligious and unsuitable for members of that church.[60]

Kelley may have been the most reviled of the antebellum female abolitionists. Some scholars have suggested that her style was too confrontational; she was not "gentle" enough, and she antagonized her audiences. Yet virtually all other female lecturers faced similar criticisms.[61] Maria Stewart faced so much hostility in Boston for her lectures that she decided to give them up and leave the city in 1833.[62] The Grimké sisters also faced severe attacks on their character. Angelina Grimké was "repeatedly characterized in the press as a 'loose woman,'" and newspaper articles referred to her as "Devil-ina." Both sisters were compared to Frances Wright, called "unnatural," and said to be on the road to "shame and dishonor" if they were not already there.[63] Lucy Stone, Jane Elizabeth Jones, Sallie Holley, Antoinette Brown Blackwell, Elizabeth Cady Stanton, Susan B. Anthony, Caroline Dall, and every other female reformer who gave public lectures in this period mentioned in letters or journals that they too faced this sort of abuse.[64]

Attackers asserted that public speaking by women was evidence of immorality and impiety, or as Lucy Stone put it, "free love, infidelity and every other bad thing." Stone noted in 1851 that at one of her antislavery meetings a church member told the congregation before her arrival that she and her fellow lecturers were all "infidels." After Sallie Holley decided in 1850 to become a lecturer, she told a friend that ladies "who had been proud of her acquaintance crossed the street to avoid . . . her, as if she had become infamous." According to opponents of female public speaking, the act of lecturing unsexed women; it made them masculine because they were usurping roles that, according to Christianity, belonged to men. Their supposed disregard for Christianity and the Bible was seen as evidence of a decline into uncivilized behavior. Without the restraining and civilizing influence of Christianity, these women were thought to become both evil and animalistic.[65]

"WHAT 'WOMAN'S SPHERE', IS THE VERY MATTER IN DISPUTE"

Criticisms of women's lecturing were always ambiguous. The same Massachusetts ministers, newspaper editors, and other writers who criticized the Grimké sisters also embraced redemptive womanhood and stressed women's special moral and religious nature and their duty to promote religion and morality inside and outside their families. The pastoral letter condemning the Grimké sisters praised woman's promotion of religion and benevolence "as becomes the modesty of her sex," but added that this modesty precluded public lecturing.[66] The same Reverend Jonathan Sterns who warned the Grimké sisters and other women that if they lectured in public they would turn Americans into a "fierce race of barbarians" also told his parishioners that "*religion* seems almost to have been entrusted to [woman's] particular custody" and that woman "stands at the *fountain* of moral action and feeling." He added that "the influence of woman is not limited to the domestic circle. *Society* is her empire, which she governs almost at will." Specifically, he noted, "the cause of benevolence is peculiarly indebted to the agency of woman. She is fitted by nature to cheer the afflicted, elevate the depressed."[67] Even as Sterns told women to remain inside their sphere, his description of women's sphere seemed to know no boundaries.

Colored American sent the same kinds of mixed messages to its readers. Even as it argued that women should not compete with men for the public limelight and that they should not lecture men in public, the paper asserted that women should engage in public moral, religious, and political debates. Many of the articles criticizing women's public lecturing were written by women. One female author, "Ellen," told women that their place was not in the lecture hall but at the "domestic fireside." But she also explained that she had to overcome her concerns about the "delicacy in a young and unknown female writing for the public press" in order to write her letter. Ellen decided that she had to send in her letter because of her great "anxiety for the elevation of my people, and the improvement of my sex."[68] Thus, she argued that the importance of her mission justified her own controversial behavior. In a letter written to tell women that public speaking was outside their sphere, Ellen used exactly the same argument female lecturers used to justify their actions.

Editorials, articles, and letters printed in the *Colored American* repeated this pattern constantly. The same editorial that asserted that female lecturers assumed "masculine views and measures" argued in the same sentence that woman's sphere ought to expand, that the editor was "anxious that woman . . . should fill the *whole* of her important and elevated sphere." Such articles told African American women that they were "naturally more moral, more loving, more caring than men," that they possessed the ability to "influence" men, and that they had a duty to use this influence to "instill into [men] true Moral and Religious principles."[69] In its first issue, the paper begged African American women to use their special womanly influence to support reform. It told female readers that "in any enterprise for the improvement of our people—either moral, or mental, our hands would be palsied without woman's influence. We ask them for an exertion of her influence."[70] The paper made a considerable effort to identify and support the efforts of African American female reformers and benevolent societies, looking far from New York City for examples of female benevolence. In February 1837, it printed the speech of Robert Banks to the Colored Female Dorcas Society in Buffalo, New York. Banks had told the society, "I believe it is admitted on all hands, that female influence is paramount to all other" and that "there is no place under the broad canopy of heaven, no condition, no situation, into which female influence may not enter, either for good or for evil, a blessing or a curse." Specifically, he added, "benevolence is a field particularly adapted to your character and feelings."[71] On one hand the paper condemned female lecturers; on the other it encouraged women, because they were women, to become more active in reform and benevolent organizations.

Well-known reformer, educator, and domestic advice-book author Catharine Beecher also strongly opposed the Grimké sisters' 1837 lecture tour. Beecher exchanged public letters with Angelina Grimké, arguing about both abolition and the meaning of woman's sphere. Beecher's criticism of the sisters' lectures seemed to stem mostly from her belief that women should not participate in "divisive" political causes like abolition. Beecher believed that women must redeem the nation because men were leading it down a path toward "self-destruction . . . disunion and civil wars." In such an environment, she wrote, "it surely has become the duty of every female instantly to relinquish the attitude of a partisan, in every matter of clashing interests, and to assume the office of a mediator, and an advocate of peace."[72] Beecher, like all others in this debate, stressed the importance of women's duty to redeem the nation. She objected only to the divisiveness of some reformers' approach.

The lives and beliefs of Catharine and her two politically active younger sisters, Harriet Beecher Stowe and Isabella Beecher Hooker, suggest both the power and the ambiguity of the ideology of redemptive womanhood. All three sisters embraced the notion that it was woman's job to redeem the troubled nation, but they all disagreed about how women were to accomplish this feat. Catharine, Harriet, and Isabella devoted much of their lives to "elevating women's status and expanding women's influence in American society." They believed that "womanhood carried with it a particular and unique agency for shaping American society." Yet in spite of their shared sense of woman's special moral and spiritual mission, they differed on what exactly the elevation of women and the expansion of their sphere would entail. For example, Isabella, and eventually Harriet, embraced women's right to vote, while Catharine thought voting or any involvement in partisan politics was outside woman's sphere.[73]

As the controversy over the Grimké sisters suggests, debates about the boundaries of woman's sphere had no clear answers. Reformers quickly found this weakness and used it to undermine the notion that woman's sphere could be defined in a way that limited women's actions. When Catharine Beecher wrote to Angelina Grimké that a "woman may seek the aid of co-operation and combination among her own sex, to assist her in her appropriate offices of piety [and] charity," but that she must not take an active role in a "divisive" cause like abolition, Angelina Grimké responded, "Appropriate offices! Ah! here is the great difficulty. What are they? Who can point them out? Who has ever attempted to draw a line of separation between the duties of men and women, as moral beings, without committing the grossest inconsistencies on the one hand, or running into the most arrant absurdities [on] the other?" Angelina also pointed out to Amos A. Phelps that "the attempt to draw a line of demarcation [sic] between the duties of men and women always failed." A writer calling himself "Justice," in his 1840 letter to the *Boston Courier*, illuminated some of the "absurdities" that had emerged in a recent public lecture on women. The lecturer, he claimed, had used the standard argument against female speakers, that woman's sphere is "different" from man's and that hence she should not perform actions contained in man's sphere. But Justice pointed out that this argument was a piece of circular reasoning. Not only was this definition of woman's sphere negative in that it described only what the sphere was not, but it was irrefutable, because any woman who dared argue with the point was engaging in a "male" activity and thus was out of her sphere.[74]

In a similar vein, Abby Kelley complained in a letter to the *Liberator* that most women had no idea what the conventional limits of woman's sphere were supposed to be. She asserted that some women "do not dare to do any thing for fear they may get out of their 'sphere;' not having a very distinct idea of the limits of this 'sphere,' they think it hazardous to take even one step on the ground in which there has been such a 'hue-and-cry' set up about 'sphere.'"[75] Angelina Grimké and Kelley suggest that opponents of women's lecturing could never say what the boundaries of woman's sphere were; instead, they simply labeled specific activities as inside or outside that sphere. They argued that actions were beyond woman's sphere when they seemed indelicate and unfeminine, but those definitions did nothing to clarify the situation. If virtually all Americans seemed to accept the notion that women had a sphere, they were perpetually arguing over the nature and limits of that sphere.

Adding to the confusion about woman's sphere was the notion that the sphere was constantly expanding. Supporters and critics of female lecturers and women's rights continually pointed out that notions of woman's appropriate activities changed at different places and times and had expanded in progressive "Christian nations" like the United States. Antebellum Americans considered their women and their nation the most advanced in the world, and they believed that like the nation women ought to always be progressing to a higher, more civilized plane. Even those, like Reverend Jonathan Sterns, who held conservative positions on woman's sphere believed that because Christianity had elevated woman from her low state in "barbarous and savage lands . . . [to her] true dignity as the *companion* and *equal* of man, . . . the true sphere of female usefulness will be constantly expanding." According to Maine Universalist minister Daniel Smith, another opponent of women lecturers, "our females owe their present exalted stand, to the Gospel of the blessed Son of God."[76]

Supporters of female lecturing and women's rights used this same point to argue in favor of female lecturers and women's rights in general. As one participant at the national woman's rights convention at Worcester in 1850 wrote, "What *'woman's sphere'* IS, is the very matter in dispute. In different climates and among different races of men, and different conditions of social progress, woman's sphere differs immensely." And as minister and woman's rights activist Antoinette Brown noted, "The sphere of woman never yet remained fixed or permanent for any considerable length of time."[77] If woman's nature was to be pious, moral, and nurturing, there could be endless disagreement over what actions such a nature would require or prevent, and nineteenth-century Americans knew this. Using ideas about woman's nature to securely define her sphere of action was virtually impossible. Thus, those who disapproved of female lecturers found themselves in the awkward position of agreeing with women's rights supporters that women were responsible for the moral and spiritual welfare of the nation and that as civilization progressed woman's sphere would naturally expand, while arguing against a particular expansion of that sphere. Margaret Fuller noted the irony of this, pointing out that even those men with the narrowest conception of woman's sphere always took great pride in saying how much Christianity had advanced women.[78] On one hand, they told women not to give public lectures to mixed-sex audiences because that would be usurping male authority. On the other hand, they stressed the vital importance of women's involvement in reform movements, telling women that their special womanly influence knew no boundaries. The issue up for debate, then, was not whether women would participate in the redemption of the nation, but how they would accomplish it.

ANGELS BY DEFAULT

Widespread confusion over the meaning of woman's sphere created a curious situation. Unable to determine whether a female reformer was inside or outside her sphere by her actions, Americans looked to her character and her motives to find the answer, just as they had with alleged murderesses and "fallen" women. In 1846, Ohio doctor C. B. Judd wrote a letter to Amos

Phelps, a general agent of the Massachusetts Anti-Slavery Society and a total stranger, for help in making just such a determination regarding Abby Kelley's public lectures in his state. Judd asked Phelps for information on the nature of Kelley's "*true* principles, character or acts":

> For some time past this section has been agitated by the paradoxical effusions of a Lecturess in the person of Miss Abby Kelley, but more recently, Mrs Abby Foster, the latter being the surname of a Husband who is Hierophant in the work of propagating the tenets of her universally *negative* faith. She passes from place to place among us, attacking every institution we cherish as the Civil Government, the Church, the Ministry, our Fathers . . . all parties, sects and men. . . . She creates quite a sensation in the Church and out of it, for she appears in the garb of a devout Christian, quotes scripture and claims for her defence the qualities of morality and piety; Various reports follow her, some asserting her to be immoral, infidel and pernicious: others denying the same. . . . If the former be true, she should be stopt, as she is wielding a dangerous influence upon the common cause of our country, posterity and the race; if the latter, she may proceed, and we await the eliciting of order out of confusion, by the providence of Him who worketh all things of the councils of his own will.[79]

This conflicted letter reveals Judd's inability to judge Kelley by her actions. He was clearly disturbed by her behavior. Yet, in spite of his obvious hostility toward Kelley and his evident disgust at what he saw as her usurpation of male roles, Judd felt he could do nothing to stop her. He wrote to Phelps that he was willing to admit her duty to perform such disruptive work if only he could be sure that she was a pious and moral woman doing her Christian duty.

In Judd's mind, a woman performing such a disruptive public task would be justified if she was a moral and pious Christian. Her motivation was the key to her actions. The problem, he wrote, was that he could not determine whether Kelley's motives were good or evil. Yet he would have to guess that Phelps, a leader in the antislavery movement, would not tell him that Kelley was "immoral, infidel and pernicious."[80] Judd appeared to resign himself to the notion that Kelley had to be allowed to lecture, whatever chaos she caused. She looked pious and moral and she quoted the Bible, so Judd could not believe she was infidel and immoral. Yet he was not at ease with this idea. He was so disturbed by the way she undermined the social structure that he wrote to a total stranger to ask about her character. Almost against his will, it appears from his letter, he felt compelled to allow Kelley to continue to lecture.

Because Americans could not securely define or determine the nature of women like Abby Kelley, they could never agree on any physical sphere appropriate to women, however much they tried. Directly confronted with a publicly speaking woman dressed modestly and quoting scripture, they found it extremely difficult to believe her an infidel, a prostitute, a Jezebel, even when they expected she would be such a creature. Margaret Fuller noted this phenomenon in the experience of Abby Kelley. In *Woman in the Nineteenth Century*, Fuller reproduced an extract from a letter that described Kelley's encounter with a hostile crowd. When Kelley arrived at the event described in the letter, a violent mob was prepared to harass her as a "female out of her sphere." But she quietly walked to the front of the hall and took her seat, like a "gentle hero . . . with mild decision and womanly calmness." Her womanliness and her "moral power" "subdued the prejudices of hearers." Fuller was certain that, when angry crowds attended women's lectures, if the speakers acted in a sacred or moral cause they would inevitably "excite an interest proportionate to the aversion with which it had been their purpose to regard them." The crowds apparently could not retain their hostility toward female lecturers in the presence of moral and pious speakers.[81]

When Kelley made another lecture tour in Connecticut in 1842, a Baptist minister refused to open his meeting hall to her because he had heard reports of her "Fanny Wrightism &c." But after the minister heard Kelley speak, he apologized to her in a letter and assured her that he would do all he could to help her "just and holy causes" in the future. Kelley had many similar experiences on her lecture tours. One Rhode Island woman wrote to her, "I was not prepared to love thee, not even to respect thee, for calumny and slander had preceded thee in thy visit. But how did their hateful influences vanish, before thy silent yet eloquent preaching of thy consistent and unblamable deportment." Because Kelley acted like a redemptive woman, this writer accepted her as a public speaker. In the Rhoda Bement church trial, local attorney and abolitionist Ansel Bascom noted that although "Abby Kelley was tried and tried over and over again, . . . the attempt to represent Miss Kelley unfavorably upon the record was an utter failure." The witnesses had been to Kelley's lectures and refused to testify that Kelley had done or said anything immoral on those occasions, despite all the rumors that she was immoral and impious. This difficulty in believing that even the most reviled woman could be evil if one saw her looking and acting pious and moral was characteristic of the reaction to antebellum female lecturers.[82]

Author and editor Sarah Josepha Hale found it difficult to condemn the actions of female lecturers and women's rights activists, just as she had been unable to condemn George Sand for her "life of license."[83] Hale was always ready to point out that she had "no sympathy with those who are wrangling for 'woman's rights.'" In 1839, she published a novel, *The Lectures; or, Woman's*

Sphere, the story of a young wife whose marriage and life were destroyed by her insistence on lecturing in public after she married. But even as Hale disavowed women's rights, she took great pains to demonstrate that woman's "moral sense" was "better developed and more active than is found in the other sex." Hale had compiled *Woman's Record*, an account of women from "the Creation to A.D. 1854 " nearly one thousand pages long, in order to show that "in the moral progress of mankind, woman has been God's most efficient agent."[84] For Hale, there was a direct link between women's ability to exert their moral influence and the moral character of society as a whole. Despite the fact that Hale had written an entire novel condemning women's public lecturing and had asserted many times that she strongly disapproved of women's rights, her descriptions of real women involved in these activities were strangely sympathetic. While Hale believed that publicly speaking abolitionist and women's rights supporter Lucretia Mott's theories tended to promote infidelity and would "disorganize society," she nonetheless wrote that Mott was "sincere and earnest in her endeavors to do good" and possessed an excellent "private character." Harriet Martineau, Frances Wright, Margaret Fuller, Lydia Maria Child, and a number of other women whose actions Hale hinted would lead to social disorder also became slightly misguided geniuses with noble souls in *Woman's Record*.[85]

One also can see this growing acceptance of women's activism in the changing concerns of female abolitionist writers and speakers. As Lyde Cullen Sizer has pointed out, "By the late 1850s, rationales for writing or speaking were no longer as central as they had been for women antislavery writers." In the 1830s women such as Lydia Maria Child and Maria Stewart had felt it necessary to engage in long justifications of their actions, apologizing for or explaining why they, as women, wrote or spoke out on slavery. By the 1850s, as a growing national crisis made women's duty to save the nation seem increasingly vital, these justifications became less and less central to the arguments of female abolitionists and often dropped out of their writing. Instead, such women simply began to assume that readers and listeners understood they had the right and duty to take part in political life.[86]

Antebellum gender ideology was not an ideology constructed by men to contain women in the private sphere of the home; it was a belief promoted by women as well as men, a belief in woman's moral and spiritual superiority, and her corresponding duty to uphold morality and religion in the family and society. Female lecturers argued that they were acting on this duty. They faced numerous attacks on their character, yet these negative labels never securely defined them. They were able to assert their status as good women, Christian martyrs, and modern Joans of Arc. Many Americans did disapprove of women speaking in public, particularly at the start of the antebellum era, but their logic never made it clear why women should not lecture. Those who argued against female lecturing claimed it was outside of woman's sphere, that it usurped male authority, but at the same time they argued that women had a special duty to redeem the nation. In this way opponents of female lecturing undermined their own arguments. As a result, by the last half of the antebellum era, Americans were becoming less and less critical—though not completely uncritical—of publicly speaking women.

Female public speakers and other publicly active reformers increased in number in the late 1840s and 1850s. Sallie Holley, Caroline Dall, Frances Ellen Watkins, and Mary Ann Shadd Cary all began their lecture careers in the 1850s. If Americans still did not agree about their character, they found it easier to believe that these women were moral and pious than the opposite. Because of the binary opposition inherent in redemptive womanhood, women who claimed respectability tended to become respectable almost by default. Unable to imagine that this growing number of women speaking out against sin and evil could actually be a pack of Jezebels, Americans gradually became accustomed to female lecturers and other politically active women the more they were exposed to them. Just as it was difficult for juries to imagine that the demure, weeping woman on trial for murder in front of them was a depraved she-devil or tigress, it was difficult for Americans generally to see and hear female lecturers like the Grimké sisters, Abby Kelley, and Lucy Stone—dressed simply and modestly, quoting scripture, and pleading with their audience to end the sin of slavery—and still believe them to be depraved and licentious infidels. And if these women were not depraved, they must be virtuous.

The Impending Crisis, Male Immorality, and Female Heroism

CHAPTER

FIVE

If the affairs of the Nation had been under woman's joint control, . . . I think the Fugitive Slave Bill would never have been an Act. Woman has some respect for the natural law of God.

—Theodore Parker, *A Sermon on the Public Function of Woman*[1]

The Reverend Byron Sunderland was no supporter of women's rights. In one 1857 sermon, he explained to his congregation the difference between "true women" and "strong-minded women." The true woman, he asserted, "feareth the Lord. There is a certain intuition whereby she knows her place and keeps it." Strong-minded women, on the other hand, were "infidels, or act on the principle of infidelity. . . . They have grown wiser in their own esteem than the word of God; and, casting this light away, they rush out in the darkness of their own un-aided reason, making disgrace of the very name of woman, so that all the world laughs after them." Yet in the same sermon, this Washington, D.C., Presbyterian minister also admitted that he could not tell a particular woman what the limits of her sphere were, since God might call a woman to any "high or lowly mission . . . like Deborah of the Old, or like Dorcas of the New Testament; like the Maid of Orleans, or like the mother of Washington."[2]

It is striking that in such a sermon two of the four exemplars of proper womanhood—Deborah and Joan of Arc—were leaders of armies. This focus on historical and biblical female warriors was no accident. Sunderland, like many Americans in the second half of the antebellum era, was convinced that women must actively fight to save the nation from corrupt and selfish men who seemed bent on destroying it. And also, like many others, he invoked extremely aggressive and publicly active historical, literary, and living heroines in an effort to support his argument. In addition to the four women mentioned above, in other sections of the sermon Sunderland lauded English prison reformer Elizabeth Fry, nurse Florence Nightingale, and even transcendentalist author Margaret Fuller. Sunderland used these specific examples of female heroes to convince his female parishioners that they and other American women must fight to "preserve the . . . foundations of society from decay and dissolution": "I invoke your earnest aid, your unceasing vigilance, in every noble, Christian and patriotic work. . . . I call upon you to correct the evil and the disorders of our social life and manners. . . . I call upon you to roll back the dark and bitter tide of vice, and crime, and wretchedness and desolation, which is breaking out, alas, on every hand."[3] The belief that America, ruled solely by men, was being overcome by a "bitter tide of vice" and that women must step in to stem that tide had become common in the second half of the antebellum era. References to historical, literary, and living heroines who could and did save nations were also becoming routine in even the most conservative discussions of women and womanhood in the same period.

The ideology of redemptive womanhood made woman's nature and her role in society of central importance to antebellum Americans. If it was woman's duty to protect and preserve the morality and piety of the nation, then she must fulfill this duty or America would "break up and become a chaos of disjointed and unsightly elements."[4] If this responsibility for the moral and religious health of the nation gave women the right and duty to be interested in the moral and religious welfare of those outside their families, then it demanded that women act in extremely assertive and public ways when the virtue of their nation seemed threatened.

By the mid-1840s, many Americans believed that the virtue of the nation was directly threatened. There had been signs of growing tension between the North and South as early as the Missouri Compromise debate of 1819–1820. But this debate ended in a seemingly airtight agreement covering all U.S. territories not already carved into states: it delineated which territories could become slave states, and which must be free. The problem over the admittance of new states seemed to be resolved permanently. Although tensions over new states had dissipated, in the 1830s significant signs suggested that the North and South were heading into further conflict: South Carolina's attempt to nullify federal tariffs, sectional debate over Southern Indian removal, the rise of radical abolition societies in the North, the flooding of Congress with antislavery petitions and the subsequent "gag rule" against bringing such petitions forward, the proliferation of antislavery literature throughout the North and South, Southern legal crackdowns on free speech and the rights of enslaved and free blacks, and debate over the admission of Texas into the union. But to most Americans, these conflicts did not seem to be a direct or immediate threat to the nation's survival.

This changed beginning in the mid-1840s with the conflict over the introduction of new territory into the United States. William Appleman Williams has argued that after about 1844 Americans became less and less optimistic about resolving the problems engendered by the rise of a market-dominated economy within the territorial United States. In 1844, the term Manifest Destiny was coined, and from that time on Americans looked more and more to the frontier as the place that would allow all citizens access to an independent economic existence and thus would make possible the maintenance of American freedom and democracy. This expansion created both internal conflicts between the North and the South and external conflicts, most notably the Mexican-American War of 1846–1848.[5]

The United States had finally annexed Texas as a slave state in 1845 after years of debate. Almost immediately that annexation and the state's dispute over its boundary with Mexico led the United States into the Mexican-American War. This war, more popular in the South than in the North, led to the addition of a vast amount of territory to the United States. Because this new land was not covered by the Missouri Compromise, the acquisition reopened the dispute over slave and free states. Each attempt to admit a new state led to increasingly bitter battles between Northerners and Southerners, each new compromise created more problems than it solved, and soon the situation turned violent. By 1856, battles over the admission of new states had turned into warfare both on the frontier and in Congress. As Northern and Southern settlers murdered one another and burned towns to decide the issue in Kansas, South Carolina representative Preston Brooks beat Massachusetts senator Charles Sumner unconscious for suggesting in his speech "The Crime against Kansas" that Brooks's uncle, South Carolina senator Andrew Butler, was in bed with the "harlot, Slavery."[6]

The worsening atmosphere of war and crisis after the mid-1840s led Americans to fear that there were no peaceful solutions, that their nation might well be speeding toward civil war and destruction. The ideology of redemptive womanhood had prepared Americans to understand this growing sense of national crisis, these tensions engendered by a market-oriented economy, as the product of male immorality, selfishness, and greed. It was in this context that Americans further highlighted women's active role as the moral regenerators of society.[7]

The ideology of redemptive womanhood took a more activist turn in the 1840s for another reason. Starting in the 1820s, the ideology had stimulated an explosion of literature by and about woman that focused specifically on women's duty to family and society. Histories of women, domestic novels, and yellow-backed pamphlet fiction, which frequently detailed the exploits of female fiends and heroines, all became popular. These literary explorations of woman's nature and actions both facilitated and were facilitated by the public actions of actual women in antebellum America. Antebellum reformers drew strength from these literary images of womanhood, which also gave them a way to understand and justify their public actions, and in some cases they created images of womanhood that others would later emulate. Histories and novels about heroic women gave more and more women a sense that they could and should perform heroic actions as part of their duty to preserve the moral and religious health of the nation. The literature also gave them ways to imagine the specifics of female heroism. Then, as fears of a national crisis grew in the 1840s and 1850s, these literary heroines generally became more active and assertive. Before 1845, the ideology of redemptive womanhood was already encouraging woman's public activism and the proliferation of literature about assertive and publicly active heroines. After 1845, amid a growing atmosphere of crisis, redemptive womanhood would make assertive and publicly active women seem increasingly natural to Americans.

"SELFISHNESS . . . IS PREACHED AS GOSPEL AND ENACTED AS LAW"

There was a flip side to antebellum Americans' argument that women were particularly moral: it was that men generally lacked moral fiber. Countless writers asserted that men, who lacked women's refined moral and religious sensibilities, at best ignored and more frequently promoted the sins of society. According to Catharine Beecher, "the day when most men would be motivated by benevolence was a 'millennial point beyond our ken.'" The members of the Dorchester Female Anti-Slavery Society believed that history showed that the "salvation or destruction" of the nation depended mostly on women: "If every female anti-slavery society and other benevolent societies were disbanded, . . . sin and infidelity would no doubt triumph, in spite of all our brethren could do." Because men shirked their moral and religious duty, women must perform theirs or society would face destruction. Abolitionist Nathaniel Rogers suggested that men, rather than women, ought to lecture, write, and publish in the cause of reform, yet he contended that because men had shirked their duty, it had also become women's. He asserted that if women "have any peculiar province and sphere, it is to head this moral reformation. . . . Men ought, as custom is, do the public lecturing and the editing and printing. But if they won't do it, woman must. . . . Do your duty. That is your sphere."[8]

Men's refusal to do their moral duty demanded that women act in their place. An article in the November 1838 issue of the moral reform journal *Friend of Virtue* made this argument in defense of women who had been labeled Amazons for attending "Female Conventions." In addition to making the point that these women were in their sphere because they were working to "preserve moral purity," the author asserted that they were acting because men were failing to:

> I will acknowledge, that, according to one literal definition of the word, such women may be Amazons. That is, women are called Amazons who perform the duties of men; and that they are frequently obliged to do their own share of the work as well as that from which men should relieve them is too true to admit of denial, . . . but what name shall we find for the other sex who shrink from the performance of their own duty, and suffer women to bear the heat and burthen of the day[?][9]

Transforming the slur "Amazon" into a positive expression, these reformers focused on the female warrior's heroic bravery and attention to duty rather than her supposed unnatural physical resemblance to a man. These women believed that the existence of great sin freed them to do whatever was necessary to fight evil.

As the political crisis between the North and the South escalated in the 1840s, the idea that male immorality threatened the nation's future seemed increasingly reasonable. In the 1840s and 1850s, the rhetoric of male irresponsibility and immorality was far more damning than it had been in the 1830s. In the 1830s, reformers had criticized men for shirking their duty to speak out against slavery and for slandering female abolitionists; in the 1840s, reformers began to accuse men of active involvement in the destruction of the nation. A number of reformers argued that many of the problems America faced in the late 1840s and 1850s were a direct result of women's less than full participation in public political life. Statements like Thomas Wentworth Higginson's, that "we need the feminine element in our public affairs to make us better," were routine.[10] But many writers took the argument further, asserting that male-dominated public life was putting the nation in serious danger that could be remedied only by allowing women more of a public political role. Samuel J. May preached in 1845 that "the *men* of our nation presumed to plunge us into multiform calamities, crimes and expenditures of war, without so much as consulting the women, who will have to share equally, if not to endure a larger part of the losses and sufferings, that are inevitable upon such a measure of folly and wickedness." And when men governed alone in "folly and wickedness," they would eventually drive their countries into severe national crises:

> In great emergencies, at those crises which have decided the fates of nations, women have been allowed, encouraged, nay summoned to lend their aid—both in council, and on the field of battle. Now, I believe, if they were admitted to equal advantages of education, and permitted at all times to influence counsels, and assist in the administration of affairs of state—I believe those terrible emergencies, which shake nations at their centres, would much less frequently, if ever, arise; and the redemption of the world would sooner be accomplished.[11]

In another sermon, Theodore Parker also stressed the problems created by the exclusion of American women from politics. He asserted that in the nineteenth-century,

> Selfishness . . . is preached as gospel and enacted as law. It is thought good political economy for a strong people to devour the weak nations—for "Christian" England and American to plunder the "Heathen" and annex their land; for a strong class to oppress and ruin the feeble class—for the capitalists of England to pauperise the poor white laborer, . . . for the capitalists of America to enslave the poorer black laborer; . . . I fear we shall never get beyond this theory and this practice, until woman has her natural rights as the equal of man, and takes her natural place in regulating the affairs of the family, the community, the Church and the State. It seems to me that God has treasured up a reserved power in the nature of women to correct many of those evils which are Christendom's disgrace to-day.[12]

As Parker had it, America was a nation drenched in selfishness and greed. And it was so selfish precisely because men ran the country. Without women's involvement, men made selfish, immoral decisions. Men made the Fugitive Slave Bill a law; men exterminated Indians and stole their land; men allowed the exploitation of wage workers and slaves. Such things could never happen if women, with their purer natures, participated in politics and government.[13]

According to women's rights supporter Mary Anne Johnson of Philadelphia, because women were excluded from "public counsels, . . . the legislation of the country is deprived of the purifying, elevating, unselfish feminine element, which is essential to the enactment of just and beneficent laws." But, she asserted, American women were beginning to awaken from their "slumbers":

They weary of senseless talk of "woman's sphere," when that sphere is so cir-
cumscribed that they may not exert their full influence and power to save their
country from the war, intemperance, slavery, licentiousness, ignorance,
poverty and crime, which man, in the mad pursuit of his ambitious schemes,
unchecked by their presence and counsel, permits to desolate and destroy all
that is fair and beautiful in life and fill the world with weeping, lamentation
and woe.

Here again, men, apparently selfish by nature, were responsible for the evils of
American life, which would never be corrected without women's help. For
Mary Ann Johnson, this was why woman must "demand" her rights, specifically
the right to "equal freedom with her brother to raise her voice and exert her influence directly for the removal of all the evils that afflict the race; and that she
be permitted to do this in the manner dictated by her own sense and propriety
and justice."[14] In another appeal, Mrs. C. M. Steele, principal of a female seminary, exclaimed, "How would every mother and daughter's heart leap for joy, if
by her right of suffrage she could arrest the tide of moral desolation, which
threatens to engulf in one common ruin our country, famed otherwise for ex-
ampled prosperity!"[15]

By the 1850s, women's justifications for their public actions had become increasingly frequent and forceful. The sheer number of women's rights conventions from the first one in 1848 through 1860 is evidence of women's growing
activism.[16] Additionally, the tone of their calls to action became more urgent,
and the nation's need for redemption became ever more desperate in these accounts. The idea that without women's intervention men were actively destroying the country became commonplace in a variety of written forms: history, biography, philosophical tracts on women, domestic novels, and the more
sensational pamphlet fiction of the period. The number of representations of
moral and pious publicly active women in nonfiction and fiction increased dramatically after 1830, and by the 1850s the women depicted in such accounts
were becoming increasingly active and assertive.

We tend to think of history, domestic novels, and sensational pamphlet fiction in the antebellum era as discrete and disparate entities, yet these genres
shared much in common.[17] Beginning in the 1830s and increasingly in the
1840s and 1850s, all three exhibited a fascination with strong, assertive, and
sometimes violent women. Furthermore, authors frequently wrote in more
than one of these genres. For example, Lydia Maria Child, Maria McIntosh,
Sarah Josepha Hale, Harriet Beecher Stowe, Elizabeth Oakes Smith, Susan
Warner, and Caroline Dall all wrote domestic fiction as well as nonfictional
works on woman's heroism, past and current.

While historians and literary critics have tended to separate the presumably female-authored domestic novel from supposedly male-dominated pamphlet fiction, as David Reynolds points out, "Several male authors were among the most prolific authors of sentimental-domestic fiction, while certain female writers produced lurid, sensational literature." Thus, Reynolds concludes, no "single kind of fiction . . . can be absolutely designated as 'woman's fiction.'" Ann S. Stephens wrote domestic novels like *Mary Derwent* and *The Old Homestead*, edited several ladies magazines, and wrote tales for sensational story papers, as well as authoring the first Beadle dime novel, *Malaeska, the Indian Wife of the White Hunter.* Timothy Shay Arthur, Charles J. Peterson, and even *El Dorado* author Bayard Taylor wrote domestic novels. Maturin Murray Ballou, author of countless sensational tales of piracy and murder, including the immensely popular *Fanny Campbell, the Female Pirate Captain,* also published the lengthy *Notable Thoughts about Women.*[18] E. D. E. N. Southworth novels such as *The Hidden Hand,* with a daring, adventurous heroine who captured criminals and saved women from forced marriages, led Reynolds to call Southworth a "sensational" writer rather than a domestic novelist. To many literary historians she was a domestic novelist; to others she was a sensationalist. Others distinguished between her early "lurid" tales and her later, more conservative works. The problem of categorizing Southworth reveals the murkiness of the distinction between sensational and domestic writers.[19] I consider these genres together because writers of history, domestic fiction, and sensational pamphlets consistently explored the meaning of woman's moral and religious duty to herself, her family, and her nation.

HISTORICAL AND BIBLICAL HEROINES

Until recently, scholars have neglected the vast body of history written by and about women in nineteenth-century America. However, in the last several years, Nina Baym and Mary Kelley have pointed out the vital importance of this first wave of American women's history. As Baym describes them, the female authors of these histories "were Christian republican woman, proud of themselves, and jubilantly on the march."[20] According to Kelley, American women wrote women's history to uncover "a past that provided them and their contemporaries with subjects for emulation" and to advocate some expansion of opportunities available to women. All these histories, no matter how varied, focus on "female achievement." Kelley and Baym discovered that the authors linked these achievements to women's "essential spirituality" and selflessness and assumed that historical heroines did not "pursue learning for personal ends," but used their education and their skills to "serve others."[21]

This focus on women's piety and their selfless efforts to care for and help others resonates with the ideology of redemptive womanhood. The women's history of the era moved women, as writers and historical subjects at least, into public life. In addition to focusing on piety and selflessness, all these histories stressed woman's active bravery and heroism, particularly in times of crisis. Baym and Kelley trace the roots of this interest in American women's history to the aftermath of the American Revolution, linking it with the ideology of republican motherhood.[22]

If American women's history started in the 1790s, histories about women were few and far between before the 1830s. But by the 1850s the genre had exploded. Beginning with Lydia Maria Child's five-volume Ladies Family Library, which culminated with her 1835 *History of the Condition of Women, in Various Ages and Nations,* histories of women proliferated. Sarah Josepha Hale, Jesse Clement, Maria McIntosh, Elizabeth Ellet, Caroline Dall, and many others published histories of women in the decade before the Civil War. Other works on women during this era also frequently included discussions of woman's history, including Margaret Fuller's *Woman in the Nineteenth Century,* Eliza Farnham's *Woman and Her Era* (published in 1864, but begun in 1856), and Edward Mansfield's *Legal Rights, Liabilities, and Duties of Women.*[23] If women's history had its origins in the world of the republican mother, it had its heyday as Americans embraced the more activist gender ideology of redemptive womanhood. By the 1840s and 1850s, Americans were using these histories to assert not just that women were or could be public actors, but that they *must* be public actors in order to redeem the nation. Histories of women created and disseminated role models for active, assertive, ethical, and pious redemptive women in the figures of Aspasia, Joan of Arc, Anne Hutchinson, heroines of the American Revolution, Margaret Fuller, Dorothea Dix, Harriet Martineau, and many others.

Some authors of these histories specifically disavowed that they wrote to promote "woman's rights," yet all implicitly or explicitly argued for women's participation in public life by demonstrating that women had in the past performed a number of important, even heroic, public actions. Lydia Maria Child wrote in her preface that her history of women was "not an essay on woman's rights," but between the accounts of women's bravery and heroics she wrote, "The time will come, when it will be seen that the moral and intellectual condition of woman must be . . . in exact correspondence with that of man." As Mary Kelley pointed out, Sarah Josepha Hale was never in favor of "woman's rights"; however, she was certainly a part of the movement to improve and enlarge women's educational and work opportunities. In favor of female colleges, doctors, teachers, and authors and married women's rights to their property and their children, Hale used her history of women to show how great were the accomplishments of learned women throughout history. Like that of physician Elizabeth Blackwell, who was unnerved by her future sister-in-law Lucy Stone's "bloomerism, abolitionism [and] woman's rightism," Hale's disapproval of women's public speaking did not keep her from espousing new rights, roles, and duties for women both in *Woman's Record* and as editor of *Godey's Lady's Book*.[24]

Starting in the late 1840s, one way women's history more forcefully promoted women's participation in public life was through a new focus on female heroism. In the histories of women written in the United States before 1850, I could find no woman's history with *heroine* or *heroism* in its title. But in the 1850s, such titles suddenly became common. In addition to such books as *Heroic Women of the West*, *Heroines of the Crusades*, and *Heroines of Methodism*, three different Americans published histories of women with exactly the same title, *Heroines of History*, in 1852, 1854, and 1855.[25] This focus on heroines, however, was not limited to books with one of those words in their titles. Between 1848 and 1852, Elizabeth Fries Ellet produced a three-volume work, *The Women of the American Revolution*; another book on the Revolution, *Domestic History of the American Revolution*; and *Pioneer Women of the West*. Ellet's work represented part of the general explosion of interest in American female heroism in the Revolution and at other critical historical moments.[26]

By the 1850s, American women's history was filled with accounts of woman's public activism and heroism, whether it was written by those who advocated women's rights or those who opposed them.[27] If the women's histories of the 1830s tended to be accounts of "good wives" or "pious," "distinguished," or "celebrated" women or histories of the general conditions under which women lived in different times and places, the histories of women in the late 1840s and 1850s were filled with tales of women's "boldness," "daring," and physical as well as moral heroism.[28]

Elizabeth Ellet's *Women of the American Revolution* is filled with hundreds of stories of morally upright women who raised war heroes, sustained men's patriotism, hid or destroyed supplies to keep them out of British hands, concealed male relatives or soldiers from the enemy, worked as spies and couriers, and occasionally fought in battle. These women used their "influence" to "animate the courage, and confirm the self-devotion of those who ventured all in the common cause." But they also acted themselves, especially when men were unavailable or insufficiently patriotic. Ellet recounted stories of women who stepped in and rallied frightened soldiers to continue fighting when they were about to flee from battle. She told several stories of women who frightened off or even captured British troops when all the men were away from home. The women of Groton, Massachusetts, for example, dressed up in their absent husbands' clothes and, carrying muskets and pitchforks, guarded the bridge into town. While at this post, they stopped and captured a British courier who was carrying important messages.[29]

Even when Ellet felt a woman had gone too far, she was remarkably mild in her criticism. In her discussion of Deborah Sampson, a young woman who enlisted in the Continental Army and served for two years disguised as a man, Ellet described Sampson's courage and heroism for fourteen pages, comparing her to Joan of Arc and stressing her great patriotism and moral purity. In closing she added, "The career to which her patriotism urged her cannot be commended as an example; but her exemplary conduct after the first step will go far to plead her excuse." Even as Ellet told women they should not follow Sampson's example, she made Sampson into a noble, heroic figure who never lost her virtue or "purity." It is difficult to imagine that Ellet's portrait of Sampson would dissuade any woman from following her example.[30] While Ellet did not advocate woman's rights, she argued through historical example that women must be active in public life, particularly in times of crisis.

Jesse Clement's *Noble Deeds of American Women*, published soon after Ellet's work, focused even more on aggressive forms of female heroism. While including accounts of more sedate figures, such as the mother and the wife of George Washington, Clement also recounted a number of violent encounters women had with Indians, writing, for example, of the 1697 "noble deed" of Hannah Dustan, who, with the help of two others, scalped ten of her Indian captors, six of whom were children.[31] He included a number of stories, some taken from Ellet, of women fighting, spying, and scouting in the Revolution, as well as several more accounts of women who spurred men on to battle when their spirits flagged. Female heroism in these histories consisted of raising virtuous children and "influencing" one's husband, but also of engaging in violent action to protect one's family and one's country when men could not or would not do it by themselves.[32]

Laura McCall has pointed out that *Godey's Lady's Book*, long stereotyped as a stronghold of an ideology of female submissiveness and passivity, actually was filled with stories of active and assertive heroines. In the late 1840s, for example, Godey's published a series of engravings titled "Heroic Women of America." If these heroines did not often wield weapons, they frequently were active participants in wars. Women, in these accounts, could stop violence simply by asserting the moral force they contained within them. For example, one *Godey's* heroine was Miss Newman, a beautiful and well-to-do young woman who lived during the American Revolution. One day, a wounded American soldier who was being chased by a British officer ran into her house. The American begged her to protect him. Miss Newman simply ordered the British soldier to "stop." According to *Godey's*, "Had she been at the head of his regiment, in full uni-

form, her voice could not have been more firm, her gesture more command-
ing." The officer then "stopped instinctively" and yielded to the lady. Soon after this, the British officer was captured. He was paroled and returned to England, and he vowed that "he would never fight against a people whose women
could subdue him."[33] An American woman, then, could stop violence, and even
end war, simply by asserting her moral authority. She did not need guns to fight
in the war; her weapon was her redemptive nature, which she could use to
"command" men.

In another account of female heroism in *Godey's*, several Indian women
performed a similar feat. They protected James Dean, a white man who had
been adopted years earlier by their tribe, from being murdered to avenge the
death of an Indian killed by an unknown white man. In this account, the Indians showed up Dean's door, explaining that they must kill him to avenge the
other murder. Dean "calmly commenced reasoning with them . . . enforc[ing]
his arguments with all the skill he was master of; but still he could see no
prospect of making any impression upon them." He was saved from death
when three women of his tribe came in and demanded that Dean be spared
because he was an adopted son of the tribe. When the chiefs "bade them to
begone," the women pulled out knives and declared that they would kill
themselves if Dean was murdered. The chiefs "immediately" decided to spare
Dean.[34] In this case also, women could end violence and save others when
men could not. If this was a racially stereotypical, more passionate version of
female heroism (presumably the women had to threaten suicide because the
more passionate Indian men would heed nothing less), the moral of the story
was very similar: women could influence men to stop violence in situations
where men were powerless to do so.

Other supposedly conservative women's journals also contained a variety of
articles on women's wartime heroism and publicly active women. The *Ladies
Repository*, the women's journal of the Methodist Episcopal Church, was openly
opposed to the woman's rights movement. It published articles informing
women they should "cease to strive for the ballot box and the senate and content [themselves] with forming character which shall govern both."[35] Yet it provided women with numerous examples of ways they might widen their sphere
and perform public work. For the *Repository*, woman's sphere did not include
voting or holding political office, but the journal did urge that

> woman be taught to *feel* that she is indeed the companion and fellow-laborer
> *with* man in the great moral and intellectual world. Let her be taught to put
> forth her indomitable energies in the attainment of all that is good and great,
> her power of perseverance and endurance will accomplish the object. We should

soon participate in the benefits such a change would create. Her high and holy purpose and lofty aim would soon produce about us an atmosphere of pure moral excellence. (emphasis in original)[36]

Such a statement hardly confined women to the home, or anywhere else for that matter. Rather, it encouraged women to do whatever was necessary in order to attain "all that is good and great" in the world to improve the moral character of society.

Even as articles in the *Ladies Repository* overtly disavowed the claims of the women's rights movement, they portrayed women as vital to public life. Like *Godey's*, the *Repository* published excerpts from Elizabeth Ellet's *Women of the Revolution* in the 1850s. In addition, the *Repository* published several articles on Joan of Arc between 1845 and the start of the Civil War, and many others in which she is mentioned. It printed articles about other historical heroines and numerous female philanthropists.[37] Such articles praised women for their work in public life even as some of these pieces also asserted that home was woman's proper sphere. In an article on British prison reformer Sarah Martin titled "A Model Female Philanthropist," the author began by claiming that "the home is a sufficient sphere for the woman who would do her work nobly and truly there." Immediately thereafter the author added, "Still, there are the helpless to be helped, and when generous women have been found among the helpers, are we not ready to praise them, and to cherish their memory?" The rest of the lengthy article lauded Martin for her "noble and heroic" activities in reform work, refuting the original point that the home is a "sufficient sphere" for all women.[38]

While many antebellum women's historians separated themselves from women's rights, some made their histories explicit arguments in favor of that cause. In 1860, Massachusetts abolitionist, public lecturer, and women's rights supporter Caroline Dall published *Historical Pictures Retouched*. She wrote this anecdotal history of eminent women from antiquity to the nineteenth century explicitly to promote the women's rights movement. As one reviewer put it, the book presents "a strong-minded woman's thoughts concerning strong-minded women." Dall rewrote the history of powerful and publicly active women whom she thought had been misrepresented in the past. In almost every instance, she argued that such women had been categorized as evil and immoral by historians, but that in reality they were pure and noble. Dall did admit that not every famous historical woman was virtuous: she described Lucretia Borgia, a fifteenth-century Italian woman accused of incest and murder, as a "fog-light" warning other women away. Nonetheless, she did not condemn Borgia so severely as other historians had; her portrayal was sympathetic enough that one reviewer complained that she had "vindicated" her.[39]

Beginning in ancient Greece with Aspasia, whom she called "the first woman who endeavored *systematically* to elevate the condition of her sex," Dall created a history of moral, pious, and intelligent women struggling against popular prejudices to improve themselves, womanhood, and society. She wrote that previous histories of Aspasia had charged her with impiety: they asserted that she had convinced Pericles to divorce his wife, had brought on the Peloponnesian War, and had founded a "school of courtezans" at Athens. Dall refuted all these charges, arguing that they stemmed not from her immorality but from prejudice against her. She was charged with infidelity and licentiousness because "she walks the streets of Athens unveiled; she sits at the table with men; . . . she talks about one sole Creator." Dall helped her readers make the leap from Aspasia's time to their own by comparing criticism of Aspasia directly to "the riot which a Bloomer skirt will attract in our own city": "Look at the scandal of that day!—was it not the counterpart of this of ours? At first she was 'odd;' then 'bold, setting the conventions of decent society at defiance.'—'Who but a courtezan would sit in the presence of men, unveiled?'—'What but a sensual supremacy could explain the power of her words over Pericles?'"[40] Because of popular prejudice, Dall argued, men, in the past and in the present, could not envision a woman as virtuous yet independent, or as able to wield political power other than through sexual influence. Dall consistently argued that publicly active women whom previous historians had labeled evil were, in reality, good.

This was a very personal argument for Dall, who felt that she had often been attacked and slandered because of her own strong commitment to reform, her independence, and her unwillingness to submit to male authority. She wrote in her private journal of the "popular prejudice" that followed her when she gave public lectures: she resented being called "a hurricane of a woman" and being treated as if she were an "adder" for speaking in public.[41] She also faced a great deal of conflict in her private life because of her assertive behavior. She defied her beloved father, who demanded when Dall was twenty-nine that she promise never to "directly [or] indirectly to aid the cause of freedom for the slave," and she was devastated by the effect this had on their relationship. She married her husband, Charles, a Unitarian minister, in 1844. The couple had numerous conflicts over her role and duties as the minister's wife, and her active role in what many church members considered to be Charles's sphere created resentment in more than one of his parishes. These conflicts had escalated so much by 1855 that Charles left her and their two children to work as a missionary in Calcutta, where he lived for the rest of his life, returning to America only for a few short visits. Even at a women's rights convention in 1855 a number of participants objected to Dall being named vice president, since they had heard that

she "makes so much trouble for her husband everywhere." After a friend defended her, Dall commented sadly in her journal, "she could not see, that I
have made trouble for my husband simply by being stronger than he."[42] Dall
believed that like the women she studied she was slandered because the public
had little tolerance for strong, assertive, and independent women. In *Historical
Pictures Retouched*, Dall vindicated historical publicly active women and transformed them into heroines in order to vindicate the 1850s women's movement,
herself, and her own public activism.

A "MORAL JOAN OF ARC": REFORMERS' USE OF WOMEN'S HISTORY

To justify women's public activism, many female lecturers, like Caroline
Dall, both created new histories of women and reinterpretations of biblical
heroines and drew upon those that proliferated in the antebellum era. Scholars
have illuminated the power of negative labeling—in particular, the charge of
Fanny Wrightism—to keep antebellum women from speaking in public and
from questioning their religious beliefs, but historians have not explored the
importance of positive labeling to reformers and their supporters.[43] While
names like Fanny Wright, Jezebel, and servant of Satan kept some women out
of reform movements, comparisons to early Christian martyrs, Joan of Arc, and
the heroines of the American Revolution encouraged other women to participate in public life. For example, Maria Chapman compared the Grimké sisters'
heroism to that of Anne Hutchinson, and William Lloyd Garrison wrote in a
letter to Abby Kelley, "Of all the women who have appeared upon the historic
stage, I have always regarded you as peerless—the moral Joan of Arc of the
world."[44] Appealing to historical and literary heroines, female reformers described each other as courageous heroines fighting a holy war. These arguments were so readily available to reformers because they were at the same
time being articulated in women's history and fiction.

As early as 1833, Maria Stewart referred to a history of women, *Sketches of
the Fair Sex*, to demonstrate that respectable women had participated in public
life throughout history and to defend her own public speaking.[45] A few years
later, Sarah Grimké appealed to Lydia Maria Child's *History of the Condition of
Women* to assert women's superior morality and their right to speak in public.
The Dorchester Female Anti-Slavery Society asserted, "From the history of the
past, we have reason to believe much may and can be done by females to purify
and elevate the public morals of our nation."[46]

By the late 1840s and 1850s, these appeals to women's history had become
commonplace in reform literature. Virtually every public assertion of women's
right to act and speak in public included references to biblical or secular histor-

ical heroines. The proceedings of woman's rights conventions from 1848 through the 1850s and other public speeches on women's rights were filled with references to such women.[47] Lucretia Mott, for example, asserted women's right to speak and act in public by reminding her listeners of Old Testament heroines like Deborah, who had "led the armies of Israel," and Jael, "the wife of Heber, . . . who drove the nail into the head of [Sisera,] the Canaanite General." According to Mott, although Jael's act was "revolting to Christianity, it is recognized as an act befitting women of the day." These biblical heroines, she argued, "were looked up to and consulted in times of exigency, and their counsel was received."[48]

As part of his argument for women's rights, Thomas Wentworth Higginson produced a long list of educated and publicly active women from antiquity to the present. Reformer Paulina Wright Davis pointed out that women had been healers and copyists as far back as the Middle Ages and hence would make excellent doctors, clerks, and printers in the nineteenth century. In one address, Elizabeth Cady Stanton reminded her listeners that women of the past and present had "guided great movements of charity, established missions, edited journals, published works on history, economics and statistics, . . . governed nations, led armies, filled the professor's chair, . . . discovered planets, [and] piloted ships across the sea"; therefore, they deserved the same rights as men. Margaret Fuller drew on previous histories of women in her *Woman in the Nineteenth Century* to argue that women have always had public power "wherever Man is sufficiently raised above extreme poverty or brutal stupidity."[49]

Lucy Stone appealed to a historical event that had occurred a short time before when she spoke in 1857 before the Judiciary Committee of the Massachusetts State Senate in favor of woman's suffrage. She described a story just published in the newspapers about a Mrs. Patton, "the heroine of the sea." Mrs. Patton, having studied navigation "for pleasure," took command of her husband's ship when he became ill. She thwarted an attempted mutiny by the incompetent first mate, who resented her command, by reasoning with the crew and appealing to their good judgment and their loyalty to her husband. The crew accepted her leadership and later offered to make another voyage with the captain, "if [he] would take his wife with him." Stone argued that the experiences of Mrs. Patton both proved woman's competence in activities defined as masculine and illustrated "the influence of woman, even upon the rudest men." She used this example to show that such activities did not damage a woman's character, then she connected Mrs. Patton's successful navigation of the masculine world of the sea to women's ability and right to participate in the masculine world of voting.[50]

Fictional Heroines

Like their counterparts in history, fictional heroines became more aggressive and publicly active in even the most conventional literature of the antebellum era, especially in the 1840s and 1850s. David Reynolds, in his study of American religious literature, notes that before 1820 the vast majority of female characters in religious literature had been angelic but "passive recipients of divine instruction." After about 1835, these fictional "angelic characters became more actively redemptive." Many "possessed the capacity to struggle and endure, to rescue others and teach them." From the 1830s through the 1850s, Reynolds asserts, these characters became increasingly "tough" and self-reliant women who observed "the code of Arminian heroism in the secular sphere of daily experience."[51]

A number of historians and literary critics have noted the domestic novel's rising importance in the antebellum period, in the 1840s and especially the 1850s. While some, most notably Ann Douglas, have stressed the passivity of the female characters in these works, others, as far back as Helen Waite Papashvily, have focused on the active and assertive qualities of the heroines of these novels. Virtually all heroines of domestic novels suffer severe trials, Nina Baym has noted. The heroine always has to learn to rely on herself and God for spiritual, physical, and financial support and protection because men have failed to protect her.[52] In Mary Kelley's words, "Man was the threat to the domestic dream. At times he is indifferent to his family's welfare, forgets or refuses to be a provider, neglects his children, and fails to abide by his wife's moral example. At other times he is well-meaning but weak and irresponsible, incapable of performing his assigned role." In such cases, women have to learn to become "strong, active and independent . . . to serve family and community" or they will be destroyed, both morally and physically.[53]

These novels are stories in which men are commonly absent, ineffectual, or evil—explorations of what happens in a society in which men often cannot or will not protect and maintain their families. Invariably the answer is that women must learn to take care of themselves. The absence of adequate male protection places these young women into situations in which they are forced to choose between good and evil, situations that bring out their true character. They either have to bravely resist the commands of sinful adults, often their guardians, or weakly submit to them and embrace sin themselves. Of course, because they are heroines, they never submit to evil, although their foils, littered throughout such novels, often do. Thus, even heroines who seem to do very little are engaged in the most important battle of all to the antebellum American mind: "the saving or damning of the soul."[54] Forced to choose between good and evil, all these heroines fight to keep their souls pure, an act that frequently requires them to directly disobey their parents or guardians in order to follow their conscience. Here too, woman's nature, her duty, is not to blindly obey authority, not to be passive and submissive, but to be virtuous, to look inside herself for the meaning of her duty and to do whatever that entails.

David Reynolds points out the centrality of active and assertive women to the domestic novel. He labels its heroines "moral exemplars" and "adventure feminists": "In some of her manifestations the American moral exemplar was gentle, but more often she was notably spunky and active. . . . In some works she became so bold as to fight, explore, command, or shoot just like a man, creating an androgynous stereotype I call the adventure feminist." Reynolds also notes the connection between the aggression and action of the female moral exemplars and the lack of "reliable male authority figures," arguing that "the female moral exemplar became a chief means of reconstructing moral values in a world of devalued, amoral males." This description resonates with the types of stories Laura McCall describes in her study of *Godey's Lady's Book* between 1830 and 1860. McCall focuses on *Godey's* specifically because it has long been a target for those who claim woman's literature in antebellum America "preached the gospel of purity, piety and domesticity . . . and feminine submission." In her statistical analysis, McCall could not identify a single story in which the protagonist "possessed all four features that purportedly made up the 'true woman.'" What she did find, however, is that the vast majority of heroines are depicted as "intelligent," "physically strong," "independent," and "emotionally strong," and that the magazine contains "a number of tales depicting feminine heroism." McCall's, Mary Kelley's, and David Reynolds's evidence, as well as my own, points to the importance in antebellum fiction and history of extremely assertive and heroic women who saved themselves, their families, and sometimes their country. And domestic novelists did more than simply approve of active and assertive women. They "rarely praised" passivity, and they often condemned it. In general, domestic novelists were openly hostile to female passivity and indicated that it was ill suited to life in modern times.[55]

As Mary Kelley points out, Catharine Maria Sedgwick's *Hope Leslie* is an "investigation into . . . what it meant in America to be a moral *woman*." In the novel, published in 1827, the moral American woman is emphatically not passive. Sedgwick sets her story in the seventeenth century, which she refers to as "an age of undisputed masculine supremacy," contrasting the women of that era to the "less passive" women of the nineteenth century. Throughout the novel, Sedgwick is extremely critical of the supposedly Puritan "virtue" of female passivity. On several occasions the title character, Hope Leslie, defies Puritan authorities to do what her conscience deems right. She rescues two Indian women from jail and probable or certain death, and she herself escapes captivity twice.

Hope is constantly berated by Puritan authorities for her lack of docility, and Sedgwick always makes it clear that Hope is in the right. When Governor Winthrop tells Hope Leslie's guardian, Mr. Fletcher, that "she hath not . . . that passiveness, that, next to godliness, is a woman's best virtue," Mr. Fletcher rejoins, "I should scarcely account . . . a property of soulless matter, a virtue." In *Hope Leslie*, Sedgwick creates her vision of the modern American heroine, an active woman who will do anything in order to promote what she believes was right, no matter which male authority opposes her.[56]

Already in 1827 Catharine Maria Sedgwick had described American female morality as emphatically active and assertive. If in *Hope Leslie* Sedgwick links the strength and action of American female morality to the experience of the wilderness and contact with Native Americans, in her other books she connects this female strength to the instability of life in the modern market-oriented economy. For example, in her first novel, the 1822 *A New-England Tale*, the "resilient, secure and independent" heroine, Jane Elton, is brought up in wealth until her father suddenly dies in bankruptcy when she is twelve. Jane has to learn to act independently after her father's death in order to sustain and protect her family because her mother, an extremely passive figure, can do nothing without her husband.[57] Domestic novelists after Sedgwick, many of whom set their stories in the present, focused on the same questions: the nature of American female morality in an economically unstable society in which women often could not or should not depend on men. In such cases, female passivity and submission to male authority was a serious problem. Novelists who wrote about women, both those categorized as domestic novelists and those categorized as sensational writers, were self-consciously engaged in creating a moral woman who was strong enough to survive and protect others in a world filled with sudden bankruptcy and men in authority who seemed to have little use for morality and religion.

E. D. E. N. Southworth's book sales were "the greatest of any female author in American History," according to literary historian John Tebbel. Southworth, a Washington, D.C., native, wrote her most famous novel, *The Hidden Hand*, in 1859.[58] Capitola Black, the heroine of the story, is a young orphaned heiress who engages in a series of exciting and dangerous adventures over the course of the novel. Among other things, she saves herself from various men who want to kill her, rape her, or force her into marriage, and she even outwits and captures the notorious outlaw Black Donald and challenges another villain to a duel after he slanders her honor. When he refuses to fight, she shoots him with the grapeshot in her pistol, publicly humiliating him but not harming him.

Many historians and literary critics have commented on Capitola's active heroism, but *The Hidden Hand* is also littered with examples of the dangers of

female passivity.[59] All three of the other major female characters in the novel—
Marah Rocke, the abandoned wife of Capitola's guardian; Capitola's mother,
who has been locked away for years in an insane asylum; and Clara Day, who
narrowly avoids a forced marriage—are passive and submissive women who
are victimized by men who have legal control of them. Southworth, who was
abandoned by her own husband and left to raise their two children on her
own, was well aware of the dangers facing women who depended on men. All
of Southworth's good but passive female characters pay dearly for their behavior, except Clara, who is lucky enough to be saved by Capitola.[60] Capitola's mother is eventually rescued from the asylum, and Marah Rocke is reunited with her husband, but these two women have to wait years for men to
do their duty. Southworth suggests that passive women are not meant for the
modern world. They will always be at the mercy of men, who do not protect
women as they should.[61]

Author Susan Warner began her professional writing career after her father's
bankruptcy, and her heroines faced similar problems in her novels.[62] Fleda
Ringgan, the heroine of her 1852 novel, *Queechy*, had lived happily in the country with her grandfather until he died when she was ten years old. She was then
sent to live with her rich aunt and uncle, Mr. and Mrs. Rossitur. Six years later,
Mr. Rossitur goes bankrupt, and the family moves to the country and rents
Queechy, the farm where Fleda had lived with her grandfather. Mr. Rossitur is
so demoralized by his business disaster that from the moment they move to the
farm he makes virtually no effort to support his family, and Mrs. Rossitur de-
clares herself incapable of doing any work in the house or on the farm. Fleda
steps in and, at the age of sixteen, learns to manage the farm profitably. For the
next few years, she supports the entire family, with only the help of her sickly
cousin Hugh. She also sustains her aunt, uncle, and cousin spiritually through
the period. Warner indicates that, if Fleda had been passive and submissive,
both she and the family of her guardian would have ended up homeless and
starving. Fleda is finally rescued from her tiring life when Mr. Carelton, the
one man in the novel who is both decent and competent, proposes to her. Con-
veniently, he is rich and solves her uncle's financial problems as well. In the
end, a man does save Fleda from her life of drudgery, but Fleda supports herself
and a family almost single-handedly in the years before this occurs. To make it
clear that Fleda does not marry to escape her difficult life, Warner allows her to
receive and refuse other proposals before Carelton's. Unpleasant though her
life is in many ways, she manages it and would continue to do so if necessary.[63]

Fleda is never masculinized by her embrace of the man's role in her family.
Warner depicts her as a model of female grace and beauty. She stresses that
motivations are the key to Fleda's character. In the market but never of it, Fleda

takes financial responsibility for her family in order to take care of them. She handles money, but this never corrupts her because she never acts for greedy or selfish reasons. She works to fulfill the most important duty a woman ever has: the physical and spiritual protection and maintenance of others. For novelists like Warner, Sedgwick, and Southworth, the best woman is the one who is motivated by religion, morality, and the selfless nurture of others. Like female reformers, these characters do whatever is necessary in the name of their womanly duty.

Male domestic novelists created equally or even more assertive heroines in their stories, and they appealed to historical and biblical heroines as well. Charles Peterson, the Philadelphia publisher of *Peterson's Lady's Magazine*, for example, wrote a number of stories about women in the antebellum era. These novels were invariably accounts of young women trying to do their duty in the face of a number of trials. Kate Aylesford, the heroine of Peterson's 1855 novel by the same name, is a fearless and patriotic rich young orphan living in the midst of the American Revolution. She helps to save herself and others in a treacherous shipwreck, a circumstance that leads her future husband to exclaim, "Most of her sex, at such times, I'm told, lose all presence of mind, and I don't wonder at it. But she seems as courageous as Joan of Arc." While Kate does not fight in the war, she does escape from an evil British officer who has kidnapped her, and she rescues another young girl in the process. Throughout the story, male characters marvel at her bravery, comparing her to both Joan of Arc and Molly Pitcher. Four years later, Peterson published another novel, *The Old Stone Mansion*, in which the future husband of novel's heroine compares her to Joan of Arc too because of her fearlessness and bravery.[64]

Helen Papashvily once wrote that domestic novelists were engaged in an "undeclared war against men." There was certainly a war, but it was not undeclared, and it did not simply pit women against men. This war centered on the theme that American men, immersed in a market-oriented society, had in large numbers become selfish, greedy, and immoral and were corrupting the virtue of the nation in general and the women who depended upon them in particular. Mary Kelley notes that "Materialistic, individualistic immoral man appears again and again in [the novels] as the . . . diseased product of a society obsessed with the money that brought privilege and power."[65] Domestic novels were filled with sudden bankruptcies caused by men's speculation and with orphans thrown upon the mercy of immoral guardians or strangers. In such situations, novelists argued, heroines had to be assertive and independent, or they would lose their virtue. But this was not only a complaint of female domestic novelists; it was a general critique of American society, not just of men per se, and it was shared by many Americans, male and female. In this light, it should be no surprise that the domestic novel arose in the 1820s, as the market economy became increasingly central in American society, and that it had its heyday in the 1840s and 1850s, as national crisis, engendered by the constantly expanding, profit-driven market, began to seem inevitable.

THE FIGHTING HEROINES OF SENSATIONAL FICTION

The assertive and heroic qualities of domestic heroines were magnified further in "sensational" pamphlet fiction. The pamphlet fiction of the 1840s and 1850s was filled with tales of heroic and virtuous women who literally saved men and their country, as well as spiritually redeeming them. These works frequently focused on the bravery of women in wartime or other physically dangerous situations, while domestic novels more commonly portrayed heroic struggles of young women away from literal battlefields, at least that is until the Civil War. The heroines of pamphlet fiction tended to be more physically assertive and aggressive than most heroines of domestic novels, but they shared important similarities. As David Reynolds points out, "debates about women's issues . . . were as apt to occur in sensational literature as in domestic fiction."[66] Sensational heroines also stepped in to do their duty as ethical, Christian women where men could not or would not.

Women who fought in wars and who killed in order to save their families and their country were not new to American history or literature in the mid-1840s. They were part of a long tradition from early modern "female warrior" ballads and seventeenth-century captivity narratives to eighteenth- and early-nineteenth-century stories and songs about female soldiers, and they did appear in print from time to time.[67] But stories of such heroines increased dramatically in number in the mid-1840s.

The pamphlet novel *Fanny Campbell, the Female Pirate Captain* provides one early example of the new popularity of these tales. Its author, Maturin Murray Ballou, the son of prominent Boston Universalist minister Hosea Ballou, published the cheap pamphlet under the pseudonym Lieutenant Murray in 1844. *Fanny Campbell* was the first story Ballou ever published. It was incredibly successful, selling 80,000 copies in its first few months in print.[68] *Fanny Campbell* is a historical romance about a respectable young woman engaged to an American sailor during the Revolutionary War. When her fiancé is captured and unjustly thrown into a Cuban prison, the navy will not rescue him, so Campbell does. She dresses as a man and signs on as a sailor on a British ship. At sea, she discovers that the captain plans to impress all the sailors into the British navy. Campbell takes part in a mutiny and becomes captain of the ship. In her naval career, she manages to capture another British ship, killing a man in the process, and she finally rescues her fiancé. She then returns to America and is married, and she and her husband turn one of the captured ships into an American privateer, hunting down other English ships until the war's end.

Ballou describes Fanny Campbell as a "noble looking girl." She is beautiful, extremely intelligent, pious, and well-educated, and she writes poetry. Yet she also "could row a boat, shoot a panther, ride the wildest horse in the province or do almost any brave and useful act." She can perform any number of so-called masculine feats, yet still remain "womanly." As a ship's captain she is extremely kind to her men and even to her prisoners. She dislikes violence, but is willing to use it when she feels she has no alternative. She kills one British sailor who has been participating in an attempted mutiny, but she fires only after he purposefully disobeys her command to put down his weapon. As well as caring for wounded shipmates, she always tries to prevent violence. In one instance, she pardons a British officer whom her shipmates want put to death, deciding that he is an honorable man, loyal to his king. She unchains him and reasons with him, soon convincing him that the colonies have been unjustly treated by England. He then becomes "an ardent supporter" of the Americans and withdraws from the war effort.[69]

If readers wondered whether Fanny Campbell could remain a virtuous woman after having such violent and daring adventures, they could find their answer in the way the other characters treat her. Virtually every one of them loves and venerates her in the end. Even her would-be rapist is later thankful that only he is hurt when she repulses his attack. Campbell's parents, trusting her judgment entirely, approve of her adventures. Her father comforts her mother, saying, "Let us trust in Heaven wife, it is a holy cause she is engaged in." Others consider her an angel. One man she sails with refers to her as "a holy spirit." An English captain who had lusted after her when he knew her as a woman falls entirely in love when he discovers her disguised as a pirate captain. He proposes, then tells her, "Thou art an angel, nevertheless," when she rejects him.[70]

Ballou depicts Fanny Campbell as an angel in the world; she can do the work of men, even be a sea captain, and she can do these things better than a man. She moves in a "man's" world, but her character is that of a woman. Fanny Campbell thus retains the key aspects of redemptive womanhood: piety, morality, and nurture. It is not her actions that determine her character, but her motivations. She goes to sea to save her fiancé when no one else will. She fights for her country in its war for independence. She is always pious, she is kind and nurturing to her crew, and she keeps her chastity, even to the point of stabbing and nearly killing an attempted rapist. She is motivated by a selfless love of her family and her country and by her duty to protect both of these.

Fanny Campbell is an incredibly publicly active and aggressive paragon of womanhood. She was also an extremely popular paragon. Ballou was well aware of how much he owed to *Fanny Campbell*. His second novel, *The Naval Officer*, is the story of Fanny's oldest son, Herbert, in his career as a naval officer in the War of 1812. Although Fanny Campbell plays no role in the novel's plot, Ballou brings up her name from time to time as if to remind the reader that this book is linked somehow to her exciting tale. For example, a member of Herbert's crew suddenly observes as he watches Herbert: "That's a remarkable woman, the mother of our captain."[71] *Fanny Campbell*, which went through several editions, launched Ballou's career as a successful writer and publisher of story papers and, later, as founder of the *Boston Globe*.[72] It also led at least one literary historian to label him "the father of the dime novel."[73]

Beginning with *The Female Warrior* in 1843, female soldiers appeared in pamphlet fiction in great numbers. Leonora Siddons, the heroine of *The Female Warrior*, is the daughter of a wealthy merchant who dies fighting in Mexico. His dying words are for her "to serve her country by whatever means fortune may place in her power." She decides to fulfill this duty by dressing as a man and enlisting in the U.S. Army to take his place. She fights in a bloody battle and shoots at least one foe through the heart before being captured and jailed in Mexico. Before she is to be whipped and shot, her sex is discovered, and a captor offers to let her live if she will be his mistress. She pretends to be unsure in order to gain time to escape. After she escapes, killing a guard in the process, she makes her way back home to the United States.[74]

Another heroine, Amelia Sherwood, runs away from a well-to-do family in New York to marry a man of whom her parents disapprove. Another man soon tricks her into sailing to California, but even so, she thwarts his attempts to rape her. When pirates attack the ship, she saves the captain's life by killing his would-be murderer. Sherwood lands in California right before Sutter discovers gold there. Instead of going back to New York, she travels to gold country to see what it is like. In this violent, greedy masculine world, Amelia breaks up fights between men by using "gentle persuasion." Her fiancé, not knowing she is there, also travels to California, where eventually they are reunited and happily become married.[75]

Fanny Templeton Danforth is the "well educated" daughter of rich parents who live in the country outside Philadelphia. Fanny falls in love with a lieutenant in the U.S. Navy, Harry Danforth, who proposes to her on the day he has to leave port to chase a pirate ship. Months pass and Fanny worries constantly about Harry. Her parents suggest she take a trip to improve her health, and she agrees, secretly planning to disguise herself as a navy officer to go to sea and find Harry. On the ship, she gets into an argument with an Englishman who claims that the American navy is full of cowards. The Englishman challenges Fanny to a duel. Fanny, knowing he is a much better shot, insists they fire from two feet apart, so that she can kill him as he kills her. The Englishman is so frightened at the prospect of certain death that he misses Fanny entirely. Fanny, on the other hand, is brave and calm and kills her opponent easily. If dueling is morally problematic, Fanny is careful to point out that she was forced into it because she could not resist defending the honor of her country and her fiancé, a naval officer. She describes the Englishman as a "duelist"; hence by killing him, she prevents him from forcing others into duels in the future. She also depicts him as a man who is so evil that no one mourns him. After the duel, everyone on the ship "toasted and feasted [her] as a hero who had redeemed the honor of my countrymen and rid the earth of a scoundrel."[76] By killing one man, then, Fanny redeems many others.

Soon after the duel, Fanny's ship is captured by the pirates Harry Danforth had been sent to hunt. The pirates offered her a choice: to join them or to die. Of course Fanny chooses death. When the pirates reach an island, they determine to roast Fanny alive, but just after they light the fire, Harry Danforth rushes in with his men, saves her and defeats the pirates. Fanny also saves Harry from death, although she is still tied, by warning him of a man sneaking up behind him with a sword. When she reveals herself to Harry, "instead of reproving me for my rashness . . . he imprinted a kiss upon my lips, and said we should never be parted again in life—for such love as mine was worthy of every earthly sacrifice he could make." Harry gives up his commission, and they marry and settle on her father's estate. Fanny Templeton Danforth, Fanny Campbell, Amelia Sherwood, Leonora Siddons, and many others like them dress as men, fight pirates, and kill men, but all of them remain virtuous and moral, if adventure-loving, women. They try to avoid violence, but they are willing to fight evil wherever they find it if they see no other choice. They save people when men cannot or will not.[77]

These sensational novels, like virtually all writing on women in the antebellum era, were explorations of what makes a woman good or evil. Many of these pamphlets were published by the same firms that had begun only a few years earlier to publish accounts of apparently respectable female fiends. Publishers like E. E. Barclay, Frank Gleason, A. R. Orton, H. M. Rulison, C. W. Kenworthy, and T. B. Peterson were all heavily involved in writing and publishing tales of adventurous female fiends and heroines in the 1840s and 1850s.[78] The aggressive and violent female fiends differed from the new heroines in only one aspect: motive. Both types of protagonists were assertive, powerful, and often violent, but the female fiend, usually a murderer, was entirely depraved, while the heroine was moral, even angelic, since she fought and killed for a "good" cause.

Publisher E. E. Barclay, for example, published his first pamphlet novel, *Narrative and Confessions of Lucretia P. Cannon*, the murderess, in 1841. This began Barclay's highly successful publishing career, which ended only with his death in 1888. In 1843, Barclay published *The Female Warrior*, his heroic account of Leonora Siddons. Until the end of the Civil War, the subjects of Barclay's pamphlets and short novels were usually young women who left their homes and went on a series of adventures, often dressing as men or serving as soldiers.[79] Some of these heroines were portrayed as moral women, like Leonora Siddons, while others were depicted as evil fiends, like Lucretia Cannon. Yet all of them managed to kill at least one person in the course of their adventures.[80]

The fundamental difference between the women depicted as depraved murderesses and those portrayed as heroines in this fiction is their moral, religious, and selfless nature. Lucretia Cannon is a selfish, immoral infidel. She scorns religion and gives in to every selfish and base passion she feels. She is licentious, violent, and greedy. She destroys her own family and others in the exercise of these passions, killing her husband, for example, when he discovers her depravity. Heroines like Fanny Campbell, Leonora Siddons, Amelia Sherwood, Fanny Templeton Danforth, and a number of other young women engage in the same kinds of activities as fiendish women, including murder and piracy, yet they remain decent. They are chaste, kind, and loving Christian women who perform actions atypical for women in order to protect both people and those societal values closely associated with women.[81]

The pamphlet novels Barclay published in the 1840s and 1850s address the same question over and over: What is the nature, the character, of a young woman who defies authority and enters the world on her own, taking care of herself and others even to the point of killing someone? These stories never resolve the issue. Read together, they reveal yet again the inability of antebellum Americans to clearly identify the limits of proper female behavior, even in fiction. All might have agreed that the fictional Lucretia Cannon is an evil fiend because they learned of her evil deeds through the device of an omnipotent narrator, a convention unavailable in the cases of actual women. But even if good women were distinguished from fiends in a single book, they were not easily separated from one another in the literature as a whole. From the mid-1840s on, women as aggressive and as capable of violence as the murderess Lucretia Cannon began to appear with increasing frequency in these pamphlet novels as heroines rather than fiends.

These fighting heroines of sensational fiction reinforced the point that a woman's character centered on the purity of her motives, rather than her actions. They also supported the notion that society now required more assertive and active women than it had in earlier times. In story after story in sensational pamphlet novels and domestic novels, young women suddenly were orphaned, penniless, or both and were faced with the task of saving themselves and sometimes their families to avoid being destroyed physically or morally. In that unstable modern era, fortunes were made and lost quite suddenly and almost inexplicably in the sorts of speculations that littered the pages of these works. It was a world in which if one did become bankrupt in a large city, one could not rely on neighbors, whom one might not even know. Older networks of protection had broken down. Seducers could no longer easily be forced into marrying their victims; they could simply leave town. Orphans could not always find a place with lifelong neighbors or relatives in such a fast-moving society.

Domestic novels and pamphlet fiction reveal a growing sense that a new ideal of a more active and even cunning woman was required for survival in the impersonal, dangerous, and chaotic modern world. As society changed rapidly, women raised with notions of woman's sphere that were suited to older and more stable times had difficulty functioning in the modern world. This dangerous new environment required an ideal of a stronger and more assertive woman in order for women to retain their piety, morality, and selflessness. The new woman of the mid-1840s had to learn to negotiate the male world of the market without ever embracing its values.[82]

Like histories and biographies of women, these adventure tales were never fantasies unrelated to the lives of actual women. They were part of a larger critique of a society run by men according to the dictates of self-interest. They were a cry for the reinfusion of republican virtue into American life, through the increasing participation of women (and hence of so-called women's values) in public life. Female reformers, domestic novels, pamphlet fiction, and histories of women all created justifications for the public activism of respectable women. Embracing women's duty to promote and maintain religiosity, ethicality, and selfless nurture in society as well as their own families, they declared that women might go anywhere and do anything if duty called them to it. In the last part of the antebellum era, Americans seemed to yearn for heroines who would go to any extreme, including fighting in wars, to protect and preserve the nation's virtue.

Female moral and spiritual superiority had always implied male moral and spiritual inadequacy. But with increasing frequency in the late 1840s and 1850s, Americans expressed concern over the problems created by male self-interest. As a number of historians have pointed out, the passage of legislation such as antiseduction acts and married women's property acts were linked to Americans' fear that men were no longer attending to the physical and moral health of the nation's women.[83] Domestic novels, sensational fiction, and histories of women in the period explored the very same problem and suggested a radical solution. Men could no longer be expected to protect their families or the country. They were too self-interested. Therefore women must step into public life and do whatever was necessary to protect and sustain the virtue of the republic and its citizens—even if this meant going into battle.

As the Civil War approached, women were more and more often cast as the saviors of American society. It was up to them to prevent violence, or if they could not, to help fight the holy war. When the Civil War began, women, at least in the North, immediately embraced an extremely active and public role in the war effort. The war was the national crisis they had been expecting for years. Women simply assumed that, because they were women, duty required them to collect supplies, to nurse, to fight, and to perform virtually any action that would help win the war and save the country.

"Like a Second Joan of Arc"

Imagining Women's War

There is one result to be hoped for from all this waste of human life. The demand for laborers, and the necessity of self support among women . . . will compel them to enter upon business avocations heretofore closed to them.

—Paulina W. Davis, 25 December 1854 [1]

*T*n the last few years there has been a tremendous upsurge of interest in women and the American Civil War, with historians and literary critics beginning to investigate in detail what the war meant for women, North and South. Of the several important studies that have explored the effects of the Civil War on the position of women in American society, most have assumed that the realities of war were a direct challenge to antebellum gender ideology; they have posited either explicitly or implicitly a disjuncture between antebellum gender ideology and women's work in the war. Historians of both Northern and Southern women in the war generally have assumed that antebellum notions of separate spheres required women to be submissive and private, or domestic, in order to be proper women. Most have argued that women who became public actors in the war as nurses, sanitary workers, doctors, or soldiers challenged such ideas and hastened the destruction of the ideology of true womanhood or separate spheres.[2] A few scholars have begun to complicate these claims. For example, Judith Ann Giesberg, Lyde Cullen Sizer, and Elizabeth Young have explored important parallels between women's prewar activism and writing and the ways women reacted to the Civil War, but they still see the war as a dramatic turning point in gender ideology. Giesberg, for example, argues that the U.S. Sanitary Commission can be understood as a "missing link" between women's prewar and postwar activism. She stresses the war's effect in transforming women into political actors, contrasting women's prewar "moral reform" work with their postwar "political" work.[3] Yet antebellum women's prewar moral reform work was explicitly political well before the Civil War.

The Civil War was an event of immense importance to Americans, and understanding it as a challenge to antebellum gender ideology, particularly in the North, overlooks the continuity between prewar ideals of selfless female heroism and women's wartime activities. At its heart, antebellum gender ideology centered on the belief that women were responsible for the redemption of the nation. In the North, in the critical times of the 1840s and 1850s, women's role as the moral and religious foundation of the country made their aggressive and public actions more palatable, and even desirable to Americans of that region. And like their antebellum predecessors, female Civil War workers understood themselves as redeemers called to protect their nation in a time of crisis.

Instead of depicting the war as an event so powerful that it challenged and overwhelmed ideology, I argue that gender ideology, as well as the events, shaped Northern women's responses to the war. Like the work of Ann Rose, mine asserts "the power of culture to shape war" in addition to being shaped by it.[4] Antebellum writings about woman and war specifically shaped the way in which American women understood and described the Civil War and their role in it. While this treatment of the war deals primarily with Northern women, it occasionally makes use of Southern writings. Southerners also read about and created assertive and public heroines in fictional and nonfictional writings in the antebellum and Civil War eras. In addition, of course, Southerners read Northern literature and Northerners read Southern literature.[5]

Scholars' tendency to see women's experiences in the war as the cause of a transformation to a new gender ideology mirrors the claims nineteenth-century American women and men themselves made about the war. Lyde Cullen Sizer recently pointed out that Northern women writers of the late 1860s consistently asserted that the war had ushered in a new era for women. "As a result of the war, they claimed, women had demonstrated their abilities in a public sphere in a variety of ways, and henceforth they should be offered the freedoms and the rights in that sphere that they had previously been denied." Sizer also notes that the authors of the 1881 *History of Woman Suffrage* picked up on this argument, stating that the Civil War had caused "a revolution in woman herself."[6] Nearly every female war worker who wrote or lectured on her war experiences in the postwar period made a similar claim. Historians and literary critics have used such evidence to suggest that the experience of war changed America's gender system. Yet women's postwar claims that the war had transformed ideas about women have a curious similarity to women's prewar comments about what a war would mean for women. In 1854, for example, women's rights advocate Paulina Wright Davis almost seemed to hope for a war because of the good it would do for women's rights. Although she asserted that war was a "waste of human life," this did little to diminish her excitement as she imagined the new opportunities a war would open up for women: "The demand for laborers, and the necessity for self support among women and the still more urgent demand for the helpless, the aged and young, will compel them to enter upon business avocations heretofore closed to them."[7] Writers like Davis did not need to experience a war to know what it would mean for American women. They had decided beforehand that a war would prove women were capable of performing work and duties commonly identified as masculine, and thus it would open up new rights and opportunities in public life. Such expectations shaped American women's understanding of and participation in the Civil War in fundamental ways.

Women's postwar statements that the war had transformed women's roles, then, may have been the continuation of a prewar strategy to assert that woman's sphere knew no geographical boundaries; women's actions in the war provided another piece of evidence for the preexisting argument that women should participate in all avenues of public life. This is not to suggest that the war did not change many women's lives: the war changed American society and individual lives in countless ways. Yet it did not destroy or undermine antebellum gender ideology. Rather, women and men understood women's duty during the Civil War through the lens of the dominant prewar gender ideology—that of redemptive womanhood.

IMMERSED IN A CULTURE OF HEROISM

By 1860, a generation of Americans, North and South, had been raised on stories of female heroics that had taken place in the home, on the battlefields of Texas, in California during the Gold Rush, and in historical settings from ancient Greece and Rome to the American Revolution. From childhood, American girls and women read fictional and nonfictional accounts of brave and virtuous heroines who did whatever duty required, no matter how difficult, to preserve family, morality, religion, and country. These literary accounts both stimulated and were reinforced by the activities of reform-minded women. In the North particularly, the ideology of redemptive womanhood with which antebellum girls were raised prepared them to understand the Civil War almost instantly as a call to action. Having been fed on a steady diet of selfless, brave, self-sacrificing moral heroines, it is no surprise that many of the women who became nurses and other kinds of public war workers seem almost to have been waiting for the challenge. Exposed to the debates over women's public activism and to domestic novels, pamphlet fiction, and a series of histories of women in the 1840s and 1850s, Northern women and men had become increasingly comfortable with the conception of an aggressive and publicly active redemptive woman. For Northern women, the war presented not a challenge to gender ideology, but the perfect opportunity to exercise their redemptive nature. It was the national crisis for which they had been preparing.

Yet when Northern women took their duty to redeem the nation seriously during the war and ventured into formerly male spaces in greater numbers than ever before, Americans did not always embrace their actions. These female war workers faced the same sorts of problems as their antebellum reformer counterparts. Contemporaries, apprehensive about their presence in armies and on battlefields, scrutinized their actions and character in an effort to determine whether they were virtuous women or fiends. Yet, as before, it was virtually impossible to securely label a woman evil if she claimed to have pure motives.

The war created a situation in which, for the first time, vast numbers of Northern women acted on their duty to redeem the nation in an extremely visible and assertive manner. Throughout the antebellum era, the redemptive woman's duty had undermined older ideas of male hierarchy and female subordination inside the family and in the body politic.[8] But the crisis of war made it even more clear to Americans that redemptive womanhood tended to free women from male control. Many Americans were disturbed by women's public war work during the Civil War not because it was a challenge to gender ideology, but because some of the implications of redemptive womanhood were, and always had been, disturbing to them. Much of the writing on womanhood, especially from the late 1840s on, asserted that women were more capable of running the public affairs of the nation than men.[9] Such writing was becoming increasingly accepting of women's assertive action in the name of duty as "anxiety and anger" grew in the North. According to Lyde Cullen Sizer, the writers of domestic novels, for example, made a "palpable shift" in tone in the mid-1850s: whereas they had attempted to effect social change through "love," now they were "promising vengeance if justice is not served."[10] When women tried to enter public war work in large numbers, many men and women saw these increasingly assertive women as a threat not only to male domination, but even to male participation in public life.

Women growing up in the antebellum North were immersed in a culture fixated on women's moral and religious nature and duty. Americans were bombarded with histories, among them both fictional and journalistic accounts that highlighted woman's special nature and special duties. If women growing up at this time faced conflicting ideas of woman's sphere of action, they inevitably imbibed the notion that women, ideally, were noble creatures and had a special mission to uphold the virtue of the nation.

The examples of female reformers and the stories of female heroism gave women ways of imagining an active, even heroic life for themselves, and it also encouraged in many the desire for such a life. The histories, biographies, and novels discussed in the last chapter all played an important role in the ways female Civil War workers would see themselves, as well as in the ways other Americans would understand their actions. Joan of Arc, the women of Sparta, the women of the American Revolution, and Florence Nightingale were only some of the most common exemplars of female heroism that men and women drew from the fictional and nonfictional writings of the antebellum era.

From the very start of the war, female war workers and future war workers frequently compared themselves to such heroines. Louisa May Alcott, for example, noted in May 1861 that seeing soldiers made her feel "very martial and Joan-of-Arc-y." Kate Cumming, a Confederate nurse, wrote in her journal that men "constantly" compared the nurses to "the women of '76 and Sparta." Anna Dickinson, an abolitionist and wartime public lecturer, was frequently described in the press as another Joan of Arc. One confederate woman wrote in 1864 that Elizabeth Ellet's *Women of the American Revolution* was "so suited to the times [that it] quite nerves me up to undergo anything." The wartime press was filled with general comparisons of women of the Revolution to women of the Civil War. In her *Address to the Women of the United States*, Ann Stephens lauded the achievements of "the women of '76" and pleaded with Northern women to "follow their example, and take up, cheerfully, the . . . burdens that the welfare of our country demands."[11]

Ladies Repository, the Methodist Episcopal Church–affiliated women's journal, which had lauded female heroines in the 1850s, continued this trend in the war. The *Repository* came out quite clearly in favor of the Union cause. Several articles early in the war contained harsh criticisms of the Lincoln administration, claiming that it had "failed to prosecute the war."[12] The *Repository* also told women what they could do for the war effort. Of course they could knit mittens and socks for soldiers at home, but they also might go to hospitals and battlefields and nurse wounded soldiers, or perhaps, the journal hinted, even fight themselves. Women might emulate "Mrs. Reynolds," an Illinois woman who followed her soldier husband to the battlefield, nursed the wounded, and was commissioned as a major in the army for her work. An 1862 piece suggested they could also follow the lead of the Spanish "Maid of Saragossa," Augustina Zaragoza, who fought in defense of her town when it was under siege. In a career that would have reminded readers immediately of Revolutionary War heroine Molly Pitcher, Augustina began her war work by carrying water to soldiers firing the cannons, but when these soldiers were killed and other men were afraid to take their places, Augustina rushed in and began firing, "vowing never to quit it alive during the siege." Her bravery "infused new courage" into the men and they fought with her.[13] Such a comment alerted readers to the fact that Augustina remained a proper woman: she retained her redemptive nature—she made men better, more courageous—even as she fought in battle.

As the Reverend D. W. Clark, the editor of the *Repository*, put it in his 1862 commencement address to the Ohio Female College, women such as Hannah More, Harriet Beecher Stowe, and Florence Nightingale had made great contributions to literature, politics, science, and benevolence. Such contributions were not beyond women's proper sphere, he asserted; rather, they "ennobled the sphere of women." As Clark pointed out: "In the more public spheres of literature of science, of art, or of public life, only a very small portion of the race, whether of men or of women engage; but in this wider and even more important sphere, lying as it does at that very foundation of all good to the race, all may enter and all may labor."[14] Here Clark explicitly stated that the "public" sphere is the property of women and men equally. Women must take part in that sphere if they are to work for the betterment of society. This sort of reasoning, these examples of women's wartime heroism, only reinforced the prewar depictions of female heroism that had permeated this and other women's journals in the late 1840s and 1850s.

Florence Nightingale and the Crimean Example

At the beginning of the Civil War, the wartime model for a publicly active redemptive woman was embodied most popularly in English nurse Florence Nightingale, who had become famous in the Crimean War of 1854–1856. Mary Poovey suggests that Florence Nightingale's involvement in professional nursing was "potentially destabilizing" to gender ideology, but argues that these destabilizing implications were largely resolved in Britain. Nightingale was primarily, for Poovey, a woman who was able to make work for unmarried middle-class women seem normal and nonthreatening by making "the hospital a home." Poovey finds in Nightingale's writings a tendency to identify herself as both a gentle motherly figure and as a soldier; she points out that "the domestic ideal always contained an aggressive element." But, she argues, this "masculine" side of Nightingale's personality "simply disappeared from popular representations." Poovey also notes that while Nightingale herself disavowed feminism and woman's rights, English feminists were able to read in her actions a profeminist "proof of women's capabilities." In the end, however, Nightingale's image worked to sustain racism, classism, and sexism.[15] If this was the case in England, Nightingale's image took on quite different meanings in the United States.

Florence Nightingale's *Notes on Nursing* was first published in America in 1860, but she was already well known in the United States by 1856. Nightingale was a perfect heroine for both North and South in the Civil War, not only because she presented herself as a selfless, pious, hardworking, and efficient surrogate mother to wounded soldiers, but also because she was British and thus could be easily embraced by both sides. Nightingale provided Americans with compelling evidence that nursing was compatible with femininity, morality, and religion.

The American fascination with Florence Nightingale was more than a result of the wartime need for more nurses. Soon after Nightingale began her work in the Crimea in 1854, Americans began to follow her career closely. Northern female reformers were some of her earliest American admirers. Caroline Dall recorded in her journal in January 1855 that an acquaintance had informed her that Catharine Maria Sedgwick was in correspondence with someone in England who had read Nightingale's letters from the Crimea. Apparently even such a tangential connection with Nightingale was noteworthy. Dall then repeated a story about Nightingale's long working hours, her gentle, motherly care of the wounded, and her piety. Dall also included Nightingale in her series of lectures on women and the law, education, and labor, which she wrote in 1860 and 1861 and later transformed into a book, *The College, the Market, and the Court*. She contended that Nightingale was "no exception in the history of her sex" and used her, Mary Wollstonecraft, Margaret Fuller, and many other publicly active women as examples of women whose lives "have modified public opinion."[16]

In 1856, Julia Ward Howe, future author of "The Battle Hymn of the Republic," published a book of poetry that included two works on Nightingale alluding to her great popularity in America. In the first, "To Florence Nightingale," she revealed both her admiration for Nightingale and her fear that Nightingale would be "deafened with plaudits, vexed to answer them," so incessantly did everyone praise her. Another poem, "Florence Nightingale and Her Praisers," begins with the following lines:

> If you debase the sex to elevate
> One of like soul and temper with the rest,
> You do but wrong a thousand fervent hearts,
> To pay full tribute to one generous breast.

In both poems Howe revealed her frustration with the contrast between the public's constant praise of Nightingale and its disinterest in the achievements of other women who performed similar work. These lines also pointed to Americans' tendency to see Nightingale as an exceptional woman capable of work no ordinary woman could do. Howe, like Dall, believed that Nightingale was noble, but not unusual. Nursing, she asserted, had been women's duty since "ancient days."[17]

Northern reform-minded people immediately recognized Nightingale's career as powerful evidence that women were suited to be professional nurses, and many, like Dall, considered it as evidence that women were capable of more than just nursing.[18] African American schoolteacher and future Civil War worker Charlotte Forten attended a lecture in 1857 on "Ancient and Modern Chivalry" in which the speaker focused on Elizabeth Fry, Florence Nightingale, Harriet Beecher Stowe, and a few other women as examples of modern chivalry, also linking Nightingale's work as a nurse in the Crimea to other women's reform activities. As reformer Wendell Phillips put it: "If Florence Nightingale, taking up the problems of confused and troubled England, carries peace and contentment and efficient arrangement to the camp of the Crimes [sic], it is because God made woman capable of the highest offices of civil and social life." For many in America, by the late 1850s, the name Florence Nightingale had become a synonym for any kind of female hero. For example, Thomas Wentworth Higginson called escaped slave Harriet Tubman "braver than Florence Nightingale" in 1858 for her work as a "conductor" on the underground railroad.[19] More conservative Americans described the impact of Nightingale's achievements in much the same way. In a January 1857 sermon, the Reverend Byron Sunderland lumped Florence Nightingale, Elizabeth Fry, and Margaret Fuller together as evidence of the various kinds of great work women were capable of performing within their sphere.[20]

When the issue became more pressing with the start of the Civil War, Nightingale's name appeared in the press and in novels, letters, and diaries as a justification for women's wartime nursing. According to one historian, Nightingale "was one of the most important woman icons of the war period."[21] Virtually every Civil War nurse was at some point likened to Nightingale or claimed to be inspired by her example. A September 1862 article in *Harpers Weekly* noted, "This war of ours has developed scores of Florence Nightingales, whose names no one knows, but whose reward . . . is the highest guerdon woman can win." Civil war nurse and author Louisa May Alcott referred to Superintendent of Nurses Dorothea Dix as "our Florence Nightingale." Drew Faust noted that Nightingale's example encouraged Southern women to become wartime nurses because she made nursing seem compatible with feminine respectability and high social standing. Linus Brockett and Mary Vaughan, in their massive history *Woman's Work in the Civil War*, argued that Northern women responded immediately to the war, "fired by the noble example of Florence Nightingale." Frank Moore, in the other major postwar compilation about Northern women workers in the Civil War, *Women of the War*, wrote that Nightingale had "proved" that women were fit "for a life of effective beneficence among homeless and suffering men," and he asked, "Who shall say how many noble aspirations and unselfish plans have been inspired by the golden record of that English girl?" Southerner Kate Cumming wrote that Nightingale's example inspired her to believe that she and other women were capable of effectively nursing the wounded: "I knew that what one woman had done another could."[22]

Civil War nurses also were constantly likened to angels. Some were labeled "the Angel of the Battlefield," and a battlefield angel was the central figure on the seal of the U.S. Sanitary Commission, a Civil War soldiers' aid organization headed primarily by men but staffed mostly by women.[23] One might expect that constant comparisons of American women to Florence Nightingale and to angels would lead to an image of loving, gentle, and nonthreatening women in military hospitals and on battlefields in the United States, as Poovey argues that these associations did in England. Judith Giesberg has also suggested that in the American context, because the angel is "a heavenly incarnation of an idealized, eternal femininity," it "effaces the work of real women" and therefore "reinforced the self-proclaimed subordination of the nurse." Thus the nurse became nonthreatening because her power "was ultimately controlled by her male superiors."[24] However, war novels suggest that the battlefield angel could take very powerful and threatening forms both before and during the Civil War. In such cases, the image of the angel could legitimate women's war work even as it stressed the threat of such work. These angels did more than threaten male power; they took it in both public and private life.

Americans had been making comparisons between women and angels long before the war began.[25] Heroines of antebellum sensational fiction were frequently depicted as angelic. The author of *Fanny Campbell, the Female Pirate Captain* frequently referred to his heroine, who participated in the Revolutionary War, as an angel or a "holy spirit." The narrator of Fanny Templeton Danforth's story compared her to "an angel descending from heaven."[26]

If the "Angel in the Home" was a common trope in the antebellum era, by 1850 so too was the angel who moved through the world and even onto battlefields. The author of the 1850 novel *Amelia Sherwood, or Bloody Scenes at the California Gold Mines* highlights the heroine's goodness by stressing the bad character of the gold regions of California—a land of immorality and sin, full of "robberies, fighting, and other lawless outbreaks" and a place where the "most disgraceful outrages" occurred.[27] Like many other accounts of California in the 1850s, *Amelia Sherwood* portrays the mines as a battleground where men fought a war over gold.[28] In one incident in the novel, Amelia displays "great daring and cool courage." She finds two men fighting over a piece of gold. When each pulls out a "bowie-knife" and they move toward each other, Amelia jumps between the two and "by words of gentle persuasion, calmed their ruffled passion, and prevented the unnecessary effusion of blood." The woodcut depicting this scene shows Amelia standing with her arms held up between the two knife-wielding men, bathed in rays of light shining directly on her from above, presumably emanating from heaven. The caption reads: "Unparalleled heroism of Amelia—she rushes between combatants in their quarrel about the Gold." The author does not use the word *angel* to describe Amelia in the text, but does say that she possesses the ability to stop male violence through "gentle persuasion"— a clear sign for readers of Amelia's status as a virtuous woman. In addition, the woodcut portrays Amelia bathed in heavenly light. She is not on an official battlefield, but she is on an informal one, endangering her life to stop violence. Like Fanny Campbell and others, Amelia Sherwood is an extremely assertive figure who consistently disobeys male authority. She is "self-will[ed]" and "wayward," and she disobeys her father, running away from home to follow her lover, Frank Richards, to New Orleans. Furthermore, she does not have to pay a price for this disobedience: in the end she finds and marries Richards in California.[29]

Not all the heroines of sensational fiction were explicitly labeled angels, but all were portrayed as moral, religious, active, patriotic, and brave "true" women. These heroines did more than nurse soldiers, controversial as that could be. Fanny Campbell, Leonora Siddons, and others fought in battles, shot their weapons, and killed foes in defense of their country.[30] Other periodicals and books described the adventures of nonfictional historical heroines, most notably Joan of Arc. These were aggressive avenging angels who belied the notion that antebellum gender ideology required women to be passive and submissive in order to be good. Antebellum women incorporated these angelic and aggressive heroines into their understandings of woman's duty in the Civil War, just as they had embraced stories of Florence Nightingale.

Stories of wartime angels reached a new level after the start of the Civil War. For example, in 1861, E. E. Barclay, publisher of *Amelia Sherwood, The Female*

Warrior, and many other sensational pamphlets, switched to a new topic: women on Civil War battlefields. These pamphlet novels were so successful that by 1863 the author of most of them, C. W. Alexander, left Barclay to establish his own firm and continued churning out tales of women in the war. Some of these heroines dressed as men and enlisted as soldiers, one protected her home and the flag, others remained in female attire and worked as battlefield nurses, and some worked in all three capacities at different moments, but all of them were "refined as well as educated."[31]

One heroine, "Pauline of the Potomac," starts her wartime career as a field nurse, but she soon "thirsted . . . for a more important part in the great drama." She cannot imagine what this will be until suddenly, "like an electric spark, an idea suggested itself to her": she will go to the Union general McClellan and offer her services as a spy. Pauline engages in a number of daring adventures and is extremely successful. One general tells her that she has "brilliantly accomplished that which the shrewdest and most experienced government detectives and scouts had failed to compass." Still, Pauline does not lose her feminine decency by engaging in her controversial work; rather, she is selfless, noble, tender, and even angelic. For example, she goes "round like an angel" to tend wounded Confederate soldiers despite the fact that she hates the Confederacy. Her decision to become a spy seems itself almost like a call from God. She made no rational choice; the idea came to her like an "electric spark."[32]

The same author soon wrote another pamphlet, *The Angel of the Battle-Field,* which is even more explicit about threats to male authority and in its comparison of nurses to angels. Its heroine, Eleanor Poindexter, defies her Southern family to support the Union in the Civil War. The first half of the novel contains scene after scene in which Eleanor and her father and brother engage in battles of will that almost turn physically violent. In one incident, her father finds out that Eleanor has freed her slave Rosa. The father sees Rosa and vows to whip her. As he picks up the whip, Eleanor points a revolver at her own chest and cocks the weapon. Seeing this, her father drops his whip. As the author puts it, "The stern, self-devoting, and unyielding heroism of his daughter overcame Mr. Poindexter, when everything else failed." Eventually, having antagonized the neighborhood with her pro-Union sympathies, Eleanor decides to move North and to do her "solemn duty" as a battlefield nurse, and she soon becomes known as the angel of the battlefield.[33]

This angelic imagery permeated pamphlet fiction. In the same year, another author, in the pamphlet novel *Miriam Rivers,* described the heroine Miriam's decision to become a "lady soldier": "Miriam . . . sat with clasped hands looking away into the distance, and that glorious light in her eyes which made her so beautiful. She was revolving some glorious plan in her mind—perhaps, like a second Joan of Arc, the angels were whispering to her a plan to save her country."[34]

Comparisons to Florence Nightingale, angels, and warrior-heroines like Joan of Arc and Fanny Campbell helped make female war workers' actions more palatable to Americans; they helped bolster women's claim to redemptive womanhood as they traveled from battlefield to battlefield. If some of these exemplars were extremely aggressive and capable of violence, their violence was always described as necessary action in defense of what is right. Such models allowed female workers to believe they had a vital role in the war effort, even on the battlefield. In practice, it encouraged them to behave at times in extremely assertive ways: arguing with surgeons and government bureaucrats, fighting fearlessly in battle, spying, joining regiments with male relatives, and even sometimes disguising themselves as men and enlisting in the army themselves.[35]

Such female characters were exciting, but could also be extremely threatening, since in many ways they hinted—and sometimes explicitly stated—that men were less competent, less capable, and less virtuous than women. Fanny Campbell could fight better than a man, and she also possessed the virtue associated with the ideal woman. The same was true for wartime heroines Pauline of the Potomac, Eleanor Poindexter, and Miriam Rivers. Men wrote all three of those sensational stories, but Lyde Cullen Sizer has noted this tendency in women's Civil War writing as well. According to Sizer, during the war women wrote numerous stories of fighting heroines who were "hybrids" possessing "the best traits of both genders," thus suggesting that "a woman can be all that a man can be and still retain the virtues of womanhood." Actual women who dressed as men and joined Civil War armies depicted themselves as just this sort of gender hybrid. While Sizer suggests that "gender was more a matter of appearance than of existential difference," one existential difference did remain in the picture: women's superior virtue.[36] If the only real difference between men and women is women's redemptive nature, and not physical strength or bravery, men would seem to have little to offer society. These accounts of women who retain their redemptive qualities yet take on the best qualities of men as well threaten to make men superfluous to public life. This might seem to be only a literary threat, but the boundary between literature and the lives of Civil War women was a permeable one.

Literary Heroines and the Experiences of Female Soldiers

In what seems to be no coincidence, the two women who wrote and published stories of their wartime experiences as ostensibly male soldiers both claimed that reading stories of female heroism played an important part in their decision to dress as men and enlist in the army.[37] Whatever role their reading played in their decision to go to war, these women used romantic novels and histories to assert that their actions were within woman's sphere, that they were doing nothing new or unnatural. These stories established a precedent for their actions. Presumably each woman believed the public would be more sympathetic if she justified her "unfeminine" actions by suggesting that she would not have dreamed of dressing as a man and going to war until she had read of a noble and heroic woman doing so.

Canadian-born Sarah Emma E. Edmonds's career as a Civil War soldier is quite well documented. She was eventually granted an army pension for approximately two years of service as Franklin Thompson in the Union army. Edmonds wrote a loosely autobiographical and highly popular account of her experiences in 1864, entitled *Nurse and Spy in the Union Army*.[38] Edmonds failed to point out in that book that, when she joined the army as a field nurse, she enlisted as a male soldier; her autobiography contains no explanation of her reasons for enlisting as a man. Edmonds does mention later in the narrative that she dressed as a man at times, at first on some spying expeditions, and halfway through the book she notes in passing, "At this time I was in military uniform . . . and was acting orderly." However, she seems to have made a point of glossing over the issue and avoiding making any explanations; in the book it is never clear that she enlisted as a man.[39]

Years later, in order to obtain an army pension, Edmonds publicly admitted that she had served as a male soldier. When a newspaper reporter interviewed her about her wartime experiences, she traced her decision to fight in the Civil War back to an event that had occurred in about 1854 when she was thirteen years old and living in eastern Canada. After her mother fed a peddler and provided him with lodging for the night at the family farm, the peddler gave Edmonds a book as a present: *Fanny Campbell, the Female Pirate Captain.* Calling the day she received the book "the most wonderful day in all my life," she remembered:

> All the latent energy of my nature was aroused, and each exploit of the heroine thrilled me to my finger tips. . . . When I read where "Fanny" cut off her brown curls and donned the blue jacket, and stepped into the freedom and glorious independence of masculinity, I threw up my old straw hat and shouted, as I have since heard McClellan's soldiers do, when he rode past the troops.[40]

A few years later, Edmonds wrote, when her father tried to force her to marry an older neighbor, she left home secretly, disguised herself as a man, and found employment as a traveling bookseller. In 1859, she went to the United States and continued selling books there. At the time the war broke out in 1861, she

was living in Flint, Michigan, as Franklin Thompson. She almost immediately
enlisted as a private in the 2nd Michigan Infantry.[41]

Although there were at least seven years between the time Edmonds read
Fanny Campbell and the time she became a soldier, she insisted that the book
was the origin of that decision. As one of her biographers notes, Edmonds may
have used *Fanny Campbell* as a model for her own wartime autobiography:
"When writing her memoirs, Emma never allowed herself to forget Ballou's
heroine for too long and sometimes it seems almost as though 'Fanny' is Emma
and 'Frank' is Captain Channing."[42] Whatever Edmonds's reasons were for disguising herself as a man and becoming a soldier, she linked her actions to those
of the fictional Fanny Campbell. Her story reads in many places like a novel,
and at times its similarities to *Fanny Campbell* are striking.[43] Edmonds positioned herself in a tradition of warrior heroines to justify her actions. Like virtually all fictional and real female Civil War workers, she linked her duty to her
country with her desire for an exciting and independent life. Edmonds first explained that she wished to nurse soldiers to perform her duty to her adopted
country, but then she made her desire for excitement clear: she was not going
to be a hospital nurse whose job it was to "sit quietly and fan the patients";
rather, she would "go to the front and participate in all the excitement of the
battle scenes . . . [as] a 'FIELD NURSE.'"[44] But it had not taken an event as mo-
mentous as the Civil War to start Edmonds on this road. She disguised herself
as a man and left home at least two years before the war began, initially applying the example of Fanny Campbell to the more mundane career of a traveling
book peddler. Women like Edmonds did not need a war to emulate Fanny
Campbell: the prospect of an unwanted marriage was enough for her. The war
certainly escalated women's desire and duty to be publicly active, but they felt
and acted on these longings before the Civil War.

Loreta Janeta Velazquez began her narrative of her Civil War service as a
soldier and spy with a six-page minihistory of female warriors, from Old Testament heroine Deborah to female soldiers of the nineteenth century. For Velazquez, "the greatest and noblest" of all these women was Joan of Arc. Velazquez directly linked her fascination with Joan of Arc to her desire to become
a soldier. She wrote: "From early childhood, Joan of Arc was my favorite heroine; and many a time has my soul burned with an overwhelming desire to emulate her deeds of valor." As a young girl in New Orleans, she explained,

> I expended all my pocket money, not in candies and cakes, as most girls
> are in the habit of doing, but in the purchase of books which related to
> the events in the lives of kings, princes and soldiers. The story of the
> siege of Orleans, in particular, I remember, thrilled my young heart, fired

my imagination, and sent my blood bounding through my veins with excitement. Joan of Arc became my heroine, and I longed for an opportunity to become such another as she.

Velazquez described her early life as a long waiting period for the chance to be another Joan of Arc. She claimed that she immediately understood the Civil War as "an opportunity . . . for me to carry out my long cherished ideas" and soon joined the Confederate war effort as Harry T. Buford. In the rest of the book, she recounted her daring and courageous adventures as a soldier and later a Confederate spy.[45]

Although her war narrative may have been highly fictionalized, Velazquez did exist, and she probably served in the Confederate army. Historian Richard Hall has documented parts of her life as Harry Buford. Velazquez's foreign surname, as well as her assertion that she had been born in Cuba and was descended from a noble Spanish family, would seem to indicate that she grew up in a different milieu from that of Anglo-American women, but evidence suggests that she invented her Spanish name and background. She most likely was American born and a native English speaker. One contemporary noted, "Her appearance and voice are those of an American woman, and bear no resemblance to those of a cultivated Spanish lady." Additionally, in her incarnation as Harry Buford, Velazquez made no attempt to appear Spanish, and she apparently had no accent to conceal.[46]

Both Velazquez and Edmonds traced their service as Civil War soldiers to their desire to emulate the female heroines they had read about in their youth. By appealing to the examples of moral heroines like Fanny Campbell and Joan of Arc, these women established a precedent for their soldiering, arguing that it was compatible with proper womanhood. Both used other strategies as well to present themselves as respectable women. Edmonds most notably glosses over her service as a soldier in her book, focusing on her motherly role as a nurse instead. Velazquez asserts in her preface that there was "nothing essentially improper" in her military service as a man because she was "courageous" in battle and "never did aught to disgrace the uniform I wore." Later she adds that she came out of the war "with my womanly reputation unblemished by even a suspicion of impropriety."[47] Thus Velazquez too portrayed herself as possessing all the best qualities of both a woman and a man.

"WHEN WE WERE LITTLE CHILDREN, WE USED TO WISH WE HAD LIVED IN THE OLD WAR OF THE REVOLUTION"

Most female war workers did not dress as men and serve secretly as soldiers, but they too referred to literary and historical heroines to justify their participation in the war effort. They also consistently referred to the heroism of their own ancestors. They described childhoods filled with tales of the exploits of their soldier ancestors in the American Revolution, the Indian wars, and the War of 1812. Mary Livermore's father, "always a great patriot," served in the War of 1812, and his father fought in the Revolution. Clara Barton never tired of telling people that her father had served under "Mad Anthony Wayne" in the Indian wars. Nurse Catherine Lawrence claimed to be a direct descendent of War of 1812 hero Captain James Lawrence, and according to her autobiography, in moments of crisis she routinely exclaimed to herself and others "Lawrence won't give up the ship!" Louisa May Alcott harkened back to the Revolutionary War heritage of her mother's family when she described her excitement over the war with the announcement that "The blood of the Mays is up!" Caroline Dall wrote an article for a Boston journal during the war in which she reminisced about her childhood daydreams of wartime heroism: "When we were little children, we used to wish we had lived in the old war of the Revolution. . . . We read Peter Parley and envied Mrs. Dammer riding a bare-backed horse . . . that she might warn Washington of the approach of Cornwallis." Linus Brockett, Mary Vaughan, and Frank Moore made similar connections in their histories of women's work in the Civil War, noting whenever female war workers had relatives who fought in the Revolution or other American wars.[48]

Some future war workers even created their own stories of self-sacrificing heroic women in the years before the Civil War. Future hospital matron Hannah Ropes, for example, wrote *Cranston House*, a novel in which a heroic young nurse is caught in a fictional war between pioneers and Mormons. Louisa May Alcott wrote a number of plays and potboilers in the 1850s, including the stories "Bandit's Bride" and "The Moorish Maiden's Vow," which were similar to the sensational tales she later attributed to Jo March in *Little Women*. Southern domestic novelist Augusta Jane Evans, later famous for *Macaria*, the story of a wealthy planter's daughter who devotes herself to nursing Confederate soldiers during the war, had already explored women's duty in times of crisis in the books she wrote before that war. In her first novel, *Inez*, set in the Mexican-American War, Evans told the story of two American girls in Texas and the young Mexican woman, Inez, who saves them from the treachery of a Spanish priest during the war. In *Beulah*, Evans's first popular novel, published in 1859, the heroine nurses her neighbors through a yellow fever epidemic when even many doctors are afraid to help and nurses are not available "for any sum." When Beulah is told that she will probably die of the fever, she answers, "I have thought of it all, sir, and determined to do my duty."[49]

Evans's *Macaria*, written during the war and published in 1864, was quickly "hailed as the most popular book in the Confederacy." *Macaria* is the story of two young women who devote all their energy to the Confederate cause. One participates in spying missions, and both eventually become nurses in military hospitals. Evans wrote *Macaria* with the hope that it would encourage Southern women to take an active role in the war effort, especially as nurses. As Drew Faust points out, "Nearly every Confederate woman who discussed her reading in a diary or in her correspondence mentioned *Macaria*." At least one Southern woman volunteered at a local hospital the day after she read the book. Even the army recognized the book's power to influence individuals. As one scholar points out, the book "was considered so incendiary in its support for the Confederacy that it was literally burned by military leaders in Northern army camps."[50]

Drew Faust argues of *Macaria* in particular and of Southern wartime novels in general that "in fiction [Southern] women could invent new lives and could imagine new selves, new identities, and new meanings that seemed too frightening to contemplate outside the world of literary fantasy."[51] In the North, however, the situation was somewhat different. There literary heroines were reinforced, rather than undermined, by the publicly active female reformers of the antebellum era. The proliferation of histories of women had been a part of Northern reform-minded women's search for historical foremothers. In the North by the 1850s, the assertive and publicly active redemptive woman was frequently a real figure as well as a fictional one. The actions of antebellum female reformers, Crimean and American nurses, and fictional and historical heroines of the period established a precedent in the North for women's ongoing public action before and during the Civil War.

Antebellum narratives of women and war—sensational novels, domestic fiction, histories, journal articles, and stories passed down orally from parent to child—taught antebellum women that if war came they would have a central place in the conflict. These accounts were further reinforced when the war started, and stories about women in the Civil War proliferated. According to many of these accounts, it would be women's job to save the nation, and they could fulfill this duty in a variety of capacities: as nurses, doctors, spies, and soldiers, and perhaps by filling formerly "male" jobs on the home front. The stories taught women that they were more just and often more capable than men in war, and that women would have to be willing to disobey male authority when it conflicted with their own sense of right. Like domestic novels and women's histories in general, the writing on war in the late 1840s and 1850s suggested that women could not rely on men to fix bad situations. If men were so unreliable, immoral, or incompetent, women could freely disregard their authority.

These war stories also encouraged women to expect and to desire meaningful, stimulating, and even heroic work. The existence of such adventurous and daring heroines seems to have engendered in many future female war workers a desire to participate in the kind of crisis that would call out women's strength, bravery, and selfless heroism. Antebellum literature—fictional and nonfictional—continually informed women they were the nation's saviors, that they were noble, brave, and capable of heroism in a crisis. Such narratives could give women extremely high expectations. By the time the war started, many Northern women were eager to participate, not only because they had been taught it was their duty, but also because they had been told from childhood that their destiny was to save the world. What ordinary life could measure up to such expectations? As a number of future female war workers described it in their letters and journals, life seemed drab and often meaningless before the war. They saw the war, in part, as a solution to this problem: it was each woman's chance, finally, to show the world she was "a second Joan of Arc."

Angels on the Battlefield

I've often longed to see a war, and now I have my wish. I long to be a man; but as I can't fight, I will content myself with working for those who can.

—Louisa May Alcott, April 1861[1]

*T*t was not an inevitable result of the realities of the Civil War that more than twenty thousand Northern women left home during the course of the war to nurse wounded and sick soldiers, while many others joined loyalty leagues and worked for sanitary commissions and a few became spies or soldiers. As Drew Faust notes, Southern and Northern women responded to the war differently. Southern women did not enter the hospitals in nearly the same numbers that Northern women did, although the war was fought on their own territory. Even those who did work in the hospitals usually "wrote their memoirs and faded away" after the war, unlike many of their Northern counterparts, who continued in public work.[2] Why did Northern women's actions and their attitudes about the war follow the specific course they did? In the North, antebellum accounts of female heroism, in conjunction with antebellum women's increasing presence in public life, encouraged large numbers of women to look for a way to participate in the war immediately after it began. Southern women's war experiences were generally different. Yet women in the two regions did share some things: Southern Civil War literature, like *Macaria*, and published diaries and letters of Southern nurses suggest certain commonalities of belief between Northern and Southern women that merit further exploration. In the North and the South, debates over women's duty in wartime were structured around many of the same themes, even if the results of the debates often differed.

For a number of Northern female reformers, participation in the Civil War was merely the continuation of a public career in reform. Elizabeth Leonard argues that Annie Wittenmyer, long active in local benevolent activities, saw her war work in the Iowa Sanitary Commission as "not so much a break with her normal life, as a shift into a new field of labor." After the war ended, Wittenmyer remained active in public work: she continued her work for Iowa Soldiers' Orphans' Homes, which she had begun during the war; from 1874 to 1879 she was the first president of the Women's Christian Temperance Union, soon to be the largest women's organization in the world; and later she became president of the Women's Relief Corps.[3] Dorothea Dix, appointed superintendent of woman nurses in June 1861, had long been famous for her work in mental hospitals. At the end of the war, Dix returned to her prewar labors.[4] By the time Eliza Farnham died while nursing sick and wounded soldiers in the winter of 1864, she had already written several books, including a lengthy tract on female superiority, *Woman and Her Era*; worked as the head matron at the women's prison in Sing Sing; and led an unsuccessful "Mission of Redemption" to California in 1850, in which she tried to send a number of respectable young women to gold country to marry and "civilize" the forty-niners.[5]

Worcester, Massachusetts, sisters Lucy and Sarah Chase had grown up in a family immersed in reform movements. They had attended abolition and temperance lectures, dinners, and conventions from childhood. At age fifteen, in boarding school in Rhode Island, Lucy Chase filled her school composition books with essays on the evils of slavery. Her family's correspondence to her during her stay at school included accounts of recent antislavery meetings and lectures interspersed with admonitions to "pay particular attention" to her algebra.[6]

At an early age, the Chase sisters embraced women's public duty to redeem society. They heard and admired the speeches of Abby Kelley, Lucretia Mott, and many more female lecturers. When Lucy Chase attended a Unitarian convention in October 1844, she noted that Lucretia Mott was allowed to speak, but only after voting was concluded on an issue. On the last day of the convention, she complained in her journal that "The time is yet to come when woman's right to join in the service of her maker will be recognized. The Bible is perverted into opposition to her public teaching." Lucy's role in antebellum reform went far beyond attending events. She participated in antislavery sewing circles, worked at antislavery fairs, and went door-to-door obtaining signatures for petitions on antislavery and other reform causes.[7]

The Chase sisters wasted no time at all in trying to enter the war effort. On 20 April 1861, just five days after Lincoln issued the first call for volunteers, Sarah Chase wrote to her father asking for permission to go "South with the nurses." Sarah received permission from her father, but permission from others was harder to obtain, and she never worked as a Civil War nurse. Instead, in December 1862 she and her sister Lucy finally obtained a commission from the Boston Educational Commission to teach freed slaves on the South Carolina Sea Islands. They set off immediately and arrived in January 1863. Lucy taught in African American schools in various locations in the South until 1869, but Sarah retired in 1866 because of poor health.[8]

Sojourner Truth, an antislavery lecturer before the war, began her war work lecturing at pro-Union meetings, then began collecting food and supplies locally for a black regiment. According to one friend, Truth asserted that she would have become a field nurse, "if she was ten years younger." In 1864, Truth moved to Washington and began working with the freed slaves. She spent four years there working for various freedmen's organizations.[9] Black abolitionist and author Harriet Jacobs also worked in Washington during the war for the National Freedmen's Aid Association.[10] Mary Livermore had been a teacher, an abolitionist, and a reporter and associate editor of a journal her husband edited before the Civil War. At the beginning of the war, she immediately volunteered for the Chicago Sanitary Commission, and she soon became one of the leaders of the U.S. Sanitary Commission. In that role, she traveled through the North and West giving lectures and raising funds. On a number of occasions, she also went into the field to nurse soldiers and to inspect the sanitary conditions in camps and hospitals.[11] For physicians Esther Hill Hawks and Mary Walker also, war work was an extension of their controversial peacetime profession.[12] For other prewar reformers who did their war work in the North, like Lucy Stone, Caroline Dall, Anna Dickinson, Elizabeth Cady Stanton, and Susan B. Anthony, involvement in Civil War benevolent organizations was frequently less controversial than their earlier ventures into the public eye.[13]

Civil War hospital and field nurse Catherine Lawrence's experience was typical of women's movement from antebellum reform into Civil War work. Lawrence, born and raised in central New York, decided at age twelve that she wanted to become a missionary. Soon after this, she began her first benevolent work: establishing a Sabbath school for the "natives living on the mountain, a few miles from my native village." After a short teaching career, Lawrence supported herself until the Civil War by traveling as a lecturer on temperance, antislavery, and other moral issues and selling books "of a moral and religious character."[14] Lawrence faced much criticism for her public speaking. At one Fourth of July temperance celebration in the 1840s, she was told that "it was quite out of place for a lady to make herself so public." In response to this, Lawrence asserted, "I had to take up the point and define woman's sphere for two-thirds of an hour." In her memoirs, Lawrence recounted numerous similar confrontations that occurred during her antebellum lecturing career. She always defended her right as a woman to speak in public and to be active in causes of religion and morality. She reported that "I have almost always felt that I was public property," and when the Civil War came, she enlisted as an army nurse almost immediately.[15]

African American teacher, public lecturer, and journalist Mary Ann Shadd Cary's Civil War work was also a logical extension of her prewar activities. Cary began her teaching career at age sixteen, and she launched her writing career at age twenty-six, publishing the pamphlet "Hints to the Colored People of the North" in 1849. Soon after the 1850 fugitive slave law was passed, Cary emigrated to Canada. In 1853 she cofounded a newspaper, the *Provincial Freeman*, and went on the lecture circuit promoting both black emigration to Canada and her newspaper. She faced the usual problems of female lecturers: at the 1853 Colored National Convention, "she had to win a debate with the male convention leaders before she was allowed to speak publicly." In her newspaper, as one scholar explains, she consistently argued that "'woman's sphere' should be enlarged to include any activity a woman wanted to pursue." During the war, Cary was "commissioned as an Army recruiting agent." As such, she traveled around the Northern United States and interviewed black would-be soldiers. After the war, she returned permanently to the United States, at first to teach African American students in Washington, D.C. Later she worked as a school principal, and eventually she became a lawyer.[16]

"I HAVE CONSTANTLY A LONGING FOR SOMETHING HIGHER AND NOBLER, THAN I HAVE KNOWN"

If some women embraced war work as a continuation of long careers in reform, for many others the war seemed to offer a long-awaited answer to their search for meaningful activity. They had been told since childhood that women had important, essential work to do in the name of morality and religion. They read numerous stories of fearless heroines who saved families, communities, and entire nations. The distance between the heroines they read about and their own role as the moral and religious foundation of American society, on the one hand, and their limited outlet for any kind of meaningful work, on the other, created a crisis for a number of Northern women in the years before the

Civil War. As serious national problems arose, a number of women were convinced they could help solve them if only they were allowed. Their frustration
did not arise out of some natural desire to participate in public, but rather from
the disjuncture between their position as the guardians of morality and religion
and their lack of outlets for performing that role.[17]

Many Northern female war workers, whether they had been abolitionists or
had hated abolitionism, shared a prewar longing for active, useful, interesting,
and meaningful labor, a desire for work that challenged their physical and moral
strength, work that would reveal the heroism they believed they possessed. The
letters, journals, and other recorded reminiscences of Northern and some
Southern female Civil War workers that cover the period before the war frequently reveal these women's frustration with their sphere of action and their
longing for useful employment. Their desire for meaningful lives often took a
romantic turn. Drawing from both fact and fiction, they envisioned themselves
as heroines called by God and country into moral and religious battles.

One of many such women was Civil War nurse Hannah Ropes of Massachusetts, who was born in 1809 and whose father was a prominent lawyer from an
old New England family. At least eight years before the start of the war, Ropes
was stricken with frustration at the social constraints she felt prevented her
from becoming involved in meaningful work. She wrote to her mother in 1853,

> What a coterie I could gather around me of intelligence and high purpose . . . if
> but the power of my own will, were not held in check, by the elements of time
> and space. . . . Why did you give this homely hen, the *wings* of an *eagle*? Behold
> they flap heavily against her sides, for the want of proper use—and fret away the
> life which as yet finds no fit element—or finding, cannot, dare not accept.[18]

Dissatisfied with a narrow conception of woman's sphere, Ropes could not yet
see a way into a more fulfilling field of action, at least not one she could accept.
She, like many other women of her time, had been raised to have high expectations of her usefulness. Her mother, she complained, had trained her to be an
eagle in a world in which she was condemned to live as a hen. She had been
taught that woman's duty was to be the moral and religious foundation of the
nation, to guard the purity of family and country, yet when she searched for a
field in which to exercise that high moral and religious purpose, her opportunities seemed extremely limited.

Although in 1853 Ropes was hesitant to engage in certain activities for fear
of overstepping the bounds of propriety, she had already established that, for
her, those boundaries were flexible. More than fifteen years earlier, she had
shown that, like antebellum female reformers, she believed that it was her duty

as a morally accountable being to make her own moral and religious decisions, and to act on them whatever the cost. Ropes began attending meetings with the Swedenborgians, a Christian sect with an emphasis on spirituality, in 1837 and joined the church in 1839. Immediately after she began associating with the Swedenborgians, she noted a negative effect on her reputation. In writing to her parents that one minister had shaken hands with her "as though I had not been a woman with a *filthy Faith*," she revealed how the rest treated her. As one historian notes, she "seemed to find this [disapproval] stimulating." Not only did her new doctrine sustain her in the face of public disdain and abuse, the abuse itself became a badge of her heroism. Thus, like female public speakers in the same years, she braved personal attacks in order to perform what she considered to be her religious duty, and she even embraced such attacks as tests of her faith.[19]

While the antebellum notion of woman as the moral and religious foundation of the nation offered a justification for women's public action, this concept always required that there be a moral or religious problem before women could act. Ropes acted in the context of a personal religious crisis in 1837; in 1853, she seems to have been actively searching for another crisis. In 1855, Ropes found it in the struggle over slavery in Kansas. Her son Edward, a Free-Soiler, went to Kansas to homestead that year. Ropes and her daughter Alice soon joined him; Ropes was eager to help Edward and to "bolster the freesoil presence" there. The settlement in Lawrence, Kansas, was apparently a sickly one. According to Ropes's own account, from the moment of her arrival she spent most of her time in Kansas nursing sick settlers, when she was not sick herself.[20]

In a climate of increasing violence, Ropes returned to Massachusetts in 1856 and published two accounts based on her experiences in the West. The first was a nonfictional collection of her letters, *Six Months in Kansas*, published in 1856. The second was *Cranston House: A Novel*, published in 1859. While Ropes herself had nursed the sick rather than those who were wounded in the violence in Kansas in 1855 and 1856, in *Cranston House* she transformed her experience into that of a battlefield nurse in a war between Western settlers and the Mormons. In that novel, published two years before the Civil War, Ropes created her version of a national moral crisis that justified, even demanded, women's public action. The words she wrote for the young nurse in *Cranston House* suggest Ropes's resolution of the feelings of uselessness she had expressed in that 1853 letter to her mother:

> O woman! chafing against the walls of thy home, and crying out for a larger sphere of action and enterprise, behold this little girl of fifteen summers, in whose simple wisdom there stirs but one emotion, instilled by a Christian mother,—the love of the Lord and the love of the neighbor. Not only is she the star of brightness and beauty to those prostrate men, but the anchor of hope . . . without which they faint and die.[21]

If Ropes did not make it explicit in her letter to her mother, here she directly linked woman's frustration to a limited sphere of action, and here she proposed an answer to the problem: nursing wounded soldiers.

Cranston House was not only a fictional resolution of Ropes's own search for meaningful activity; it was also an envisioning of the Civil War itself, and of women's role in that conflict. That she transformed her own care of the sick into her heroine's care for those wounded in battle emphasized her particular concern with women's wartime nursing. In nursing, women selflessly took care of the physical and the spiritual natures of men. In this war, the female nurse did more than heal men. She boosted their morale, encouraged them to fight. She was an active participant in a battle between good and evil. This fictional battlefield nurse proved herself womanly by selflessly nurturing men wounded in a "just" war. The war was against the Mormons, a group routinely depicted as depraved by most Americans—and whose supposed depravity had been explicitly linked to slavery in 1856 by the Republican Party, which had labeled "polygamy a 'barbarism' equal to slavery."[22] Hence, Ropes's heroine was a nurturing crusader in the cause of religion, morality, and the nation, fighting in a war that presaged the Civil War. When that war began, Ropes immediately recognized it as the kind of crisis she had envisioned in *Cranston House*. As soon as she could make arrangements, she traveled to Washington to become a nurse in a military hospital. She worked as the matron of a military hospital until she died of typhoid pneumonia in January 1863.[23]

Ropes presented nursing as woman's duty, but she also suggested it as a solution for women frustrated by the lack of meaningful work. These two threads—duty and desire—ran through the writings of virtually all women war workers. It was clear that wartime nursing was not only the self-sacrificing performance of women's duty. It also fulfilled women's desire for action, adventure, and excitement. Danger and hardship allowed them the opportunity to be heroic, to test their strength and bravery. These two themes were not necessarily incompatible: a woman ought to desire to fulfill her moral and religious duty. Yet there was always a tension between the two, since desire had connotations of selfishness.

When reading Clara Barton's letters and diaries, one sometimes has the impression that she spent the first forty years of her life waiting for the Civil War or some other great event to give her life meaning and purpose. Barton too was deeply frustrated by the disjuncture between her desires and the opportunities available to her as a woman. Even as a young woman she seemed to long for tests of courage and moral heroism that her rural Massachusetts life did not provide. She dreamed of a heroic, self-sacrificing, and dangerous life, and from the age of fourteen she filled her scrapbook with clippings of tales of selfless heroism like "Sagitto, the Warrior of the Washpelong" and "Juanita; a Tale of Murat's Time." Juanita was a young Italian girl who switched places with her heartless lover, who had been condemned to death for murder. She bravely allowed herself to be hanged in his place even though he was "unmoved" by her sacrifice.[24]

When at the age of eighty-six Clara Barton wrote an autobiography of her childhood for young readers, she revealingly portrayed her early life as a series of tests of her courage, stamina, and even heroism; she described it as a struggle to triumph over two obstacles: her gender and her youth. In one instance, she recounted her great disappointment at not being allowed to learn to skate as a child because it was not proper for girls to do so. Many of her fond childhood memories, on the other hand, centered on times when she was allowed or able to perform the activities of a boy or the duties of an adult. She wrote of running through the woods, crossing rivers on rickety planks, helping the man who was hired to repaint and paper her family's house, nursing her sick brother for two years, teaching school at a very young age, and earning the respect of her male students by being better at sports than they were. She took great pleasure in telling stories of her childhood stoicism and bravery. She noted that the doctor had told her father that she "stood it like a soldier" when he bandaged her seriously wounded knee. She also related the opinion of Mrs. Fowler, wife of the famous phrenologist, who told Clara's mother that Clara "will never assert herself for herself—she will suffer wrong first—but for others she will be perfectly fearless." In her reminiscences, Barton exulted in stories of her childhood strength, bravery, and selfless care for others.[25]

Barton's autobiography conveyed a sense of usefulness and purpose that she had wished for in her early life but did not seem to possess at that time. As a young woman, she was driven to despair by the lack of a place in her life and work for courageous and independent action. Although Barton described her first teaching experience fondly in her autobiography, her letters and journals reveal that she soon tired of teaching—if she ever had found it fulfilling. Her diary entries from 1852, when she was teaching in New Jersey, are telling: "I see less and less in the world to live for. . . . There is not a living thing but would be just as well off without me. I contribute to the happiness of not a single object and often to the unhappiness of many and always my own, for I am never happy. . . . How long I am to or can endure such a life I do not know."[26] Barton did not plan to remain a teacher, but she did not know what else she, as a woman, could do. Thirty years old, she held no hope of ever finding meaningful employment. A few weeks later she added: "I know how it will be at length, I shall take a strange sudden start and be off somewhere and all will wonder at and judge and condemn, but like the past, I shall survive it all and go on working at some trifling, unsatisfactory thing, and half paid at that."[27] Obviously this was not the first time she had struggled with the problem of finding a meaningful career.

In the short term, things worked out better than Barton had expected. She moved to Washington, D.C., and in 1854 became a clerk in the patent office. She was one of the first female employees of the federal government. Paid the same wages as men in the office, she seemed pleased with her position, but in 1857 she, a Republican, was dismissed by the Democratic administration.[28] She went home to her family in Massachusetts and spent three directionless years looking for work, taking art classes, and becoming increasingly depressed. She refused to go back to teaching, which she had grown to hate, and could find no other work. As she described it in early 1860, she had been left to "wish, pine, and fret" in a "cage." At about this time she asked her brother-in-law for help, telling him she wanted to do something useful: *"something, somewhere, or anything, anywhere."* She mentioned her willingness to go to any state in the nation or any country on the continent, if only she would be allowed to "pioneer, or establish and build up Institutions." By June 1860, still unable to find meaningful work, she broke down completely, suffering "an emotional and physical collapse." Some months later, cheered by Lincoln's election, she moved back to Washington and was able to obtain temporary work at the patent office, but it was the Civil War that finally gave Clara Barton's life a sense of meaning.[29]

Much like Ropes and Barton, at age fifteen Louisa May Alcott felt like a "caged sea-gull," trapped in the family home, cooking and cleaning. Alcott wrote in her journal as early as 1859, "I . . . long for a war." At the outbreak of the Civil War, she wrote, "I've often longed to see a war, and now I have my wish. I long to be a man; but as I can't fight, I will content myself with working for those who can."[30] Unlike Jo in *Little Women*, who was "dying to go and fight with Papa" but could "only stay at home and knit like a poky old woman," Alcott decided in November 1862 to go to Washington to nurse soldiers: "Help is needed and I love nursing, and *must* let out my pent-up energy in some new way. I want new experiences, and am sure to get 'em if I go."[31] Alcott always asserted that she wanted to nurse soldiers to fulfill her patriotic duty, but also, through Jo and in her own journal, she expressed her frustrated desires for excitement and action, desires she hoped the war would enable her to fulfill.

Hannah Ropes, Clara Barton, and Louisa May Alcott were all preoccupied with a search for meaningful and interesting work in the years before the Civil War. Sense of duty and desire for independence and excitement are inseparable in their writings. Younger war workers, like twenty-five-year-old African American schoolteacher Charlotte Forten, who went to Port Royal to teach freed slaves; twenty-three-year-old Cornelia Hancock, who traveled to Gettysburg to nurse the wounded; and nineteen-year-old soldier Sarah Rosetta Wakeman shared these intertwined desires to fulfill their duty and to engage in exciting activities. Although these younger women had not spent so many years looking for meaningful work, they too found their war work a relief from the insignificance of their peacetime lives.

At the age of seventeen, Charlotte Forten seemed happy with her life as a student in Salem, Massachusetts. She wrote that her studies would "aid me in fitting myself for laboring in a holy cause, for enabling me to do much toward changing the condition of my oppressed and suffering people." Specifically, she wanted to become an antislavery lecturer. Just a few months after she wrote these lines, Forten's father summoned her home to Philadelphia, and she begged to be able to stay in Salem and complete her education. When her father relented, she wrote that she would never give him "cause to regret it" and promised that she would "spare no effort to become what he desires that I should be; to prepare myself well for the responsible duties of a teacher." Yet, as one historian notes, it is "not clear from reading the diaries whether Charlotte ever really wanted to become a teacher." She expressed this desire never as her own, but always as her father's.[32]

Shortly after she graduated from the normal school in Salem and began a career as an elementary school teacher, Forten began to voice in her journal entries dissatisfaction with teaching and with her life in general. She seems never to have been happy teaching in Salem. Little more than a week after she began, she noted: "I find a teacher's life not nearly as pleasant as a scholar's." This was only the first of many complaints about the wearying nature of her job. Her journal entries from the late 1850s also frequently recounted bouts with illness, depression, general feelings of uselessness, and a sense that she had accomplished little with her life. In September 1856, she wrote, "Sometimes I feel there is nothing to live for. Nothing! . . . I know it is not right to feel thus. But I *cannot* help it always." Throughout this same period, she consistently mentioned longing for a more meaningful life: "I have constantly a longing for something higher and nobler, than I have known. Consequently, I ask myself Cowley's question 'what shall I do to be forever known?' This is ambition I know. It is selfish, it is wrong. But oh! how very hard it is to do and feel what is right." A few months later, she continued in the same vein: "I wonder why it is that I have this strange feeling of not *living out myself:* My existence seems not full expansive enough. I must need some great emotion to arouse the dormant energies of my nature. What means this constant restlessness, longing for something, I know not what?" Much like Clara Barton, Forten seems to have found her life as a schoolteacher draining and unsatisfying. She longed for an outlet for her "dormant energies," as well as the opportunity to perform more important duties. It was not enough for Forten to hold a respectable job. She wanted to do something truly heroic, something high and noble, something "expansive" for which she would be "forever known."[33]

In October 1862, Forten arrived in Union-occupied Port Royal, in the South Carolina Sea Islands, as part of the Philadelphia Educational Commission's effort to educate freed slaves. Once she was there, her journal entries quickly became more lively. She was not entirely healthy, but she was far less frequently incapacitated by illness in South Carolina than she had been in the North. Although she was lonely at times right after her arrival, her South Carolina journal entries are not marked by the feelings of uselessness and deep depression that ran through her earlier diaries. Instead, the entries detail her busy days of work among the freed slaves and her conversations with her many friends and acquaintances around Port Royal. In addition to teaching former slaves, in times of crisis she also nursed wounded soldiers. She was still a teacher much of the time in South Carolina, but Forten's life was filled with a greater variety of activities and a sense that her work was of immediate value in the war. She was proud of her connection to the Union army and referred to the African American 1st South Carolina Volunteer Infantry as "*my regt.*" She explained playfully but proudly in a letter to her friend John Greenleaf Whittier that Thomas Wentworth Higginson, commander of that regiment, had "adopted me as the 'daughter of the regiment.'" While Forten found the heat of South Carolina's long summers oppressive, she otherwise thrived in the region. She became more self-confident during her stay there, noting in her journals that she had suddenly acquired a bravery that she had never known at home.[34]

Her work in the Sea Islands seemed to give Forten at least some of the meaning she had been searching for in the late 1850s. Never again did she write of intense longings for a different life and feelings of worthlessness and uselessness as she had when she was a teacher in Salem. Forten remained in South Carolina until May 1864, returning to Philadelphia shortly after the death of her father. She did not go back to the Sea Islands, but neither did she go back to her prewar life. In 1865, she became the secretary of the teachers committee of the New England branch of the Freedmen's Union Commission in Boston, a position she held for the next six years. Eventually, after her marriage to Francis Grimké, she devoted herself to writing.[35]

Cornelia Hancock, a young white Quaker woman from southern New Jersey, underwent perhaps an even greater transformation during the war. Although Hancock mentioned little of her life before the war, she wrote that she felt herself "a new person" after little more than a month with the army. She wrote to her mother from a field hospital at Gettysburg:

> The main reason for my staying, aside from duty, is that I am so well, if only it
> lasts. I feel like a new person, eat . . . anything that comes up and walk as straight
> as a soldier, feel life and vigor which you well know I never felt at home. . . . I can-
> not explain it, but I feel so erect, and can go steadily from one thing to another . . .
> and feel more like work at ten [P.M.] than when I got up at home.

Hancock continued to thrive on army life throughout the war. After a year with
the army, she told her mother "how strong" she had become: "I have gained
here, better than any fortune, my nearly perfect health. A boon no one can ap-
preciate until as long deprived as I have been."[36]

Hancock consistently asserted her strength, independence, health, and happiness as a nurse in a way that suggested her frustration with her earlier life.
She also reveled in the independence she gained by having her own home. Although her house was a crude log cabin at a field hospital, she praised it constantly in her letters and told her mother that she would not return to the family home after the war. Instead, she wanted her father to clear a nearby lot,
where she would "build a log house certain, as soon as I get home." By the time
the war ended, Hancock had become even more independent. She remained in
the South for eleven years after the war, teaching in African American schools,
and she never again lived in the same town as her parents.[37]

Perhaps five hundred to one thousand women disguised themselves as men
and served in the Union and Confederate armies during the Civil War.[38] Sarah
Rosetta Wakeman was one of these female soldiers. As with Hancock, there is
little existing evidence about Wakeman's life before the Civil War, but according to her letters, she enlisted at least in part because her father, a farmer in
central New York, was deep in debt. Wakeman wrote to her parents that she
had grown tired of sitting at home doing nothing to help and feeling useless
when "I knew that I could help you more to leave home than to stay there."
She secretly left, disguised herself as a man, and enlisted as a soldier to earn
money for her family. She sent them her enlistment bounty and most of her
pay. Yet duty to her family appears to have been only one of her motivations. If
Wakeman said nothing about desire for independence or excitement in her explanation for leaving home, she too expressed contentment with her life as a
soldier in a way that suggests her dissatisfaction with her earlier life. In one letter to her parents, she told them, "I [am] enjoying my self better this summer
than I ever did before in this world." Six months later, she reiterated this point
in another letter: "I have enjoyed my self best since I have gone away from
home than I ever did before in my life." Wakeman linked her newfound happiness to her independent life. In one letter she told her parents, "When I get out
of the war I will come and see you but I shall not stay long before I shall be off

to take care of my Self. I will help you all I can as long as I live."[39] After several months as a soldier, Wakeman had resolved to live independently for the rest of her life. She would help her parents like a dutiful son, but she would never again live at home like a dutiful daughter.

Women like Clara Barton, Hannah Ropes, Louisa May Alcott, Cornelia Hancock, Charlotte Forten, and Sarah Rosetta Wakeman found in their Civil War work a solution for their dissatisfaction with their prewar lives. Unfortunately, Wakeman died of illness in an army hospital in June 1864, and Ropes died of typhoid pneumonia in January 1863, but those who lived led quite different lives after the war than they had before it. Barton went on to found the American Red Cross. Hancock, who had lived with her parents in 1863, never went home again for more than a visit. She worked from 1866 to 1876 as a teacher in the South. Neither did Forten return to her previous life. In the years after the war, she worked as an official of the Freedman's Commission, as a writer, as a high school teacher, and as a clerk in the U.S. Department of the Treasury.[40]

In a sense, it was the Civil War that launched Louisa May Alcott's famous career. Alcott first gained prominence as a writer with the 1863 publication of *Hospital Sketches*, a book based on her experiences as a Civil War nurse. But in another sense, Alcott failed in her attempt to escape her prewar life by working as a nurse. In part, this is how Alcott understood her life. Of the war workers discussed in this chapter, Alcott is the only one who returned to live with her birth family. Her tenure as a nurse had been short—little more than six weeks—and afterward she endured a long convalescence with typhoid pneumonia. She suffered for the rest of her life from the effects of the mercury she received as medicine during her illness. With the exception of a few trips, Alcott stayed near her parents, sisters, and sisters' children for the rest of her life, taking care of them whenever necessary, which was quite often. While she was extremely close to her family and was very happy to give them financial security, Alcott consistently described feeling trapped in a narrow world that was too small for her. For years she told herself in her journal, "my time is yet to come," but near the end her days she admitted to herself that she would "never live my own life." Alcott had tried to use the war as a springboard to a fully independent life and had failed, but she had tried nonetheless, and she did achieve independence in her career, becoming one of the most successful authors of the nineteenth century.[41]

THE "NATURAL PREY" OF SURGEONS

If women entered the war to do their duty as redemptive women and to engage in the type of important, noble, and heroic work their gender ideology encouraged them to desire, their actions were still troubling to many Americans,

not because these women overstepped the bounds of gender ideology, but because, like alleged murderesses, fallen women, and female reformers before
them, they made it apparent just how unclear the boundaries of that ideology
were. The need for positive labels like Florence Nightingale and the Angel of
the Battlefield pointed to a level of public disapproval as well as approval of female nurses in the war. Embedded in all the glowing depictions of female war
workers was the fear that women wanted to work in hospitals or near battlefields for less than admirable reasons.[42]

Military nursing was a controversial issue for even Northern women during
the Civil War. As Elizabeth Leonard notes, in the first year of the war many
women were held back from nursing by prejudice against female nurses and a
related lack of information about opportunities. Newspapers would not print
information about nursing opportunities because of the "dominant northern
middle-class public opinion that decent women . . . did not belong in the military in any capacity." Those who did try to become nurses "confronted impas-
sioned popular condemnation." Alice Fahs points out that negative attitudes toward female nurses permeated popular literature in the North in the first year
or so of the war. Mary Livermore "found everywhere . . . the greatest prejudice" against all female nurses other than nuns at the beginning of the conflict.
Virtually every historian of Civil War nursing has noted that Dorothea Dix's famous circular calling for female nurses to work in army hospitals included the
following requirements: "No women under thirty years of age need apply to
serve in government hospitals. All nurses are required to be very plain looking
women. Their dresses must be brown or black, with no bows, no curls, no jew-
elry, and no hoop skirts."[43] These requirements were an obvious attempt to address criticisms of female nursing in the war. By specifically ensuring that in the
wards there would be no pretty young women dressed to attract men, Dix
hoped to sever the old linkage between women and soldiers in which women
who associated with soldiers were assumed to be "camp followers"—probable
or actual prostitutes. The camp-follower image was not the only problem female nurses faced. There was also the criticism that respectable women were
not supposed to live unprotected among men; if they were not prostitutes, soldiers still could prey on their innocence. And finally, even if these women
avoided sexual corruption, exposure to the horrors of war could corrupt them
in other ways. Many feared that gentle and nurturing women either would be
out of place on the violent battlefields or they would successfully adapt to the
situation, but in so doing would lose their gentleness and femininity. Concerns
about the propriety of women nurses, while serious in the North, appear to
have been even more powerful in the South. Dix was appointed superintendent of female nurses of the Union army on 10 June 1861, less than two

months after the start of the war. The Confederacy did not grant its female nurses any official status until over a year later, when the Confederates were in a more desperate situation.[44]

Virtually all women who worked in the field, as well as many hospital nurses, had to struggle to be allowed to go to these places.[45] Clara Barton involved herself in informal relief work from the very start of the war, but faced considerable obstacles when she wanted to work as a field nurse. Barton, a member of an old and well-connected Massachusetts family and forty years old at the start of the war, first received permission to go to the field from Massachusetts governor John Andrews. But Andrews later revoked the permission, apparently after talking to a doctor who convinced him that women did not belong on battlefields. After a persistent letter-writing campaign, Barton finally received the permission she needed.[46]

Louisa May Alcott, Charlotte Forten, and the Chase sisters faced similar difficulties when starting their wartime careers. Alcott lost her first opportunity to nurse soldiers in May 1862. She had been chosen by the town of Concord, Massachusetts, to be part of a delegation to Port Royal, but then "word came that unmarried women were forbidden."[47] It took her another seven months to get approval to be an army nurse in a Washington hospital, but she did not last long there. She contracted typhoid pneumonia and had to leave after about six weeks. After her recovery, she made several more attempts to go south. In one letter, Alcott informed her friend Thomas Wentworth Higginson, the commander of a black regiment, that she "was no longer allowed to nurse the whites." She also explained that she had tried to go to the South Carolina Sea Islands as a teacher but was rejected because she "had no natural protector to go with me." She proceeded to ask Higginson if she could join his regiment as "a cook, a nurse or somewhat venerable 'child' of the regiment. . . . I am willing to enlist in any capacity."[48] Despite her efforts, Alcott never made it back to the South during the war. Charlotte Forten spent much of the summer of 1862 in the Boston area with letters of recommendation in hand, trying to get approval from the Port Royal Commission to go south and teach the freed slaves. Finally, the commission informed her that "they were not sending any women at present." Forten went back to stay with her relatives in Philadelphia. She then applied to their local Port Royal Commission and was soon on her way to South Carolina.[49] Sarah Chase was well aware of the stigma attached to nursing at the start of the Civil War. When she asked her father for permission to nurse soldiers, she assured him, "No one out of the family need know of my going." Her father gave her grudging approval: he did not seem happy with her decision, fearing she might be "exposed to danger and insults," but he was willing to accept her decision if she felt duty bound to go.[50] Even so, Sarah and her sister Lucy had to wait more than a year and a half longer before they received official permission to participate in the war effort.

If it had been up to Dorothea Dix, Cornelia Hancock would never have been a Civil War nurse. When she saw Hancock, a twenty-three-year-old with "rosy cheeks," Dix took one look and refused to approve her. But while Dix stood arguing the point with the ever persistent Eliza Farnham, who had brought Hancock with her, Hancock "settled the question herself" by jumping onto the train and refusing to move until it reached Gettysburg. Hannah Ropes, a fifty-three-year-old mother of two grown children, had little trouble passing Dorothea Dix's inspection, but Ropes refused to let her own twenty-one-year-old daughter, Alice, join her. While a matron in Washington's Union Hospital, she wrote to Alice that "it would not do for you to be here. It is no place for young girls. The surgeons are young and look upon nurses as their natural prey."[51] Although she was married, when twenty-eight-year-old physician Esther Hill Hawks traveled to Washington in 1861 to offer her services as a nurse, Dix refused to accept her because she was too young. It was only after Hawks's husband, John, went to Port Royal as a member of the Freedmen's Relief Association that she was able to go south. Because her husband was already there, it was not difficult for Hawks, a former teacher as well as a doctor, to get permission to join him and teach on the Sea Islands.[52]

After overcoming these initial hurdles, female war workers could still face considerable opposition. As a hospital matron, Hannah Ropes seems to have been in a constant power struggle with surgeons, stewards, and other male hospital officials who were unwilling to recognize that she had any authority in the hospital. Other women, such as Catherine Lawrence, Cornelia Hancock, Katherine Prescott Wormeley, and Jane Stewart Woolsey, noted similar problems in their journals and letters.[53] The propriety of females being war workers was also a frequent topic of discussion. For example, Cornelia Hancock was consistently plagued with complaints from her mother, sister, and concerned neighbors in her hometown of Salem, New Jersey, about her life as a field nurse. They were, in Hancock's words, in a "perfect panic about the 'way' I live." This controversy went on for months in Hancock's letters and died down somewhat only after townspeople read a laudatory article about her in the *New York Tribune* that stressed her "lady-like" nature and the soldiers' respect for her.[54] Sarah Rosetta Wakeman's decision to become a soldier disturbed her parents and her neighbors in New York a great deal. Obviously responding to their complaints, she wrote her parents: "I don't want you to mourn about me for I can take care of my self and I know my business as well as other folks know it for me. I will Dress as I am a mind to . . . and if they don't let me Alone they will be sorry for it." As much as she tried to ignore the criticisms, she obviously spent time thinking about them. Six months later, she told her parents, "I don't care anything about Coming home for I [am] ashamed to Come and sometimes think I will never go home in the world."[55]

Surprisingly, family and neighbors reacted quite similarly to Cornelia Hancock's work as a field nurse and to Wakeman's as a soldier. Wakeman's family and apparently the entire town knew that she was in the army, but no one informed on her; they simply gossiped and worried. Like Hancock's mother, Wakeman's parents tried to convince her to return home, telling her that the life was too dangerous and that her good reputation was at risk, but they tolerated her decision. They continued to write to her, to lecture her on proper behavior, and to accept the money she sent.[56] The similar treatment of Wakeman and Hancock reveals the extent to which women could use the ideology of redemptive womanhood to justify any action they took in the name of duty to family or country. The entrance of women into public war work—especially work that threw them into close contact with men—was controversial throughout the Civil War. Yet, like antebellum women in the public eye, these women were virtuous almost by default. They claimed to have such impeccable motives that other Northerners could not be certain they were immoral no matter what they did.

MOTHERS, SISTERS, AND SOLDIERS

All female war workers were quite conscious of public scrutiny of their morals and motives. These women understood themselves and described themselves to others in ways that reveal their attempts to refute criticisms directed at them and to situate themselves as redemptive woman. In their letters, conversations, and published accounts they constantly presented themselves as duty-bound, selfless, pious, moral, and patriotic women. Frequently, they described themselves as surrogate mothers or sisters to the soldiers, justifying their actions in terms of nonthreatening family roles.[57] Yet these women just as frequently portrayed themselves as soldiers or as soldierlike, regardless of whether they fought in any battles. Aware that aggressive women were threatening to many Americans, female war workers sometimes seemed apprehensive about appearing too aggressive, but in spite of this, they continued to depict themselves as both mothers and soldiers in many of their writings. As the war continued, the Northern public seemed to grow increasingly comfortable with women's presence in military hospitals and on battlefields. As one scholar puts it, "by late 1862 and 1863 an increasing number of Northern popular articles, illustrations, and stories reflected approvingly on women's nursing, which had been controversial earlier in the war."[58]

In C. W. Alexander's 1862 pamphlet novel, *Pauline of the Potomac*, written under the pseudonym Wesley Bradshaw, the heroine joins the war as a field nurse for the Union army and later becomes a spy. At one point when she is serving as a nurse, Pauline comforts a dying young man. In his delirium, he murmurs "Mother! mother!" smiles faintly, and dies. In *Angel of the Battle-Field*, published three years later, heroine Eleanor Poindexter has a similar encounter with a delirious dying young soldier, who cries out to her, "I knew you would come, mother! I've been praying for you to come all day! Kiss me mother!" She does kiss him, and immediately after this he dies quietly, "with a satisfied smile."[59] Almost every Civil War nurse who left letters, diaries, or a memoir of her experiences told of a similar event in which a dying soldier confused her with a female relative, usually his mother or sister.

In one of her postwar lectures, Clara Barton told of sitting up all night in the field with a dying young soldier. In his delirium, the soldier mistook Barton for his sister Mary. She knelt by him, kissed him, and let him sleep on her lap all night, though she noted that she could not bring herself to commit a direct lie by calling him "brother." The newspaper reviewers who attended Barton's lectures quoted from this story more consistently than from any other part of her speeches. For them, this was the most poignant moment of her lectures.[60] Hannah Ropes, Catherine Lawrence, and Mary Livermore all told similar stories of nursing delirious young men who confused them with their mothers. In Ropes's novel *Cranston House*, two wounded men confuse their heroic young nurse with the same woman, Sallie Cranston. Sallie is the beloved cousin and surrogate mother and sister to one of these men and the future wife of the other. Ropes later described a similar encounter in her own experience as a Civil War nurse, in which she comforted a delirious, dying young man who thought she was his mother.[61] Sarah Emma Edmonds related the sentimental story of a young man she knew, who, as he was dying, confused the nurse at his side with his mother: "Drawing her toward him with all his feeble power, he nestled his head in her arms, like a sleeping child, and thus died with the sweet word, 'Mother,' on his lips."[62]

Other nurses wrote that some soldiers called them Mother routinely, and frequently the nurses referred to soldiers as their boys or sons. Nurse Mary Bickerdyke was so commonly called Mother Bickerdyke that postwar biographers often referred to her that way rather than using her given name. Hannah Ropes called the soldiers under her care her "poor children." Harriet Hawley, who had traveled with the regiment of her soldier-husband as a nurse, wrote that after she returned to her home in Connecticut she was "homesick" to go back, explaining, "My 'boys' (for so we learn to call the soldiers) seem to call me constantly, from their beds of pain." Louisa May Alcott also routinely called sick and wounded soldiers her boys. In Mary Livermore's words, "As the soldiers were brought in, we fell into maternal relations with them as women instinctively do when brought into juxtaposition with weakness, and were soon addressing them individually as 'my son,' 'my boy,' or 'my child.'"[63]

Even as they described themselves and were described by others as surrogate mothers, wives, and sisters to the soldiers, the same women also portrayed themselves as soldiers fighting in the war. Cornelia Hancock wrote to her mother a few weeks after Gettysburg that she was now used to the "screams of agony" of wounded men because "soldiers take everything as it comes." A few weeks later, when she joked in a letter to her sister that she was in danger of being thrown into the guardhouse for being in camp before she was sworn in as a nurse, she remarked, "but that is only a part of soldiering if I am."[64] When field nurses described dressing wounds in the midst of battle, they stressed the danger they faced of being wounded or captured by the enemy. Invariably, women who wrote about experiences in battle described bullets whizzing by inches away from them.

Sarah Emma Edmonds wrote that while she was nursing soldiers during the first battle of Bull Run, one shot "struck my poor little flask of brandy which lay near me." At the end of the same battle, after she had eluded many more minnie balls, Edmonds found that she was alone. While she had been preoccupied with caring for the wounded, the rest of the army had retreated to Washington. Edmonds was forced to sneak back to Washington alone, a distance of more than twenty miles. On the journey, she was chased by rebels and narrowly escaped capture. Even after this, when she came upon a military hospital that had been deserted by the medical staff, she stayed and cared for the men, but they urged her to leave so she would not be captured. After bringing them fresh drinking water, she fled again and continued on her way to Washington, sick and exhausted. Edmonds risked both capture and death in battle in order to perform her duty. If this duty was to act as a surrogate sister or mother to the soldiers, it also required that she face the dangers of a soldier. Edmonds wrote that her conscience would not allow her to leave wounded soldiers to die of thirst in an abandoned hospital; she cared for them even at the risk of her life, although the medical staff had been unwilling to do so. Women, then, were needed on battlefields because their more-refined moral sensibilities would not allow them to desert the sick and wounded the way men, even doctors, had. Yet at the same time, women on the battlefield had to be like soldiers: brave and strong enough to endure the dangers they faced there. In this way, their duty as surrogate mothers, wives, and sisters turned them into soldiers.[65]

This understanding of female war workers—as both angels of mercy and fearless warriors—could be quite threatening. Sarah Emma Edmonds had good reason to gloss over the fact that she was a soldier disguised as a man when she wrote her autobiography, *Nurse and Spy in the Union Army*. But if Edmonds worried about public attitudes toward some of her most unconventional behavior, she could not have been excessively alarmed. She did relate numerous spying adventures, including one in which she disguised herself as a black male "contraband," and in the last part of the book she described some of her adventures as an "orderly" dressed in military attire.[66] One biographer of the famous actress and Union spy Pauline Cushman made a point of explaining to readers how female war workers could be both womanly and soldierlike at the same time:

> Dashing, charming, fearless, yet lady-like, she combines in herself all the daring of the soldier with the tenderness and modesty of the woman. Not one of the milk-and-water women of the day, whose only thought is of dress and amusement, but one of the women of old, whose soul was in their country's good and whose fearless, yet womanly, because *noble*, actions shall live forever.[67]

There was always a tension between these two images. The author's need to explain how a woman could be soldierlike and womanly at the same time suggested as much. Female violence was always problematic in this period, but it was not invariably condemned. Women's duty to work for the "country's good" could require just about anything. By identifying Cushman explicitly with republican virtue, the author implied that her soldierlike behavior was completely proper for a decent woman. He, like the antebellum debaters on woman's sphere, pointed out that the key to a woman's virtue was the purity of her motives. Cushman was noble and patriotic, in contrast to the typical women of the times, who were described as selfish and vain, concerned only with "dress and amusement." Those women had embraced the values of the market, while Cushman remained true to the republic.

Some female war workers were attached to regiments as "vivandieres."[68] These women, who did not disguise themselves as men, generally enlisted with soldier-husbands. They might work as regimental nurses, bear the regimental colors, and at times fight in battles. When Frank Moore compared one of these women, Bridget Divers, to both Joan of Arc and Florence Nightingale, he made one thing clear: if saint and angel were not easily separated, neither were warrior and nurse. Annie Etheridge was a vivandiere, or "daughter of the regiment," in at least three Michigan regiments, for a period of more than four years. According to Linus Brockett and Mary Vaughan in their history of women in the war, Etheridge worked primarily as a field nurse for her regiments, but when necessary she participated in battles. At the Battle of Spottsylvania, she saw Union soldiers retreating from the fight. She immediately went to stop them. She "expostulated with them, at last shamed them into doing their duty, by offering to lead them back into the fight, which she did under heavy fire." Brockett and Vaughan noted that this was not an unusual incident for Etheridge: "She had done the same thing more than once on other battlefields . . . by inspiring men to deeds of valor by her own example, her courage, and her presence of mind." Annie Etheridge's position as a vivandiere—living with strange men and participating in battles—"placed [her] in circumstances of peculiar moral peril," but, Brocket and Vaughan argued, "her goodness and purity of character were so strongly marked that she was respected and beloved . . . by all." The soldiers nicknamed her Gentle Annie. Yet even as the authors praised women like Annie Etheridge, they hinted at unresolved tensions. Their repeated defenses of Etheridge's morality implied that her status as a moral woman was under attack.[69]

If Annie Etheridge appeared to sidestep "moral peril" and reconcile her duties as a soldier and nurse, such tensions were not always easily glossed over. Frank Moore's biography of another vivandiere, Kady Brownell, who was attached to a Rhode Island regiment, reveals a more problematic picture. Moore related a story in which Brownell was nursing an unconscious wounded Confederate soldier. At first this seemed to be an example of selfless womanhood: a Union nurse who overlooked the fact that a man was an enemy because he was wounded and needed care. But the Confederate soldier soon woke up and began to swear at Brownell. She was so enraged that she leapt up and tried to stab him with a bayonet, "but as she was plunging the bayonet at his breast, a wounded Union soldier, who lay near, caught the point of it in his hand; remonstrated against killing a wounded enemy no matter what he said; and in her heart the woman triumphed and she spared him, ingrate that he was."[70] The apparent resolution of this story in the "triumph" of her woman's heart would hardly have masked for nineteenth-century readers the fact that Brownell had become so masculine—non-nurturing and consumed with selfish rage—that a man had to remind her not to stab a helpless wounded man to death. To Moore, Brownell had become a sort of double self in which the masculine side was gaining over the feminine, yet in the end he could only affirm her tender womanly heart, no matter what she did. Moore labeled her a redemptive woman because he was not certain she was truly evil. Nonetheless, his description of Brownell suggests that he had grave doubts about her character and found her extremely troubling.

Unlike Kady Brownell, Clara Barton was adroit at managing the tensions between female respectability and public action. From the very beginning of the war, Barton had fed and nursed soldiers in the Washington, D.C., area. She traveled home to Massachusetts to nurse her dying father in early 1862, and it was during that time that she made arrangements to become a battlefield nurse. On 20 March 1862, she wrote to Massachusetts governor John A. Andrew asking him for permission to go to Roanoke and "administer comfort to our brave men." Barton knew that the propriety of her request to travel alone with an army of men would be an issue. In addition to identifying herself with her "old Soldier father," she explained that, "If I know my own heart, I have none but right motives. I ask neither pay nor praise, simply a soldier's fare, and the sanction of Your Excellency." In closing, she added that more than forty of the young men she hoped to join in Roanoke were her former pupils.[71]

In this short letter, Barton naturalized her potentially unfeminine desire to work on battlefields by describing herself as the dutiful daughter of her soldier father, as well as a surrogate mother to the "boys" whose teacher she had been. She thus diffused arguments that she might be going for selfish reasons: to gain fame or glory, to meet a man, or to earn money. She positioned herself as a soldier as well as a surrogate mother. Apparently her arguments were convincing: by July 1862, she had managed to procure a pass to bring supplies and to nurse soldiers at Fredericksburg.[72]

Tender enough to care for soldiers and strong enough to withstand the horrors of the battlefield, Barton, like many late antebellum and Civil War fictional heroines, depicted herself as having the best qualities of both a man and a woman. Her letters, journals, and postwar speeches about her wartime experiences seem to be divided in precisely the same way: first, Barton asserted that she was fulfilling her womanly duty to nurture the sick and wounded, and second, she described herself as a soldier, constantly braving all sorts of dangers and living a life of excitement and daring. She was able to emphasize either her nurturing or her soldierly qualities according to the situation, yet both were always present. In her letters to friends, family, and the Northern women who sent her supplies, this sense of herself as a soldier came through quite clearly, although in letters to officials or in speeches to the general public after the war, she was much more guarded about calling herself a soldier. In those she tended to stress the more stereotypically feminine explanations for her motivations and actions.

In private letters to friends and family, Barton was unreserved about presenting herself as a soldier. In one 1863 letter to a friend, she wrote, "I am a *U.S. Soldier* you know and therefore not supposed to be susceptible to fear." Before she left for the field she had written in jest to her sister, "Well—here I am at War again. I knew t'would be so when I signed that treaty on the previous page. [She had promised on that page to stop writing about the war.] I'm as bad as England, the fight is in me, and I will find a pretext." Barton seemed at times desperate to take part in battle. She struggled for a year and a half after the war began to "find a pretext" to enter it, and when she finally succeeded, she appeared to exult in the danger she expected to face. Before her first trip to the field, she sent off a quick letter to her brother and sister-in-law. "I leave immediately for the Battlefield don't know when I can return," she wrote. "If anything happens to me you David must come and take all my effects home with you and Julia will know how to dispose of them."[73] This dramatic note conveyed a sense of a life so filled with important duties that she had no time for letter writing; the note communicated only feelings of danger, hurry, and excitement, rather than information.

Barton also frequently drew attention to her soldierlike bravery. In a letter to the commissioner of patents, she wrote, "It is not for those accustomed to face death twenty times a day, in nearly all possible shapes, to become appalled by the prospect of a little *future* want." On another occasion, she wrote to some friends, telling of her brushes with danger. While she and another female nurse were caring for the wounded, soldiers warned them that the arrival of Confederate troops was "imminent." The other nurse immediately left, supposedly to get stores, but Barton was not convinced by her excuse: "I knew *I* should *never leave a wounded man there* if I knew it, though I were taken prisoner forty times."[74] Here and elsewhere, Barton contrasted herself with "typical" women, asserting her bravery and fearlessness in the face of extreme danger. When duty called, she would stand firm. Yet she always asserted that as a woman she added something to the war effort that brave and fearless men could not: womanly nurture and care for the sick and wounded. Because she was performing her duty as a redemptive woman, she asserted that she remained within the bounds of female propriety, no matter how masculine her actions seemed.

For Civil War workers like Clara Barton, Hannah Ropes, Charlotte Forten, Cornelia Hancock, Louisa May Alcott, and Sarah Rosetta Wakeman, the war was the answer to their search for a more meaningful and challenging life. For other women, like Catherine Lawrence, Mary Ann Shadd Cary, Mary Livermore, Dorothea Dix, Eliza Farnham, Annie Wittenmyer, Harriet Jacobs, Sarah and Lucy Chase, Frances Gage, and Sojourner Truth, war work was the continuation of their earlier lives in public reform. All of these women created meaningful lives for themselves by becoming professional saviors. As one female abolitionist had written more than twenty years before the war, "The crisis *has* come when it would be sin for woman to stay at home and remain silent." The Civil War justified, and demanded, public action for large numbers of Northern women. They were, as Clara Barton later put it, the natural "nurses, consolers, and saviors of men."[75] When war came, these women were eager and able to tap into images of powerful, publicly active women, which had proliferated in the antebellum period.

When women like Clara Barton went into the field, depicting themselves as substitute mothers and sisters and also as soldiers, this space had already been carved out for them in literature and history. Historical and fictional nurses, soldiers, and spies were integral to and inseparable from the experiences of actual women who performed such work. There was Florence Nightingale, as well as American women like Hannah Ropes, who had gone to Kansas in 1854 to support the Free-Soilers and ended up nursing sick and wounded men. There was also the proliferation of literary accounts of women serving on the battlefield in one capacity or another. Clara Barton collected stories of heroic women, and Hannah Ropes created them. Writers like Maturin Murray Ballou and C. W. Alexander created fictional heroines who would go to any length to protect and save their families and the nation.

These literary accounts and the experiences of actual women were always intertwined. Mary Poovey has illustrated, once Florence Nightingale became famous, she had little control over others' representations of her. The myth of Nightingale as the gentle mother of the British army obscured Nightingale's own representation of herself as soldierlike. American women drew on literary narratives of women in battle to create a place for themselves in war. Women who served in the Civil War created their own narratives, fictional and nonfictional, of battlefield heroines, while writers of fictional accounts of women in battle drew on well-known accounts of real women in that situation. These fictional stories, as well as accounts of actual antebellum heroines, gave Northern women an ideology of redemptive womanhood that was remarkably assertive and public, encouraging them to participate in the Civil War in every imaginable domain.

Conclusion

The Legacies of Redemptive Womanhood

*I*n 1853, Thomas Wentworth Higginson, in an essay inscribed to the members of the Massachusetts Constitutional Convention, asserted that women should be allowed to vote and hold political office. As he put it: "In the disorder now sometimes exhibited at our caucuses and town-meetings, there is plainly an argument, not for the exclusion, but for the admission of women." According to Higginson, women's absence from formal politics had led to disorder in politics and government. The logical answer to this problem, he reasoned, was to bring women into politics: "Such is my faith in the moral power of woman, that I fear we cannot spare her from these scenes of temptation. . . . We need the feminine element in public affairs to make us better. . . . We need in our politics and our society a little more heart."[1] For Higginson, women were the answer to the nation's political problems. He was certain that women's inclusion in politics would bring order, morality, and even "heart" into government.

Higginson, like virtually all antebellum Americans, believed that women were more moral than men. And like an increasing number of Americans in the 1850s, he argued that this moral nature gave women a special duty to redeem the nation: they must participate in politics to make politics better. As Higginson's call suggests, the ideology of redemptive womanhood did not require a woman to be passive and submissive, but it did demand her virtue and selfless care of others. It did not preclude a woman from participating in a world beyond her home, nor did it stop her from performing any specific actions. In the antebellum era, women used their belief in woman's redemptive mission to justify any action they took, however public or assertive. In some ways, the effects of antebellum gender ideology on women's lives were the opposite of what one would expect. The rise and dominance of a gender system that rigidly divided women into two oppositional categories—good or evil, true or untrue—did *not* limit women to certain material spheres of action. Rather, the shift to a concept of gender that defined women by their essential nature, by their thoughts and motivations rather than their actions, freed women to imagine that any action they might perform could be proper as long as their motives were proper, that is, as long as they tried to nurture others or promote morality or religion.

Of course, even without material limitations on woman's sphere, such a gender ideology was, and still is, limiting in other ways. It can be limiting as well as empowering to think of oneself as a noble heroine or a martyr; it can be limiting to spend one's life attempting to be a pillar of moral authority. But as much as many current Americans prefer to link a limiting gender ideology with Victorianism or a long-ago past, these limits are not peculiar to the nineteenth century. America's gender system has shifted over the last century and a half, but it has not been destroyed. Numerous scholars have suggested that antebellum gender ideology was undermined and finally destroyed by the challenges posed to it by antebellum female reformers, and later by women's Civil War experiences. But the ideology of redemptive womanhood did not die out in or after the Civil War.

Women who were publicly active after the Civil War continued to justify their behavior by alluding to their special womanly redemptive nature, just as Maria W. Stewart, Abby Kelley, and the Grimké sisters had in the 1830s. As Kathryn Kish Sklar argues, in the late nineteenth century Americans shared "a vision of women as the embodiment of virtue within civil society," and female reformers in general used this powerful belief to justify their involvement in politics. Other scholars of the post–Civil War era have long noted that organizations such as the Women's Christian Temperance Union (WCTU) and the National American Woman Suffrage Association (NAWSA) and reformers such as Florence Kelley, Frances Willard, and Jane Addams justified their political activism in terms of women's special mission to make society better. The WCTU, founded in 1874, soon became the largest women's organization in the world. Its first president, Annie Wittenmyer, a Midwesterner like many of the WCTU's founding members, was already well known in the region for her work in the Civil War with the Iowa Sanitary Commission and her postwar work founding soldiers' orphans' homes.[2] For her, the temperance crusade was just one more part of women's special mission to redeem society.

Under the leadership of its second president, Frances Willard, the WCTU quickly expanded to address other political issues as well as temperance on the grounds of women's special moral mission to protect families and society. The organization argued for woman's suffrage by calling for the "Home Protection Ballot."[3] Women needed the vote, they argued, in order to fulfill their duty to protect their families physically, morally, and spiritually.

On an individual level, virtually all nineteenth-century women active in politics and reform work shared this notion of redemptive womanhood. Nancy Cott points out that female suffragists and other female reformers agreed until the 1910s that women's presence in politics would be marked by their "nurturant service and moral uplift." Jane Addams, who founded Hull House in 1889, was by the early twentieth century the most famous woman in the nation. Throughout her career, Addams justified women's involvement in politics and reform organizations as part of a proper woman's duty to society: their activities were "legitimate" forms of "municipal housekeeping and political extensions of motherhood."[4] She laid out a detailed justification for this belief in her book on women's relief work and peace activism in World War I, *Peace and Bread in Time of War.* There she argued that women had been the world's "first agriculturists." Woman's "desire to grow food for her children led to a fixed abode, and to the beginning of a home, from which our domestic morality and customs are supposed to have originated." Such developments, Addams suggested, created a particular type of woman: the moral "fostering Mother."

For Addams, political participation was a natural and necessary expansion of the duties of the fostering mother. She asserted that "women entered into politics when clean milk and the premature labor of children became factors in public life." The international food shortages of World War I, she claimed, demanded that women also enter international politics, as "international affairs . . . at last were dealing with such human and poignant matters as food for starving people who could only be fed through international activities." Women in international politics were not out of "woman's sphere"; they were simply acting on their traditional role as fostering mothers.[5] The notion that women needed to be politically active to redeem society was accepted almost without question in late-nineteenth-century America; Addams and other women used the idea, as they had since the 1830s, to justify their participation in politics.

But this consensus on women's redemptive nature did not last forever. Jane Addams was deeply troubled by the new women of the flapper generation, who she believed privileged their individual "desire over and above any notion of civic responsibility." That is, they were more concerned with personal, self-in-terested goals than with making the world a better place. The sexually expres-sive and fun-loving flapper, scholars suggest, had her origins in the white urban working classes, both immigrant and native born. The quintessential flapper movie, the 1927 silent comedy *IT*, explicitly contrasted the sexually expressive working-class flapper heroine with two older images of womanhood: the depen-dent and sexually passive upper-class woman (the heroine's rival), and the inde-pendent, middle-class, asexual female "welfare workers" who tried to impose their moral judgment on the heroine. The trend of the new self-expressive flap-per soon spread, with the help of movies and advertising, to include middle-class and suburban whites.[6] The self-expressive new woman, who cast off notions of female moral superiority in favor of the pursuit of fun, had political as well as cultural manifestations. As Nancy Cott notes, by the 1910s a younger generation of female reformers, whom she calls feminists, discarded the notion that women had a special moral mission in political life. Women like Alice Paul and Harriot Stanton Blatch abandoned the traditional argument that women needed the vote to make society a better place, asserting instead that women should get the vote simply because they are equal to men and deserve equal rights.[7]

In addition to these new models of white womanhood, another "new woman" arose in the African American community in the 1920s. The "new Ne-gro" of the Harlem Renaissance was a model for both men and women. Ac-cording to the intellectuals of the Harlem Renaissance, the new Negro was "primarily an artist"—and a particular type of artist. As African American soci-ologist Robert Park had it, "the real Negro . . . was 'an artist, loving life for its own sake.'" According to W. E. B. DuBois, new Negroes' art would contain, "a certain spiritual joyousness; a sensuous tropical love of life, in vivid contrast to the cool and cautious New England reason." As writers, they tackled "un-seemly" topics; as musicians they played jazz and sang the blues.[8] African American women were important figures in this new vision of artistic blackness, particularly in music. As Amiri Baraka points out, "the great classic blues singers were women." In this context, women like Ma Rainey and Bessie Smith became idealized symbols of African American womanhood.[9] The African American new woman, like the flapper, was extremely physically independent and self-expres-sive; she too was a reaction against older notions of women as moral, passive, and dependent. But in addition to being independent and self-expressive, she was also described as physically powerful. This focus on physical strength was built on stereotypes of black women that developed in slavery, particularly that of the an-tebellum black "Mammy," who "was the woman who could do anything and do it better than anyone else."[10] This African American new woman seemed larger than life, stronger and not at all like "respectable" white women.

Whether black or white, well-to-do or poor, the vast majority of nineteenth-century American women who left printed records embraced a belief that women were the moral and religious foundation of American society. Maria W. Stewart, Mary Ann Shadd Cary, Harriet Jacobs, Harriet Wilson, Hannah Crafts, Frances Watkins Harper, and Charlotte Forten Grimké, as well as virtually all the editors and contributors to the antebellum black press in the United States and Canada, asserted that African Americans were capable of morality and respectability and that virtue was, or could be, embodied in their women. African American women, freeborn and former slaves, middle-class and working-class, did participate in the development of mainstream nineteenth-century gender identities. Yet African American and working-class women continue to be marked as outside the dominant gender ideology and hence excluded from the main narrative of American women's history. Much of this stems from the cultural shift of the 1920s to an emphasis on the physical and cultural differences between black and white, middle-class and working-class women.

New women—from first-wave white middle-class feminists to self-expressive working-class flappers and African American female blues singers—did not replace the more traditional female reformers. Instead, from the 1920s to the 1960s, the ideals of "liberated" women existed in tension with older notions of moral womanhood. Even today, the idea that women are more moral than men has not disappeared inside or outside of feminist circles. Scholars from Carol Gilligan to Elizabeth Fox-Genovese have stressed women's differences from men in terms of women's moral nature and their duty to nurture—referring, for example, to "women's special responsibility for children."[11] Nonfeminists and antifeminists, such as ERA opponent Phyllis Schlafly, also have appealed to women's essential difference from men. According to Schlafly, a "Positive Woman cannot defeat a man in a . . . boxing match, but she can motivate him, inspire him, encourage him, teach him, restrain him, reward him, and have power over him that he can never achieve over her with all his muscle." Schlafly has celebrated women's moral influence over men as a core element in her call for a return to so-called traditional gender roles.[12]

By the 1920s, the notion that women are more moral, nurturing, and religious than men was no longer an unquestioned assumption; it had become a topic of heated debate. This debate has flared up a number of times, most notably in the 1960s, and it continues to this day. Yet the ideology of redemptive womanhood has never died. Because it developed hand in hand with a market-oriented society in the United States, we should not expect that its death is imminent, even in an age of women's personal freedom and references to broken glass ceilings. The ideology of redemptive womanhood was and is a way Americans have coped with their desire to maintain a virtuous republic—a moral society—in a market-oriented world.[13]

Although the issue of women's ability to lecture in public and to work as hospital nurses was resolved, at least partially, in the North by the end of the Civil War, Americans' attempts to understand a woman's actions through her nurturing, moral, and religious nature remain common. As a recent article in *Time* magazine has it, women have begun to earn top executive positions in the airline industry because of that industry's new appreciation of the value of their "feminine" qualities: "Airline CEOs say that while many of their male managers have emphasized hardware and thought of their job as moving planes efficiently from place to place, women executives seem to understand more clearly that they are in a service business—and that happy workers make for happy customers."[14] As the airlines' leaders see it, women are more caring and nurturing than men, and thus better suited to keeping workers and customers happy. The assumptions about women's appropriate sphere continue even now: if the job had remained merely one of "moving planes efficiently," the airlines would have had no reason to hire women as managers. Airline CEOs feel it is necessary to explain why women are now suited for these jobs.

Herein lies one of the limits of redemptive womanhood for today: in 1830, when many Americans would criticize a woman for giving public lectures, performing wage work, participating in formal politics, or attending college, women's opportunities to engage in such activities were extremely limited. Women used the ideology of redemptive womanhood and played on nineteenth-century beliefs about women's differences from men to justify their entrance into public life. Far from attempting to challenge or destroy the ideals of redemptive womanhood, women used this ideology to expand their educational, career, and political opportunities immensely over the course of the nineteenth and twentieth centuries. In this context, the limits the ideology imposed on women were far less confining than they are now.[15] Today women have equal access to higher education; they vote and are elected to political office; they work in virtually all career fields. While gender inequalities still exist, few formal legal barriers remain against women's full participation in public life. Yet the movement of women into male-dominated jobs continues to be justified with reference to women's caring or moral nature.

It is troubling that after nearly two hundred years, we still are asking exactly the same question about women in public life: does this woman belong in this particular public space? Much has changed in these debates since 1865: an increased preoccupation with biological difference and normative sexuality, and the privileging of scientific knowledge over moral and religious knowledge in the twentieth century have altered the debates in ways I cannot begin to do justice to without writing another book. Yet women still find themselves in a defensive position in the public sphere.

Frequently we hear in the mainstream media that America has lost its family values, that American society is in a period of moral decline. Such fears are curiously reminiscent of the anxieties of Americans in the 1820s and 1830s: they too feared that social change was destroying families and communities. For many, their old social system, which relied heavily on kinship ties, social policing, and an ideal of republican virtue in public life, no longer seemed to function in the new, market-oriented society. Young men, they feared, would flee to cities to avoid marrying their pregnant lovers. Parents worried that they could not watch over the virtue of their daughters or sons who left home to work in factories. Native-born Americans feared immigration would lead to the decline of American wages and values. Slavery seemed to be destroying the families and morality of both slaves and slave owners. Where would morality lie in a society that seemed to revel in unbridled greed and self-interest? In the 1830s, the answer was that morality would lie in women. Moral women would protect this new, market-oriented society from ruin. Most white middle-class Americans believed that these moral women would generally be white middle-class women, but American women from other backgrounds also embraced the ideology.

But this ideal of a gender-balanced moral economy was never completely satisfying to begin with, and it became considerably less satisfying over time for two reasons. First, it gave women precisely the power to engage in the public sphere that it seemed to deny them. Second, after a time it could be seen as doing little more than effecting a gendered hypocrisy: a marriage of bad men and good women, which did not seem to be making men, or the world, any better. This became particularly apparent after 1920 when women gained the right to vote but the United States did not become a more moral place as a result.

If the 1920s began to call into question the solution for preserving a moral society that was worked out in the antebellum era, the social movements of the 1960s further undermined this gender-based moral economy. If women now had the same relationship to the market as men, many Americans feared that women could not remain moral. Civil rights forced whites to stop excluding other racial or ethnic groups from participation in society, but many whites still believed nonwhites were less moral and feared society itself would become less moral with this expansion of membership. If everyone became a full and equal participant in the amoral market society, where could morality lie? These questions are still unresolved today.

Fears of societal decay, today as in the 1830s, are fears about capitalism, fears that the values of the marketplace—self-interest and profit taking—will replace all other values. Since the antebellum era, fears about the marketplace have almost overwhelmingly been articulated as threats to the family, and the family has been closely linked to women. This highly gendered language about family, marriage, and illicit sexuality reveals how closely our gender, economic, and so-cial systems were and are still intertwined. This is why, for example, discussions of civil rights so often turn into conversations about interracial sex: gender is the language through which Americans understand their social system. Sexual relationships, perceived or real, between black men and white women are still symbolic, for many whites, of the moral corruption of the virtuous nation.

Because Americans have not yet resolved how to ensure the existence of a moral society in the modern world, woman's nature and her sphere are once again at the center of public discussion. If publicly lecturing women, female criminals, and Civil War workers were at the center of controversy in the nine-teenth century, feminists and feminism are in a similar spot today. Current at-tacks on feminism and confusion surrounding the meanings of feminism are in-dicative of larger debates over the meanings of womanhood in American society. In both eras, women's behavior has been read as a sign of the fragmen-tation and destruction of the nation—and as its only hope for redemption.

Almost one hundred fifty years ago, Thomas Wentworth Higginson argued that women were more moral, "better" than men; therefore, if they participated in politics they would make politics better; they would give it "heart." At the beginning of the twenty-first century, when the major airlines had trouble with customer relations and worker morale, they too decided they need more heart. And like Higginson, they believed that caring, compassionate women, this time in managerial positions, were the answer to their problems. The problem with this reasoning—in 1853 and in 2002—is that it assumes men are self-interested and individualistic. For both Higginson and the airline CEOs, women *are* morality. According to this line of thinking, if women are not different from men, morality itself seems to disappear from the social order. The only ques-tion this lets us ask about women (and men) is, "Are women self-interested like men, or are they better than men?" It is time for us to interrogate the question itself, as well as the larger cultural and economic systems that brought this question into being in the first place.

Notes

Introduction:
Angels, Devils, and Redemptive Womanhood

1. *The Early Life and Complete Trial of Mary, Alias Polly Bodine* (New York: n.p., 1846), 5, 16, 17.

2. "Reminiscences of Mrs Abby Kelley Foster," *Woman's Journal*, 7 February 1891, 42; Sarah Baker for the Dorchester Female Anti-Slavery Society to Abby Kelley for the Lynn Female Anti-Slavery Society, 31 May 1838, Abby Kelley Foster Papers, American Antiquarian Society, Worcester, Massachusetts. On this general point, see James Stewart, *Holy Warriors: The Abolitionists and American Slavery* (New York: Hill and Wang, 1976).

3. George G. Foster, *New York by Gas-light and Other Urban Sketches* (1850; reprint, Berkeley: University of California Press, 1993), 131.

4. Caroline Dall, *Women's Right to Labor; or, Low Wages and Hard Work* (Boston: Walker, Wise, and Co., 1860), reprinted in *Low Wages and Great Sins: Two Antebellum Views on Prostitution and the Working-Girl*, ed. David Rothman and Sheila Rothman (New York: Garland, 1987), 25, 29–30.

5. *Newark Daily Advertiser*, 8 October 1851.

6. Carolyn Lawes makes exactly this point about current scholarship, specifically in reference to the concept of separate spheres: that is, the idea that Americans could clearly distinguish between proper and improper women by ascertaining whether they were inside or outside the woman's sphere. Carolyn Lawes, *Women and Reform in a New England Community, 1815–1860* (Lexington: University of Kentucky Press, 2000), 2n2, 189–90.

7. Barbara Welter, "The Cult of True Womanhood, 1820–1860," *American Quarterly* 16 (1966): 152.

8. On perceptions of antebellum working women as outside the ideology of true womanhood, see Gerda Lerner, "The Lady and the Mill Girl: Changes in the Status of Women in the Age of Jackson, 1800–1840," *Midcontinent American Studies Journal* 10 (1969): 5–15; Christine Stansell, *City of Women: Sex and Class in New York, 1789–1860* (Urbana: University of Illinois Press, 1982); Alice Kessler-Harris, *Out to Work: A History of Wage-Earning Women in the United States* (New York: Oxford University Press, 1982); Karen V. Hansen, *A Very Social Time: Crafting Community in Antebellum New England* (Berkeley: University of California Press, 1994); Mary Blewett, *Men, Women, and Work: Class, Gender, and Protest in the New England Shoe Industry, 1780–1910* (Urbana: University of Illinois Press, 1988), 69, 78–96, especially 78 and 92–93; and Lyde Cullen Sizer, *The Political Work of Northern Women Writers and the Civil War, 1850–1872* (Chapel Hill: University of North Carolina Press, 2000), 10–11.

On African American women as outside the ideology, see, for example, Paula Giddings, *When and Where I Enter: The Impact of Black Women on Race and Sex in America* (1984; reprint, New York: Bantam, 1996), 47; Julie Roy Jeffrey, *The Great Silent Army of Abolitionism: Ordinary Women in the Antislavery Movement* (Chapel Hill: University of North Carolina Press, 1998), 179, 182; James Oliver Horton and Lois E. Horton, *In Hope of Liberty: Culture, Community, and Protest among Northern Free Blacks, 1700–1860* (New York: Oxford University Press, 1997), 74, 147; Hazel Carby, *Reconstructing Womanhood: The Emergence of the Afro-American Woman Novelist* (New York: Oxford University Press, 1987), 59–61; Shirley Yee, *Black Women Abolitionists: A Study in Activism, 1828–1860* (Knoxville: University of Tennessee Press, 1992), 156; Jean Fagan Yellin, *Women and Sisters: The Antislavery Feminists in American Culture* (New Haven, Conn.: Yale University Press, 1989), 78, 96; Elizabeth Raul Bethel, *The Roots of African American Identity: Memory and History in Antebellum Free Communities* (New York: St. Martin's Press, 1997), 170; and Sizer, *Political Work of Northern Women Writers*, 11.

9. On antebellum gender ideology as a white ideology that did not suit the needs of African Americans who tried to fit into it, see Yee, *Black Women Abolitionists*, 4, 54; Maria W. Stewart, *Maria W. Stewart: America's First Black Woman Political Writer*, ed. Marilyn Richardson (Bloomington: Indiana University Press, 1987), 22; Dorothy Sterling, ed., *We are Your Sisters: Black Women in the Nineteenth Century* (New York: W. W. Norton, 1984), x–xi, xiii; James Oliver Horton, "Freedom's Yoke: Gender Conventions among Antebellum Free Blacks," *Feminist Studies* 12, no. 1 (1986): 60, 64, 70, and *Free People of Color: Inside the African American Community* (Washington, D.C.: Smithsonian Institution Press, 1993), 95; Jeffrey, *Great Silent Army*, 192; and Jacqueline Jones Royster, *Traces of a Stream: Literacy and Social Change among African American Women* (Pittsburgh: University of Pittsburgh Press, 2000), 180.

10. Lori Ginzberg, *Women and the Work of Benevolence: Morality, Politics, and Class in the Nineteenth-Century United States* (New Haven, Conn.: Yale University Press, 1990), 2–3, and Jeffrey, *Great Silent Army*, 6–7. U.S. history textbooks that demonstrate this understanding include Mary Beth Norton and Ruth M. Alexander, eds., *Major Problems in American Women's History*, 2nd ed. (Lexington, Mass.: D.C. Heath, 1996), 108; Nancy Woloch, *Women and the American Experience: A Concise History*, 2nd ed. (Boston: McGraw Hill, 2002), 71–77; Edward L. Ayers, Lewis Gould, David Oshinsky, and Jean Soderland, *American Passages: A History of the United States*, vol. 1 (Fort Worth, Tex.: Harcourt, 2000), 318–19. For some recent works that continue to use the separate spheres concept, see Sizer, *Political Work of Northern Women Writers*, 10–11; Catherine E. Kelly, *In the New England Fashion: Reshaping Women's Lives in the Nineteenth Century* (Ithaca, N.Y.: Cornell University Press, 1999); and John F. Marszalek, *The Petticoat Affair: Manners, Mutiny, and Sex in Andrew Jackson's White House* (Baton Rouge: Louisiana State University Press, 2000 [1997]) 53. For a recent popular account of nineteenth-century gender ideology as confining and repressive, see Rene Denfeld, *The New Victorians: A Young Woman's Challenge to the Old Feminist Order* (New York: Warner Books, 1995), 133. According to Denfeld, the "ideal of feminine spiritual purity was used effectively against women in the Victorian era; they were told that, for [women] . . . prayer was the only appropriate means of improving the world."

11. On this point for Southern middle- and upper-class women, see Elizabeth Varon, *We Mean to Be Counted: White Women and Politics in Antebellum Virginia* (Chapel Hill: University of North Carolina Press, 1998), 1, 101; and for Northern middle-class women in Worcester, Massachusetts, see Lawes, *Women and Reform*, 191n5. Years earlier, Nancy Hewitt noted that, even within the white middle class, women shared no single notion of woman's sphere because of differences in their material conditions. That Hewitt could find three different notions of woman's sphere, of woman's appropriate locations and behaviors, inside a single middle-class community suggests the limited usefulness of the concept of woman's sphere as a physical or geographical boundary. Nancy Hewitt, "Beyond the Search for Sisterhood: American Women's History in the 1980s," *Social History* 10 (October 1985): 315, and *Women's Activism and Social Change: Rochester, New York, 1822–1872* (Ithaca, N.Y.: Cornell University Press, 1984). Linda Kerber also points out the indeterminacy of historians' definitions of separate spheres, but retains the idea that the geographical or behavioral boundaries of woman's sphere might be known at a specific time and place. Linda Kerber, "Separate Spheres, Female Worlds, Woman's Place: The Rhetoric of Women's History," *Journal of American History* 75 (1988): 9–39.

12. On the active nature of protagonists of domestic novels, see, for example, Mary Kelley, "The Sentimentalists: The Promise and Betrayal of the Home," *Signs* 4, no. 3 (1979): 434–46; David S. Reynolds, "The Feminization Controversy: Sexual Stereotypes and the Paradoxes of Piety in Nineteenth-Century America," *New England Quarterly* 53, no. 1 (1980): 96–106; Myra Jehlen, "The Family Militant: Domesticity versus Slavery in Uncle Tom's Cabin," *Criticism* 31, no. 3 (1989): 383–400, especially 390; and Jane Tompkins, *Sensational Designs: The Cultural Work of American Fiction, 1790–1860* (New York: Oxford University Press, 1985). On histories of women, see Nina Baym, *American Women Writers and the Work of History, 1790–1860* (New Brunswick, N.J.: Rutgers University Press, 1995), and Mary Kelley, "Designing a Past for the Present: Women Writing Women's History in Nineteenth-Century America," *Proceedings of the American Antiquarian Society* 105, part 2 (1995): 314–46.

13. Nancy Cott, *The Bonds of Womanhood: 'Woman's Sphere' in New England, 1780–1835* (New Haven, Conn.: Yale University Press, 1977), 140.

14. Ruth Bloch, "The Gendered Meanings of Virtue in Revolutionary America," *Signs* 13, no. 1 (1987): 37–58. On republican motherhood or wifehood, see also Linda Kerber, *Women of the Republic: Intellect and Ideology in Revolutionary America* (New York: Norton, 1980), and Jan Lewis, "The Republican Wife," *William and Mary Quarterly* 44 (October 1987): 689–721. On the connection between republican motherhood and antebellum gender ideology, see Bloch, "Gendered Meanings," 57–58; Jeanne Boydston, *Home and Work: Housework, Wages, and the Ideology of Labor in the Early Republic* (New York: Oxford University Press, 1990), 56–57; and Stansell, *City of Women*, 20–22.

15. I have taken my definition of *market society* from Amy Dru Stanley's article, "Home Life and the Morality of the Market." Stanley uses C. B. Macpherson's notion that "where labour has become a market commodity, market relations so shape and permeate all social relations that it may properly be called a market society, not merely a market economy." C. B. Macpherson, *The Political Theory of Possessive Individualism:*

Hobbes to Locke (New York: Oxford University Press, 1962), 272, quoted in Amy Dru Stanley, "Home Life and the Morality of the Market," in *The Market Revolution in America: Social, Political, and Religious Expressions, 1800–1880*, ed. Melvyn Stokes and Stephen Conway (Charlottesville: University Press of Virginia, 1996), 75.

16. Ted Steinberg, "Down to Earth: Nature, Agency, and Power in History," *American Historical Review* 107 (June 2002): 807–808. See also the discussion of antiprostitution reformers' concern for young women in rural areas in chapter 2 of this book.

17. Historians since Gilbert Barnes have linked antebellum reform to a sense of moral and religious crisis in American society. Gilbert Barnes, *The Anti-Slavery Impulse: 1830–1844* (New York: Appleton-Century, 1933). See, for example, Whitney R. Cross, *The Burned-Over District: The Social and Intellectual History of Enthusiastic Religion in Western New York, 1800–1850* (Ithaca, N.Y.: Cornell University Press, 1950); Clifford Griffin, *Their Brothers' Keepers: Moral Stewardship in the United States* (New Brunswick, N.J.: Rutgers University Press, 1960), x, 44, 177; and Stewart, *Holy Warriors*, 44–45. Recently scholars have argued that reform movements were more popular in the antebellum South than historians had previously suggested. See, for example, Douglas Carlson, "'Drinks He to His Own Undoing': Temperance Ideology in the Deep South," *Journal of the Early Republic* 18, no. 4 (1998): 659–91.

18. Thomas Wentworth Higginson, *Woman and Her Wishes; an Essay: Inscribed to the Massachusetts Constitutional Convention* (Boston: R. F. Wallcut, 1853), 24.

19. On the link between moral womanhood and the amoral market-oriented man, see Brian Roberts, *American Alchemy: The California Gold Rush and Middle-Class Culture* (Chapel Hill: University of North Carolina Press, 2000), 224–30, and E. Anthony Rotundo, *American Manhood: Transformations in Masculinity from the Revolution to the Modern Era* (New York: Basic Books, 1993), 22–25. On the relationship between the nineteenth-century true woman and the self-made man, see especially Barbara Welter, "The Cult of True Womanhood," 151–52; Nancy Cott, "Passionlessness: An Interpretation of Victorian Sexual Ideology, 1790–1850," in *A Heritage of Her Own: Toward a New Social History of American Women*, ed. Nancy Cott and Elizabeth Pleck (New York: Simon & Schuster, 1979), 162–81; Carroll Smith-Rosenberg, "The Beauty, the Beast and the Militant Woman," in *Disorderly Conduct: Visions of Gender in Victorian America* (New York: Oxford University Press, 1985), 109–128; and Mary Ryan, *Cradle of the Middle Class: The Family in Oneida County, New York, 1790–1865* (New York: Cambridge University Press, 1981), 146–55.

20. Editorial, *Colored American*, 14 September 1839, quoted in Horton, "Freedom's Yoke," 53.

21. Boydston, *Home and Work*, 142–63; Roberts, *American Alchemy*, 69–118, 169–95.

22. Stanley, "Home Life and the Morality of the Market," 78. On the concept of the deputy husband and her role in the colonial era, see Laurel Thatcher Ulrich, *Good Wives: Image and Reality in the Lives of Women in Northern New England, 1650–1750* (New York: Oxford University Press, 1980). On gold-rush women taking over their husband's roles, see Roberts, *American Alchemy*, 87–90. On the increasing distance in relations between employers and employees, see Ryan, *Cradle of the Middle Class;* Paul Johnson, *A Shopkeeper's Millennium: Society and Revivals in Rochester, New York, 1815–1837*

(New York: Hill and Wang, 1978); Sean Wilentz, *Chants Democratic: New York City and the Rise of the American Working Class* (New York: Oxford University Press, 1984); and Stuart Blumin, *The Emergence of the Middle Class: Social Experience in the American City, 1760–1900* (New York: Cambridge University Press, 1989).

23. *New York Courier and Enquirer*, 11 June 1830, quoted in William Randall Waterman, *Frances Wright*, (New York: Columbia University, 1924), 186. See also Blanche Glassman Hersh, *The Slavery of Sex: Feminist-Abolitionists in America* (Urbana: University of Illinois Press, 1978), 136.

24. Donald H. Meyer, *The Instructed Conscience: The Shaping of the American National Ethic* (Philadelphia: University of Pennsylvania Press, 1972), 72, 76.

25. "Religion in Woman," *Colored American*, 24 November 1838.

26. Meyer, *Instructed Conscience*, 80, 143, 51, 85–86; David Brion Davis has also noted antebellum Americans' obsession with moral certainty. David Brion Davis, *Homicide in American Fiction, 1798–1860: A Study in Social Values* (Ithaca, N.Y.: Cornell University Press, 1957), 12.

27. Historians have long noted that women were generally considered more moral and religious than men in the antebellum era. See, for example, Smith-Rosenberg, "Beauty"; Ginzberg, *Women and the Work of Benevolence*, 11–12; Catherine A. Brekus, "Let Your Women Keep Silence in the Churches: Female Preaching and Evangelical Religion in America, 1740–1845" (Ph.D. diss., Yale University, 1993), 178; Yee, *Black Women Abolitionists*, 114–15; and Nancy Hewitt, "Feminist Friends: Agrarian Quakers and the Emergence of Woman's Rights in America," *Feminist Studies* 12 (spring 1986): 27–49, 29.

28. Mary Beth Norton, *Founding Mothers and Fathers: Gendered Power and the Forming of American Society* (New York: Alfred A. Knopf, 1996), 404–5. On the privatization of women in the eighteenth century, see also Ulrich, *Good Wives*, 48–50.

29. Jonathan Sterns, *Rev. Mr. Sterns' Discourse on Female Influence, and the True Christian Mode of Its Exercise* (Newburyport, Mass.: John G. Tilton, 1837), 23, 9, 10, 12.

30. "What Have Women to Do with Slavery?" *Liberator*, 1 November 1839, 174.

31. Varon, *We Mean to Be Counted*, 101. Julie Roy Jeffrey also mentions that by 1856, "in New York State, women comprised half those attending [Republican party] rallies." Jeffrey, *Great Silent Army*, 169. See also Glenna Matthews, *The Rise of Public Woman: Woman's Power and Woman's Place in the United States, 1630–1970* (New York: Oxford University Press, 1992), 118–19; and Melanie Susan Gustafson, *Women and the Republican Party, 1854–1924* (Urbana: University of Illinois Press, 2001).

32. Kessler-Harris, *Out to Work*, chapters 3 and 4, esp. 50–52, 75.

33. Blewett, *Men, Women, and Work*, 78, 92–93.

34. Yellin, *Women and Sisters*, 87; Carby, *Reconstructing Womanhood*, 30–32; and Yee, *Black Women Abolitionists*, 156.

35. See in particular Yee, *Black Women Abolitionists*, 4, 40, 54, 58–59; Stewart, *Maria W. Stewart* (edited by Marilyn Richardson), 22; Horton, "Freedom's Yoke," 60, 64, 70; and Sterling, ed., *We Are Your Sisters*, x–xi, xiii.

36. Nell Irvin Painter, *Sojourner Truth: A Life, a Symbol* (New York: W. W. Norton, 1996), 257–63. On the exceptional nature of antebellum female lecturers,

see Nancy Cott, *The Bonds of Womanhood;* Hewitt, "Feminist Friends," 28–29; Smith-Rosenberg, "Beauty"; and Yellin, *Women and Sisters,* 26, 94, 154. By linking women like Sojourner Truth, Maria Stewart, the Grimkés, and Abby Kelley Foster to a tradition of female preachers, Catherine Brekus and Nell Painter have argued that antebellum female lecturers were not as exceptional as historians have portrayed them to be. Painter, *Sojourner Truth,* 72–73; Brekus, "Let Your Women Keep Silence," 12, 202, 318–19.

37. As Suzanne Lebsock has pointed out, black and white women might have shared a "distinctive women's value system or culture" even where there were no communicative bonds between them. Suzanne Lebsock, *Free Women of Petersburg: Status and Culture in a Southern Town* (New York: W. W. Norton, 1985), xix.

38. Horton and Horton, *In Hope of Liberty,* xii.

39. Horton, "Freedom's Yoke," 58.

40. On this growing sense of crisis, see William Appleman Williams, *The Contours of American History* (1966; reprint, New York: Norton, 1988), 270–76, 285–90; Michael Paul Rogin, *Fathers and Children: Andrew Jackson and the Subjugation of the American Indian* (1975; reprint, New Brunswick, N.J.: Transaction Publishers, 1991), 296–313; and David Potter, *The Impending Crisis, 1848–1861* (New York: Harper and Row, 1976).

41. Jesse Clement, *Noble Deeds of American Women,* new edition revised (Auburn and Buffalo, N.Y.: Miller, Orton & Mulligan, 1854; original edition published in 1851).

42. Henry Nash Smith, *Virgin Land: The American West as Symbol and Myth* (Cambridge, Mass.: Harvard University Press, 1950), 87–88. Maturin Murray Ballou [pseud. Lieutenant Murray], *Fanny Campbell, the Female Pirate Captain: A Tale of the Revolution* (1844; reprint, Boston: F. Gleason, 1845). On Civil War soldier Sarah Emma Edmonds's account of reading *Fanny Campbell,* see Betty Fladeland, "Alias Frank Thompson," *Michigan History* 42, no. 3 (1958): 436.

1: "Drunk with Murderous Longing"

1. *Narrative and Confessions of Lucretia P. Cannon* (New York: E. E. Barclay, 1841. The identical quote is also in William H. Jackson, *The Life and Confession of Sophia Hamilton* (Fredrickton, N.B.: n.p., 1845), 5; and Ann Walters, *Confession of Ann Walters, the Murderess* (Boston: Printed for the Proprietor, 1850), 3.

2. John D. Lawson, ed., "The Trial of Bathsheba Spooner . . . for the Murder of Joshua Spooner," *American State Trials,* ed. John D. Lawson, vol. 2 (St. Louis: Thomas Law Books, 1914), 189–91. *The Last Words and Dying Speech of Ezra Ross, James Buchanan, and William Brooks,* in *Massachusetts Broadsides of the American Revolution,* ed. Mason I. Lowance Jr. and Georgia B. Bumgardner (Amherst: University of Massachusetts Press, 1976).

3. Published accounts exist for ten accused murderesses in the eighteenth century. Seven were charged with infanticide of illegitimate children. Two of the accused were black slaves; one was an Indian servant. Of the white women, four were servants, two were of unclear background, and one, Bathsheba Spooner, was well-to-do.

4. This assessment comes from an examination of Thomas McDade's bibliography of published works on American murderers, *The Annals of Murder: A Bibliography*

of Books and Pamphlets on American Murders from Colonial Times to 1900 (Norman: University of Oklahoma Press, 1961).

    5. Lawson, "Trial of Bathsheba Spooner," 189–91, and *Last Words*.

    6. Lawson, "The Trial of Bathsheba Spooner," 191. On the Spooner case, see also Thaddeus Maccarty, *The Guilt of Innocent Blood Put Away: A Sermon Preached . . . on the Occasion of the Execution of James Buchanan, William Brooks, Ezra Ross, and Bathshua* [sic] *Spooner* (Worcester, Mass.: Isaiah Thomas & Company, 1778), and Nathan Fiske, *A Sermon Preached at Brookfield . . . on the day of the Internment of Mr. Joshua Spooner* (Norwich, Conn.: Green & Spooner, 1778). Karen Halttunen notes that the Spooner case "generated no narrative of the peculiar heinousness of female crime" as husband-murder cases would in the nineteenth century. Karen Halttunen, *Murder Most Foul: The Killer and the American Gothic Imagination* (Cambridge, Mass.: Harvard University Press, 1998), 152.

    7. Peleg W. Chandler, *American Criminal Trials*, vol. 2 (1844; reprint, Freeport, N.Y.: Books for Libraries Press, 1970), v, 8–9.

    8. Chandler, *American Criminal Trials*, 55. Since Chandler's time, writers have continued to understand Spooner's crime, and the crimes of all women who commit murder, in highly gendered terms. For example, Deborah Navas, in her recent account of the Spooner case, asserts that "murder is a more aggressive, masculine act." Deborah Navas, *Murdered by His Wife: An Absorbing Tale of Crime and Punishment in Eighteenth-Century Massachusetts* (Amherst: University of Massachusetts Press, 1999), 103.

    9. Halttunen, *Murder Most Foul*, 3–6, 57, 152–55.

    10. Ibid., 168, and Dawn Keetley, "Victim and Victimizer: Female Fiends and Unease over Marriage in Sensational Fiction," *American Quarterly* 51, no. 2 (1999): 376, 364. Amy Gilman Srebnick and Patricia Cline Cohen have dealt with gender issues extensively in the case of nineteenth-century female murder victims, but cases of women accused of murder are quite different. Because female murder victims were by definition no longer alive, they did not present the same problems for antebellum Americans as did women on trial for murder. See Amy Gilman Srebnick, *The Mysterious Death of Mary Rogers: Sex and Culture in Nineteenth-Century New York* (New York: Oxford University Press, 1995); Patricia Cline Cohen, "Unregulated Youth: Masculinity and Murder in the 1830s City," *Radical History Review* 52 (1992): 33–52; and Patricia Cline Cohen, *The Murder of Helen Jewett: The Life and Death of a Prostitute in Nineteenth-Century New York* (New York: Vintage, 1999).

    11. Karen Halttunen, "Early American Murder Narratives: The Birth of Horror," in *The Power of Culture: Critical Essays in American History*, ed. Richard Wrightman Fox and T. J. Jackson Lears (Chicago: University of Chicago Press, 1993), 70. See also Halttunen, *Murder Most Foul*, chapter 1; Daniel Cohen, *Pillars of Salt, Monuments of Grace: New England Crime Literature and the Origins of American Popular Culture, 1674–1860* (New York: Oxford University Press, 1993), 184. For further discussion of the relationship between belief in innate depravity and attitudes toward murderers see David Brion Davis, *Homicide in American Fiction, 1798–1860: A Study in Social Values* (Ithaca, N.Y.: Cornell University Press, 1957); Richard Slotkin, "Narratives of Negro Crime in New England, 1675–1800," *American Quarterly* 25 (1973): 3–31; and Daniel E. Williams, "'Behold a Tragic Scene Strangely Turned into a Theater of Mercy': The Structure and Significance of Criminal Conversion Narratives in Early New England," *American Quarterly* 38, no. 5 (1986): 827–47.

12. Cotton Mather, *Pillars of Salt: A History of Some Criminals Executed in This Land for Capital Crimes* (1699), *Declaration and Confession of Esther Rodgers* (Boston, 1701), and *A Faithful Narrative of the Wicked Life and Remarkable Conversion of Patience Boston* (Boston, 1738), all reprinted in Daniel Williams, ed., *Pillars of Salt: An Anthology of Early American Criminal Narratives* (Madison, Wisconsin: Madison House, 1993), 71–72, 96, 120.

13. Henry May, *The Enlightenment in America* (New York: Oxford University Press, 1976); Halttunen, "Early American Murder Narratives," 80; Davis, *Homicide in American Fiction*, 28–29; and Daniel Cohen, *Pillars of Salt*, 89.

14. Perry Miller, *The New England Mind: From Colony to Province* (Cambridge, Mass.: Harvard University Press, 1953), 462; May, *Enlightenment in America*, 58; Davis, *Homicide in American Fiction*, 5; Edwin Gaustad, *The Great Awakening in New England* (New York: Harper, 1957); and Halttunen, "Early American Murder Narratives," 80.

15. Daniel E. Williams, "Introduction," in *Pillars of Salt: An Anthology of Early American Criminal Narratives*, ed. Daniel E. Williams (Madison, Wisconsin: Madison House, 1993), 13–14. See, for example, *An Authentic and Particular Account of the Life of Francis Burdett Personel* (New York, 1773), *The Dying Declaration of James Buchanan, Ezra Ross, and William Brooks* (Worcester, Mass., 1778), *A Faithful Narrative of Elizabeth Wilson* (Philadelphia, 1786), and *The Confession and Dying Words of Samuel Frost* (Worcester, Mass., 1793), all reprinted in *Pillars of Salt: An Anthology of Early American Criminal Narratives*, ed. Daniel E. Williams (Madison, Wisconsin: Madison House, 1993), 219–32, 271–82, and 337–42; Stephen Mix Mitchell, *A Narrative of the Life of William Beadle* (Hartford: Bavil Webster, 1783); *The Life and Confession of Charles O'-Donnel, Who Was Executed at Morgantown, June 19, 1797, for the Wilful Murder of His Son* (Lancaster, [Pa.]: W. & R. Dickson, 1797); and *Narrative of the Life, Last Dying Speech, and Confession of John Young* (New York: n.p., 1797). Ministers continued to write execution sermons, but they too focused on secular motives rather than innate depravity. See Maccarty, *Guilt of Innocent Blood*; Fiske, *Sermon Preached at Brookfield*; and Nathan Strong, *A Sermon Preached in Hartford . . . At the Execution of Richard Doane* (Hartford, [Conn.]: Elisha Babcock 1797).

16. Donald Meyer, *The Instructed Conscience: The Shaping of the American National Ethic* (Philadelphia: University of Pennsylvania Press, 1972), 10.

17. Davis, *Homicide in American Fiction*, 13–14.

18. See, for example, *Narrative of the Life of William Beadle* and the novels of Charles Brockden Brown, especially *Wieland; or, The Transformation* (1798; reprint, New York: Anchor, 1973).

19. Nancy Cott, "Passionlessness: An Interpretation of Victorian Sexual Ideology, 1790–1850," in *A Heritage of Her Own: Toward a New Social History of American Women*, ed. Nancy Cott and Elizabeth Pleck (New York: Simon & Schuster, 1979), 162–81; 164. See also Ruth Bloch, "The Gendered Meanings of Virtue in Revolutionary America," *Signs* 13, no. 1 (1987): 38.

20. Francis Hutcheson, quoted in Davis, *Homicide in American Fiction*, 18, 20–21. On this general trend, see also Meyer, *Instructed Conscience*, 35–42.

21. Bloch, "Gendered Meanings of Virtue," 49–50, 53.

22. On republican motherhood or wifehood, see Bloch, "Gendered Meanings of Virtue"; Linda Kerber, *Women of the Republic: Intellect and Ideology in Revolutionary America* (New York: Norton, 1980); and Jan Lewis, "The Republican Wife," *William and Mary Quarterly* 44 (October 1987): 689–721. On the linkage between reason and morality and the shift to an emotion-based morality, see also Meyer, *Instructed Conscience*, 35–42, and Davis, *Homicide in American Fiction*, 20–21. On the popular idea that virtue consisted of "piety (love of God) and morality (love of man)," see Meyer, *Instructed Conscience*, 72.

23. Bloch, "Gendered Meanings of Virtue," 38.

24. *The Confession of Mary Cole, Who Was Executed on Friday, 26th June; at Newton, Sussex County, N.J., for the Murder of Agnes Teaurs, Her Mother* (New York: Printed for the Purchasers, 1812[?]), 3–4.

25. John Kirn, ed., *Sketch of the Trial of Mary Cole for the Willful Murder of Her Mother, Agnes Thuers* (New Brunswick, N.J.: Printed for the Publisher, 1812), 10–13.

26. Ibid., 6.

27. Ibid., 9.

28. By all accounts Cole's lawyers were competent. One, Theodore Frelinghuysen, was later Henry Clay's running mate for vice president. John T. Cunningham, ed., *Murder Did Pay: Nineteenth-Century New Jersey Murders* (Newark: New Jersey Historical Society, 1982), 5.

29. Karen Halttunen argues that antebellum Americans commonly linked external appearances to "inner virtues." She also notes that, because of their supposed "superior sensibility," women were believed to be "incapable" of simulating a virtuous exterior if the interior was corrupt. Karen Halttunen, *Confidence Men and Painted Women: A Study of Middle-Class Culture in America, 1830–1870* (New Haven, Conn.: Yale University Press, 1982), 40, 57–58.

30. The vast literature on the antebellum gender ideology dichotomizing women as true and untrue begins with Barbara Welter, "The Cult of True Womanhood, 1820–1860," *American Quarterly* 16 (1966): 151–74, and Gerda Lerner, "The Lady and the Mill Girl: Changes in the Status of Women in the Age of Jackson," *Midcontinent American Studies Journal* 10 (1969): 5–15. For an extended discussion of the historiography of true womanhood, see the introduction to the present volume.

31. On the rise of a new print culture and its fascination with murder, see Patricia Cline Cohen, "Unregulated Youth," 45–46; Daniel Cohen, *Pillars of Salt*, 35–38, 195–96, 278n173; and David S. Reynolds, *Beneath the American Renaissance: The Subversive Imagination in the Age of Emerson and Melville* (Cambridge, Mass.: Harvard University Press, 1988), 169, 170, 171–76, 209. On middle-class men and women as readers of sensational murder literature, see Keetley, "Victim and Victimizer," 345–46.

32. These figures come from an examination of Thomas McDade's exhaustive bibliography of published works on American murderers (and a few of my own additions to his list). I say "allegedly nonfiction" because although McDade focused primarily on accused murderers who appeared to have existed, intentionally excluding a number of murderers who seemed to be fictional, he noted that a few of the accused murderesses whose cases he included may be fictional. McDade, *Annals of Murder*.

33. Mary Hartman has noticed a similar trend in Victorian England and France. Mary Hartman, *Victorian Murderesses: A True History of Thirteen Respectable French and English Women Accused of Unspeakable Crimes* (New York: Schocken, 1977). Dawn Keetley studied antebellum fictional accounts of women who murdered their husbands and found that in this fiction women were invariably white, "young and attractive." Keetley, "Victim and Victimizer," 345.

34. See Harry Watson, *Liberty and Power: The Politics of Jacksonian America* (New York: Noonday Press, 1990), 51–54; Roland Berthoff, "Conventional Mentality: Free Blacks, Women, and Business Corporations as Unequal Persons, 1820–1870," *Journal of American History* 76 (1989): 753–84; Nancy Cott, *The Bonds of Womanhood: 'Woman's Sphere' in New England, 1780–1835* (New Haven, Conn.: Yale University Press, 1977), 98–99; Edmund Morgan, *American Slavery, American Freedom: The Ordeal of Colonial Virginia* (New York: Norton, 1975), 338–87; and Reginald Horsman, *Race and Manifest Destiny: The Origins of Racial Anglo-Saxonism* (Cambridge, Mass.: Harvard University Press, 1981).

35. On this point, see Brian E. Roberts, *American Alchemy: The California Gold Rush and Middle-Class Culture*, (Chapel Hill: University of North Carolina Press, 2000), chapter 9, and E. Anthony Rotundo, *American Manhood: Transformations in Masculinity from the Revolution to the Modern Era* (New York: Basic Books, 1993), 22–25. On the relationship between the true woman and the self-made man in general, see Welter, "Cult of True Womanhood," 151–52; Cott, "Passionlessness"; Carroll Smith-Rosenberg, "The Beauty, the Beast, and the Militant Woman," in *Disorderly Conduct: Visions of Gender in Victorian America*, by Carroll Smith-Rosenberg (New York: Oxford University Press, 1985), 109–28; and Mary Ryan, *Cradle of the Middle Class: The Family in Oneida County, New York, 1790–1865* (New York: Cambridge University Press, 1981), 146–55.

36. *The Early Life and Complete Trial of Mary, Alias Polly Bodine* (New York: n.p., 1846), 5; D. Wilson, *Henrietta Robinson* (New York: Miller, Orton & Mulligan, 1855), 11; and A. R. Orton [pseud. O. R. Arthur], ed., *The Three Sisters; or, The Life, Confession, and Execution of Amy, Elizabeth, and Cynthia Halzingler* (Baltimore: A. R. Orton, 1855), 22. See also *Narrative and Confessions of Lucretia P. Cannon*; Walters, *Confession of Ann Walters*; Hamilton, *The Life and Confession of Sophia Hamilton*; *The Private History and Confession of Pamela Lee* (Pittsburgh: Lucas & Grant, 1852); and *Trial and Conviction of Eliza Dawson* (Halifax, Nova Scotia: J. B. Finnerty, 1850).

37. Wilson, *Henrietta Robinson*, 11, 16–21; *Trial and Conviction of Eliza Dawson*, 6, 7; Orton, *Three Sisters*, 22; *Narrative and Confessions of Lucretia P. Cannon*; *Confession of Ann Walters*; and Hamilton, *Life and Confession of Sophia Hamilton*; *Private History and Confession of Pamela Lee*, 6, 7; *Ellen Irving, The Female Victimizer* (Baltimore: A. R. Orton, 1856), 30; *Trial, Conviction, and Confession of Mary Thorn* (Norfolk, Va.: William C. Murdock, 1854), 6, 27; *Estelle Grant; or, The Lost Wife* (New York: Garrett, Dick & Fitzgerald, 1855); and *Annals of Murder; or, Daring Outrages* (John Perry, 1845), 10, 18.

38. John D. Lawson, ed., "The Trial of Lucretia Chapman for the Murder of William Chapman," in *America State Trials*, ed. John D. Lawson, vol. 6 (St. Louis: Thomas Law Books), 169, 286, 234–35.

39. John D. Lawson, ed., "Trial of Emma Augusta Cunningham, for the Murder

of Dr. Harvey Burdell," *American State Trials*, vol. 5 (St. Louis: Thomas Law Books, 1916), 99–101, 194–95.

40. *Early Life and Complete Trial of Mary, Alias Polly Bodine*, 17; *Narrative and Confessions of Lucretia P. Cannon*, 11.

41. *Ellen Irving*, 45–46.

42. John D. Lawson, ed., "Trial of Henrietta Robinson," *American State Trials*, ed. John D. Lawson, vol. 11 (St. Louis: Thomas Law Books, 1919), 531, 584, 609, 554, 558.

43. Wilson, *Henrietta Robinson*, 11–12. Karen Halttunen also stresses the mystery of Robinson's past, but the one point on which all popular accounts agree is that her social standing had once been quite high. Halttunen, *Murder Most Foul*, 113.

44. Wilson, *Henrietta Robinson*, 12, 21, 41.

45. "Trial of Henrietta Robinson," 609. See also *Trial and Conviction of Eliza Dawson*; Orton, *Three Sisters*; *Narrative and Confessions of Lucretia P. Cannon*; Walters, *Confession of Ann Walters*; Hamilton, *Life and Confession of Sophia Hamilton*; *Private History and Confession of Pamela Lee*; *Ellen Irving*; *Trial, Conviction, and Confession of Mary Thorn*; and *Estelle Grant*.

46. On fictional murderesses see, for example, Orton, *Three Sisters*; Walters, *Confession of Ann Walters*; Hamilton, *Life and Confession of Sophia Hamilton*; *Private History and Confession of Pamela Lee*; *Ellen Irving*; *The Life, Career, and Awful Death by the Garote of Margaret C. Waldegrave* (New Orleans: A. R. Orton, 1853); *Trial, Conviction, and Confession of Mary Thorn*; *Estelle Grant*; *Trial and Conviction of Eliza Dawson*; and J. S. Calhoun, *Life and Confession of Mary Jane Gordon* (Covington, Ky.: Benjamin True, 1849).

47. *Niles Weekly Register*, 25 May 1829, 202.

48. On this blurring between law and literature, see Alexis de Tocqueville, *Democracy in America*, edited by Richard D. Heffner (New York: Mentor, 1956), 123–28; Perry Miller, *The Life of the Mind in America* (New York: Harcourt, Brace and World, 1965), 96–265; Robert A. Ferguson, *Law and Letters in American Culture* (Cambridge, Mass.: Harvard University Press, 1984), 11–15, 20; and Daniel Cohen, *Pillars of Salt*, 168, 196, 198, 297n47.

49. This supports Myra Jehlen's argument that, as a form, novels offer resolution of tensions. Myra Jehlen, "The Novel and the Middle Class in America," in *Ideology and Classic American Literature*, ed. Sacvan Bercovitch and Myra Jehlen (New York: Cambridge University Press, 1986). Amy Srebnick also noted this phenomenon in novelistic accounts of the murder of Mary Rogers. Srebnick, *Mysterious Death of Mary Rogers*.

50. Ann Jones, *Women Who Kill* (New York: Holt, Reinhart, and Winston, 1980), 108. Lawson, "Trial of Henrietta Robinson," 619. These claims are based on my findings and on analysis of statistics from McDade, *Annals of Murder*.

51. See almost daily accounts in the *New York Herald* and *New York Daily Tribune*, 1–21 January 1844.

52. Charles W. Leng and William T. Davis, *Staten Island and Its People, 1609–1929*, vol. 1 (New York: Lewis Historical Publishing Company, 1930), 218, 241; *New York Herald*, 3 January 1844.

53. *New York Herald*, 3 January 1844, 1 and 3 April 1845; *Early Life and Complete Trial of Mary, Alias Polly Bodine*, 5.

54. Henry L. Clinton, *Extraordinary Cases* (New York: Harper & Brothers, 1896), 15, 21; *New York Herald*, 7 April 1845, 3 January 1844. See also the *New York Herald*,

New York Daily Tribune, and *Newark Daily Advertiser* in general for the months of January 1844, June 1844, March–April 1845, and April 1846.

55. On the press's focus on the particularly horrible nature of her crime, see, for example, the *New York Herald*, which called Bodine's crime the worst "that has ever occurred in this country." *New York Herald*, 8 January 1844. See also John D. Lawson, ed., "Official Report of the Trial of Laura D. Fair" in *American State Trials*, ed. John D. Lawson, vol. 17 (St. Louis: Thomas Law Books, 1936), 303.

56. *New York Herald*, 3 January 1844, 21 March 1845. On the *New York Sun*'s claims, see *New York Herald*, 5 January 1844; *National Police Gazette*, 27 December 1845, 147, 148, 160; 3 January 1846, 160; and *New York Daily Tribune*, 21 March 1845. *Sotheby's Important Americana: Furniture and Folk Art*, New York, 18 January 1998, no. 1519.

57. *New York Herald*, 10 April 1845, 5 April 1845, 1 April 1845. See also daily accounts of the trial in the *New York Herald* and *New York Daily Tribune* for March–April 1845.

58. Clinton, *Extraordinary Cases*, 21; *New York Herald*, 3 April 1845; *National Police Gazette*, 27 December 1845, 147; *New York Herald*, 11 April 1845. On the name Polly, see "Records of the United Brethren Congregation . . . Staten Island Baptism and Births," in *Collections of the New York Genealogical and Biographical Society*, vol. 4: *Staten Island Church Records*, ed. Tobias Wright (New York: Printed for the Society, 1909), 121; and *New York Herald*, 21 March 1845.

59. "Verdict of the Jury", *New York Herald*, 12 April 1845; Clinton, *Extraordinary Cases*, 15–23.

60. Clinton, *Extraordinary Cases*, 19; *National Police Gazette*, 3 January 1846, 160.

61. Lawson, "Trial of Henrietta Robinson," 584–85.

62. Calhoun, *Life and Confession of Mary Jane Gordon*, 25–26.

63. See also the story of Mary Moriarty, a "poor, friendless," pregnant Irish immigrant who was tried for the murder of her lover. Having been seduced with promises of marriage, she killed her lover to defend her honor. A jury acquitted her after two minutes of deliberation. Jones, *Women Who Kill*, 153, 154–57.

64. *Newark Daily Advertiser*, 6 August 1851 and 8 October 1851.

65. John Costin Eames, *Innocence Rewarded; or, The Successful Triumph of Margaret Garrity, Who Was Tried for the Murder of a False Lover, at Newark, New-Jersey, United States of America, in the Month of October 1851*, (Newark, N.J.: n.p., 1851).

66. Melton McLaurin, *Celia, a Slave*, (Athens: University of Georgia Press, 1991), 90–91. There is a great deal of evidence linking African American women to ideals of redemptive womanhood. See, for example, Dorothy Sterling, ed., *We Are Your Sisters: Black Women in the Nineteenth Century* (New York: W. W. Norton, 1984); Nell Irvin Painter, *Sojourner Truth: A Life, a Symbol* (New York: W. W. Norton, 1996), 257–63; and Jean Fagan Yellin and John C. Van Horne eds., *The Abolitionist Sisterhood: Women's Political Culture in Antebellum America* (Ithaca, N.Y.: Cornell University Press, 1994), chapters 7 and 8. See also chapter 3 of this book for an extended discussion of this issue.

67. Steven Weisenburger points out that the case quickly became "nationally famous" except in "the Deep South, where editors practically imposed a news blackout on it." He refers to three novels based on the case that were written in the 1850s: Hattia M'Keehan's *Liberty or Death; or, Heaven's Infraction of the Fugitive Slave Law*

(Cincinnati: Published by the Author, 1856); Henry Field James's *Abolitionism Unveiled; or, Its Origin, Progress, and Pernicious Tendency Fully Developed* (Cincinnati: E. Morgan and Sons, 1856); and John Jolliffe's *Chattanooga* (Cincinnati: Wrightson, 1858). Weisenburger also notes that Thomas Satterwhite Noble's 1867 painting *The Modern Medea* was inspired by the case, as were a number of poems, including one by Frances Ellen Watkins Harper. Steven Weisenburger, *Modern Medea: A Family Story of Slavery and Child-Murder from the Old South* (New York: Hill and Wang, 1998), 134–35, 264–65, 271, 272–74, 8, 286.

68. "Report on the Inquest," *Cincinnati Gazette*, 30 January 1856, and Salmon P. Chase to William Dennison, 31 December 1863, Salmon Portland Chase Papers, Reel 30, 0714, both quoted in Weisenburger, *Modern Medea*, 74, 89, and 216.

69. Weisenburger, *Modern Medea*, 244–45, 277–78.

70. Ibid., 238, and Joseph Cox, "Letter to the Editors," *Cincinnati Commercial*, 21 November 1863, quoted in Weisenburger, *Modern Medea*, 117.

71. Weisenburger, *Modern Medea*, 229; "Letter to Editor," *Liberator*, 28 March 1856, and *Cincinnati Commercial*, 31 January 1856, both quoted in Weisenburger, *Modern Medea*, 269, 263. Of course Margaret Garner was not always portrayed as a heroic mother; certainly defenders of slavery would not consider her one. Her master's lawyer at the fugitive slave trial, for example, referred to Margaret as a slave who had "barbarously murdered one of her children." Weisenburger, *Modern Medea*, 167.

2: THE "FALLEN WOMAN" IN ANTEBELLUM AMERICA

1. "Moral Reform," *Friend of Virtue* 2, no. 18, 1 October 1839, 283.

2. *First Annual Report of the New York Magdalen Society*, as quoted in Marilynn Wood Hill, *Their Sisters' Keepers: Prostitution in New York City, 1830–1870* (Berkeley: University of California Press, 1993), 18, 27.

3. For contemporary criticism of the Magdalen report, see *The Phantasmagoria of New York, a Poetical Burlesque upon a Certain Libellous Pamphlet, Written by a Committee of Notorious Fanatics, Entitled the Magdalen Report* (New York: n.p., n.d. [1831?]); and *Orthodox Bubbles; or, A Review of the First Annual Report . . . of the Magdalen Society* (Boston: Printed for the Publishers, 1831). Although the Magdalen Society disbanded in 1831, many of its members helped to form a new society in 1833, which soon evolved into the long-lasting New York Female Moral Reform Society.

4. Hill, *Their Sisters' Keepers*, chapter 1. See also Timothy Gilfoyle, *City of Eros: New York City, Prostitution, and the Commercialization of Sex, 1790–1920* (New York: W. W. Norton, 1992), and Christine Stansell, *City of Women: Sex and Class in New York, 1789–1860* (Urbana: University of Illinois Press, 1982).

5. I link the terms *fallen woman* and *prostitute* because antebellum Americans did. They tended to see prostitution as the end result, the logical conclusion, of all illicit female sexual activity. Christine Stansell has argued that all classes closely linked prostitution with female "ruin." Stansell, *City of Women*, 175.

6. Jane H. Pease and William H. Pease, *Ladies, Women, and Wenches: Choice and Constraint in Antebellum Charleston and Boston* (Chapel Hill: University of North Carolina

Press, 1990), 150; Hill, *Their Sisters' Keepers*, 16–17; and Gilfoyle, *City of Eros*, 29–31. Mary Ryan, *Cradle of the Middle-Class: The Family in Oneida County, New York, 1790–1865* (New York: Cambridge University Press, 1981), 122.

7. For example, Timothy Gilfoyle notes that according to William Sanger's *History of Prostitution* (New York: Harper & Brothers, 1859), "the overwhelming majority in Sanger's sample belonged to families with middle-class (41%) or skilled artisanal (31%) parents," yet he makes little of this fact. Instead, Gilfoyle lapses back into a conception of prostitution as a choice that an urban working-class woman made in a world of limited opportunities. Gilfoyle, *City of Eros*, 66, 74–75. See also Hill, *Their Sisters' Keepers*, 60–62; Marybeth Hamilton Arnold, "The Life of a Citizen in the Hands of a Woman," in *Passion and Power: Sexuality in History*, eds. Kathy Peiss and Christina Simmons (Philadelphia: Temple University Press, 1989); and Stansell, *City of Women*, 178.

8. Lori D. Ginzberg, *Women and the Work of Benevolence: Morality, Politics, and Class in the Nineteenth-Century United States* (New Haven, Conn.: Yale University Press, 1990), 24; Stansell, *City of Women*, 171–72.

9. Adrienne Siegel, *The Image of the American City in Popular Literature, 1820–1870* (Port Washington, N.Y.: Kennikat Press, 1981) 38, 81, 94.

10. David S. Reynolds, *Beneath the American Renaissance: The Subversive Imagination in the Age of Emerson and Melville* (Cambridge, Mass.: Harvard University Press, 1988), 64, 362.

11. Gilfoyle, *City of Eros*, 148, 146.

12. Ginzberg, *Women and the Work of Benevolence*, 22; Stansell, *City of Women*, 192; and Charles Loring Brace, *The Dangerous Classes of New York*, 118, as quoted in Stansell, *City of Women*, 192.

13. New York Magdalen Society, *First Annual Report of the Executive Committee of the New York Magdalen Society, Instituted January 1, 1830* (New York: Printed for the Society by J. Seymour, 1831), 10.

14. J. R. McDowall, *Magdalen Facts* (New York: J. R. McDowall, 1832), 19–21, 24–27.

15. Caroline H. Dall, *Women's Right to Labor; or, Low Wages and Hard Work* (Boston: Walker, Wise, and Co., 1860), *Low Wages and Great Sins: Two Antebellum Views on Prostitution and the Working-Girl*, ed. David Rothman and Sheila Rothman (New York: Garland, 1987), 18, see also 14.

16. Joseph Tuckerman, *An Essay on the Wages Paid to Females for Their Labour* (Philadelphia, 1830), reprinted in *Low Wages and Great Sins: Two Antebellum Views on Prostitution and the Working-Girl*, ed. David Rothman and Sheila Rothman (New York: Garland, 1987), 35. On Tuckerman, see also William H. Pease and Jane H. Pease, *Web of Progress: Private Values and Public Styles in Boston and Charleston, 1828–1843* (New York: Oxford University Press, 1985), 150.

17. For details surrounding the Jewett case and its fame, see Patricia Cline Cohen, "Unregulated Youth: Masculinity and Murder in the 1830s City," *Radical History Review* 52 (1992): 33–52; Patricia Cline Cohen, *The Murder of Helen Jewett: The Life and Death of a Prostitute in Nineteenth-Century New York* (New York: Vintage, 1999); and, Hill, *Their Sisters' Keepers*, 9–16.

18. Hill, *Their Sisters' Keepers*, 12. *New York Sun*, 11 April 1836, and *New York Herald*, 12 April 1836, as quoted in Hill, *Their Sisters' Keepers*, 13. On Jewett's correspondence, see Hill, *Their Sisters' Keepers*, 9–16.

19. Dall, *Women's Right to Labor*, 125; J. H. Ingraham, *Frank Rivers; or, The Dangers of the Town* (Boston: E. P. Williams, 1843), 8. Reynolds, *Beneath the American Renaissance*, 362.

20. George Foster, *New York by Gas-light and Other Urban Sketches* (1850; reprint, Berkeley: University of California Press, 1990), 82–83.

21. George Thompson, *The Countess; or, Memoirs of Women of Leisure*, (Boston: Berry & Wright, 1849), 3.

22. Thompson, *Countess*, 37; Foster, *New York by Gas-light*, 99; Ingraham, *Frank Rivers*, 42; David Brion Davis, *Homicide in American Fiction, 1798–1860: A Study in Social Values* (Ithaca, N.Y.: Cornell University Press, 1957), 170.

23. Foster, *New York By Gas-light*, 94–96; see also George Lippard, *New York: Its Upper Ten and Lower Million* (1853; reprint, New York: Irvington, 1993); George Lippard, *The Quaker City; or, The Monks of Monk Hall* (1844; reprint, New York: Odyssey Press, 1970); George Thompson, *Countess*; Ralph Wardlaw, *Lectures on Magdalenism: Its Nature, Extent, Effects, Guilt, Causes, and Remedy* (New York: Redfield, 1843); and McDowall, *Magdalen Facts*. See also numerous articles in the periodicals *Advocate of Moral Reform* and *Friend of Virtue*.

24. Tuckerman, *Essay*, 52.

25. Foster, *New York by Gas-light*, 96, 82–83.

26. McDowall, *Magdalen Facts*, 79.

27. *The Flash*, 18 September 1842, 1. On the linkage of prostitution to fears of racial amalgamation, see Pease and Pease, *Ladies, Women, and Wenches*, 153.

28. Sanger, *History of Prostitution*, 550–51, 557, 564–65.

29. Foster, *New York by Gas-light*, 96.

30. Hill, *Their Sisters' Keepers*, 93; Gilfoyle, *City of Eros*, 146.

31. *Diary of George Templeton Strong*, entry of 12 April 1836, 1:15; quoted in Hill, *Their Sisters' Keepers*, 34; Tuckerman, *Essay*, 30; *Magdalen Report*, 8.

32. Wardlaw, *Lectures on Magdalenism*, 35; Tuckerman, *Essay*, 30–31.

33. Ingraham, *Frank Rivers*, 17, 31–35, and Osgood Bradbury, *Ellen Grant; or, Fashionable Life in New York* (New York: Dick & Fitzgerald, [1853?]).

34. Anonymous [George W. Dixon?], *Trial of Madame Restell* (New York, 1846), 5; James Mohr, *Abortion in America: The Origins and Evolution of National Policy, 1800–1900* (New York: Oxford University Press, 1978), chapter 3, 46–85; and Carroll Smith-Rosenberg, "The Abortion Movement," *Disorderly Conduct: Visions of Gender in Victorian America* (New York: Oxford University Press, 1985), 221, 226–27.

35. Clifford Browder, *The Wickedest Woman in New York: Madame Restell, the Abortionist* (Hamden, Conn.: Archon, 1988), 127; Mohr, *Abortion in America*, 123–25.

36. See, for example, numerous articles in *Advocate of Moral Reform*; sensational reform journals like the *National Police Gazette* and George W. Dixon's *New York Polyanthos*; medical journals like the *New York Medical and Surgical Reporter* and the *Boston Medical and Surgical Journal*; and newspapers, including the *New York Herald*,

New York Daily Tribune, New York Commercial Advertiser, New York Sun, Boston Daily Times and the *Bostonian*.

37. Anonymous [George W. Dixon?], *Trial of Madame Restell, Alias Ann Lohman for Abortion and Causing the Death of Mrs. Purdy* (New York: n.p., 1841), 8.

38. Lippard, *New York: Its Upper Ten and Lower Millions*, 123–24.

39. Rodney Hessinger, "Victim of Seduction or Vicious Woman? Conceptions of the Prostitute at the Philadelphia Magdalen Society, 1800–1850," *Pennsylvania History* 66 (1999): 201, 206.

40. Laurel Thatcher Ulrich, *A Midwife's Tale: The Life of Martha Ballard, Based on Her Diary, 1785–1812* (New York: Knopf, 1990), 149–50, 157, 149–60.

41. Ibid., 157.

42. McDowall, *Magdalen Facts*, 19–21.

43. Tuckerman, *Essay*, 35, 27; Ingraham, *Frank Rivers*, 8.

44. Ulrich, *Midwife's Tale*, 149–60. The law did not force the couple to marry, but it did force a man to support the child he had fathered, and marriage was the common result.

45. Ulrich, for example, points out that a civil seduction case did not fare well in Hallowell during the period when community policing seemed to be working effectively. Ulrich, *Midwife's Tale*, 159.

46. Reynolds, *Beneath the American Renaissance*, 362.

47. Gilfoyle, *City of Eros*, 155; Hill, *Their Sisters' Keepers*, 217–18; Davis, *Homicide in American Fiction*, 160; Stansell, *City of Women*, 191; Hessinger, "Victim of Seduction," 216–17.

48. Reynolds, *Beneath the American Renaissance*, 85. See also Siegel, *Image of the American City*, 170.

49. Bradbury, *Ellen Grant*, 8, 11, 92.

50. Ibid., 11.

51. Osgood Bradbury, *Female Depravity; or, The House of Death* (New York: R. M. De Witt, 1857), 34.

52. Cecilia Mayo, *Life and Sufferings of Cecilia Mayo: Founded on Incidents in Real Life* (Boston: M. Aurelius, 1843), 9, 21.

53. Sarah Josepha Hale, *Woman's Record; or, Sketches of All Distinguished Women from the Creation to A.D. 1854*, 2nd rev. ed. (New York: Harper, 1855), 641–42. Lydia Maria Child to Francis G. Shaw, Wayland [Mass.], 1870, in Lydia Maria Child, *Letters of Lydia Maria Child* (Boston: Houghton, Mifflin, 1883), 205.

54. Journal entries of 16 January, 8 March, and 30 October 1864, quoted in Mary Boykin Chesnut, *A Diary from Dixie*, edited by Ben Ames Williams (1949; reprint, Cambridge, Mass.: Harvard University Press, 1980), 361, 390, 446.

55. *Newark Daily Advertiser*, 19 January 1844.

56. Margaret Fuller, *Woman in the Nineteenth Century, and Kindred Papers Relating to the Sphere, Condition, and Duties of Woman* (1855; reprint, New York: W. W. Norton, 1971), 148–49.

57. *Newark Daily Advertiser*, 19 January 1844; *New York Herald*, 19 January 1844.

58. *New York Herald*, 2 and 3 November 1843; *New York Daily Tribune*, 2 and 4 November 1843.

59. Hill, *Their Sisters' Keepers*, 142. Both Hill and Gilfoyle also assume that Nor-

man was a prostitute. Hill, *Their Sisters' Keepers*, 170; and Gilfoyle, *City of Eros*, 82.

60. *New York Daily Tribune*, 17 January 1844; *Newark Daily Advertiser*, 18 January 1844. On crowds in court, see *New York Herald*, *New York Daily Tribune*, and *Newark Daily Advertiser*, 17–20 January 1844.

61. *New York Herald*, 17 and 18 January 1844.

62. Lydia Maria Child, "Uncollected Letter," in Lydia Maria Child, *A Lydia Maria Child Reader*, ed. Carolyn Karcher (Durham, N.C.: Duke University Press, 1997), 371.

63. *New York Herald*, 20 January 1844.

64. Child, "Uncollected Letter," 367–68; *New York Herald*, 20 January 1844.

65. *New York Herald*, 20 January 1844; Child, "Uncollected Letter," 370; Hill, *Their Sisters' Keepers*, 141.

66. *New York Tribune*, 22 January 1844.

67. Child, "Uncollected Letter," 371.

68. *Newark Daily Advertiser*, 22 January 1844; Child, "Uncollected Letter," 372.

69. See chapter 1 for examples of women acquitted of murder in these circumstances.

70. For discussions of anti-seduction laws, see Carroll Smith-Rosenberg, "The Beauty, the Beast, and the Militant Woman," in *Disorderly Conduct: Visions of Gender in Victorian America*, by Carroll Smith-Rosenberg, 109–28; and Mary Ryan, *Women in Public: Between Banners and Ballots, 1825–1880* (Baltimore: Johns Hopkins University Press, 1990), 95–129.

71. "What Good Has the Advocate Done?" *Advocate of Moral Reform*, 2 January 1843, 2–3.

72. "Review of *Woman as She Should Be and Woman in Her Social Character*, by Rev. Hubbard Winslow and Mrs. John Sanford," *Friend of Virtue*, January 1838, 24–25. Cambridge Female Moral Reform Society, *Constitution of the Cambridge Female Moral Reform Society* (Boston, 1837), 1.

73. "Another Warning to the Young and Ignorant," *New York Daily Tribune*, 22 June 1844.

74. "Female Conventions," *Friend of Virtue*, November 1838, 173.

75. Fuller, *Woman in the Nineteenth Century*, 132, 140–41, 96.

76. Dall, *Women's Right to Labor*, 25.

77. *Life and Sufferings of Cecilia Mayo*.

78. Ibid., 9.

79. Emma Cole, *Life and Sufferings of Miss Emma Cole: Being a Faithful Narrative of Her Life* (Boston: M. Aurelius, 1844).

80. Ibid., 20.

81. E. D. E. N. Southworth, *The Hidden Hand; or, Capitola the Madcap*, with an introduction by Joanne Dobson (1859; reprint, New Brunswick, N.J.: Rutgers University Press, 1988), 305, 296–311.

3: Redemptive Womanhood and African Americans in the Antebellum North

1. "Religion and the Pure Principles of Morality . . . Delivered in Boston, October 1831," from Maria W. Stewart, *Productions of Mrs Maria W. Stewart, Presented to the*

First African Baptist Church and Society of the City of Boston (Boston: Friends of Freedom and Virtue, 1835), reprinted in *Spiritual Narratives*, ed. Henry Louis Gates Jr. (New York: Oxford University Press, 1988), 6.

2. "Colored Females," *Colored American*, 17 November 1838.

3. "Moral Influence of the Wife on the Husband," "Woman's Kindness," "Woman's Eloquence," *Colored American*, 17 November 1838.

4. "Female Education," *Colored American*, 23 November 1839.

5. On African American women living outside of or being less affected by the ideology of true womanhood, see Paula Giddings, *When and Where I Enter: The Impact of Black Women on Race and Sex in America* (1984; reprint, New York: Bantam, 1996), 47; Julie Roy Jeffrey, *The Great Silent Army of Abolitionism: Ordinary Women in the Antislavery Movement* (Chapel Hill: University of North Carolina Press, 1998), 179, 182; James Oliver Horton and Lois E. Horton, *In Hope of Liberty: Culture, Community, and Protest among Northern Free Blacks, 1700–1860 (New York: Oxford University Press, 1997)*, 74, 147; Hazel Carby, *Reconstructing Womanhood: The Emergence of the Afro-American Woman Novelist* (New York: Oxford University Press, 1987), 59–61; Shirley Yee, *Black Women Abolitionists: A Study in Activism, 1828–1860* (Knoxville: University of Tennessee Press, 1992), 156; Jean Fagan Yellin, *Women and Sisters: The Antislavery Feminists in American Culture* (New Haven, Conn.: Yale University Press, 1989), 78, 96; Elizabeth Raul Bethel, *The Roots of African American Identity: Memory and History in Antebellum Free Communities* (New York: St. Martin's Press, 1997), 170; and Lyde Cullen Sizer, *The Political Work of Northern Women Writers and the Civil War, 1850–1872* (Chapel Hill: University of North Carolina Press, 2000), 11.

6. On antebellum gender ideology as a "white" ideology that did not fit the needs of African Americans who tried to fit into it, see Yee, *Black Women Abolitionists*, 4, 54; Maria W. Stewart, *Maria W. Stewart: America's First Black Woman Political Writer*, edited by Marilyn Richardson (Bloomington: Indiana University Press, 1987), 22; and Dorothy Sterling, ed., *We Are Your Sisters: Black Women in the Nineteenth Century* (New York: W. W. Norton, 1984), x–xi, xiii; James Oliver Horton, "Freedom's Yoke: Gender Conventions among Antebellum Free Blacks," *Feminist Studies* 12, no. 1 (1986): 60, 64, 70; James Oliver Horton, *Free People of Color: Inside the African American Community* (Washington, D.C.: Smithsonian Institution Press, 1993), 95; Jeffrey, *Great Silent Army*, 192; and Jacqueline Jones Royster, *Traces of a Stream: Literacy and Social Change among African American Women* (Pittsburgh: University of Pittsburgh Press, 2000), 180.

7. Here Romero was referring specifically to women such as public lecturer Maria W. Stewart and Harriet Wilson, author of *Our Nig*. Lora Romero, *Home Fronts: Domesticity and Its Critics in the Antebellum United States* (Durham, N.C.: Duke University Press, 1997), 112, 27–28, 29–30, 63–64. On the New York City black community's stress on female morality, see Leslie M. Harris, *In the Shadow of Slavery: African Americans in New York City, 1626–1863* (Chicago: University of Chicago Press, 2003), 178–81, 202–4.

8. On ideas about African American inferiority, see James McPherson, *The Struggle for Black Equality: Abolitionists and the Negro in the Civil War and Reconstruction* (Princeton: Princeton University Press, 1964), 134; Winthrop Jordan, *White over Black:*

American Attitudes toward the Negro, 1550–1812 (New York: Norton, 1968); and Roland Berthoff, "Conventional Mentality: Free Blacks, Women, and Business Corporations as Unequal Persons, 1820–1870," *Journal of American History* 76 (1989): 753–84.

9. Hutton says little about gender ideology, but she does assert that the way black newspapers countered racist images was by "reporting the females' good deeds and community service." These would be obvious signifiers of a woman's redemptive nature. Frankie Hutton, *The Early Black Press in America, 1827–1860* (Westport, Conn.: Greenwood Press, 1993), 57–58.

10. Yee, *Black Women Abolitionists*, 87.

11. "Mrs Stewart's Farewell Address to her Friends . . . September 21, 1833," and "Religion and the Pure Principles of Morality . . . Delivered in Boston, October 1831," in Stewart, *Productions of Mrs Maria W. Stewart*, 75–76, 12–13, 6.

12. "Matilda," Letter to the Editors, *Freedom's Journal*, 10 August 1827.

13. These were not the only black newspapers of the antebellum era, but they were some of the most well known and widely read. According to Benjamin Quarles, seventeen different black newspapers were published in the antebellum period, but many of these periodicals, like white abolitionist papers, were "short-lived" due to financial problems. Benjamin Quarles, *Black Abolitionists* (New York: Da Capo, 1969), 85–86.

14. "Proposals for Publishing the Freedom's Journal," *Freedom's Journal*, 16 March 1827; Editorial, *Weekly Advocate*, 7 January 1837; and "Editorial Correspondence, F.D. to 'My Dear Nell, Lynn Mass., 5 February 1848,'" *North Star*, 11 February 1848.

15. See "Free People of Color," *Weekly Advocate*, 11 February 1837, on the link between education and respectability in the antebellum Northern black community in general.

16. *Philanthropist*, 11 March 1836, and Ann Plato, *Essays: Including Biographies and Miscellaneous Pieces, in Prose and Poetry*, edited by Henry Louis Gates Jr. (1841; reprint, New York: Oxford, 1988), xv, xviii. See also Editorial, "Colored Orphan Asylum," *Colored American*, 28 October 1837.

17. "A True Woman," *Frederick Douglass' Paper*, 24 December 1854, and "The Late Colored Concerts. From the National Era," *Frederick Douglass' Paper*, 1 December 1854.

18. "The Black Swan Again" and "From our NY Correspondent," *Frederick Douglass' Paper*, 18 December 1851 and 9 March 1855, respectively. On Greenfield's background, see Arthur R. LaBrew, *The Black Swan: Elizabeth T. Greenfield, Songstress: Biographical Study* (Detroit: n.p., 1969).

19. "W. S.," Letter to the Editor, "Christianity," and "'Died of Starvation,' by Miss Frances Ellen Watkins," *Provincial Freeman*, 2 September 1854; and "From Our Philadelphia Correspondent. No. III. The Black Swan in Baltimore—Narrative—Escapes, &c.," *Provincial Freeman*, 21 April 1855.

20. "The Black Siddons," *Provincial Freeman*, 12 May 1855, and "A Novelty," *Provincial Freeman*, 5 May 1855. See also Hutton, *The Early Black Press in America*, 74–75.

21. "Women's Sphere," *North Star*, 17 March 1848; "The Rights of Woman," *North Star*, 10 May 1850; "Lectures," *Provincial Freeman*, 17 March 1855; "Marriage of Lucy Stone under Protest," *Provincial Freeman*, 12 May 1855; "Woman," *North Star*, 26 May 1848; "One of Hungary's Heroines," *Frederick Douglass' Paper*, 31 July 1851.

22. Sarah Forten, quoted in Sterling, ed., *We Are Your Sisters*, 114.

23. Henry Louis Gates Jr. "Introduction," in Harriet E. Wilson, *Our Nig; or, Sketches from the Life of a Free Black* (New York: Random House, 1983), xiv, xviii; xxxv–xxxvii.

24. Wilson, *Our Nig*, 30; 68; 86–88; 94; 56–61; 111–15; 22.

25. Ibid., 124–25.

26. In Romero, *Home Fronts*, see 27–28 on *Our Nig*, and 20–22 and 25 on domesticity as antipatriarchal. Sedgwick did link her arguments against patriarchy with arguments against slavery, even though that was not her central focus. See, for example, Catharine Maria Sedgwick, *The Linwoods; or, "Sixty Years Since" in America* (1835; reprint, Hanover, N.H.: University Press of New England, 2002), 136–39.

27. Nell Irvin Painter, *Sojourner Truth: A Life, a Symbol* (New York: W. W. Norton, 1996), 22, 87, 103, 147, 4.

28. Ibid., 164–78, 121–29, 7, 154–57.

29. Ibid., 181, 187, 257. On historians' continuing tendency to see Truth as outside the ideology of true womanhood, see Yellin, *Women and Sisters*, 96; Yee, *Black Women Abolitionists*, 156; Jeffrey C. Stewart, "Introduction," in Sojourner Truth, *Narrative of Sojourner Truth*, ed. Henry Louis Gates Jr. (New York: Oxford University Press, 1988), xxxvi.

30. Harriet Jacobs [pseud. Linda Brent], *Incidents in the Life of a Slave Girl* (1861; reprint, New York: Harcourt, Brace, Jovanovich, 1973), 54–55, 56–58.

31. Carby, *Reconstructing Womanhood*, 49, 59; Yellin, *Women and Sisters*, 78–79, 88, 92–96. Lyde Cullen Sizer reiterates this point in *Political Work*, 68.

32. Carby, *Reconstructing Womanhood*, 58. Harriet Jacobs to Amy (Kirby) Post, June 21, [no year], #90, Post Papers, University of Rochester, on Black Abolitionist Papers reel 16:0676.

33. Donald Gibson, "Harriet Jacobs, Frederick Douglass, and the Slavery Debate: Bondage, Family, and the Discourse of Domesticity," in *Harriet Jacobs and Incidents in the Life of a Slave Girl*, ed. Deborah Garfield and Rafia Zafar (New York: Cambridge University Press, 1996), 166.

34. F. Gabriella Foreman, "Manifest in Signs: The Politics of Sex and Representation in Incidents in the Life of a Slave Girl," in *Harriet Jacobs and Incidents in the Life of a Slave Girl*, ed. Deborah Garfield and Rafia Zafar (New York: Cambridge University Press, 1996), 92; Sandra Gunning, "Reading and Redemption in Incidents in the Life of a Slave Girl," in *Harriet Jacobs and Incidents in the Life of a Slave Girl*, ed. Deborah Garfield and Rafia Zafar (New York: Cambridge University Press, 1996), 150.

35. For other discussions of *Incidents* that rely on Carby and Yellin's interpretations, see articles in Deborah Garfield and Rafia Zafar, eds., *Harriet Jacobs and Incidents in the Life of a Slave Girl* (New York: Cambridge University Press, 1996): Deborah Garfield, "Earwitness: Female Abolitionism, Sexuality, and *Incidents in the Life of a Slave Girl*"; Ernest, "Motherhood beyond the Gate"; Anne Bradford Warner, "Carnival Laughter: Resistance in *Incidents*"; and Stephanie Smith, "The Tender of Memory: Restructuring Value in Harriet Jacobs's *Incidents in the Life of a Slave Girl*," 127n35, 181–83, 189, 228, 254, 260–61. For an exception to this reading of Jacobs, see Mary Titus, "This Poisonous System: Social Ills, Bodily Ills, and *Incidents in the Life of a Slave Girl*," also in *Harriet Jacobs and Incidents*, ed. Garfield and Zafar, 211–12.

36. Romero, *Home Fronts*, 27–28.

37. Hannah Crafts, *The Bondwoman's Narrative*, edited and with an introduction by Henry Louis Gates Jr. (New York: Warner Books, 2002), xxxiii, lxxi–lxxii.

38. Ibid., 5–6, 10–12. The strikethroughs in these quotes are Hannah Crafts's. As editor, Henry Louis Gates Jr. left them intact.

39. Ibid., 82–83, 80.

40. Ibid., 99–100.

41. Ibid., 105–6.

42. Ibid., 102–3.

43. Ibid., 153, 152.

44. Ibid., 204–5, 206, 237–39.

45. "Declaration of Sentiments on the Sin of Slavery," *Colored American*, 17 June 1837. See also "The Beauties of Slavery!" *Weekly Advocate*, 31 January 1837.

46. Myra Jehlen, "The Family Militant: Domesticity versus Slavery in Uncle Tom's Cabin," *Criticism*, 31, no. 4 (1989): 397–98; Jeanne Boydston, Mary Kelley, and Anne Margolis, eds., *The Limits of Sisterhood: The Beecher Sisters on Women's Rights and Woman's Sphere* (Chapel Hill: University of North Carolina Press, 1988), 159–62.

47. Harriet Beecher Stowe, *Uncle Tom's Cabin* (1851–1852; reprint, New York: Bantam, 1981), 90, 75–91, 366–69, 393–94, 429. On the link between Eliza and Mrs. Bird, see also Sizer, *Political Work*, 56.

48. Frances Ellen Watkins, *Poems on Miscellaneous Subjects* (Boston: J. B. Yerrington, 1854), 9–11. *The Public Years of Sarah and Angelina Grimké*, edited and annotated by Larry Ceplair (New York: Columbia University Press, 1989), 337; on the similarity of Angelina's testimony to Sarah's, see 338–49. The Grimkés' testimony appeared in Theodore Dwight Weld, ed., *American Slavery as It Is: Testimony of a Thousand Witnesses* (New York: American Anti-Slavery Society, 1839). See also Jean Fagan Yellin's description of Lydia Maria Child's fiction, in which "all [female] slaves are patriarchy's true woman." Yellin, *Women and Sisters*, 53.

49. The newspaper lasted until 1829, when Russwurm emigrated to Liberia. Cornish then published another paper, *The Rights of All*, which ceased operation after a few months.

50. "Thoughts," *Freedom's Journal*, 13 April 1827; "Varieties—Woman," *Freedom's Journal*, 11 April 1828.

51. "What Does Your Sugar Cost? A Cottage Conversation on the Subject of British Negro Slavery," *Freedom's Journal*, 17 August 1827; "Miss Wright's Philanthropy," *Freedom's Journal*, 11 May 1827; "Summary," *Freedom's Journal*, 12 December 1828; and "Woman," *Freedom's Journal*, 14 February 1829.

52. For an extended discussion of this point, see chapter 4.

53. "To the Females of Colour" *Weekly Advocate*, 7 January 1837; "An Address Delivered before the Female Branch Society of Zion," *Colored American*, 3 June 1837.

54. *Colored American*, 17 November 1838. See also "Speech of Robert Banks . . . ," *Weekly Advocate*, 11 February and 18 February 1837; "A Word to Ladies" *Colored American*, 18 March 1837; and letter "For the Colored American," *Colored American*, 21 October, 1837.

55. "Woman's Eloquence," *Colored American*, 17 November 1838. For an extended discussion of coverage of the Grimké sisters in the *Colored American*, see chapter 4.

56. I have skipped several years here because the *Colored American*, like many other black newspapers in the antebellum period, succumbed to financial difficulties; it published its last issue in 1841. The next long-lasting black paper did not appear until 1847, when Frederick Douglass entered the newspaper business.

57. Benjamin Quarles, *Frederick Douglass* (New York: Atheneum, 1968), 87–95, and William McFeely, *Frederick Douglass* (New York: Norton, 1991), 164–65, 182. The newspaper survived the 1850s, but financial difficulties finally forced it to close in 1860.

58. "Woman," *North Star,* 25 May 1848; "Selections from the Washington County Journal. Woman's Influence," *North Star,* 2 June 1848. See also "Woman's Sphere," *North Star,* 17 March 1848; "Addressed to Husbands," *North Star,* 28 April 1848; "Woman's Devotion," *North Star,* 9 March 1849; "The Rights of Woman," *North Star,* 7 April 1849; and "Woman," *North Star,* 13 April 1849.

59. "The Rights of Women," *North Star,* 28 July 1848; and "Woman's Sphere," *North Star,* 17 March 1848.

60. For coverage of these issues in the second half of 1848, see "Selections from the Washington County Journal," 2 June 1848; "Presentation to the U.C.A. Association, Cincinnati," 25 August 1848; "Woman's Protection Union," 15 September 1848; "Women," 22 September 1848; and "Women's Rights Defended by a Young Lady of Sixteen," 13 October 1848, all in the *North Star.*

61. Black Canadians founded or attempted to found at least six newspapers before the Civil War. Some of these newspapers may never have been published; others lasted for a few months at most. The two exceptions were the *Voice of the Fugitive* and the *Provincial Freeman. The Black Abolitionist Papers: Canada, 1830–1865,* vol. 2, edited and with an introduction by C. Peter Ripley (Chapel Hill: University of North Carolina Press, 1986), 367.

62. "Mary E. Bibb to [Gerritt Smith] 8 November 1850," in *Black Abolitionist Papers,* 2:108–9; 2:111n3; 2:109n1.

63. In Syracuse, New York, Ward had published the *True American* from 1847 to 1848 and the *Impartial Citizen* from 1849 to 1851. See editorial note in *Black Abolitionist Papers,* 2:265; and 2:293n7.

64. The Provincial Freeman stopped publication for a short period in 1857, then restarted in 1858, this time under the editorship of Cary's brother Isaac Shadd. The newspaper went out of business in late 1860 or the first part of 1861. *Black Abolitionist Papers,* 2:192n10, 2:237n26, and 2:293n7.

65. In his introduction to *Black Abolitionist Papers,* C. Peter Ripley notes that the *Provincial Freeman* provided "extensive commentary on women's rights and responsibilities" (2:23).

66. "Women's Labor," 29 April 1854; "Woman's Rights," 12 August 1854; "Make Your Girls Independent," 4 November 1854; untitled item, 23 December 1854; and "Man's Sphere. By Mrs. Swisshelm," 23 September 1854, all in *Provincial Freeman.* Sylvia D. Hoffert, "Jane Grey Swisshelm, Elizabeth Keckley, and the Significance of Race Consciousness in American Women's History," *Journal of Women's History,* 13, no. 3 (2001): 16.

67. "The Famous Horse Tamer," *Provincial Freeman,* 26 August 1854.

68. I do not mean to suggest that a female editor was not a controversial figure. Cary was attacked for stepping out of her proper sphere by working as a newspaper editor. But the fact that she had this job at all points to the existence a very different climate from that of the 1830s.

4: PUBLIC WOMEN

1. John Quincy Adams, address to the House of Representatives, quoted in Harriet Martineau, *The Martyr Age of the United States* (1839; reprint, New York: Arno Press, 1969), 78–79.

2. Lydia Maria Child to E. Carpenter, 20 March 1838, quoted in Jean Fagan Yellin, *Women and Sisters: The Antislavery Feminists in American Culture* (New Haven, Conn.: Yale University Press, 1989), 29.

3. On the centrality of debates over female lecturing in the antebellum era, see Shirley Yee, *Black Women Abolitionists: A Study in Activism, 1828–1860* (Knoxville: University of Tennessee Press, 1992), 114–15; Yellin, *Women and Sisters*, 44–46. Frank Mott, and more recently Lyde Cullen Sizer, have commented on the ubiquity of public discussions of woman's sphere in the 1850s. I suggest that the issue became ubiquitous by the mid-1830s. Frank Mott, *History of American Magazines* 1, as cited in Lyde Cullen Sizer, *The Political Work of Northern Women Writers and the Civil War, 1850–1872* (Chapel Hill: University of North Carolina Press, 2000), 57.

4. On Southern approval of women's participation in benevolent organizations and partisan politics, see Elizabeth Varon, *We Mean to Be Counted: White Women and Politics in Antebellum Virginia* (Chapel Hill: University of North Carolina Press, 1998), 1, 101, and Douglas Carlson, "'Drinks He to His Own Undoing': Temperance Ideology in the Deep South," *Journal of the Early Republic* 18, no. 4 (1998): 659–91.

5. A number of scholars have noted that antebellum critics of female lecturers often compared such women to prostitutes and other types of "sexually deviant" women. For example, see Dorothy Sterling, *Ahead of Her Time: Abby Kelley and the Politics of Anti-Slavery* (New York: Norton, 1991), 173, 182, 232, 311; Nancy Isenberg, *Sex and Citizenship in Antebellum America* (Chapel Hill: University of North Carolina Press, 1998), 46; and Lori Ginzberg, "'The Hearts of Your Readers Will Shudder': Fanny Wright, Infidelity, and American Freethought," *American Quarterly*, 46, no. 2 (June 1994): 204. Julie Roy Jeffrey makes the same point about female antislavery petitioners. Julie Roy Jeffrey, *The Great Silent Army of Abolitionism: Ordinary Women in the Antislavery Movement* (Chapel Hill: University of North Carolina Press, 1998), 91.

6. Sarah Baker, for the Dorchester Female Anti-Slavery Society, to Abby Kelley, for the Lynn Female Anti-Slavery Society, 31 May 1838, Abby Kelley Foster Papers, American Antiquarian Society (AAS).

7. John Quincy Adams, quoted in Harriet Martineau, *The Martyr Age*, 78–79. While some scholars have considered this a "very narrow definition of women's right to petition" that described women "as social rather than political beings," I suggest that to define women primarily as moral and religious beings in the antebellum era was to define them as inside politics. See Isenberg, *Sex and Citizenship*, 65–66.

8. On the exceptional nature of antebellum female lecturers and women's rights activists, see Carroll Smith-Rosenberg, "The Beauty, the Beast, and the Militant Woman," in *Disorderly Conduct: Visions of Gender in Victorian America*, by Carroll Smith-Rosenberg (New York: Oxford University Press, 1985), 109–28; Nancy Hewitt, "Feminist Friends: Agrarian Quakers and the Emergence of Woman's Rights in America," *Feminist Studies* 12 (spring 1986): 28–29; Debra Gold Hansen, *Strained Sisterhood: Gen-*

der, Class, and Conflict in the Boston Female Anti-Slavery Society, 1833–1840 (Amherst: University of Massachusetts Press, 1993), 148–49; Yellin, *Women and Sisters*, 26, 60–61, 94, 154; Susan Hill Lindley, *"You Have Stept Out of Your Place": A History of Women and Religion in America* (Louisville, Ky.: Westminster John Knox Press, 1996), 52, 56; Sizer, *Political Work*, 9–10; Jeffrey, *Great Silent Army*, 7–8, 214; Isenberg, *Sex and Citizenship*, 69–72; Sylvia D. Hoffert, *When Hens Crow: The Woman's Rights Movement in Antebellum America* (Bloomington: Indiana University Press, 1995); and Lora Romero, *Home Fronts: Domesticity and Its Critics in the Antebellum United States* (Durham, N.C.: Duke University Press, 1997), 25.

9. Varon, *We Mean to Be Counted*, and Carolyn Lawes, *Women and Reform in a New England Community, 1815–1860* (Lexington: University of Kentucky Press, 2000), 191n5. By linking antebellum female lecturers to a tradition of female preachers, Nell Painter and Catherine Brekus argue that antebellum female lecturers were not as exceptional as historians have portrayed them to be. Nell Irvin Painter, *Sojourner Truth: A Life, a Symbol* (New York: W. W. Norton, 1996), 72–73; Catherine A. Brekus, "Let Your Women Keep Silence in the Churches: Female Preaching and Evangelical Religion in America, 1740–1845" (Ph.D. diss., Yale University, 1993), 12, 202, 318–19. Karlyn Kohrs Campbell also mentions a major expansion in female lecturers beginning in the 1830s. Karlyn Kohrs Campbell, ed., *Women Public Speakers in the United States, 1800–1925: A Bio-Critical Sourcebook* (Westport, Conn.: Greenwood Press, 1993), xiv.

10. Lawes, *Women and Reform*, 2, 189–90. Some recent works that continue to use the separate spheres concept are Sizer, *Political Work*, 10–11; Catherine E. Kelly, *In the New England Fashion: Reshaping Women's Lives in the Nineteenth Century* (Ithaca, N.Y.: Cornell University Press, 1999); John F. Marszalek, *The Petticoat Affair: Manners, Mutiny, and Sex in Andrew Jackson's White House* (1997; reprint, Baton Rouge: Louisiana State University Press, 2000), 53.

11. Painter, *Sojourner Truth*, 257–63.

12. On the antebellum Northern black community's acceptance of redemptive womanhood, see chapter 3 of this book.

13. Until recently, historians agreed that as the antebellum era progressed, women were pushed out of public life. See, for example, Mary Ryan, *Cradle of the Middle Class: The Family in Oneida County, New York, 1790–1865* (New York: Cambridge University Press, 1981), 146; and Lori Ginzberg, *Women and the Work of Benevolence: Morality, Politics, and Class in the Nineteenth-Century United States* (New Haven, Conn.: Yale University Press, 1990). A few historians have recently challenged this notion, suggesting that the American public became *more* accepting of women's presence on the public lecture platform in the 1840s and especially the 1850s. See, for example, Jeffrey, *Great Silent Army*, 198; Glenna Matthews, *The Rise of Public Woman: Woman's Power and Woman's Place in the United States, 1630–1970* (New York: Oxford University Press, 1992), 115; Campbell, ed., *Women Public Speakers*, xiv; and Varon, *We Mean to Be Counted*, 101.

14. Amanda Vickery, "Golden Age to Separate Spheres? A Review of the Categories and Chronology of English Women's History," *Historical Journal* 36, no. 2 (1993): 400.

15. Brekus, "Let Your Women Keep Silence," 4, 7, 13, 146, 163.

16. Jarena Lee, *Religious Experience and Journal of Mrs. Jarena Lee, Giving an Account of Her Call to Preach the Gospel* (1836; revision, Philadelphia: J. Lee, 1849), reprinted in Henry Louis Gates Jr., ed., *Spiritual Narratives*, (New York: Oxford University Press, 1988), 10, 11.

17. Zilpha Elaw, *Memoirs of the Life, Religious Experience, Ministerial Travels, and Labours of Mrs. Zilpha Elaw, an American Female of Colour* (London, 1846), reprinted in *Sisters of the Spirit: Three Black Women's Autobiographies of the Nineteenth Century*, ed. William L. Andrews (Bloomington: Indiana University Press, 1986), 73, 75–79; 82.

18. Almond H. Davis, *The Female Preacher; or, Memoir of Salome Lincoln* (1843; reprint, New York: Arno Press, 1972), 36, 37, 38–40.

19. Linda Kerber, *No Constitutional Right to Be Ladies: Women and the Obligations of Citizenship* (New York: Hill and Wang, 1998), xxiii. Disapproval of female lecturing can be traced back to eighteenth-century American gender ideology, which did exclude women from public life. Mary Beth Norton, *Founding Mothers and Fathers: Gendered Power and the Forming of American Society* (New York: Alfred A. Knopf, 1996), 404–5.

20. Kerber, *No Constitutional Right*, xxiii, 146, 305. Nancy Isenberg has also noted that at the start of the antebellum era "inherited arguments—religious, political and legal—already existed that were used to justify women's difference and their subordinate status." Isenberg, *Sex and Citizenship*, xiii.

21. On the "antipatriarchal nature" of antebellum gender ideology, see Romero, *Home Fronts*, 20.

22. Campbell, *Women Public Speakers*, xiv.

23. Blanche Hersh, in her study of fifty-one prominent antebellum feminist-abolitionists, found that all of these women "felt 'called' to a special vocation, usually at an early age." Blanche Glassman Hersh, *The Slavery of Sex: Feminist-Abolitionists in America* (Urbana: University of Illinois Press, 1978), 138.

24. "Mrs Stewart's Farewell Address to Her Friends . . . September 21, 1833," in Maria W. Stewart, *Productions of Mrs Maria W. Stewart, Presented to the First African Baptist Church and Society of the City of Boston* (Boston: Friends of Freedom and Virtue, 1835), reprinted in Henry Louis Gates Jr., ed., *Spiritual Narratives*, (New York: Oxford University Press, 1988), 74–75, 6.

25. Sarah Grimké, quoted in Gerda Lerner, *The Grimké Sisters from South Carolina: Pioneers for Woman's Rights and Abolition* (New York: Schocken, 1971), 144; see also pp. 136, 138; Catherine Birney, *The Grimké Sisters: Sarah and Angelina Grimké, the First Women Advocates of Abolition and Woman's Rights* (Boston: Lee and Shepard, 1885), 31, 56, 62, 128, 130, 149; and *The Public Years of Sarah and Angelina Grimké: Selected Writings, 1835–1839*, edited and annotated by Larry Ceplair (New York: Columbia University Press, 1989), 16, 142.

26. Sarah and Angelina Grimké to Henry C. Wright, 27 August 1837, Brookline, [Mass.], in Gilbert H. Barnes and Dwight L. Dumond, eds., *Letters of Theodore Dwight Weld, Angelina Grimké Weld, and Sarah Grimké, 1822–1844*, vol. 1 (1934; reprint, Gloucester Mass.: Peter Smith, 1965), 437.

27. Abby Kelley Foster to Alla Foster, 1883, Abby Kelley Foster Papers, Worcester Historical Society; "Reminiscences of Mrs Abby Kelley Foster," *Woman's Journal*, 7

February 1891, 42; and Abby Kelley Foster to Anne W. Weston, 29 May 1839, Weston Sisters Papers, Boston Public Library.

28. Eleanor Flexner, *A Century of Struggle: The Women's Rights Movement in the United States* (Cambridge, Mass.: Harvard University Press, 1959), 44; see also Yellin, *Women and Sisters*, 47.

29. Stewart, "Mrs Stewart's Farewell Address to her Friends . . . September 21, 1833," and "Religion and the Pure Principles of Morality . . . Delivered in Boston, October 1831," in Stewart, *Productions of Mrs Maria W. Stewart*, 75–76, 12–13, 16.

30. Sarah Grimké, *Letters on the Equality of the Sexes and Other Essays*, edited by Elizabeth Ann Bartlett (New Haven, Conn.: Yale University Press, 1988), 38; see also Angelina Grimké, *Letters to Catharine E. Beecher* (1838; reprint, New York: Arno Press, 1969), 115.

31. *Proceedings of the Anti-Slavery Convention of American Women Held in the City of New York, May 9th, 10th, 11th, and 12th, 1837* (New York: W. S. Dorr, 1837), 9.

32. Abby Kelley, "The Woman Question," *Liberator,* 27 March 1840, 52.

33. Boston Female Anti-Slavery Society [Maria W. Chapman], *Right and Wrong in Boston: The Annual Report of the Boston Female Anti-Slavery Society . . . in 1837* (Boston: Isaac Knapp, 1837), 75.

34. Letter to the editor, *Liberator,* 6 March 1840, 88.

35. Lydia Maria Child, "Speaking in the Church," *National Anti-Slavery Standard,* 15 July 1841, 22, quoted in Lydia Maria Child, *A Lydia Maria Child Reader,* edited by Carolyn Karcher (Durham, N.C.: Duke University Press, 1997), 356–57.

36. On women's increasing involvement in party politics in the 1840s and 1850s, see Varon, *We Mean to Be Counted,* 101. Julie Roy Jeffrey mentions that by 1856, half of the people attending Republican Party rallies in New York state were women. Jeffrey, *Great Silent Army,* 169. See also Matthews, *The Rise of Public Woman,* 118–19.

37. Sarah Baker, for the Dorchester Female Anti-Slavery Society, to Abby Kelley, for the Lynn Female Anti-Slavery Society, 31 May 1838, Abby Kelley Foster Papers, AAS.

38. Ernestine Rose speech in *Proceedings of the Woman's Rights Convention Held at Worcester, October 15th and 16th, 1851* (New York: Fowler and Wells, 1852), 46–47; Lucy Stone, "An Address before the Female Moral Reform Society of Gardiner, Mass., about 1850," Blackwell Family Papers, Library of Congress; and "What Have Women to Do with Slavery," *Liberator,* 1 November 1839, 174.

39. Maria W. Stewart, "An Address Delivered before the Afric-American Female Intelligence Society of Boston" and "Farewell Address," in Henry Louis Gates Jr., ed., *Spiritual Narratives* (New York: Oxford University Press, 1988), 59; 76.

40. William Lloyd Garrison to Sarah M. Douglass, 5 March 1832, Anti-Slavery Collection, Boston Public Library.

41. Lucy M. Wright, sec. of Portage Co. Female Anti-Slavery Society to Boston Female Anti-Slavery Society, Talmadge Ohio, Aug. 11, 1836, in *Right and Wrong in Boston in 1836. Annual Report of the Boston Female Anti-Slavery Society* (Boston, 1836), 72–74; 73.

42. Speech of James Forten Jr., delivered before the Philadelphia Female Anti-Slavery Society, Philadelphia, 14 April 1836, in *The Black Abolitionist Papers: The United*

States, 1830–1846, vol. 3. Edited and with an introduction by C. Peter Ripley (Chapel Hill: University of North Carolina Press, 1985), 154–67; 162–63.

43. Ada [Sarah Forten], "Lines," *Liberator*, 6 October 1836, quoted in Yee, *Black Women Abolitionists*, 123–24.

44. Essay by "A Colored Woman," November 1839, in *Charter Oak*, Hartford, Conn., in, *Black Abolitionist Papers*, vol. 3, 326–27. See also Editorial, "Colored Orphan Asylum," *Colored American*, 28 October 1837.

45. "Extract from Dr. Channing's pamphlet entitled 'Emancipation,'" in *Ten Years of Experience: Ninth Annual Report of the Boston Female Anti-Slavery Society* (Boston: Oliver Johnson, 1842), 26–27.

46. "Selections from the Washington County Journal," *North Star*, 2 June 1848; "Presentation to the U.C.A. association, Cincinnati," *North Star*, 25 August 1848; and "The Rights of Women," *North Star*, 28 July 1848.

47. Thomas Wentworth Higginson, *Woman and Her Wishes; an Essay: Inscribed to the Massachusetts Constitutional Convention* (Boston: R. F. Wallcut, 1853), 24; and "Letter of Dr. Jos. R. Buchanan to the Woman's Rights Convention at Akron, 1851," in *The Proceedings of the Woman's Rights Convention held at Akron, Ohio, May 28th and 29th, 1851* (1851; reprint, New York: Burt Franklin, 1973), 48.

48. Lerner, *Grimké Sisters*, 163–64, 168, 169.

49. "Pastoral Letter of the . . . General Association of the Massachusetts Congregationalist Clergy" quoted in Aileen S. Kraditor, ed., *Up from the Pedestal: Selected Writings in the History of American Feminism* (Chicago: Quadrangle Books, 1968), 51–52.

50. Hubbard Winslow, *Woman as She Should Be and Woman in Her Social and Domestic Character* (Boston: T. H. Carter, 1838), 39, vi. On these ministers' sermons, see Boston Female Anti-Slavery Society [Maria W. Chapman], *Right and Wrong in Boston . . . in 1837*, 5. The powerful Congregationalists took the lead in these criticisms, but ministers from other sects joined in as well. See, for example, "Abolition Women," in the *Liberator*, 22 September 1837, and Parsons Cooke, *Female Preaching, Unlawful and Inexpedient. A Sermon by Parsons Cooke, Pastor of the First Church in Lynn* (Lynn, Mass.: James R. Newhall, 1837), 9–10.

51. Jonathan Sterns, *Rev. Mr. Sterns' Discourse on Female Influence, and the True Christian Mode of Its Exercise* (Newburyport, Mass.: John G. Tilton, 1837), 22, 23.

52. Letter to the editor, *Colored American*, 30 September 1837, and "For the *Colored American*, Lodge Nelsonville, Athens Co. O, 25th of 9th month, 1839," *Colored American*, 12 October 1839.

53. Winslow, *Woman as She Should Be*, 25–26; Cooke, *Female Preaching*, 3.

54. Ginzberg, "The Hearts of Your Readers Will Shudder," 201, 206, 199; Cooke, *Female Preaching*, 9. On the power of "Fanny Wrightism" as a negative label, see also Flexner, *Century of Struggle*, 27–28.

55. Amos Farnsworth letter to Anne W. Weston, 25 March 1838, Weston Sisters Papers; and Editorial [Samuel Cornish], "Ladies Beware," *Colored American*, 18 May 1839.

56. Elizabeth Cady Stanton, Susan B. Anthony, and Matilda Joslyn Gage, eds., *History of Woman Suffrage*, vol. 1 (New York: Fowler & Wells, 1881), 40; Abby Kelley, quoted in Sterling, *Ahead of Her Time*, 173; *Exeter Newsletter and Rockingham Advertiser*, 22 September 1846.

57. "Reminiscences of Mrs Abby Kelley Foster," *Woman's Journal*, 7 February 1891, 42.

58. Sarah Gould to Abby Kelley, Cranston, Rhode Island, 11 November 1841, Abby Kelley Foster Papers, AAS; Abby Kelley to Maria Chapman, 12 August 1843, Seneca Falls, N.Y., Weston Sisters Papers; Abby Kelley to Stephen Foster, 1 June 1843, quoted in Sterling, *Ahead of Her Time*, 170; and Abby Kelley to Stephen S. Foster, 7 June 1843, East Hampton, Abby Kelley Foster Papers, AAS. Jean Fagan Yellin has noted that women "who entered the public sphere" in the antebellum era "were routinely condemned as sexual nonconformists." Yellin, *Women and Sisters*, 65.

59. Sterling, *Ahead of Her Time*, 311; Paulina Wright Davis, letters to Abby Kelley, January–March 1843, quoted in Sterling, *We Are Your Sisters*, 160; Paulina S. Wright to Abby Kelley, August 1843, Utica, Abby Kelley Foster Papers, AAS; *North Star*, quoted in Sterling, *We Are Your Sisters*, 170; see also Yee, *Black Women Abolitionists*, 66.

60. Abby Kelley to Stephen S. Foster, 30 July 1843, Utica; Ansel Bascom, Edward Lyon, and Abraham Failing to Abby Kelley, 16 February 1844, Seneca Falls, Abby Kelly Foster Papers, AAS; Glenn Altschuler and Jan Saltzgaber, eds., *Revivalism, Social Conscience, and Community in the Burned-Over District: The Trial of Rhoda Bement* (Ithaca, N.Y.: Cornell University Press, 1983), 110–23; 133–36.

61. Jeffrey, *Great Silent Army*, 201. See also Isenberg, *Sex and Citizenship*, 61. However, not all contemporary accounts suggest that Kelley's style was so confrontational. Margaret Fuller, for example, referred to her as a "gentle hero" at one lecture. Margaret Fuller, *Woman in the Nineteenth Century, and Kindred Papers Relating to the Sphere, Condition, and Duties of Woman* (1855; reprint, New York: W. W. Norton, 1971), 110–11. There is evidence that the differences among female public speakers were more regional than class-based. In an 1843 diary entry, Massachusetts resident Lucy Chase noted with surprise that when she attended an antislavery meeting in Philadelphia, "the language used was strikingly mild in comparison with what we generally hear in N. England." Lucy Chase Diary, 30 August 1843, diaries (fragments), Chase Family Papers, American Antiquarian Society. See also Lerner, *Grimké Sisters*, 165–66.

62. James Oliver Horton, "Freedom's Yoke: Gender Conventions among Antebellum Free Blacks," *Feminist Studies* 12, no. 1 (1986): 63, 71. Horton writes that the black community was generally supportive of female lecturers, but Stewart was an exception because she criticized black men. However, other historians note that the Northern black community was frequently hostile toward women lecturers. See, for example, Yee, *Black Women Abolitionists*, 8, 114–15; and Yellin, *Women and Sisters*, 45.

63. Lydia Maria Child, *Letters of Lydia Maria Child* (Boston: Houghton, Mifflin, 1883), quoted in Lerner, *Grimké Sisters*, 8; "Pastoral Letter," in Kraditor, *Up from the Pedestal*, 51; Angelina Grimké, letter to Theodore Weld and John Greenleaf Whittier, 8 August 1837, in Barnes and Dumond, *Letters of Theodore Dwight Weld*, 1:430.

64. See, for example, Susan B. Anthony to Elizabeth Cady Stanton, Rochester, 26 May 1856, Elizabeth Cady Stanton Papers, Douglas College, Rutgers University; Caroline F. Putnam to Samuel May, 22 January 1887, Samuel J. May Papers, Massachusetts Historical Society (MHS); Antoinette Brown to Lucy Stone, late winter 1848, in Carol Lasser and Marlene Deahl Merrill, eds., *Friends and Sisters: Letters between Lucy Stone and*

Antoinette Brown Blackwell, 1846–1893 (Urbana: University of Illinois Press, 1987), 35; Caroline Dall, journal entries of 27 February 1856 and 16 April 1857, Caroline Dall Papers, Massachusetts Historical Society; ? to Abby Kelley Foster, 23 January 1857, Abby Kelley Foster Papers, AAS; Lucy Stone to Samuel J. May, 9 July 1851, Samuel J. May Papers, Boston Public Library (BPL); and Abby Kelley Foster to Maria Chapman, 12 August 1843, Weston Sisters Papers.

65. Lucy Stone to Susan B. Anthony, 9 January 1857, Blackwell Family Papers; Lucy Stone to Samuel J. May, West Brookfield, 9 July 1851, Samuel J. May Papers, BPL; Caroline Putnam to Samuel May, Lottsburg, Virginia, 22 January 1887, Samuel J. May Papers, MHS.

66. "Pastoral Letter" in Kraditor, *Up from the Pedestal*, 51–52.

67. Sterns, *Rev. Mr. Sterns' Discourse on Female Influence*, 11, 9–10.

68. Ellen, "Female Influence," *Colored American*, 30 September 1837.

69. Editorial [Samuel Cornish], "Ladies Beware," *Colored American*, 18 May 1839; Editorial, *Colored American*, 14 September 1839, quoted in James Oliver Horton, "Freedom's Yoke," 55; Ellen, "Female Influence," *Colored American*, 30 September 1837.

70. "To the Females of Colour," *Weekly Advocate*, 7 January 1837.

71. "Address Delivered before the Colored Female Dorcas Society of the City of Buffalo by Robert Banks, a Colored Man—Part 1" *Weekly Advocate*, 11 February 1837.

72. Kathryn Kish Sklar, *Catharine Beecher: A Study in American Domesticity* (New York: Norton, 1976 [1973]), 135, 132, 134; Catharine Beecher, *An Essay on Slavery and Abolitionism: With Reference to the Duty of American Females* (Philadelphia: Henry Perkins, 1837), 128.

73. Jeanne Boydston, Mary Kelley, and Anne Margolis, eds., *The Limits of Sisterhood: The Beecher Sisters on Women's Rights and Woman's Sphere* (Chapel Hill: University of North Carolina Press, 1988), 1, 7. Boydston, Kelley, and Margolis agree that nineteenth-century Americans were "almost continually at odds over the proper place of females."

74. Catharine Beecher, *Essay on Slavery and Abolitionism*, 102. Angelina Grimké, *Letters to Catharine Beecher*, 108; Angelina E. Grimké to Amos A. Phelps, 2 September 1837, Brookline, Massachusetts, Amos A. Phelps Papers, Boston Public Library; "Justice," letter to the editor, *Boston Courier*, reprinted in *Liberator*, 27 November 1840, 189. On the indeterminacy of woman's sphere, see also Lucy Stone, "The Province of Woman," undated [the words "early essay" are handwritten on the manuscript], Lucy Stone file, Blackwell Family Papers.

75. Abby Kelley to William L. Garrison, *Liberator*, 20 September 1839, 150.

76. Sterns, *Rev. Mr. Sterns' Discourse on Female Influence*, 12; Daniel D. Smith, *Lectures on Domestic Duties* (Portland, Maine: S. H. Colesworthy, 1837), 91.

77. H. H. Amringe, "Woman's Rights in Church and State," *Proceedings of the National Women's Rights Convention held at Worcester, October 23rd and 24th 1850* (Boston, 1851), 36–37; Antoinette Brown speech, *Proceedings of the Woman's Rights Convention, held at Worcester, October 15th and 16th, 1851*, 89.

78. Fuller, *Woman in the Nineteenth Century*, 48.

79. Dr. C. B. Judd to Amos A. Phelps, 4 March 1846, Amos A. Phelps Papers.

80. Even if Judd was aware of the controversy over female lecturers in the anti-slavery movement, he still could not have expected Phelps to call a female abolitionist "pernicious."

81. Fuller, *Woman in the Nineteenth Century*, 110–11.

82. Benjamin Barney to John Collins and Abby Kelley, 16 October 1842[?], Westport, Conn., Abby Kelley Foster Papers, WHS; Sarah Gould to Abby Kelley, 11 November 1841, Cranston, and Ansel Bascom et al. to Abby Kelley, 16 February 1844, Abby Kelley Foster Papers, AAS.

83. See chapter 2 for a discussion of Hale's treatment of Sand.

84. Sarah Josepha Buell Hale, *The Lecturess; or, Woman's Sphere* (Boston: Whipple and Damrell, 1839), and *Woman's Record; or, Sketches of All Distinguished Women from the Creation to A.D. 1854*, 2nd rev. ed. (New York: Harper, 1855), xxxvi, xlviii, xl.

85. Hale, *Woman's Record*, xxxvi, xlviii, xl, 619–20, 641–42, 666, 739–40, 752–53.

86. Sizer, *Political Work*, 66, 60.

5: THE IMPENDING CRISIS, MALE IMMORALITY, AND FEMALE HEROISM

1. Theodore Parker, *A Sermon on the Public Function of Woman . . . March 27, 1853* (Boston, 1853), 17.

2. Byron Sunderland, *Discourse to Young Ladies: A Sermon by Rev. Byron Sunderland, Pastor of the First Presbyterian Church . . . Delivered the 22nd Day of January, 1857* (Washington, D.C.: C. Wendell, 1857), 27.

3. Ibid., 18, 12, 30–31.

4. Jonathan Sterns, *Rev. Mr. Sterns' Discourse on Female Influence, and the True Christian Mode of Its Exercise* (Newburyport, Mass.: John G. Tilton, 1837), 23.

5. William Appleman Williams, *The Contours of American History* (1966; reprint, New York: Norton, 1988), 270–76, 285–90. See also Michael Paul Rogin, *Fathers and Children: Andrew Jackson and the Subjugation of the American Indian* (1975; reprint, New Brunswick, N.J.: Transaction Publishers, 1991), 296–313; and David Potter, *The Impending Crisis, 1848–1861* (New York: Harper and Row, 1976). For fictional accounts of the inability to solve the problems of modern urban society except by abandonment of that society, see two of George Lippard's extremely popular books, *The Quaker City; or, The Monks of Monk Hall* (1844; reprint, New York: Odyssey Press, 1970), and *New York: Its Upper Ten and Lower Million* (1853; reprint, New York: Irvington, 1993). Both of these urban exposés reach their resolution in the final few pages when the redeemed characters moved out of the city to start new lives as country farmers.

6. Charles Sumner, "The Crime against Kansas: The Apologies for the Crime, the True Remedy, Delivered to the United States Senate, 19–20 May 1856," in *The Works of Charles Sumner* (Boston: Lee and Shepard, 1870–1873), 4:125–48, as quoted in James M. McPherson, *Battle Cry of Freedom: The Civil War Era* (1988; reprint, New York: Ballantine, 1989), 150. On Texas, the Mexican-American War, and violence surrounding Kansas, see McPherson, *Battle Cry of Freedom*, 47–58 and 145–53.

7. As Brian Roberts has argued in the context of his discussion of the California Gold Rush, the logic of antebellum gender ideology "seemed to demand that women, in

order to uphold the social fabric, constantly and repeatedly wage war on men." Brian Roberts, *American Alchemy: The California Gold Rush and Middle-Class Culture* (Chapel Hill: University of North Carolina Press, 2000), 230.

8. Catharine Beecher, "Appeal to American Women," *American Woman's Home; or, Principles of Domestic Science* (New York: J. B. Ford and Company, 1869), 468, quoted in Jeanne Boydston, Mary Kelley, and Anne Margolis, eds., *The Limits of Sisterhood: The Beecher Sisters on Women's Rights and Woman's Sphere* (Chapel Hill: University of North Carolina Press, 1988), 251; *First Annual Report of the Dorchester Female Anti-Slavery Society* (Boston: D. Clapp, 1838), 11; Nathaniel P. Rogers, *An Address Delivered before the Concord Female Anti-Slavery Society at Its Annual Meeting, 25 December 1837* (Concord, N.H.: W. White, 1838), 12–18.

9. "Female Conventions," *The Friend of Virtue: Journal of the New England Female Moral Reform Society* 1, no. 11 (1838), 173.

10. Thomas Wentworth Higginson, *Woman and Her Wishes; An Essay: Inscribed to the Massachusetts Constitutional Convention* (Boston: R. F. Wallcut, 1853), 24. On the linkage of men to market values and of women to "communal values," see also E. Anthony Rotundo, *American Manhood: Transformations in Masculinity from the Revolution to the Modern Era* (New York: Basic Books, 1993), 24–25, and Boydston, Kelley, and Margolis, *Limits of Sisterhood*, 5. Also see the introduction for more on this point.

11. Samuel J. May, *The Rights and Conditions of Women: A Sermon Preached in Syracuse, November 1845* (n.p., 1845), 1, 8.

12. Parker, *Sermon on the Public Function of Woman*, 18.

13. See also Elizabeth Cady Stanton, letter to the Woman's Rights Convention, *Proceedings of the Woman's Rights Convention Held at Worcester, October 23rd and 24th, 1850* (Boston: Prentiss & Sawyer, 1851), 52; speech of Mrs. C. J. H. Nichols, *Proceedings of the Woman's Rights Convention Held at the Broadway Tabernacle in the City of New York . . . September 6th and 7th, 1853* (New York: Fowler and Well, 1853), 58.

14. Speech of Mary Ann Johnson, Proceedings of the Woman's Rights Convention . . . West Chester, Pa., June 2d and 3d, 1852 (Philadelphia: n.p., 1852), 7, 9–10.

15. Letter from Mrs. C. M. Steele, *Proceedings of the Woman's Rights Convention Held at Akron Ohio, May 28th and 29th, 1851* (1851; reprint, New York: Burt Franklin, 1973), 39.

16. See, for example, *Report of the Woman's Rights Convention Held at Seneca Falls, N.Y., July 19th and 20th, 1848* (Rochester, N.Y.: Printed at the *North Star* Office, 1848); *Proceedings of the Woman's Rights Convention, Held at the Unitarian Church, Rochester, N.Y., August 2, 1848 . . . Revised by Amy Post* (New York : R.J. Johnston, 1870); *Proceedings of the Woman's Rights Convention Held at Worcester . . . 1850; Proceedings of the Woman's Rights Convention Held at Akron, Ohio . . . 1851; Proceedings of the Woman's Rights Convention Held at Worcester, October 15th and 16th, 1851* (New York: Fowler and Wells, 1852); *Proceedings of the Woman's Rights Convention Held at West Chester, Pa. . . . 1852; Proceedings of the Woman's Rights Convention Held at Syracuse, September 8th, 9th, and 10th, 1852* (Syracuse: J. E. Masters, 1852); *Proceedings of the Woman's Rights Convention Held at . . . New York . . . 1853; Proceedings of the Woman's Rights Convention Held at Cleveland, Ohio . . . October 5th, 6th, and 7th, 1853* (Cleveland: Gray, Beardsley, Spear, 1854); *Reports on the*

Laws of New England, Presented to the New England Meeting Convened at the Meionaon, September 19 and 20, 1855 (Boston: n.p., 1855); and *Report of the Woman's Rights Meeting at Mercantile Hall, May 27, 1859* (Boston: S. Urbino, 1859). For national conventions between 1853 and 1866, see *Proceedings of the National Woman's Rights Convention* (Cleveland: Grey, Beardsley, Spear & Co, 1853–1866).

17. Until Mary Kelley and Nina Baym recently focused on histories written by and about women in the first half of the nineteenth century, scholars had not even noticed the existence of the study of women's history in the antebellum era. For example, Aileen Kraditor asserted that nineteenth-century women "wrote as little history as they made [so] it is not surprising that historiography faithfully reflected their exclusion." Only "toward the end of the nineteenth century," she wrote, "did this begin to change." Aileen S. Kraditor, ed., *Up from the Pedestal: Selected Writings in the History of American Feminism* (Chicago: Quadrangle Books, 1968), 3; Nina Baym, "Women and the Republic: Emma Willard's Rhetoric of History," *American Quarterly* 43, no. 1 (1991): 1–23; Nina Baym, *American Women Writers and the Work of History, 1790–1860* (New Brunswick, N.J.: Rutgers University Press, 1995); Mary Kelley, "Designing a Past for the Present: Women Writing Women's History in Nineteenth-Century America," *Proceedings of the American Antiquarian Society* 105, part 2 (1995): 315–46.

18. David Reynolds, *Beneath the American Renaissance: The Subversive Imagination in the Age of Emerson and Melville* (Cambridge, Mass.: Harvard University Press, 1988), 338; Bayard Taylor, *Hannah Thurston: A Story of American Life* (New York: G. P. Putnam, 1863); Ann S. Stephens, *Malaeska, the Indian Wife of the White Hunter,* with an introduction by Frank P. O'Brien (1860; reprint, New York, The John Day Company, 1929), xiii–xvi; Henry Nash Smith, *Virgin Land: The American West as Symbol and Myth* (Cambridge, Mass.: Harvard University Press, 1950), 87. Nina Baym has also pointed out that a number of women in addition to Stephens wrote dime novels for Beadle. Nina Baym, *Woman's Fiction: A Guide to Novels by and about Women, 1820–1870* (Ithaca, N.Y.: Cornell University Press, 1978), 176. Lieutenant Murray [Maturin Murray Ballou], *Fanny Campbell, The Female Pirate Captain: A Tale of the Revolution* (1844; reprint, Boston: F. Gleason, 1845); and Maturin Murray Ballou, *Notable Thoughts about Women* (Boston: Houghton, Mifflin, 1882).

19. On Southworth, see, in particular, Dee Garrison, "Immoral Fiction in the Late Victorian Library," *American Quarterly* 28 (spring 1976): 71–80; Baym, *Women's Fiction,* 110–26; Mary Kelley, *Private Woman, Public Stage: Literary Domesticity in Nineteenth-Century America* (New York: Oxford University Press, 1984); E. D. E. N. Southworth, *The Hidden Hand; or, Capitola the Madcap,* with an introduction by Joanne Dobson (1859; reprint, New Brunswick, N.J.: Rutgers University Press, 1988).

20. Baym, *American Women Writers,* 239.

21. Kelley, "Designing a Past," 342, 346; Baym, *American Women Writers,* 219.

22. Kelley, "Designing a Past," 334, 323; Baym, *American Women Writers,* 5, 239, 6–7.

23. Lydia Maria Child, *The History of the Condition of Women, in Various Ages and Nations* (Boston: J. Allen & Co., 1835), *The Biographies of Lady Russell and Madame Guyon* (Boston: Carter, Hendee & 1832), *The Biographies of Madame de Staël and Madame Roland* (Boston: Carter and Hendee, 1832), and *Good Wives* (Boston: Carter, Hendee, &

Co., 1833), published again as *Biographies of Good Wives* in 1846. On these histories, see Sarah Josepha Buell Hale, *Woman's Record; or, Sketches of All Distinguished Women, from "the Beginning" till A.D. 1850* (New York: Harper & Brothers, 1853), later updated to 1854, then 1868; Jesse Clement, *Noble Deeds of American Women*, new edition revised (Auburn and Buffalo, N.Y.: Miller, Orton & Mulligan, 1854; original edition published in 1851); Maria McIntosh, *Woman in America: Her Work and Her Reward* (New York: D. Appleton, 1850); Elizabeth Fries Ellet, *The Women of the American Revolution*, 3 vols. (New York: Baker and Scribner, 1848–1850), *Domestic History of the American Revolution* (New York: Baker and Scribner, 1850), and *Pioneer Women of the West* (1852; reprint, Freeport, N.Y.: Books for Libraries Press, 1973); Caroline Dall, *Historical Pictures Retouched: A Volume of Miscellanies* (Boston: Walker, Wise, and Company, 1860). Margaret Fuller, *Woman in the Nineteenth-Century, and Kindred Papers Relating to the Sphere, Condition, and Duties of Woman* (1855; reprint, New York: W. W. Norton, 1971); Eliza Farnham, *Woman and Her Era* (New York: A. J. Davis, 1864); Edward Mansfield, *The Legal Rights, Liabilities, and Duties of Women with an Introductory History of their Legal Condition in the Hebrew, Roman, and Feudal Civil Systems* (Salem, Mass.: J. P. Jewett & Co., 1845).

24. Child, *History of the Condition of Women*, 1:iii, 2:211. On Hale as author of *Woman's Record*, see Kelley, "Designing a Past," 336–38; on Hale as editor of *Godey's Lady's Book*, see Laura McCall, "'The Reign of Brute Force Is Over': A Content Analysis of *Godey's Lady's Book*, 1830–1860," *Journal of the Early Republic* 9 (summer 1989): 235; Elizabeth Blackwell to Henry B. Blackwell, 27 December 1854[?], Blackwell Family Papers, Library of Congress.

25. John Frost, *Heroic Women of the West* (Philadelphia: A. Hart, 1854); Celestia Angenette Bloss, *Heroines of the Crusades* (Muscatine, Iowa: R. M. Burnett, 1852); George Coles, *Heroines of Methodism; or, Pen and Ink Sketches of the Mothers and Daughters of the Church* (New York: Carlton & Porter, 1857); Mary E. Hewitt, ed., *Heroines of History* (New York: Cornish, Lamport, 1852); Emily Owen, *The Heroines of History* (New York: Carlton & Phillips, 1854); John Stilwell Jenkins, *The Heroines of History* (Auburn, N.Y.: Alden and Beardsley, 1855). See also Frank Boott Goodrich, *Women of Beauty and Heroism from Semiramis to Eugenie* (New York: Derby & Jackson, 1859); Clement, *Noble Deeds of American Women*; and Elizabeth Starling, *Noble Deeds of Woman; or, Examples of Female Courage and Virtue* (Boston: Phillips, Sampson and Co., 1850).

26. Ellet, *The Women of the American Revolution*, *Domestic History of the American Revolution*, and *Pioneer Women of the West*. This trend continued during and after the Civil War. See, for example, Linus Brockett and Mary C. Vaughan, eds., *Woman's Work in the Civil War: A Record of Heroism, Patriotism, and Patience* (Philadelphia: Zeigler, McCurdy & Co., 1867); and Frank Moore, *Women of the War: Their Heroism and Self-Sacrifice* (Hartford, Conn.: S. S. Scranton, 1866). For the period after the Civil War, see Caroline Dall, *The College, the Market, and the Court; or, Woman's Relation to Education, Labor, and Law* (Boston: Lee and Shepard, 1867); Lydia Sigourney, *Great and Good Women: Biographies for Girls* (Edinburgh: W. P. Nimmo, 1871 [1866]); James Parton, Thomas Wentworth Higginson, and Horace Greeley, *Eminent Women of the Age: Being Narratives of the Lives and Deeds of the Most Prominent Women of the Present Generation* (Hartford, Conn.: S. M. Betts, 1868); Ballou, *Notable Thoughts about Women*; Harriet Beecher

Stowe, *Our Famous Women* (Hartford: A. D. Worthington, 1883), and *Woman in Sacred History* (New York: J. B. Ford and Co., 1874), published again later as *Bible Heroines* in 1978 (New York: Fords, Howard & Hulbert); Julia Ward Howe, *Sketches of Representative Women of New England* (Boston: New England Historical Publishing Company, 1904); and Frances Willard, *American Women: Fifteen Hundred Biographies* (New York: Mast, Crowell & Kirkpatrick, 1897).

27. As Nina Baym points out, "feminist" and "anti-feminist" writers of women's history in the first half of the nineteenth century "share ideas of women that make them seem as much alike as different." Baym, *American Women Writers*, 231.

28. Child, *Good Wives* and *History of the Condition of Women*; David Francis Bacon, ed., *Memoirs of Eminently Pious Women of Britain and America* (New Haven: D. McLeod, 1833); *Sketches of the Lives of Distinguished Females, Written for Girls, with a View to Their Mental and Moral Improvement, by an American Lady* (New York: J. & J. Harper, 1833); Samuel Lorenzo Knapp, *Female Biography; Containing Notices of Distinguished Women, in Different Nations and Ages* (New York: J. Carpenter, 1834); and George P. R. James, *Memoirs of Celebrated Women* (Philadelphia: E. L. Carey & A. Hart, 1839).

29. Ellet, *Women of the Revolution*, 1:14, 274–76; 2:147–49, 255–56.

30. Ibid., 2:122–34, 135.

31. On these details of the Dustan case, see Cotton Mather, "A Narrative of Hannah Dustan's Notable Deliverance from Captivity," in *Puritans among the Indians: Accounts of Captivity and Redemption, 1676–1724*, ed. Alden Vaughan and Edward Clark (Cambridge, Mass.: Harvard University Press, 1981), 161–64.

32. Clement, *Noble Deeds of American Women*, especially pages 108–10, 114–23, 176–77, 192–94, 237–38, 261–62, 272–74, 303–4, and 346–51; Ellet, *Pioneer Women of the West*, vii.

33. McCall, "'The Reign of Brute Force Is Over,'" 233; *Godey's Lady's Book* 34 (1847), 66–67.

34. Seba Smith, "Examples of Female Heroism," *Godey's Lady's Book* 27 (1843), 267–69.

35. Lucy Towne, "The Sphere of Woman," *Ladies Repository* 11 (July 1851), 251–52.

36. Martha Whitehouse, "Inefficiency of Woman," *Ladies Repository* 12 (July 1852), 309–10.

37. See, for example, articles in *Godey's Lady's Book* 40 (March and April 1850), and 54 (1857), 339; and *Ladies Repository* 10 (1850), 233, 265; 13 (1853), 44. For articles specifically focusing on Joan of Arc, see *Ladies Repository* 5 (October and November 1845), 13 (January 1853), 17 (July 1857), 19 (April 1859), and 21 (October 1861).

38. "A Model Female Philanthropist," *Ladies Repository* 12 (October 1852), 390.

39. Review of *Historical Pictures Retouched*, in *Conway's Dial*, and Review of *Historical Pictures Retouched*, in *Athenoeum*, 16 February 1861, both in Caroline Dall Scrapbooks, vol. 1, Caroline Dall Papers, Library of Congress.

40. Dall, *Historical Pictures Retouched*, 3, 4, 13–14.

41. Caroline Dall Journals, [Boston] Monday, 1 July 1850, and [Boston] 27 February 1856, Caroline Dall Papers, Massachusetts Historical Society (MHS).

42. Copy of letter to "Mr. Healy, Esq., Boston, Mass., in Caroline Dall Journal, Toronto Canada, 6 July 1851; and Caroline Dall Journal, West Newton, Mass., 25 September 1855, Caroline Dall Papers, MHS.

43. See Lori Ginzberg, "'The Hearts of Your Readers Will Shudder': Fanny Wright, Infidelity, and American Freethought," *American Quarterly* 46, no. 2 (1994): 195–226.

44. William L. Garrison, "Christian Heroism," in the *Liberator*, September 1835; First Annual Report of the Dorchester Female Anti-Slavery Society, 13; Boston Female Anti-Slavery Society [Maria W. Chapman], *Right and Wrong in Boston: The Annual Report of the Boston Female Anti-Slavery Society . . . in 1837* (Boston: Isaac Knapp, 1837), 61–62; William Lloyd Garrison to Abby Kelley Foster, 22 July 1859, Boston, Abby Kelley Foster Papers, American Antiquarian Society. On Lucy Stone as Joan of Arc, see undated newspaper clipping, "Rights of Women," Lucy Stone file, National American Woman Suffrage Association (NAWSA) Papers, Library of Congress. On Anna Dickinson as Joan of Arc, see James McPherson, *The Struggle for Black Equality: Abolitionists and the Negro in the Civil War and Reconstruction* (Princeton: Princeton University Press, 1964), 131.

45. Maria W. Stewart, *Productions of Mrs Maria W. Stewart, Presented to the First African Baptist Church and Society of the City of Boston* (Boston, 1835), reprinted in Henry Louis Gates Jr., ed., *Spiritual Narratives* (New York: Oxford University Press, 1988), 76.

46. Sarah Grimké, *Letters on the Equality of the Sexes and Other Essays*, edited by Elizabeth Ann Bartlett (New Haven, Conn.: Yale University Press, 1988), 37. See Nina Baym on the Grimké sisters' reliance on the new women's history in their writings in general. Baym, *American Women Writers*, 223; *First Annual Report of the Dorchester Female Anti-Slavery Society*, 11.

47. See conventions listed in note 16; *Rights and Conditions of Women*; Lucretia Mott, *Discourse on Woman . . . Delivered at the Assembly Buildings, December 17, 1849* (Philadelphia: W. P. Kildare, 1869); Ernestine Rose, *An Address on Woman's Rights . . . October 19th, 1851* (Boston: J. P. Mendum, 1851); Parker, *A Sermon on the Public Function of Woman*; Luther Lee, *Woman's Right to Preach the Gospel. A Sermon Preached at the Ordination of the Rev. Miss Antoinette L. Brown . . . Sept., 15, 1853* (Syracuse: Published by the author, 1853); Elizabeth Cady Stanton, *Address to the Legislature of New York, Adopted by the State Woman's Rights Convention, Held at Albany . . . February 14 and 15, 1854* (Albany, N.Y.: Weed, Parsons and Co., 1854); and Higginson, *Woman and Her Wishes*.

48. Lucretia Mott, *Discourse on Woman . . . December 17, 1849*, 5; "Speech of Lucretia Mott," in *Proceedings of the Woman's Rights Convention Held at Syracuse . . . 1852*, 35.

49. Higginson, *Woman and Her Wishes*, 4–5; Paulina Wright Davis, in *Proceedings of the Woman's Rights Convention Held at the Broadway Tabernacle . . . September 6th and 7th, 1853*, 29; Stanton, *Address to the Legislature of New York*, 4; Fuller, *Woman in the Nineteenth Century*, 61.

50. Handwritten speech of Lucy Stone to the "Judiciary Committee of the Massachusetts Senate, on the Memorial of a Committee of the National Woman's Rights Convention, asking that the Right of Suffrage may be granted to Woman. In the Representatives Hall, March 6, 1857," Blackwell Family Papers, LOC.

51. David S. Reynolds, *Faith in Fiction: The Emergence of Religious Literature in America* (Cambridge, Mass.: Harvard University Press, 1981), 66–67, 109–10, 111.

52. On the passivity of protagonists of domestic novels, see Ann Douglas, *The Feminization of American Culture* (New York: Avon, 1977), 11; Barbara Welter, "The Cult of True Womanhood, 1820–1860," *American Quarterly* 16 (1966): 151–74; Gerda Lerner, "The Lady and the Mill Girl: Changes in the Status of Women in the Age of Jackson," *Midcontinent American Studies Journal* 10 (1969): 5–15. On discussions of the protagonists as active and independent, see Helen Waite Papashvily, *All the Happy Endings: A Study of the Domestic Novel in America, the Women Who Wrote It, the Women Who Read It in the Nineteenth Century* (New York: Harper, 1956), esp. xvii; Mary Kelley, "The Sentimentalists: The Promise and Betrayal of the Home," *Signs* 4, no. 3 (1979): 434–46; David S. Reynolds, "The Feminization Controversy: Sexual Stereotypes and the Paradoxes of Piety in Nineteenth-Century America," *New England Quarterly* 53, no. 1 (1980): 96–106; Myra Jehlen, "The Family Militant: Domesticity versus Slavery in Uncle Tom's Cabin," *Criticism* 31, no. 4 (1989): 390; Jane Tompkins, *Sensational Designs: The Cultural Work of American Fiction, 1790–1860* (New York: Oxford University Press, 1985); Baym, *Woman's Fiction*, 11, 36; and Cathy Davidson, *Revolution and the Word: The Rise of the Novel in America* (New York: Oxford University Press, 1986).

53. Kelley, "The Sentimentalists," 443, 440. On a similar point, see Papashvily, *All the Happy Endings*, xvi.

54. Tompkins, *Sensational Designs*, 153.

55. Reynolds, *Beneath the American Renaissance*, 339, 342; McCall, "'The Reign of Brute Force Is Over,'" 221, 233–34, 231.

56. Mary Kelley, "Introduction," in Catharine Maria Sedgwick, *Hope Leslie; or, Early Times in the Massachusetts* (New Brunswick, N.J.: Rutgers University Press, 1987), xiii, xxxiv; and Sedgwick, *Hope Leslie*, 153, 16, 278, 277–80. See also Reynolds, *Beneath the American Renaissance*, 348–49.

57. Although it was *Hope Leslie* that catapulted her into national recognition, Sedgwick had written two previous novels that dealt with the same issue of female passivity and activity. On Catharine Maria Sedgwick, *A New-England Tale; or, Sketches of New England Character and Manners* (New York: Oxford University Press, 1995), see Kelley, "Introduction," in *Hope Leslie*, xx; and Baym, *Woman's Fiction*, 54–55.

58. John Tebbel, *A History of Book Publishing in the United States*, vol. 1 (New York: R. R. Bowker Co., 1972), 240.

59. Joanne Dobson, "The Hidden Hand: Subversion of Cultural Ideology in Three Mid-Nineteenth-Century American Women's Novels," *American Quarterly* 38, no. 2 (1986): 223–41.

60. See chapter 2 for a discussion of that rescue.

61. Southworth, *The Hidden Hand*, 305, 307, 312–20.

62. For an excellent discussion of the connection between the personal lives of female domestic novelists and the themes of their novels, see Kelley, *Private Woman, Public Stage*.

63. Susan Warner, *Queechy* (New York: Putnam, 1852); see also Baym, *Woman's Fiction*, 150–51.

64. Charles Peterson, *Kate Aylesford: A Story of the Refugees* (Philadelphia: T. B. Peterson, 1855), 74, 255, 74–76, and *The Old Stone Mansion* (Philadelphia: T. B. Peterson, 1859), 82. See also Reynolds, *Beneath the American Renaissance*, 338.

65. Papashvily, *All the Happy Endings*, 24; Kelley, "Sentimentalists," 443–44.

66. Reynolds, *Beneath the American Renaissance*, 338.

67. On captivity narratives, see Mather, "Narrative of Hannah Dustan's Notable Deliverance." For female soldiers in the period before 1840, see Herman Mann, *The Female Review; or, Memoirs of an American Young Lady* (Dedham [Mass.]: Nathaniel and Benjamin Heaton, 1797); Lucy Brewer, *The Affecting Narrative of Louisa Baker* (Boston: Nathaniel Coverly, 1814), and *The Adventures of Lucy Brewer (alias) Louisa Baker* (Boston: N. Coverly Jr., 1815); Almira Paul, *The Surprising Adventures of Almira Paul* (Boston: N. Coverly Jr., 1816); Cordelia Stark, *The Female Wanderer, an Interesting Tale, Founded on Fact* (n.p., 1824). Dianne Dugaw has claimed that London-published "Female Warrior" ballads were often reprinted in America in the eighteenth and early nineteenth centuries. Dianne Dugaw, *Warrior Women and Popular Balladry, 1600–1850* (Cambridge: Cambridge University Press, 1989), 87.

68. Ballou, *Fanny Campbell*; Smith, *Virgin Land*, 87.

69. Ballou, *Fanny Campbell*, 12, 57.

70. Ibid., 72, 80, 77, 79.

71. Lieutenant Murray [Maturin Murray Ballou], *The Naval Officer; or, the Pirate's Cave: A Tale of the Last War* (Boston: F. Gleason, 1845), 12.

72. Smith, *Virgin Land*, 88.

73. Ralph Admari, "Ballou, the Father of the Dime Novel," *American Book Collector* 4, no. 128 (1933): 121.

74. Leonora Siddons, *The Female Warrior. An Interesting Narrative of the Sufferings, and Singular and Surprising Adventures of Miss Leonora Siddons* (New York: E. E. & G. Barclay, 1843), 6;

75. Amelia Sherwood, *Amelia Sherwood; or, Bloody Scenes at the California Gold Mines* (Richmond, Va.: Barclay & Co., 1850), 25–26.

76. Fanny Templeton Danforth, *The Startling, Thrilling, and Interesting Narrative of the Life, Sufferings, Singular Adventures of Fanny Templeton Danforth* (Philadelphia: E. E. Barclay, 1849), 11, 12–14.

77. Ibid., 15–17, 18, 22, 35.

78. Thomas McDade, "Lurid Literature of the Last Century: The Publications of E. E. Barclay," *Pennsylvania Magazine of History and Biography* 80 (1956): 457. Most of these works were copyrighted by the publisher, and many were obviously written by the publishers themselves or members of their staff. Ballou wrote under several pseudonyms, including Lieutenant Murray and Benjamin Barker. Barclay's and Rulison's pamphlets usually were purported to have been written by the fictional protagonist, and Arthur R. Orton's were frequently "edited" by ministers with names strangely similar to his own. Rev. O. R. Arthur, ed., *The Three Sisters; or, The Life, Confession, and Execution of Amy, Elizabeth, and Cynthia Halzingler* (Baltimore: A. R. Orton, 1855).

79. McDade, "Lurid Literature," 452–53.

80. *Narrative and Confessions of Lucretia P. Cannon* (New York: E. E. Barclay, 1841); *The Burglar's Companion; or, Fatal Elopement of Sarah Williamson, the Misguided Victim of Artful Depravity* (New York: E. E. Barclay, 1841); *The Female Land Pirate; or, The Awful, Mysterious, and Horrible Disclosures of Amanda Bannorris* (Cincinnati: E. E. Barclay, 1847), 12, 18, 23, 37; Danforth, *Startling, Thrilling, and Interesting Narrative*, 17; Sherwood, *Amelia Sherwood*,

12, 23; *The Pirate's Bride; or, The Wonderful Adventures of Miss Cordelia Thompson* (Richmond, Va.: Barclay & Co., 185?); *Adeline Lane, Fearful Adventures in the Pennsylvania Wilds; or, The Startling Narrative of Adeline Lane* (Philadelphia: Barclay & Co., 1857), 14.

81. See, for example, Maturin Murray Ballou [pseud. Benjamin Barker], *The Female Spy; or, The Child of the Brigade: A Romance of the Revolution* (Boston: Gleason, 1846), *Ellen Grafton, the Lily of Lexington; or, The Bride of Liberty* (Boston: Gleason, 1845), *Mornliva; or, The Outlaw of the Forest: A Romance of Lake Wenham* (Boston: Gleason, 1846), *The Land Pirate; or, The Wild Girl of the Beach: A Tale of the New Jersey Shore* (Boston: Gleason, 1847), and *The Bandit of the Ocean; or, The Female Privateer* (New York: R. M. DeWitt, 1855); Eliza Allen, *Eliza Allen, The Female Volunteer; or, The Life and Wonderful Adventures of Miss Eliza Allen* (Ohio: H. M. Rulison, 1851); Sophia Johnson, *The Friendless Orphan. An Affecting Narrative of the Trials and Afflictions of Sophia Johnson* (New York: S. Johnson, 1841).

82. See also my discussion in chapter 2 of the two pamphlet novels published by M. Aurelius—*Life and Sufferings of Cecilia Mayo* and *The Life and Sufferings of Miss Emma Cole*—which illustrate the need for a new vision of a more assertive proper woman. Cecilia Mayo, *Life and Sufferings of Cecilia Mayo: Founded on Incidents in Real Life* (Boston: M. Aurelius, 1843). Emma Cole, *The Life and Sufferings of Miss Emma Cole: Being a Faithful Narrative of Her Life* (Boston: M. Aurelius, 1844).

83. Norma Basch, *In the Eyes of the Law: Women, Marriage, and Property in Nineteenth-Century New York* (Ithaca, N.Y.: Cornell University Press, 1982); Carroll Smith-Rosenberg, "The Beauty, The Beast, and the Militant Woman," in *Disorderly Conduct: Visions of Gender in Victorian America*, by Carroll Smith-Rosenberg (New York: Oxford University Press, 1985), 109–28; Mary Ryan, *Women in Public: Between Banners and Ballots, 1825–1880* (Baltimore: Johns Hopkins University Press, 1990), 100–101.

6: "LIKE A SECOND JOAN OF ARC"

1. Paulina W. Davis, Washington, D.C., 25 December 1854, *Una* 3, no. 1 (1855): 8, reprinted in Ann Russo and Cheris Kramarae, eds., *The Radical Women's Press of the 1850s* (New York: Routledge, 1991), 204.

2. On the war as a challenge to antebellum gender ideology in the North, see Elizabeth Leonard, *Yankee Women: Gender Battles and the Civil War* (New York: W. W. Norton, 1994), xxi–xxv, and "Civil War Nurse, Civil War Nursing: Rebecca Usher of Maine," *Civil War History* 41 (1995): 206–7; Jeanie Attie, *Patriotic Toil: Northern Women and the American Civil War* (Ithaca, N.Y.: Cornell University Press, 1998), 8–18; Elizabeth Leonard, *All the Daring of a Soldier: Women of the Civil War Armies* (New York: Norton, 1999); Elizabeth Young, *Disarming the Nation: Women's Writing and the American Civil War* (Chicago: University of Chicago Press, 1999), 2, 15; Lyde Cullen Sizer, *The Political Work of Northern Women Writers and the Civil War, 1850–1872* (Chapel Hill: University of North Carolina Press, 2000), 84–85. Lyde Cullen Sizer, "Narratives of Union Army Spies," 132; Michael Feldman, "Women and Guerrilla Warfare," 147; and Jeanie Attie, "Warwork and the Crisis of Domesticity in the North," 248, all in Catherine Clinton and Nina Silber, eds., *Divided Houses: Gender and the Civil War* (New York: Oxford University

Press, 1992). On the South, see Drew Gilpin Faust, *Mothers of Invention: Women of the Slaveholding South in the Civil War* (Chapel Hill: University of North Carolina Press, 1996); George Rabble, *Civil Wars: Women and the Crisis of Southern Nationalism* (Urbana: University of Illinois Press, 1989); and LeeAnn Whites, *The Civil War as a Crisis in Gender: Augusta, Georgia, 1860–1890* (Athens: University of Georgia Press, 1995).

3. Judith Ann Giesberg, *Civil War Sisterhood: The U.S. Sanitary Commission and Women's Politics in Transition* (Boston: Northeastern University Press, 2000), 8, 11, 15; Sizer, *Political Work*, 60, 84–85; and Young, *Disarming the Nation*, 15, 68. Ann Douglas Wood is an exception to this pattern. She emphasizes the continuity between women's role as nurses in their families and Civil War nursing. Ann Douglas Wood, "The War within a War: Women Nurses in the Union Army," *Civil War History* 18 (September 1972): 197–212.

4. Anne C. Rose, *Victorian America and the Civil War* (New York: Cambridge University Press, 1992), 2.

5. On the connections between Northern and Southern popular literary culture in the Civil War, see Alice Fahs, *The Imagined Civil War: Popular Literature of the North and South, 1861–1865* (Chapel Hill: University of North Carolina Press, 2001), 5, 6, 120.

6. Sizer, *Political Work*, 280–81, 2. Alice Fahs also argues that much of the popular literature written during the war suggested that women's war work made them full members of the "'imagined community' of the nation," Fahs, *Imagined Civil War*, 2.

7. Paulina W. Davis, Washington, D.C., 204.

8. On the exclusion of women from public life in the eighteenth century, see Mary Beth Norton, *Founding Mothers and Fathers: Gendered Power and the Forming of American Society* (New York: Alfred A. Knopf, 1996), 404–5.

9. See chapter 5 on this point. Domestic novels, pamphlet fiction, histories, biographies, and reform literature all tended to stress men's inability to properly perform their public and private duties to their families and their nation.

10. Sizer, *Political Work*, 60.

11. Louisa May Alcott, *Louisa May Alcott: Her Life, Letters, and Journals*, edited by Ednah D. Cheney (Boston: Roberts Brothers, 1889), 128; Kate Cumming journal, 13 September 1863, in Kate Cumming, *Kate: The Journal of a Confederate Nurse*, edited by Richard Harwell (Baton Rouge: Louisiana State University Press, 1959), 130; James McPherson, *The Struggle for Black Equality: Abolitionists and the Negro in the Civil War and Reconstruction* (Princeton: Princeton University Press, 1964), 131; Ellen Moore to Samuel Moore, 7 February 1864, quoted in Faust, *Mothers of Invention*, 160; Ann S. Stephens, *Address to the Women of the United States* (Washington, D.C.: Gibson Brothers, 1864), 1. See also Fahs, *Imagined Civil War*, 121.

12. "Editor's Table: Preserving the Union and Slavery," *Ladies Repository* 22 (March 1862), 190; "Editor's Table "The Nation Wanting a Man, " *Ladies Repository* 22 (February 1862): 128.

13. Harriet N. Babb, "Maggie Morton's Mittens; or, Working for the Soldiers and What Came of It," *Ladies Repository* 22 (April 1862): 219–22; "A Woman Appointed Major," *Ladies Repository* 22 (June 1862): 380; and Prof. Samuel W. Williams, "The Maid of Saragossa," *Ladies Repository* 22 (May 1862): 257–59. See also Julia Olin, "Renée of

France," *Ladies Repository* 22 (January 1862): 27–30 and 22 (February 1862): 104–108; "An Appeal to the Christian and Patriotic Women upon Their Duties in Relation to the War," *Ladies Repository* 22 (August 1862): 492–97; and "The Female Howard—Elizabeth Fry," *Ladies Repository* 22 (September 1862): 513–17.

14. D. W. Clark, "My Life and What Shall I Do with It?" *Ladies Repository* 22 (May 1862): 269–70. See also Virginia F. Townshend, "What Can They Do?" *Ladies Repository* 22 (November 1862): 657–60.

15. Mary Poovey, *Uneven Developments: The Ideological Work of Gender in Mid-Victorian England* (Chicago: University of Chicago Press, 1988), 14, 170, 172, 198, 166. Martha Vicinus also points out that popular representations of Nightingale focused on her self-sacrificing spirit and excluded all references to her "ambitiousness and her ruthlessness." Martha Vicinus, *Independent Women: Work and Community for Single Women, 1850–1920* (Chicago: University of Chicago Press, 1985), 21.

16. Caroline Dall Journal, 25 January 1855, Caroline Dall Papers, Massachusetts Historical Society; and Caroline Dall, *The College, the Market, and the Court; or, Woman's Relation to Education, Labor, and Law* (Boston: Lee and Shepard, 1867), 122, 83, 221–61.

17. Julia Ward Howe, *Words for the Hour* (Boston: Ticknor and Fields 1856), 40. Future Civil War nurse Hannah Ropes read Nightingale's *Notes on Nursing* right after its American publication in 1860. Hannah Ropes, *Civil War Nurse: The Diary and Letters of Hannah Ropes*, edited and with an introduction by John R. Brumgardt (Knoxville: University of Tennessee Press, 1980), 29. See also the Henry Wadsworth Longfellow poem "The Lady with the Lamp" in *Atlantic Monthly*, October 1857.

18. See "Miss Nightingale's Nurses in Liverpool," 1866 newspaper article by "C. H. D." in Caroline Dall Scrapbooks, Caroline Dall Papers, MHS.

19. Entry of 19 February 1857 in Charlotte L. Forten, *Journals of Charlotte Forten Grimké*, edited by Brenda Stevenson (New York: Oxford University Press, 1988), 194. On Phillips, see *Proceedings of the Ninth National Woman's Rights Convention . . . May 12, 1859* (Rochester, N.Y., 1859), 19. On Tubman, see "Speech of T. W. Higginson," in *Report of the 5th Anniversary Meeting of the New York Anti-Slavery Society* 19, no. 2 (29 May 1858), 1, quoted in Sizer, "Acting Her Part: Northern Women Spies during the American Civil War," in *Divided Houses: Gender and the Civil War*, ed. Catherine Clinton and Nina Silber (New York: Oxford University Press, 1992), 127–28.

20. Byron Sunderland, *Discourse to Young Ladies: A Sermon by Rev. Byron Sunderland, Pastor of the First Presbyterian Church . . . Delivered the 22nd Day of January, 1857* (Washington, D.C.: C. Wendell, 1857), 18.

21. Sizer, "Acting Her Part," 128.

22. Article in *Harpers Weekly*, 9 September 1862, 568–70, quoted in Jane Schultz, "The Inhospitable Hospital: Gender and Professionalism in Civil War Medicine," *Signs* 17, no. 2 (1992), 364n4; Louisa May Alcott, *Hospital Sketches*, as quoted in Dorothy Clarke Wilson, *Stranger and Traveler: The Story of Dorothea Dix, American Reformer* (Boston: Little, Brown & Co., 1975), 296; Faust, *Mothers of Invention*, 92; Linus Brockett and Mary C. Vaughan, eds., *Woman's Work in the Civil War: A Record of Heroism, Patriotism, and Patience* (Philadelphia: Zeigler, McCurdy & Co., 1867), 70; Frank Moore, *Women of the War: Their Heroism and Self-Sacrifice* (Hartford, Conn.: S. S. Scranton,

1866), 398; Kate Cumming, *Gleanings from Southland*, quoted in Cumming, *Kate*, x. Journal entries for 8 September and 10 October 1862 in Cumming, *Kate*, 55, 61. On this point, see also Wood, "The War within a War," 199. Mary Livermore also looked to Nightingale as an example of women's usefulness as military nurses. Mary Livermore, *My Story of the War: A Woman's Narrative of Four Years of Personal Experience as Nurse in the Union Army, and in Relief Work at Home, in Hospitals, in Camps, and at the Front, during the War of the Rebellion* (1887; reprint, New York: Da Capo Press, 1995), 127–28. Sarah Emma Edmonds compared Civil War nurses to Nightingale in *Nurse and Spy in the Union Army* (Hartford, Conn.: W. S. Williams & Co., 1864), 370.

23. Giesberg, *Civil War Sisterhood*, viii; and Sizer, *Political Work*, 169. The original image is from the frontispiece of Charles Stillé, *History of the United States Sanitary Commission, Being the General Report of Its Work during the War of the Rebellion* (Philadelphia: J. B. Lippincott & Co., 1866).

24. Even as Giesberg says the image of the angel made the nurse nonthreatening, she notes that the men of the Sanitary Commission still "remained conscious of that power." Giesberg, *Civil War Sisterhood*, x–xi.

25. On the commonness of angel imagery in nineteenth-century America, see Giesberg, *Civil War Sisterhood*, x.

26. Maturin Murray Ballou [pseud. Lieutenant Murray], *Fanny Campbell, the Female Pirate Captain: A Tale of the Revolution* (1844; reprint, Boston: F. Gleason, 1845), 77, 79; and Fanny Templeton Danforth, *The Startling, Thrilling, and Interesting Narrative of the Life, Sufferings, Singular Adventures of Fanny Templeton Danforth* (Philadelphia: E. E. Barclay, 1849), 35. Alice Fahs also notes the commonness of female heroines in antebellum sensational stories. Fahs, *Imagined Civil War*, 230.

27. Amelia Sherwood, *Amelia Sherwood; or, Bloody Scenes at the California Gold Mines* (Richmond, Va.: Barclay & Co., 1850), 24.

28. On nineteenth-century understandings of the gold-rush-era California frontier as "an evil place" and the "equation of masculinity with sin," see Brian E. Roberts, *American Alchemy: The California Gold Rush and Middle-Class Culture* (Chapel Hill: University of North Carolina Press, 2000), 225.

29. Sherwood, *Amelia Sherwood*, 25–26, 6–8, 27–28.

30. Ibid.; Ballou, *Fanny Campbell*, 77, 80; and Leonora Siddons, *The Female Warrior. An Interesting Narrative of the Sufferings, and Singular and Surprising Adventures of Miss Leonora Siddons* (New York: E. E. & G. Barclay, 1843). See chapter 5 for more on the angelic qualities of these fictional heroines.

31. Thomas McDade, "Lurid Literature of the Last Century: The Publications of E. E. Barclay," *Pennsylvania Magazine of History and Biography* 80 (1956): 459. See, for example, Wesley Bradshaw, *Pauline of the Potomac; or, General McClellan's Spy* (Philadelphia: Barclay, 1862), *Maud of the Mississippi, a Companion to Pauline of the Potomac* (Philadelphia: C. W. Alexander, 1863), *The Angel of the Battle-Field, a Tale of the Rebellion* (New York: American News Co., 1865), and *General Sherman's Indian Spy, a Singularly Thrilling Narrative of Wenonah* (Philadelphia: C. W. Alexander, 1865). *The Lady Lieutenant, a Wonderful Startling Narrative of the Adventures of Miss Madeline Moore* (Philadelphia: Barclay, 1862); W. D. Reynolds, *Miss Martha Brownlow; or, The Heroine of the Ten-*

nessee (Philadelphia: Barclay & Co., 1863); and M. C. P., *Miriam Rivers, the Lady Soldier; or, General Grant's Spy* (Philadelphia: Barclay, 1865). The quote is from *Miriam Rivers,* 39. Lyde Cullen Sizer argues that these sensational battlefield heroines became increasingly common in the last years of the war. She also points out connections between prewar and wartime sensational fiction. Sizer, *Political Work,* 178.

32. Bradshaw, *Pauline of the Potomac,* 45, 56, 54.

33. Bradshaw, *Angel of the Battle-Field,* 24, 69, 75.

34. M. C. P., *Miriam Rivers,* 41.

35. Leonard, *Yankee Women,* 32; Schultz, "Inhospitable Hospital," 377, 382.

36. Sizer, *Political Work,* 179–80.

37. I refer here to Loreta Janeta Velazquez, *The Woman in Battle: A Narrative of the Exploits, Adventures, and Travels of Madame Loreta Janeta Velazquez,* edited by C. J. Worthington (1876; reprint, New York: Arno Press, 1972), and Edmonds, *Nurse and Spy.* I do not include Elsa Jane Guerin's *Mountain Charley* because in her own story she is never a soldier. Her account was completed before the war began. Only accounts written by others describe her as a Civil War soldier disguised as a man. Elsa Jane Guerin, *Mountain Charley; or, The Adventures of Mrs. E. J. Guerin,* with an introduction by F. W. Mazzulla and William Kostka (1861; reprint, University of Oklahoma Press, 1968), viii–x.

38. Sizer notes that Sarah Emma Edmonds characterizes herself in her autobiography as a gender "hybrid." Sizer also notes that Edmonds's *Nurse and Spy* sold 175,000 copies. Sizer, *Political Work,* 179.

39. Edmonds, *Nurse and Spy,* 176; Sizer, "Acting Her Part," 122.

40. Richard Hall, *Patriots in Disguise: Women Warriors of the Civil War* (New York: Paragon House, 1993), 76.

41. Ibid., 76–81.

42. Sylvia G. Dannett, *She Rode with the Generals: The True and Incredible Story of Sarah Emma Seelye, alias Frank Thompson* (New York: Nelson, 1960), 106. See also Leonard, *All the Daring,* 248; Young, *Disarming the Nation,* 154–55; and Fahs, *Imagined Civil War,* 230.

43. On similarities between *Nurse and Spy* and *Fanny Campbell,* see, for example, the James V. story from Dannett, *She Rode with the Generals,* 106; Edmonds, *Nurse and Spy,* 98–100; Betty Fladeland, "Alias Frank Thompson," *Michigan History* 42, no. 3 (1958): 435–62, and "New Light on Sarah E. Edmonds," *Michigan History* 49, no. 4 (1963): 357–62.

44. Edmonds, *Nurse and Spy,* 18–19. On the mix of duty and desire in accounts of Union female spies, see Sizer, "Acting Her Part," 122.

45. Velazquez, *Woman in Battle,* 33–38, 42.

46. Elizabeth Leonard agrees with this assessment of Velazquez. Leonard, *All the Daring,* 258–59. Velazquez, *Woman in Battle,* 39–40; and Hall, *Patriots in Disguise,* 210. For another discussion of Velazquez, see Young, *Disarming the Nation,* 149–94.

47. Velazquez, *Woman in Battle,* 6, 38.

48. Livermore, *My Story of the War,* 86–87; Clara Barton to His Excellency John A. Andrew, Governor of the Commonwealth of Massachusetts, North Oxford, 20 March 1862, Clara Barton Papers, Library of Congress; Catherine S. Lawrence,

Autobiography. Sketch of Life and Labors of Miss Catherine S. Lawrence (Albany, N.Y.: Amasa J. Parker, 1893), 3; journal entry of September October 1862 in Alcott, *Louisa May Alcott*, 132; Caroline Dall, "The Times in Which We Live," article from an unknown journal, "Boston, February 22, 1865," Caroline Dall Scrapbook, Caroline Dall Papers, MHS; and Brockett and Vaughan, *Woman's Work in the Civil War*, 343; Moore, *Women of the War.*

49. Hannah Anderson Ropes, *Cranston House: A Novel* (Boston: O. Clapp, 1859); Alcott, *Louisa May Alcott*, 64; and three novels by Augusta J. Evans: *Macaria; or, The Altars of Sacrifice*, edited and with an introduction and notes by Drew Gilpin Faust (Baton Rouge: Louisiana State University Press, 1992); *Inez, a Tale of the Alamo* (New York: Harper, 1855); and *Beulah*, edited and with an introduction by Elizabeth Fox-Genovese (Baton Rouge: Louisiana State University Press, 1992), 163, 164.

50. Drew Gilpin Faust, "Introduction," in August J. Evans, *Macaria; or, The Altars of Sacrifice* (Baton Rouge: Louisiana State University Press, 1992), xvii, xvi; Gertrude Thomas Diary, 29 June 1864, Duke University Special Collections, quoted in Faust, *Mothers of Invention*, 175.

51. Faust, *Mothers of Invention*, 178. Alice Fahs, in her study of the popular war literature of the North and South, finds a similar pattern in literature. She argues that "Southern writers did not embrace women's work outside the home, including nursing, to the same extent as Northerners did during the war." Fahs, *Imagined Civil War*, 142.

7: ANGELS ON THE BATTLEFIELD

1. Louisa May Alcott, *Louisa May Alcott: Her Life, Letters, and Journals*, edited by Ednah D. Cheney (Boston: Roberts Brothers, 1889), 127.

2. Jane Schultz, "The Inhospitable Hospital: Gender and Professionalism in Civil War Medicine," *Signs* 17, no. 2 (1992): 363–64; and Drew Gilpin Faust, *Mothers of Invention: Women of the Slaveholding South in the Civil War* (Chapel Hill: University of North Carolina Press, 1996), 111. On the difference between Civil War nurses North and South, see also Schultz, "Inhospitable Hospital," 377; Faust, *Mothers of Invention*, 5–6; James McPherson, *Battle Cry of Freedom: The Civil War Era* (1988; reprint, New York: Ballantine, 1989), 480; and Richard Hall, *Patriots in Disguise: Women Warriors of the Civil War* (New York: Paragon House, 1993), 98–99. On differences in Southern and Northern attitudes toward women's roles in the war generally, see Alice Fahs, *The Imagined Civil War: Popular Literature of the North and South, 1861–1865* (Chapel Hill: University of North Carolina Press, 2001), 255.

3. Elizabeth Leonard, *Yankee Women: Gender Battles and the Civil War* (New York: W. W. Norton, 1994), 53, 83–87, 162–65.

4. Leonard, *Yankee Women*, 7; and Dorothy Clarke Wilson, *Stranger and Traveler: The Story of Dorothea Dix, American Reformer* (Boston: Little, Brown & Co., 1975).

5. Eliza Farnham, *Woman and Her Era* (New York: A. J. Davis, 1864); Eliza Farnham, *California Indoors and Out* (1856; reprint with an introduction by Madeleine B. Stern, Nieuwkoop, Netherlands: De Graaf, 1972). For an extended discussion of Farnham's mission to California, see Brian E. Roberts, *American Alchemy: The California Gold Rush and Middle-Class Culture* (Chapel Hill: University of North Carolina Press, 2000), 221–42, 268.

6. Lucy Chase, "On Slavery, No. 8," "Composition book No. 2" [183?], six volumes of composition books, Octavo Volumes, Chase Family Papers, American Antiquarian Society. Pliny E. Chase to Sister [Lucy Chase], Worcester, 12 April 1838, Pliny Earle Chase Correspondence, 1820–1886, Chase Family Papers, AAS.

7. Lucy Chase diary: 22 October 1844, 11 and 16 December 1844; diary fragments: 5 October 1844 to 5 June 1847; Lucy Chase diary: 9, 18, and 19 January 1842 (fragments); and Lucy Chase diary: 25 and 27 January 1845, 18 and 20 February 1845, and 1 and 2 March 1845, all in Chase Family Papers, AAS.

8. Unsigned [Sarah Chase] to Father [Anthony Chase], Philadelphia, 20 April 1861, Sarah Earle Chase Correspondence, 1836–1915, Chase Family Papers, AAS. Swint introduction, and Father [Anthony Chase] to Sarah [Chase], 28 April 1861, in Henry Lee Swint, ed., *Dear Ones at Home: Letters from Contraband Camps* (Nashville: Vanderbilt University Press, 1966), 5, 15–17, 7.

9. "Letter from Josephine Griffin," *Liberator*, 21 June 1861, quoted in Nell Irvin Painter, *Sojourner Truth: A Life, a Symbol* (New York: W. W. Norton, 1996), 180, see also 179, 182–84, 213.

10. Painter, *Sojourner Truth*, 184.

11. Mary Livermore, *My Story of the War: A Woman's Narrative of Four Years of Personal Experience as Nurse in the Union Army, and in Relief Work at Home, in Hospitals, in Camps, and at the Front, During the War of the Rebellion*, (1887; reprint, with an introduction by Nina Silber, New York: Da Capo Press, 1995), vi–viii.

12. On the war experiences of Dr. Mary Walker, see Leonard, *Yankee Women*, 105–57; Esther Hill Hawks, *A Woman Doctor's Civil War: Esther Hill Hawks' Diary* (Columbia: University of South Carolina Press, 1984).

13. On Lucy Stone, see Alice Stone Blackwell, *Lucy Stone: Pioneer of Woman's Rights* (Boston: Little, Brown & Co., 1930), 200. On Stanton and Anthony, see Elizabeth Cady Stanton, *Eighty Years and More: Reminiscences, 1815–1897*, introduction by Gail Parker (1898; reprint, with an introduction by Gail Parker, New York: Schocken Books, 1971), 234–44. On Caroline Dall's war work, see Caroline Dall Scrapbooks, Caroline Dall Papers, Massachusetts Historical Society. Although Dall never went South, she did long for a more active role in the war. She wrote in 1862 that if she were a man she would go to war. Caroline Dall to A. C. Avery, 11 September 1862, Caroline Dall Papers, MHS.

14. Catherine S. Lawrence, *Autobiography. Sketch of Life and Labors of Miss Catherine S. Lawrence* (Albany, N.Y.: Amasa J. Parker, 1893), 10–11, 13, 33–49, 64.

15. Ibid., 49, 66; see also 17, 19, 33, 39–40, 64, 147.

16. Rodger Streitmatter, *Raising Her Voice: African-American Women Journalists Who Changed History* (Lexington: University of Kentucky Press, 1994), 26–28, 34–35; "Great Anti-Colonization Meeting in Philadelphia," *Pennsylvania Freeman*, 29 September 1853, 3, and "Woman's Rights" *Provincial Freeman*, 12 August 1854, 2, quoted in Streitmatter, *Raising Her Voice*, 29, 31.

17. Anne Rose notes that Victorian Americans understood the Civil War in part as an opportunity to give their lives meaning in a rapidly secularizing and industrializing and increasingly anonymous world. However, this does not explain why Northern women be-

lieved that, as women, they should be in the center of the action. The ideology of redemptive womanhood and the culture that had grown up around this ideology were central to the way Northern women understood the war. Anne C. Rose, *Victorian America and the Civil War* (New York: Cambridge University Press, 1992), 5, 97–98, 236.

18. Hannah Ropes, *Civil War Nurse: The Diary and Letters of Hannah Ropes*, edited and with an introduction by John R. Brumgardt (Knoxville: University of Tennessee Press, 1980), 12.

19. Ibid., 9.

20. Hannah Anderson Ropes, *Six Months in Kansas, by a Lady* (1856; reprint, Freeport, N.Y.: Books for Libraries Press, 1972).

21. Hannah Anderson Ropes, *Cranston House: A Novel* (Boston: O. Clapp, 1859), 372–73; see also Ropes, *Civil War Nurse*, 12, and *Six Months in Kansas*, 48ff.

22. McPherson, *Battle Cry of Freedom*, 45.

23. Ropes, *Civil War Nurse*, 30, 123–24.

24. Clara Barton Scrapbook, 1835, Clara Barton Papers, Library of Congress.

25. Clara Barton, *The Story of My Childhood* (1907; reprint, New York: Arno Press, 1980), 62, 114.

26. Clara Barton, diary entries of 11 and 24 March 1852, Clara Barton Diaries, 1849–1863, Clara Barton Papers, American Antiquarian Society.

27. Barton, diary entry of 31 March 1852, Clara Barton Diaries, 1849–1863, Clara Barton Papers, AAS.

28. Stephen B. Oates, *A Woman of Valor: Clara Barton and the Civil War* (New York: Free Press, 1994), 12.

29. Clara Barton to Bernard Vassal, 13 February 1860, Clara Barton Papers, LOC; Clara Barton to Bernard Vassal, North Oxford, Mass., 26 January 1860, Clara Barton Papers, AAS; and Oates, *Woman of Valor*, 12–13.

30. Edna Cheney introduction, Louisa May Alcott journal, September 1859 and April 1861, in Alcott, *Louisa May Alcott*, xv, 104, 127.

31. Louisa May Alcott, *Little Women* (1868; reprint, New York: Signet, 1983), 5, Alcott, journal entry of November 1862, in *Louisa May Alcott*, 140.

32. Charlotte L. Forten, journal entries for 4 January 1854, 28 July 1854, 23 October 1854, in Forten, *Journals of Charlotte Forten Grimké*, edited by Brenda Stevenson (New York: Oxford University Press, 1988), 67, 92, 105. On Brenda Stevenson's analysis of Forten's attitude toward teaching, see her introduction to Forten, *Journals of Charlotte Forten Grimké*, 18.

33. Forten, journal entries of 28 June 1856, 1 September 1856, 11 October 1857, and 2 January 1858, in *Journals of Charlotte Forten Grimké*, 158, 163–64, 261, 276. This analysis of her life in Salem deals specifically with the period up to May 1859. Between 8 May 1859 and 22 June 1862, Forten made only one entry in her journal.

34. Lottie [Charlotte] Forten to My Dear Friends [John Greenleaf Whittier and Elizabeth Whittier], Seaside, 13 June 1863, Whittier Correspondence, John Greenleaf Whittier Papers, Peabody-Essex Museum; and Forten, journal entry of 2 March 1863, in *Journals of Charlotte Forten Grimké*, 431. For her war experiences in general, see Forten, journal entries for 27 October 1862–15 May 1864, in *Journals of Charlotte Forten Grimké*, 382–511.

35. Forten, journal entries of 27 October 1862–15 May 1864, in *Journals of Charlotte Forten Grimké*, 382–511; see also xxxvi–xl.

36. Cornelia Hancock to Mother, 14 August 1863 and 25 September 1864, in Cornelia Hancock, *South after Gettysburg: Letters of Cornelia Hancock from the Army of the Potomac, 1863–1865*, edited by Henrietta Stratton Jaquette (Philadelphia: University of Pennsylvania Press, 1937), 18, 152.

37. Cornelia Hancock to Mother, 2 March 1864, in Hancock, *South after Gettysburg*, 59; see also viii–x.

38. Thomas Lowry, *The Story the Soldiers Wouldn't Tell: Sex in the Civil War* (Mechanicsburg, Pa.: Stackpole, 1994), 118, as quoted in Elizabeth Leonard, *All the Daring of a Soldier: Women of the Civil War Armies* (New York: Norton, 1999), 310n2.

39. S. R. W. to Father and Mother, 5 June 1863, Alexandria, Va., and S. R. W. to Father and Mother, D.C., 28 Dec 1863, in Sarah Rosetta Wakeman, *An Uncommon Soldier: The Civil War Letters of Sarah Rosetta Wakeman*, edited by Lauren Burgess Cook (Pasadena, Md.: Minerva Center, 1994), 31, 58.

40. Lauren Burgess Cook, "Introduction," in *An Uncommon Soldier: The Civil War Letters of Sarah Rosetta Wakeman* (Pasadena, Md.: Minerva Center, 1994), 12; Forten, *Journals of Charlotte Forten Grimké*, xxxviii–xxxix, viii–x.

41. Elaine Showalter, "Introduction," in Louisa May Alcott, *Alternative Alcott* (New Brunswick, N.J.: Rutgers University Press, 1988), xx–xxi. Sarah Elbert, introduction to *Diana and Persis*, 33, and Martha Saxton, *Louisa May: A Modern Biography*, 406, quoted in Showalter, "Introduction," in *Alternative Alcott*, xxv–xxvi.

42. On this criticism of female soldiers, see Leonard, *All the Daring*, 241–45.

43. Leonard, *Yankee Women*, 6, 12, 14; Fahs, *Imagined Civil War*, 140; Mary Livermore, *My Story of the War*, 224. Dix circular quoted in Kate Cumming, *Kate: The Journal of a Confederate Nurse*, edited by Richard Harwell (Baton Rouge: Louisiana State University Press, 1959), xi.

44. Leonard, *Yankee Women*, 12–14; Cumming, *Kate*, xi. See also Faust, *Mothers of Invention*, 5–6.

45. See Elizabeth Leonard on the long lag time many Civil War nurses experienced between trying to become a nurse and starting their nursing careers. Leonard, *Yankee Women*, 5–6.

46. Clara Barton to Capt. I. W. Denney [about 30 March 1862], Clara Barton Papers, AAS.

47. Louisa May Alcott to Alfred Whitman, Concord [Mass.], 11 May 1862, in Louisa May Alcott, *The Selected Letters of Louisa May Alcott*, edited and with an introduction by Madeleine B. Stern (Boston: Little, Brown, 1987), 77.

48. Louisa May Alcott to Thomas Wentworth Higginson, Concord [Mass.], 12 November 1863, in Alcott, *Selected Letters*, 96–97.

49. Forten, journal entry of Sunday, 14 September 1862, in *Journals of Charlotte Forten Grimké*, 381. See also Forten's journal entries for August–September 1862, in *Journals of Charlotte Forten Grimké*, 371–81.

50. Sarah to Father, 20 April 1861, in Sarah Earle Chase Correspondence, Chase Family Papers, AAS; and Father to Sarah, 28 April 1861, in Swint, *Dear Ones at Home*, 15–17.

51. Hancock, *South after Gettysburg*, 3–4; Mother [Hannah Anderson Ropes] to Alice, August 1862, in Ropes, *Civil War Nurse*, 61.

52. Hawks, *Woman Doctor's Civil War*, 15, 18, 26.

53. On Lawrence, see her *Autobiography*, 102–3, 112–16. On Ropes, Hancock, Wormeley, and Woolsey, see John R. Brumgardt, "Introduction," in Hannah Anderson Ropes, *Civil War Nurse: The Diary and Letters of Hannah Ropes*, edited by John Brumgardt, 36–37. On Ropes's long battle with her chief hospital surgeon, which eventually ended in his dismissal, see Ropes, journal entry of [1–9] October 1862–8 November 1862, in Ropes, *Civil War Nurse*, 71–95. Lyde Cullen Sizer points out that although many female nurses and matrons muted their criticisms during the war, their tone changed in their postwar writings. Lyde Cullen Sizer, *The Political Work of Northern Women Writers and the Civil War, 1850–1872* (Chapel Hill: University of North Carolina Press, 2000), 205.

54. Cornelia Hancock to sister [Ellen], 30 March–April 1864; [Ellen] to Cornelia Hancock, 5 June 1864; and Mother to Cornelia, 13 June 1864, in Hancock, *South after Gettysburg*, 78, 97–98, 103–4. See also Cornelia Hancock to Mother, 27 March 1864 and 12 April 1864, in Hancock, *South after Gettysburg*, 72, 80.

55. S. R. W. to Father and Mother, Alexandria, Va., 5 June 1863; and S. R. W. to Father and Mother, D.C., 18 December 1863, in Wakeman, *Uncommon Soldier*, 31, 58.

56. S. R. W. to Father, D.C., 20 January 1864, in Wakeman, *Uncommon Soldier*, 60.

57. On the nurse as mother, see Brumgardt, "Introduction," in Ropes, *Civil War Nurse*, 33.

58. Fahs, *Imagined Civil War*, 140.

59. Wesley Bradshaw, *Pauline of the Potomac; or, General McClellan's Spy* (Philadelphia: Barclay, 1862), 36; and Wesley Bradshaw, *The Angel of the Battle-Field, a Tale of the Rebellion* (New York: American News Co., 1865), 71.

60. Clara Barton, War Lectures, 1860s, and Newspaper Clippings 1865–1905, Clara Barton Papers, LOC.

61. Ropes, *Cranston House*, 376; Ropes, *Civil War Nurse*, 67–68; Livermore, *My Story of the War*, 243, 345–46, 484; Lawrence, *Autobiography*, 88, 98–99.

62. S. Emma E. Edmonds, *Nurse and Spy in the Union Army* (Hartford, Conn.: W. S. Williams & Co., 1864), 308.

63. Livermore, *My Story of the War*, 484, 476–546, 345–46; Ropes, journal entry of 11 October 1862, in Ropes, *Civil War Nurse*, 75; Harriet W. F. Hawley to John Greenleaf Whittier, Hartford, 20 March 1864, Whittier Correspondence, John Greenleaf Whittier Papers, PEM; Alcott journal entries of December 1862–January 1863, in *Louisa May Alcott*, 141, 146.

64. Cornelia Hancock to Mother, Gettysburg, 26 July 1863, and Cornelia Hancock to Sister, 16 August 1863, in Hancock, *South after Gettysburg*, 15, 16.

65. Edmonds, *Nurse and Spy*, 40, 50–53.

66. "Pension Application for S. E. E. Seelye," *House Report 820*, 48th Congress, 1st Session (Washington, D.C., 1884); Edmonds, *Nurse and Spy*.

67. Ferdinand L. Sarmiento, *Life of Pauline Cushman* (Philadelphia: John E. Potter, 1865), 13–14.

68. Linus Brockett and Mary C. Vaughan, eds., *Woman's Work in the Civil War: A Record of Heroism, Patriotism, and Patience* (Philadelphia: Zeigler, McCurdy & Co., 1867), 770.

69. Frank Moore, *Women of the War: Their Heroism and Self-Sacrifice* (Hartford, Conn.: S. S. Scranton, 1866), 513 on Annie Etheridge, and 112 on Bridget Divers; and Brockett and Vaughan, *Woman's Work*, 747, 751–52 on Annie Etheridge, and 771–73 on Bridget Divers.

70. Moore, *Women of the War*, 61–62, and Brockett and Vaughan, *Woman's Work*, 773–74.

71. Oates, *Woman of Valor*, 14–19; Clara Barton to His Excellency John A. Andrew, Governor of the Commonwealth of Massachusetts, North Oxford, 20 March 1862, Clara Barton Papers, LOC.

72. Clara Barton to Capt. I. W. Denney, about 30 March 1862, Clara Barton Papers, AAS; Oates, *Woman of Valor*, 42, 52.

73. Clara Barton to T. W. Meighan, esq., Hilton Head, S.C., 24 June 1863, Clara Barton Papers, LOC. Clara Barton to Fannie, Washington, D.C., 9 January 1862, Clara Barton Papers, AAS. Clara Barton to David and Julia Barton, Washington, D.C., 31 August 1862, Clara Barton Papers, LOC. See also Clara Barton to Cousin Vira [Stone], 12 December 1862, Army of the Potomac Camp near Falmouth, Va., Clara Barton Papers, AAS.

74. Clara Barton to D. P. Holloway, Commn. of Patents, and Barton diary entry of 11 December 1863, Clara Barton Papers, AAS. Clara Barton to Friends, 4 September 1862, Clara Barton Papers, LOC.

75. Sarah Baker for Dorchester Female Anti-Slavery Society to Abby Kelley for Lynn Female Anti-Slavery Society, 31 May 1838, Abby Kelley Foster Papers, American Antiquarian Society. Clara Barton, "The Women Who Went to the Field," a poem given on 18 November 1892 at the Farewell Reception and Banquet of the Ladies of the Potomac Corps, Clara Barton Papers, LOC.

CONCLUSION: THE LEGACIES OF REDEMPTIVE WOMANHOOD

1. Thomas Wentworth Higginson, *Woman and Her Wishes; An Essay: Inscribed to the Massachusetts Constitutional Convention* (Boston: R. F. Wallcut, 1853), 24–25.

2. Kathryn Kish Sklar, *Florence Kelley and the Nation's Work: The Rise of Women's Political Culture, 1830–1900* (New Haven, Conn.: Yale University Press, 1995), xiii; Elizabeth Leonard, *Yankee Women: Gender Battles and the Civil War* (New York: W. W. Norton, 1994), 53, 83–87, 162–65.

3. Allison Parker, *Purifying America: Women, Cultural Reform, and Pro-Censorship Activism, 1873–1933* (Urbana: University of Illinois Press, 1997), 5.

4. Nancy Cott, *The Grounding of Modern Feminism* (New Haven, Conn.: Yale University Press, 1987), 37; Jean Bethke Elshtain, *Jane Addams and the Dream of American Democracy: A Life* (New York: Basic Books, 2002), xxi; Rebecca Edwards, *Angels in the Machinery: Gender in American Party Politics from the Civil War to the Progressive Era* (New York: Oxford University Press, 1997), 164.

5. Jane Addams, *Peace and Bread in Time of War* (1922; reprint, Urbana: University of Illinois Press, 2002), 46–47.

6. Elshtain, *Jane Addams*, 114. Kathy Peiss, *Cheap Amusements: Working Women and Leisure in Turn-of-the-Century New York* (Philadelphia: Temple University Press, 1986); John D'Emilio and Estelle Freedman, *Intimate Matters: A History of Sexuality in America* (New York: Perennial Library, 1988), chapter 11.

7. Cott, *Grounding of Modern Feminism*, 42, and Ellen DuBois, *Harriot Stanton Blatch and the Winning of Woman Suffrage* (New Haven, Conn.: Yale University Press, 1997), chapter 7.

8. David Levering Lewis, *When Harlem Was in Vogue* (New York: Oxford University Press, 1979), 46, 176, 194.

9. Imamu Amiri Baraka, *Blues People: Negro Music in White America* (1963; reprint, New York: Quill, 1999), 91.

10. Deborah Gray White, *Ar'n't I a Woman? Female Slaves in the Plantation South* (New York: Norton, 1985), 47.

11. Carol Gilligan, *In a Different Voice: Psychological Theory and Women's Development* (Cambridge, Mass.: Harvard University Press, 1982); Elizabeth Fox-Genovese, *"Feminism Is Not the Story of My Life": How Today's Feminist Elite Has Lost Touch with the Real Concerns of Women* (New York: Doubleday, 1996), 229.

12. Phyllis Schlafly, *The Power of the Positive Woman* (1977), quoted in Mary Beth Norton, ed., *Major Problems in American Women's History* (Lexington, Mass.: D.C. Heath and Company, 1989), 429.

13. On the continuity in conceptions of women's nature in the political and legal system from the nineteenth century to the present, see Linda Kerber, *No Constitutional Right to Be Ladies: Women and the Obligations of Citizenship* (New York: Hill and Wang, 1998), 307–8; and Edwards, *Angels in the Machinery*, 168–69.

14. "Inside Business: Corporate Fly Girls. Women Executives Are Changing the Way Major Airlines Do Business," *Time* 160, no. 3 (July 15, 2002), Y2–Y7.

15. Lori Ginzberg makes a similar point in *Women and the Work of Benevolence: Morality, Politics, and Class in the Nineteenth-Century United States* (New Haven, Conn.: Yale University Press, 1990), 219.

Selected Bibliography

Manuscript Collections

Antislavery Collection, Boston Public Library
Clara Barton Papers, American Antiquarian Society
Clara Barton Papers, Library of Congress
Black Abolitionist Papers, UMI Microfilms
Blackwell Family Papers, Library of Congress
Chase Family Papers, American Antiquarian Society
Caroline Dall Papers, Library of Congress
Caroline Dall Papers, Massachusetts Historical Society
Abby Kelley Foster Papers, American Antiquarian Society
Abby Kelley Foster Papers, Worcester Historical Society
Samuel J. May Papers, Boston Public Library
Samuel J. May Papers, Massachusetts Historical Society
National American Woman Suffrage Association (NAWSA) Papers,
    Library of Congress
Amos A. Phelps Papers, Boston Public Library
Elizabeth Cady Stanton Papers, Douglas College, Rutgers University
Weston Sisters Papers, Boston Public Library
John Greenleaf Whittier Papers, Peabody-Essex Museum

Newspapers and Journals

Advocate of Moral Reform
Atlantic Monthly
Boston Daily Times
Boston Medical and Surgical Journal
Bostonian
Colored American
Exeter Newsletter and Rockingham Advertiser
The Flash
Frederick Douglass' Paper
Freedom's Journal
The Friend of Virtue
Godey's Lady's Book
Impartial Citizen
Ladies Repository

Liberator
National Anti-Slavery Standard
National Police Gazette
New York Commercial Advertiser
New York Daily Tribune
New York Herald
New York Medical and Surgical Reporter
New York Polyanthos
New York Sun
Newark Daily Advertiser
Niles Weekly Register
North Star
Philanthropist
Provincial Freeman
The Rights of All
True American
United States Gazette
Voice of the Fugitive
Weekly Advocate
Woman's Journal

PRIMARY PUBLISHED SOURCES

Addams, Jane. *Peace and Bread in Time of War*. 1922. Reprint, Urbana: University of Illinois Press, 2002.

Alcott, Louisa May. *Alternative Alcott*. With an introduction by Elaine Showalter. New Brunswick, N.J.: Rutgers University Press, 1988.

———. *Little Women*. 1868. Reprint, New York: Signet, 1983.

———. *Louisa May Alcott: Her Life, Letters, and Journals*. Edited by Ednah D. Cheney. Boston: Roberts Brothers, 1889.

———. *The Selected Letters of Louisa May Alcott*. Edited and with an introduction by Madeleine B. Stern. Boston: Little, Brown, 1987.

Allen, Eliza. *The Female Volunteer; or, The Life and Wonderful Adventures of Miss Eliza Allen*. Ohio: H. M. Rulison, 1851.

An Authentic and Particular Account of the Life of Francis Burdett Personel. New York: n.p., 1773.

Annals of Murder; or, Daring Outrages. Philadelphia: John Perry, 1845.

Anonymous [George W. Dixon?]. *Trial of Madame Restell*. New York: n.p., 1846.

———. *Trial of Madame Restell, Alias Ann Lohman, for Abortion and Causing the Death of Mrs. Purdy*. New York, n.p.: 1841.

Bacon, David Francis, ed. *Memoirs of Eminently Pious Women of Britain and America*. New Haven: D. McLeod, 1833.

Ballou, Maturin Murray. *Notable Thoughts about Women*. Boston: Houghton, Mifflin, 1882.

Ballou, Maturin Murray [pseud. Benjamin Barker]. *The Bandit of the Ocean; or, The Female Privateer*. New York: R. M. DeWitt, 1855.

————. *Ellen Grafton, the Lily of Lexington; or, The Bride of Liberty.* Boston: Gleason, 1845.

————. *The Female Spy; or, The Child of the Brigade: A Romance of the Revolution.* Boston: Gleason, 1846.

————. *The Land Pirate; or, The Wild Girl of the Beach: A Tale of the New Jersey Shore.* Boston: Gleason, 1847.

————. *Mornliva; or, The Outlaw of the Forest: A Romance of Lake Wenham.* Boston: Gleason, 1846.

Ballou, Maturin Murray [pseud. Lieutenant Murray]. *Fanny Campbell, the Female Pirate Captain: A Tale of the Revolution.* 1844. Reprint, Boston: F. Gleason, 1845.

————. *The Naval Officer; or, the Pirate's Cave: A Tale of the Last War.* Boston: F. Gleason, 1845.

Barnes, Gilbert H., and Dwight L. Dumond, eds. *Letters of Theodore Dwight Weld, Angelina Grimké Weld, and Sarah Grimké, 1822–1844.* Vol. 1. 1934. Reprint, Gloucester, Mass.: Peter Smith, 1965.

Barton, Clara. *The Story of My Childhood.* 1907. Reprint, New York: Arno Press, 1980.

Beecher, Catharine. *An Essay on Slavery and Abolitionism: With Reference to the Duty of American Females.* Philadelphia: Henry Perkins, 1837.

The Black Abolitionist Papers: Canada, 1830–1865. Vol. 2. Edited and with an introduction by C. Peter Ripley. Chapel Hill: University of North Carolina Press, 1986.

The Black Abolitionist Papers: The United States, 1830–1846. Vol. 3. Edited and with an introduction by C. Peter Ripley. Chapel Hill: University of North Carolina Press, 1985.

Bloss, Celestia Angenette. *Heroines of the Crusades.* Muscatine, Iowa: R. M. Burnett, 1852.

Boston Female Anti-Slavery Society. *Ten Years of Experience: Ninth Annual Report of the Boston Female Anti-Slavery Society.* Boston: Oliver Johnson, 1842.

Boston Female Anti-Slavery Society [Chapman, Maria W.]. *Right and Wrong in Boston in 1836: Annual Report of the Boston Female Anti-Slavery Society.* Boston: Isaac Knapp, 1836.

————. *Right and Wrong in Boston: The Annual Report of the Boston Female Anti-Slavery Society . . . in 1837.* Boston: Isaac Knapp, 1837.

Bradbury, Osgood. *Ellen Grant; or, Fashionable Life in New York.* New York: Dick & Fitzgerald [1853?].

————. *Female Depravity; or, The House of Death.* New York: R. M. De Witt, 1857.

Bradshaw, Wesley. *The Angel of the Battle-Field, a Tale of the Rebellion.* New York: American News Co., 1865.

————. *General Sherman's Indian Spy, a Singularly Thrilling Narrative of Wenonah.* Philadelphia: C. W. Alexander, 1865.

————. *Maud of the Mississippi, a Companion to Pauline of the Potomac.* Philadelphia: C. W. Alexander, 1863.

————. *Pauline of the Potomac; or, General McClellan's Spy.* Philadelphia: Barclay, 1862.

Brewer, Lucy. *The Adventures of Lucy Brewer (alias) Louisa Baker.* Boston: N. Coverly Jr., 1815.

————. *The Affecting Narrative of Louisa Baker.* Boston: Nathaniel Coverly, 1814.

Brockett, Linus, and Mary C. Vaughan, eds. *Woman's Work in the Civil War: A Record of Heroism, Patriotism, and Patience.* Philadelphia: Zeigler, McCurdy & Co., 1867.

Brown, Charles Brockden. *Wieland; or, The Transformation.* 1798. Reprint, New York: Anchor, 1973.

The Burglar's Companion; or, Fatal Elopement of Sarah Williamson, the Misguided Victim of Artful Depravity. New York: E. E. Barclay, 1841.

Calhoun, J. S. *Life and Confession of Mary Jane Gordon.* Covington, Ky.: Benjamin True, 1849.

Cambridge Female Moral Reform Society. *Constitution of the Cambridge Female Moral Reform Society.* Boston: n.p., 1837.

Chandler, Peleg W. *American Criminal Trials.* Vol. 2. 1844. Reprint, Freeport, N.Y.: Books for Libraries Press, 1970.

Chesnut, Mary Boykin. *A Diary from Dixie.* Edited by Ben Ames Williams. 1949. Reprint, Cambridge, Mass.: Harvard University Press, 1980.

Child, Lydia Maria. *The Biographies of Lady Russell, and Madame Guyon.* Boston: Carter, Hendee & Co., 1832.

———. *The Biographies of Madame de Staël and Madame Roland.* Boston: Carter & Hendee, 1832.

———. *Good Wives.* Boston: Carter, Hendee & Co., 1833.

———. *The History of the Condition of Women, in Various Ages and Nations.* Boston: J. Allen & Co., 1835.

———. *Letters of Lydia Maria Child.* Boston: Houghton, Mifflin, 1883.

———. *A Lydia Maria Child Reader.* Edited by Carolyn Karcher. Durham, N.C.: Duke University Press, 1997.

Clement, J. *Noble Deeds of American Women,* new edition revised. Auburn and Buffalo, N.Y.: Miller, Orton & Mulligan 1854; original edition published in 1851.

Clinton, Henry L. *Extraordinary Cases.* New York: Harper & Brothers, 1896.

Cole, Emma. *The Life and Sufferings of Miss Emma Cole: Being a Faithful Narrative of Her Life.* Boston: M. Aurelius, 1844.

Coles, George. *Heroines of Methodism; or, Pen and Ink Sketches of the Mothers and Daughters of the Church.* New York: Carlton & Porter, 1857.

The Confession and Dying Words of Samuel Frost. In *Pillars of Salt: An Anthology of Early American Criminal Narratives,* ed. Daniel E. Williams. Madison, Wisconsin: Madison House, 1993.

The Confession of Mary Cole, Who Was Executed on Friday, 26th June; at Newton, Sussex County, N.J., for the Murder of Agnes Teaurs, Her Mother. New York: Printed for the Purchasers, 1812[?].

Cooke, Parsons. *Female Preaching, Unlawful and Inexpedient. A Sermon by Parsons Cooke, Pastor of the First Church in Lynn.* Lynn, Mass.: James R. Newhall, 1837.

Crafts, Hannah. *The Bondwoman's Narrative.* Edited by Henry Louis Gates Jr. New York: Warner Books, 2002.

Cumming, Kate. *Kate: The Journal of a Confederate Nurse.* Edited by Richard Harwell. Baton Rouge: Louisiana State University Press, 1959.

Cunningham, John T. ed. *Murder Did Pay: Nineteenth-Century New Jersey Murders.* Newark: New Jersey Historical Society, 1982.

Dall, Caroline H. *The College, the Market, and the Court; or, Woman's Relation to Education, Labor, and Law.* Boston: Lee & Shepard, 1867.

———. *Historical Pictures Retouched: A Volume of Miscellanies.* Boston: Walker, Wise, & Co., 1860.

———. *Women's Right to Labor; or, Low Wages and Hard Work.* Boston: Walker, Wise, & Co., 1860. Reprinted in *Low Wages and Great Sins: Two Antebellum Views on Prostitution and the Working-Girl,* ed. David Rothman and Sheila Rothman. New York: Garland, 1987.

Danforth, Fanny Templeton. *The Startling, Thrilling, and Interesting Narrative of the Life, Sufferings, Singular Adventures of Fanny Templeton Danforth.* Philadelphia: E. E. Barclay, 1849.

Davis, Almond H. *The Female Preacher; or, Memoir of Salome Lincoln.* 1843. Reprint, New York: Arno Press, 1972.

Declaration and Confession of Esther Rodgers. In *Pillars of Salt: An Anthology of Early American Criminal Narratives,* ed. Daniel E. Williams. Madison, Wisconsin: Madison House, 1993.

The Dying Declaration of James Buchanan, Ezra Ross, and William Brooks. Worcester, Mass.: Isaiah Thomas, 1778.

Eames, John Costin. *Innocence Rewarded; or, the Successful Triumph of Margaret Garrity, Who Was Tried for the Murder of a False Lover, at Newark, New-Jersey, United States of America, in the Month of October 1851.* Newark, N.J.: n.p., 1851.

The Early Life and Complete Trial of Mary, Alias Polly Bodine. New York, n.p.: 1846.

Edmonds, S. Emma E. *Nurse and Spy in the Union Army.* Hartford, Conn.: W. S. Williams & Co., 1865.

Elaw, Zilpha. *Memoirs of the Life, Religious Experience, Ministerial Travels, and Labours of Mrs. Zilpha Elaw, An American Female of Colour.* London, 1846. Reprinted in *Sisters of the Spirit: Three Black Women's Autobiographies of the Nineteenth Century,* ed. William L. Andrews. Bloomington: Indiana University Press, 1986.

Ellen Irving, The Female Victimizer. Baltimore: A. R. Orton, 1856.

Ellet, Elizabeth Fries. *Domestic History of the American Revolution.* New York: Baker & Scribner, 1850.

———. *Pioneer Women of the West.* 1852; reprint, Freeport, N.Y.: Books for Libraries Press, 1973.

———. *The Women of the American Revolution.* 3 Vols. New York: Baker & Scribner, 1848–1850.

Estelle Grant; or, The Lost Wife. New York: Garrett, Dick & Fitzgerald, 1855.

Evans, Augusta J. *Beulah.* Edited and with an introduction by Elizabeth Fox-Genovese. Baton Rouge: Louisiana State University Press, 1992.

———. *Inez, a Tale of the Alamo.* New York: Harper, 1855.

———. *Macaria; or, The Altars of Sacrifice.* Edited and with an introduction and notes by Drew Gilpin Faust. Baton Rouge: Louisiana State University Press, 1992.

A Faithful Narrative of Elizabeth Wilson. Philadelphia: n.p., 1786.

A Faithful Narrative of the Wicked Life and Remarkable Conversion of Patience Boston. In *Pillars of Salt: An Anthology of Early American Criminal Narratives,* ed. Daniel E. Williams. Madison, Wisconsin: Madison House, 1993.

Farnham, Eliza. *California Indoors and Out.* 1856. Reprinted with an introduction by Madeleine B. Stern, Nieuwkoop, Netherlands: De Graaf, 1972.

————. *Woman and Her Era.* New York: A. J. Davis, 1864.

The Female Land Pirate; or, The Awful, Mysterious, and Horrible Disclosures of Amanda Bannorris. Cincinnati: E. E. Barclay, 1847.

First Annual Report of the Dorchester Female Anti-Slavery Society. Boston: D. Clapp, 1838.

Fiske, Nathan. *A Sermon Preached at Brookfield . . . on the Day of the Internment of Mr. Joshua Spooner.* Norwich, Conn.: Greene & Spooner, 1778.

Forten, Charlotte L. *Journals of Charlotte Forten Grimké.* Edited by Brenda Stevenson. New York: Oxford University Press, 1988.

Foster, George G. *New York by Gas-light and Other Urban Sketches.* 1850. Reprint, Berkeley: University of California Press, 1990.

Frost, John. *Heroic Women of the West.* Philadelphia: A. Hart, 1854.

Fuller, Margaret. *Woman in the Nineteenth Century, and Kindred Papers Relating to the Sphere, Condition, and Duties of Woman.* 1855. Reprint, New York: W. W. Norton, 1971.

Gates, Henry Louis, Jr., ed. *Spiritual Narratives.* New York: Oxford University Press, 1988.

Goodrich, Frank Boott. *Women of Beauty and Heroism from Semiramis to Eugenie.* New York: Derby & Jackson, 1859.

Grimké, Angelina. *Letters to Catharine E. Beecher.* 1838. Reprint, New York: Arno Press, 1969.

Grimké, Sarah. *Letters on the Equality of the Sexes and Other Essays.* Edited by Elizabeth Ann Bartlett. New Haven, Conn.: Yale University Press, 1988.

Guerin, Elsa Jane. *Mountain Charley; or, The Adventures of Mrs. E. J. Guerin.* With an introduction by F. W. Mazzulla and William Kostka. 1861. Reprint, University of Oklahoma Press, 1968.

Hale, Sarah Josepha Buell. *The Lecturess; or, Woman's Sphere.* Boston: Whipple & Damrell, 1839.

————. *Woman's Record; or, Sketches of All Distinguished Women, from "the Beginning" till A.D. 1850.* New York: Harper & Brothers, 1853.

————. *Woman's Record; or, Sketches of All Distinguished Women from the Creation to A.D. 1854,* 2nd rev. ed. New York: Harper, 1855.

Hancock, Cornelia. *South after Gettysburg: Letters of Cornelia Hancock from the Army of the Potomac, 1863–1865.* Edited by Henrietta Stratton Jaquette. Philadelphia: University of Pennsylvania Press, 1937.

Hawks, Esther Hill. *A Woman Doctor's Civil War: Esther Hill Hawks' Diary.* Columbia: University of South Carolina Press, 1984.

Hewitt, Mary E., ed. *Heroines of History.* New York: Cornish, Lamport, 1852.

Higginson, Thomas Wentworth. *Woman and Her Wishes; an Essay: Inscribed to the Massachusetts Constitutional Convention.* Boston: R. F. Wallcut, 1853.

Howe, Julia Ward. *Sketches of Representative Women of New England.* Boston: New England Historical Publishing Company, 1904.

————. *Words for the Hour.* Boston: Ticknor & Fields, 1856.

Ingraham, J. H. *Frank Rivers; or, The Dangers of the Town.* Boston: E. P. Williams, 1843.

Jackson, William H. *The Life and Confession of Sophia Hamilton.* Fredrickton, New Brunswick: n.p., 1845.

Jacobs, Harriet [pseud. Linda Brent]. *Incidents in the Life of a Slave Girl.* 1861. Reprint, New York: Harcourt, Brace, Jovanovich, 1973.

James, George P. R. *Memoirs of Celebrated Women.* Philadelphia: E. L. Carey & A. Hart, 1839.

James, Henry Field. *Abolitionism Unveiled; or, Its Origin, Progress, and Pernicious Tendency Fully Developed.* Cincinnati: E. Morgan & Sons, 1856.

Jenkins, John Stilwell. *The Heroines of History.* Auburn, N.Y.: Alden & Beardlsey, 1855.

Johnson, Sophia. *The Friendless Orphan. An Affecting Narrative of the Trials and Afflictions of Sophia Johnson.* New York: S. Johnson, 1841.

Joliffe, John. *Chattanooga.* Cincinnati: Wrightson, 1858.

Kirn, John, ed. *Sketch of the Trial of Mary Cole for the Willful Murder of Her Mother, Agnes Thuers.* New Brunswick, N.J.: Printed for the Publisher, 1812.

Knapp, Samuel Lorenzo. *Female Biography; Containing Notices of Distinguished Women, in Different Nations and Ages.* New York: J. Carpenter, 1834.

Kraditor, Aileen S., ed. *Up from the Pedestal: Selected Writings in the History of American Feminism.* Chicago: Quadrangle Books, 1968.

The Lady Lieutenant, a Wonderful Startling Narrative of the Adventures of Miss Madeline Moore. Philadelphia: Barclay, 1862.

Lane, Adeline. *Fearful Adventures in the Pennsylvania Wilds; or, The Startling Narrative of Adeline Lane.* Philadelphia: Barclay & Co., 1857.

Lasser, Carol, and Marlene Deahl Merrill, eds. *Friends and Sisters: Letters between Lucy Stone and Antoinette Brown Blackwell, 1846–1893.* Urbana: University of Illinois Press, 1987.

The Last Words and Dying Speech of Ezra Ross, James Buchanan, and William Brooks. In *Massachusetts Broadsides of the American Revolution*, ed. Mason I. Lowance Jr. and Georgia B. Bumgardner. Amherst: University of Massachusetts Press, 1976.

Lawrence, Catherine S. *Autobiography. Sketch of the Life and Labors of Miss Catherine S. Lawrence.* Albany, N.Y.: Amasa J. Parker, 1893.

Lawson, John D., ed. "Official Report of the Trial of Laura D. Fair." In *American State Trials*, ed. John D. Lawson. Vol. 17. St. Louis: Thomas Law Books, 1936.

———. "The Trial of Bathsheba Spooner . . . for the Murder of Joshua Spooner." Pp. 175–201 in *American State Trials*, ed. John D. Lawson. Vol. 2. St. Louis: Thomas Law Books, 1914.

———. "Trial of Emma Augusta Cunningham, for the Murder of Dr. Harvey Burdell." In *American State Trials*, ed. John D. Lawson. Vol. 5. St. Louis: Thomas Law Books, 1916.

———. "Trial of Henrietta Robinson." In *American State Trials*, ed. John D. Lawson. Vol. 11. St. Louis: Thomas Law Books, 1919.

———. "The Trial of Lucretia Chapman for the Murder of William Chapman." In *American State Trials*, ed. John D. Lawson. Vol. 6. St. Louis: Thomas Law Books, 1916.

Lee, Jarena. *Religious Experience and Journal of Mrs. Jarena Lee, Giving an Account of Her Call to Preach the Gospel.* 1836. Revision, Philadelphia, 1849. Reprinted in Henry Louis Gates Jr., ed. *Spiritual Narratives.* New York: Oxford University Press, 1988.

Lee, Luther. *Woman's Right to Preach the Gospel. A Sermon Preached at the Ordination of the Rev. Antoinette L. Brown . . . Sept., 15, 1853.* Syracuse: Published by the author, 1853.

The Life and Confession of Charles O'Donnel, Who Was Executed at Morgantown, June 19, 1797, for the Wilful Murder of His Son. Lancaster [Pa.]: W. & R. Dickson, 1797.

Life and Confession of Mrs. Henrietta Robinson. Boston: H. B. Skinner, 1855.

The Life, Career, and Awful Death by the Garote of Margaret C. Waldegrave. New Orleans: A. R. Orton, 1853.

Lippard, George. *New York: Its Upper Ten and Lower Million.* 1853. Reprint, New York: Irvington, 1993.

———. *The Quaker City; or, The Monks of Monk Hall.* 1844. Reprint, New York: Odyssey Press, 1970.

Livermore, Mary. *My Story of the War: A Woman's Narrative of Four Years of Personal Experience as Nurse in the Union Army, and in Relief Work at Home, in Hospitals, in Camps, and at the Front, during the War of the Rebellion.* 1887. Reprint, with an introduction by Nina Silber, New York: Da Capo Press, 1995.

Maccarty, Thaddeus. *The Guilt of Innocent Blood Put Away: A Sermon Preached . . . on the Occasion of the Execution of James Buchanan, William Brooks, Ezra Ross, and Bathshua* [sic] *Spooner.* Worcester, Mass.: Isaiah Thomas & Company, 1778.

McDowall, J. R. *Magdalen Facts.* New York: J. R. McDowall, 1832.

McIntosh, Maria. *Woman in America: Her Work and Her Reward.* New York: D. Appleton, 1850.

Mann, Herman. *The Female Review: or, Memoirs of an American Young Lady.* Dedham [Mass.]: Nathaniel & Benjamin Heaton, 1797.

Mansfield, Edward. *The Legal Rights, Liabilities, and Duties of Women, with an Introductory History of their Legal Condition in the Hebrew, Roman, and Feudal Civil Systems.* Salem, Mass.: J. P. Jewett & Co., 1845.

Martineau, Harriet. *The Martyr Age of the United States.* 1839. Reprint, New York: Arno Press, 1969.

Mather, Cotton. "A Narrative of Hannah Dustan's Notable Deliverance from Captivity." Pp. 161–64 in *Puritans among the Indians: Accounts of Captivity and Redemption, 1676–1724,* ed. Alden Vaughan and Edward Clark. Cambridge, Mass.: Harvard University Press, 1981.

———. *Pillars of Salt: A History of Some Criminals Executed in This Land for Capital Crimes.* In *Pillars of Salt: An Anthology of Early American Criminal Narratives,* ed. Daniel E. Williams. Madison, Wisconsin: Madison House, 1993.

May, Samuel J. *The Rights and Conditions of Women: A Sermon Preached in Syracuse, November 1845.* Syracuse, Lathrop's Print, 1853?. In Library of Congress Pamphlet Collection.

Mayo, Cecilia. *Life and Sufferings of Cecilia Mayo: Founded on Incidents in Real Life.* Boston: M. Aurelius, 1843.

Mitchell, Stephen Mix. *A Narrative of the Life of William Beadle.* Hartford: Bavil Webster, 1783.

M'Keehan, Hattia. *Liberty or Death; or, Heaven's Infraction of the Fugitive Slave Law.* Cincinnati: Hattia M'Keehan, 1858.

Moore, Frank. *Women of the War: Their Heroism and Self-Sacrifice.* Hartford, Conn.: S. S. Scranton, 1866.

Mott, Lucretia. *Discourse on Woman . . . Delivered at the Assembly Buildings, December 17, 1849.* Philadelphia: W. P. Kildare, 1869.

Narrative and Confessions of Lucretia P. Cannon. New York: E. E. Barclay, 1841.

Narrative of the Life, Last Dying Speech, and Confession of John Young. New York: n.p., 1797.

New York Magdalen Society, *First Annual Report of the Executive Committee of the New York Magdalen Society, Instituted January 1, 1830.* New York: Printed for the Society by J. Seymour, 1831.

Orthodox Bubbles; or, A Review of the First Annual Report . . . of the Magdalen Society. Boston: Printed for the Publishers, 1831.

Orton, A. R. [pseud. O. R. Arthur], ed. *The Three Sisters; or, The Life, Confession, and Execution of Amy, Elizabeth, and Cynthia Halzingler.* Baltimore: A. R. Orton, 1855.

Owen, Emily. *The Heroines of History.* New York: Carlton & Phillips, 1854.

P., M. C. *Miriam Rivers, the Lady Soldier; or, General Grant's Spy.* Philadelphia: Barclay, 1865.

Parker, Theodore. *A Sermon on the Public Function of Woman . . . March 27, 1853.* Boston: R. F. Wallcut, 1853.

Parton, James, Thomas Wentworth Higginson, and Horace Greeley. *Eminent Women of the Age: Being Narratives of the Lives and Deeds of the Most Prominent Women of the Present Generation.* Hartford, Conn.: S. M. Betts, 1868.

Paul, Almira. *The Surprising Adventures of Almira Paul.* Boston: N. Coverly Jr., 1816.

"Pension Application for S. E. E. Seelye." *House Report 820.* 48th Congress, 1st Session (Washington, D.C., 1884).

Peterson, Charles J. *Kate Aylesford: A Story of the Refugees.* Philadelphia: T. B. Peterson, 1855.

———. *The Old Stone Mansion.* Philadelphia: T. B. Peterson, 1859.

The Phantasmagoria of New York, a Poetical Burlesque upon a Certain Libellous Pamphlet, Written by a Committee of Notorious Fanatics, Entitled the Magdalen Report. New York: n.p., n.d. [1831?].

The Pirate's Bride; or, The Wonderful Adventures of Miss Cordelia Thompson. Richmond, Va.: Barclay & Co., [185?].

Plato, Ann. *Essays: Including Biographies and Miscellaneous Pieces, in Prose and Poetry.* 1841. Reprint, New York: Oxford University Press, 1988.

The Private History and Confession of Pamela Lee. Pittsburgh: Lucas Grant, 1852.

Proceedings of the Anti-Slavery Convention of American Women Held in the City of New York, May 9th, 10th, 11th, and 12th, 1837. New York: W.S. Dorr, 1837.

Proceedings of the National Woman's Rights Convention. Cleveland: Grey, Beardsley, Spear & Co, 1853–1866.

Proceedings of the Ninth National Woman's Rights Convention, Held in New York City . . . May 12, 1859. Rochester, N.Y.: A. Strong, 1859.

Proceedings of the Woman's Rights Convention Held at Akron, Ohio, May 28th and 29th, 1851. 1851. Reprint, New York: Burt Franklin, 1973.

Proceedings of the Woman's Rights Convention Held at Cleveland, Ohio . . . October 5th, 6th, and 7th, 1853. Cleveland: Gray, Beardsley, Spear, 1854.

Proceedings of the Woman's Rights Convention Held at Syracuse, September 8th, 9th, and 10th, 1852. Syracuse: J. E. Masters, 1852.

Proceedings of the Woman's Rights Convention Held at the Broadway Tabernacle in the City of New York . . . September 6th and 7th, 1853. New York: Fowler & Wells, 1853.

Proceedings of the Woman's Rights Convention Held at the Unitarian Church, Rochester, N.Y., August 2, 1848 . . . Revised by Amy Post. New York: R.J. Johnston, 1870.

Proceedings of the Woman's Rights Convention Held at West Chester, Pa., June 2d and 3d, 1852. Philadelphia: n.p., 1852.

Proceedings of the Woman's Rights Convention Held at Worcester, October 15th and 16th, 1851. New York: Fowler & Wells, 1852.

Proceedings of the Woman's Rights Convention Held at Worcester, October 23rd and 24th, 1850. Boston: Prentiss & Sawyer, 1851.

The Public Years of Sarah and Angelina Grimké: Selected Writings, 1835–1839. Edited and annotated by Larry Ceplair. New York: Columbia University Press, 1989.

Report of the Woman's Rights Convention Held at Seneca Falls, N.Y., July 19th and 20th, 1848. Rochester, N.Y.: Printed at the *North Star* Office, 1848.

Report of the Woman's Rights Meeting at Mercantile Hall, May 27, 1859. Boston: S. Urbino, 1859.

Reports on the Laws of New England, Presented to the New England Meeting Convened at the Meionaon, September 19 and 20, 1855. Boston: n.p., 1855.

Reynolds, W. D. *Miss Martha Brownlow; or, The Heroine of the Tennessee.* Philadelphia: Barclay & Co., 1863.

Rogers, Nathaniel P. *An Address Delivered before the Concord Female Anti-Slavery Society at Its Annual Meeting, 25 December 1837.* Concord, N.H.: W. White, 1838.

Ropes, Hannah Anderson. *Civil War Nurse: The Diary and Letters of Hannah Ropes.* Edited and with an introduction by John R. Brumgardt. Knoxville: University of Tennessee Press, 1980.

———. *Cranston House: A Novel.* Boston: O. Clapp, 1859.

———. *Six Months in Kansas, by a Lady.* 1856. Reprint, Freeport, N.Y.: Books for Libraries Press, 1972.

Rose, Ernestine. *An Address on Woman's Rights . . . October 19th, 1851.* Boston: J. P. Mendum, 1851.

Russo, Ann, and Cheris Kramarae, eds. *The Radical Women's Press of the 1850s.* New York: Routledge, 1991.

Sanger, William W. *History of Prostitution: Its Extent, Causes, and Effects throughout the World.* New York: Harper & Brothers, 1859.

Sarmiento, Ferdinand L. *Life of Pauline Cushman.* Philadelphia: John E. Potter, 1865.

Scruggs, Lawson Andrew. *Women of Distinction: Remarkable in Works and Invincible in Character.* Raleigh, N.C.: L. A. Scruggs, 1893.

Sedgwick, Catharine Maria. *Hope Leslie, or Early Times in the Massachusetts.* With an introduction by Mary Kelley. New Brunswick, N.J.: Rutgers University Press, 1987.

———. *The Linwoods; or, "Sixty Years Since" in America.* 1835. Reprint, Hanover, N.H.: University Press of New England, 2002.

———. *A New-England Tale; or, Sketches of New England Character and Manners.* New York: Oxford University Press, 1995.

Sherwood, Amelia. *Amelia Sherwood; or, Bloody Scenes at the California Gold Mines.* Richmond, Va.: Barclay & Co., 1850.

Siddons, Leonora. *The Female Warrior. An Interesting Narrative of the Sufferings, and Singular and Surprising Adventures of Miss Leonora Siddons.* New York: E. E. & G. Barclay, 1843.

Sigourney, Lydia. *Great and Good Women: Biographies for Girls.* Edinburgh: W. P. Nimmo, 1871 [1866].

Sketches of the Lives of Distinguished Females, Written for Girls, with a View to Their Mental and Moral Improvement, by an American Lady. New York: J. & J. Harper, 1833.

Smith, Daniel D. *Lectures on Domestic Duties.* Portland, Maine: S. H. Colesworthy, 1837.

Southworth, E. D. E. N. *The Hidden Hand; or, Capitola the Madcap.* With an introduction by Joanne Dobson. 1859. Reprint, New Brunswick, N.J.: Rutgers University Press, 1988.

Stanton, Elizabeth Cady. *Address to the Legislature of New York, Adopted by the State Woman's Rights Convention, Held at Albany . . . February 14 and 15, 1854.* Albany, N.Y.: Weed, Parsons & Co., 1854.

———. *Eighty Years and More: Reminiscences, 1815–1897.* 1898. Reprint, with an introduction by Gail Parker, New York: Schocken Books, 1971.

Stanton, Elizabeth Cady, Susan B. Anthony, and Matilda Joslyn Gage, eds. *History of Woman Suffrage.* Vol. 1. New York: Fowler & Wells, 1881.

Stark, Cordelia. *The Female Wanderer, an Interesting Tale, Founded on Fact.* N.p., 1824.

Starling, Elizabeth. *Noble Deeds of Woman; or, Examples of Female Courage and Virtue.* Boston: Phillips, Sampson & Co., 1850.

Stephens, Ann S. *Address to the Women of the United States.* Washington, D.C.: Gibson Brothers, 1864.

———. *Malaeska, the Indian Wife of the White Hunter,* with an introduction by Frank P. O'Brien. 1860. Reprint, New York: The John Day Company, 1929.

Sterns, Jonathan. *Rev. Mr. Sterns' Discourse on Female Influence, and the True Christian Mode of Its Exercise.* Newburyport, Mass.: John G. Tilton, 1837.

Stewart, Maria W. *Maria W. Stewart: America's First Black Woman Political Writer.* Edited by Marilyn Richardson. Bloomington: Indiana University Press, 1987.

———. *Productions of Mrs Maria W. Stewart, Presented to the First African Baptist Church and Society of the City of Boston.* Reprinted in Henry Louis Gates Jr., ed. *Spiritual Narratives.* New York: Oxford University Press, 1988.

Stillé, Charles J. *History of the United States Sanitary Commission, Being the General Report of Its Work during the War of the Rebellion.* Philadelphia: J. B. Lippincott & Co., 1866.

Stowe, Harriet Beecher. *Bible Heroines.* New York: Fords, Howard & Hulbert, 1878.

———. *Our Famous Women.* Hartford: A. D. Worthington, 1883.

———. *Uncle Tom's Cabin.* 1851–1852. Reprint, New York: Bantam, 1981.

———. *Woman in Sacred History.* New York: J. B. Ford & Co., 1874.

Strong, Nathan. *A Sermon Preached in Hartford . . . at the Execution of Richard Doane.* Hartford [Conn.]: Elisha Babcock, 1797.

Sunderland, Byron. *Discourse to Young Ladies: A Sermon by Rev. Byron Sunderland, Pastor of the First Presbyterian Church, . . . Delivered the 22nd Day of January, 1857.* Washington, D.C.: C. Wendell, 1857.

Swint, Henry Lee, ed. *Dear Ones at Home: Letters from Contraband Camps.* Nashville: Vanderbilt University Press, 1996.

Taylor, Bayard. *Hannah Thurston: A Story of American Life.* New York: G. P. Putnam, 1863.

Thompson, George. *The Countess; or, Memoirs of Women of Leisure.* Boston: Berry & Wright, 1849.

Tocqueville, Alexis de. *Democracy in America.* Edited by Richard D. Heffner. New York: Mentor, 1956.

Trial and Conviction of Eliza Dawson. Halifax, Nova Scotia: J. B. Finnerty, 1850.

Trial, Conviction, and Confession of Mary Thorn. Norfolk, Va.: William C. Murdock, 1854.

Truth, Sojourner. *Narrative of Sojourner Truth.* With an introduction by Jeffrey C. Stewart. New York: Oxford University Press, 1988.

Tuckerman, Joseph. *An Essay on the Wages Paid to Females for Their Labour.* Philadelphia, 1830. Reprinted in *Low Wages and Great Sins: Two Antebellum Views on Prostitution and the Working-Girl,* ed. David Rothman and Sheila Rothman. New York: Garland, 1987.

Velazquez, Loreta Janeta. *The Woman in Battle: A Narrative of the Exploits, Adventures, and Travels of Madame Loreta Janeta Velazquez.* Edited by C. J. Worthington. 1876. Reprint, New York: Arno Press, 1972.

Wakeman, Sarah Rosetta. *An Uncommon Soldier: The Civil War Letters of Sarah Rosetta Wakeman.* Edited by Lauren Burgess Cook. Pasadena, Md.: Minerva Center, 1994.

Walters, Ann. *Life and Confession of Ann Walters, the Murderess.* Boston: Printed for the Proprietor, 1850.

Wardlaw, Ralph. *Lectures on Magdalenism: Its Nature, Extent, Effects, Guilt, Causes, and Remedy.* New York: Redfield, 1843.

Warner, Susan. *Queechy.* New York: Putnam, 1852.

Watkins, Frances Ellen. *Poems on Miscellaneous Subjects.* Boston: J. B. Yerrington & Son, 1854.

Weld, Theodore, ed. *American Slavery as It Is: Testimony of a Thousand Witnesses.* New York: American Anti-Slavery Society, 1839.

Willard, Frances. *American Women: Fifteen Hundred Biographies.* New York: Mast, Crowell & Kirkpatrick, 1897.

Williams, Daniel E., ed. *Pillars of Salt: An Anthology of Early American Criminal Narratives.* Madison, Wisconsin: Madison House, 1993.

Wilson, D. *Henrietta Robinson.* New York: Miller, Orton & Mulligan, 1855.

Wilson, Harriet E. *Our Nig; or, Sketches from the Life of a Free Black.* Edited and with an introduction by Henry Louis Gates Jr. New York: Random House, 1983.

Winslow, Hubbard. *Woman as She Should Be and Woman in Her Social and Domestic Character.* Boston: T. H. Carter, 1838.

Wright, Tobias, ed. *Collections of the New York Genealogical and Biographical Society.* Vol. 4. *Staten Island Church Records.* New York: Printed for the Society, 1909.

Selected Secondary Sources

Admari, Ralph. "Ballou, the Father of the Dime Novel." *American Book Collector* 4, no. 128 (1933): 121–29.

Altschuler, Glenn, and Jan Saltzgaber, eds. *Revivalism, Social Conscience, and Community in the Burned-Over District: The Trial of Rhoda Bement.* Ithaca, N.Y.: Cornell University Press, 1983.

Arnold, Marybeth Hamilton. "The Life of a Citizen in the Hands of a Woman." In *Passion and Power: Sexuality in History*, ed. Kathy Peiss and Christina Simmons. Philadelphia: Temple University Press, 1989.

Attie, Jeanie. *Patriotic Toil: Northern Women and the American Civil War.* Ithaca, N.Y.: Cornell University Press, 1998.

———. "Warwork and the Crisis of Domesticity in the North." In *Divided Houses: Gender and the Civil War*, ed. Catherine Clinton and Nina Silber. New York: Oxford University Press, 1992.

Baraka, Imamu Amiri. *Blues People: Negro Music in White America.* 1963. Reprint, New York: Quill, 1999.

Barnes, Gilbert. *The Anti-Slavery Impulse: 1830–1844.* New York: Appleton-Century, 1933.

Basch, Norma. *In the Eyes of the Law: Women, Marriage, and Property in Nineteenth-Century New York.* Ithaca, N.Y.: Cornell University Press, 1982.

Baym, Nina. *American Women Writers and the Work of History, 1790–1860.* New Brunswick, N.J.: Rutgers University Press, 1995.

———. *Woman's Fiction: A Guide to Novels by and about Women, 1820–1870.* Ithaca, N.Y.: Cornell University Press, 1978.

———. "Women and the Republic: Emma Willard's Rhetoric of History." *American Quarterly* 43, no. 1 (1991): 1–23.

Berthoff, Roland. "Conventional Mentality: Free Blacks, Women, and Business Corporations as Unequal Persons, 1820–1870." *Journal of American History* 76 (1989): 753–84.

Bethel, Elizabeth Raul. *The Roots of African American Identity: Memory and History in Antebellum Free Communities.* New York: St. Martin's Press, 1997.

Birney, Catherine. *The Grimké Sisters: Sarah and Angelina Grimké, the First Women Advocates of Abolition and Woman's Rights.* Boston: Lee & Shepard, 1885.

Blackwell, Alice Stone. *Lucy Stone: Pioneer of Woman's Rights.* Boston: Little, Brown & Co., 1930.

Blewett, Mary. *Men, Women, and Work: Class, Gender, and Protest in the New England Shoe Industry, 1780–1910.* Urbana: University of Illinois Press, 1988.

Bloch, Ruth. "The Gendered Meanings of Virtue in Revolutionary America." *Signs* 13, no. 1 (1987): 37–58.

Blumin, Stuart. *The Emergence of the Middle Class: Social Experience in the American City, 1760–1900.* New York: Cambridge University Press, 1989.

Boydston, Jeanne. *Home and Work: Housework, Wages, and the Ideology of Labor in the Early Republic.* New York: Oxford University Press, 1990.

Boydston, Jeanne, Mary Kelley, and Anne Margolis, eds. *The Limits of Sisterhood: The Beecher Sisters on Women's Rights and Woman's Sphere*. Chapel Hill: University of North Carolina Press, 1988.

Brekus, Catherine A. "Let Your Women Keep Silence in the Churches: Female Preaching and Evangelical Religion in America, 1740–1845." Ph.D. diss., Yale University, 1993.

Browder, Clifford. *The Wickedest Woman in New York: Madame Restell, the Abortionist*. Hamden, Conn.: Archon, 1988.

Brumgardt, John R. "Introduction." In Hannah Anderson Ropes, *Civil War Nurse: The Diary and Letters of Hannah Ropes*. Edited by John Brumgardt. Knoxville: University of Tennessee Press, 1980.

Campbell, Karlyn Kohrs, ed. *Women Public Speakers in the United States, 1800–1925: A Bio-Critical Sourcebook*. Westport, Conn.: Greenwood Press, 1993.

Carby, Hazel. *Reconstructing Womanhood: The Emergence of the Afro-American Woman Novelist*. New York: Oxford University Press, 1987.

Carlson, Douglas. "'Drinks He to His Own Undoing': Temperance Ideology in the Deep South." *Journal of the Early Republic* 18, no. 4 (1998): 659–91.

Clinton, Catherine, and Nina Silber, eds. *Divided Houses: Gender and the Civil War*. New York: Oxford University Press, 1992.

Cohen, Daniel. *Pillars of Salt, Monuments of Grace: New England Crime Literature and the Origins of American Popular Culture, 1674–1860*. New York: Oxford University Press, 1993.

Cohen, Patricia Cline. *The Murder of Helen Jewett: The Life and Death of a Prostitute in Nineteenth-Century New York*. New York: Vintage, 1999.

———. "Unregulated Youth: Masculinity and Murder in the 1830s City." *Radical History Review* 52 (1992): 33–52.

Cook, Lauren Burgess. "Introduction." In *An Uncommon Soldier: The Civil War Letters of Sarah Rosetta Wakeman*. Pasadena, Md.: Minerva Center, 1994.

Cott, Nancy. *The Bonds of Womanhood: 'Woman's Sphere' in New England, 1780–1835*. New Haven, Conn.: Yale University Press, 1977.

———. *The Grounding of Modern Feminism*. New Haven, Conn.: Yale University Press, 1987.

———. "Passionlessness: An Interpretation of Victorian Sexual Ideology, 1790–1850." Pp. 162–81 in *A Heritage of Her Own: Toward a New Social History of American Women*, ed. Nancy Cott and Elizabeth Pleck. New York: Simon & Schuster, 1979.

Cross, Whitney R. *The Burned-Over District: The Social and Intellectual History of Enthusiastic Religion in Western New York, 1800–1850*. Ithaca, N.Y.: Cornell University Press, 1950.

Cunningham, John T. ed. *Murder Did Pay: Nineteenth-Century New Jersey Murders*. Newark: New Jersey Historical Society, 1982.

Dannett, Sylvia G. *She Rode with the Generals: The True and Incredible Story of Sarah Emma Seelye, alias Frank Thompson*. New York: Nelson, 1960.

Davidson, Cathy. *Revolution and the Word: The Rise of the Novel in America*. New York: Oxford University Press, 1986.

Davis, David Brion. *Homicide in American Fiction, 1798–1860: A Study in Social Values.* Ithaca, N.Y.: Cornell University Press, 1957.

D'Emilio, John, and Estelle Freedman. *Intimate Matters: A History of Sexuality in America.* New York: Perennial Library, 1988.

Denfeld, Rene. *The New Victorians: A Young Woman's Challenge to the Old Feminist Order.* New York: Warner Books, 1995.

Dobson, Joanne. "The Hidden Hand: Subversion of Cultural Ideology in Three Mid-Nineteenth-Century American Women's Novels." *American Quarterly* 38, no. 2 (1986): 223–42.

Douglas, Ann. *The Feminization of American Culture.* New York: Avon, 1977.

DuBois, Ellen. *Harriot Stanton Blatch and the Winning of Woman Suffrage.* New Haven, Conn.: Yale University Press, 1997.

Dugaw, Dianne. *Warrior Women and Popular Balladry, 1600–1850.* Cambridge: Cambridge University Press, 1989.

Edwards, Rebecca. *Angels in the Machinery: Gender in American Party Politics from the Civil War to the Progressive Era.* New York: Oxford University Press, 1997.

Elshtain, Jean Bethke. *Jane Addams and the Dream of American Democracy: A Life.* New York: Basic Books, 2002.

Fahs, Alice. *The Imagined Civil War: Popular Literature of the North and South, 1861–1865.* Chapel Hill: University of North Carolina Press, 2001.

Faust, Drew Gilpin. "Introduction." In Augusta J. Evans, *Macaria; or, The Altars of Sacrifice.* Baton Rouge: Louisiana State University Press, 1992.

———. *Mothers of Invention: Women of the Slaveholding South in the Civil War.* Chapel Hill: University of North Carolina Press, 1996.

Feldman, Michael. "Women and Guerrilla Warfare." In *Divided Houses: Gender and the Civil War,* ed. Catherine Clinton and Nina Silber. New York: Oxford University Press, 1992.

Ferguson, Robert A. *Law and Letters in American Culture.* Cambridge, Mass.: Harvard University Press, 1984.

Fladeland, Betty. "Alias Frank Thompson." *Michigan History* 42, no. 3 (1958): 435–62.

———. "New Light on Sarah E. Edmonds." *Michigan History* 49, no. 4 (1963): 357–62.

Flexner, Eleanor. *A Century of Struggle: The Women's Rights Movement in the United States.* Cambridge, Mass.: Harvard University Press, 1959.

Foreman, F. Gabriella. "Manifest in Signs: The Politics of Sex and Representation in Incidents in the Life of a Slave Girl." In *Harriet Jacobs and Incidents in the Life of a Slave Girl.* New York: Cambridge University Press, 1996.

Fox-Genovese, Elizabeth. *"Feminism Is Not the Story of My Life": How Today's Feminist Elite Has Lost Touch with the Real Concerns of Women.* New York: Doubleday, 1996.

Garfield, Deborah, and Rafia Zafar, eds. *Harriet Jacobs and Incidents in the Life of a Slave Girl.* New York: Cambridge University Press, 1996.

Garrison, Dee. "Immoral Fiction in the Late Victorian Library." *American Quarterly* 28 (spring 1976): 71–89.

Gates, Henry Louis, Jr. "Introduction." In Harriet E. Wilson, *Our Nig; or Sketches from the Life of a Free Black.* 1859. Reprint, edited by Henry Louis Gates Jr., New York:

Random House, 1983.

Gaustad, Edwin. *The Great Awakening in New England*. New York: Harper, 1957.

Gibson, Donald. "Harriet Jacobs, Frederick Douglass, and the Slavery Debate: Bondage, Family, and the Discourse of Domesticity." Pp. 156–78 in *Harriet Jacobs and Incidents in the Life of a Slave Girl*, ed. Deborah Garfield and Rafia Zafar. New York: Cambridge University Press, 1996.

Giddings, Paula. *When and Where I Enter: The Impact of Black Women on Race and Sex in America*. 1984. Reprint, New York: Bantam, 1996.

Giesberg, Judith Ann. *Civil War Sisterhood: The U.S. Sanitary Commission and Women's Politics in Transition*. Boston: Northeastern University Press, 2000.

Gilfoyle, Timothy. *City of Eros: New York City, Prostitution, and the Commercialization of Sex, 1790–1920*. New York: W. W. Norton, 1992.

Gilligan, Carol. *In a Different Voice: Psychological Theory and Women's Development*. Cambridge, Mass.: Harvard University Press, 1982.

Ginzberg, Lori. "'The Hearts of Your Readers Will Shudder': Fanny Wright, Infidelity, and American Freethought." *American Quarterly* 46, no. 2 (1994): 195–226.

———. *Women and the Work of Benevolence: Morality, Politics, and Class in the Nineteenth-Century United States*. New Haven, Conn.: Yale University Press, 1990.

Griffin, Clifford. *Their Brothers' Keepers: Moral Stewardship in the United States*. New Brunswick, N.J.: Rutgers University Press, 1960.

Gunning, Sandra. "Reading and Redemption in Incidents in the Life of a Slave Girl." In *Harriet Jacobs and Incidents in the Life of a Slave Girl*, ed. Deborah Garfield and Rafia Zafar. New York: Cambridge University Press, 1996.

Gustafson, Melanie Susan. *Women and the Republican Party, 1854–1924*. Urbana: University of Illinois Press, 2001.

Hall, Richard. *Patriots in Disguise: Women Warriors of the Civil War*. New York: Paragon House, 1993.

Halttunen, Karen. *Confidence Men and Painted Women: A Study of Middle-Class Culture in America, 1830–1870*. New Haven, Conn.: Yale University Press, 1982.

———. "Early American Murder Narratives: The Birth of Horror." In *The Power of Culture: Critical Essays in American History*, ed. Richard Wrightman Fox and T. J. Jackson Lears. Chicago: University of Chicago Press, 1993.

———. *Murder Most Foul: The Killer and the American Gothic Imagination*. Cambridge, Mass.: Harvard University Press, 1998.

Hansen, Debra Gold. *Strained Sisterhood: Gender, Class, and Conflict in the Boston Female Anti-Slavery Society, 1833–1840*. Amherst: University of Massachusetts Press, 1993.

Hansen, Karen V. *A Very Social Time: Crafting Community in Antebellum New England*. Berkeley: University of California Press, 1994.

Harris, Leslie M. *In the Shadow of Slavery: African Americans in New York City, 1626–1863*. Chicago: University of Chicago Press, 2003.

Hartman, Mary. *Victorian Murderesses: A True History of Thirteen Respectable French and English Women Accused of Unspeakable Crimes*. New York: Schocken, 1977.

Hersh, Blanche Glassman. *The Slavery of Sex: Feminist-Abolitionists in America*. Urbana:

University of Illinois Press, 1978.

Hessinger, Rodney. "Victim of Seduction or Vicious Woman? Conceptions of the Prostitute at the Philadelphia Magdalen Society, 1800–1850." *Pennsylvania History* 66 (1999): 201–17.

Hewitt, Nancy. "Beyond the Search for Sisterhood: American Women's History in the 1980s." *Social History* 10 (October 1985): 299–321.

———. "Feminist Friends: Agrarian Quakers and the Emergence of Woman's Rights in America." *Feminist Studies* 12 (spring 1986): 27–49.

———. *Women's Activism and Social Change: Rochester, New York, 1822–1872.* Ithaca, N.Y.: Cornell University Press, 1984.

Hill, Marilynn Wood. *Their Sisters' Keepers: Prostitution in New York City, 1830–1870.* Berkeley: University of California Press, 1993.

Hoffert, Sylvia D. "Jane Grey Swisshelm, Elizabeth Keckley, and the Significance of Race Consciousness in American Women's History." *Journal of Women's History* 13, no. 3 (2001): 8–33.

———. *When Hens Crow: The Woman's Rights Movement in Antebellum America.* Bloomington: Indiana University Press, 1995.

Horsman, Reginald. *Race and Manifest Destiny: The Origins of Racial Anglo-Saxonism.* Cambridge, Mass.: Harvard University Press, 1981.

Horton, James Oliver. *Free People of Color: Inside the African American Community.* Washington, D.C.: Smithsonian Institution Press, 1993.

———. "Freedom's Yoke: Gender Conventions among Antebellum Free Blacks." *Feminist Studies* 12, no. 1 (1986): 51–76.

Horton, James Oliver, and Lois E. Horton. *In Hope of Liberty: Culture, Community, and Protest among Northern Free Blacks, 1700–1860.* New York: Oxford University Press, 1997.

Hutton, Frankie. *The Early Black Press in America, 1827–1860.* Westport, Conn.: Greenwood Press, 1993.

Isenberg, Nancy. *Sex and Citizenship in Antebellum America.* Chapel Hill: University of North Carolina Press, 1998.

Jeffrey, Julie Roy. *The Great Silent Army of Abolitionism: Ordinary Women in the Antislavery Movement.* Chapel Hill: University of North Carolina Press, 1998.

Jehlen, Myra. "The Family Militant: Domesticity versus Slavery in Uncle Tom's Cabin." *Criticism* 31, no. 4 (1989): 383–400.

———. "The Novel and the Middle Class in America." In *Ideology and Classic American Literature*, ed. Sacvan Bercovitch and Myra Jehlen. New York: Cambridge University Press, 1986.

Johnson, Paul. *A Shopkeeper's Millennium: Society and Revivals in Rochester, New York, 1815–1837.* New York: Hill & Wang, 1978.

Jones, Ann. *Women Who Kill.* New York: Holt, Reinhart, & Winston, 1980.

Jordan, Winthrop. *White over Black: American Attitudes toward the Negro, 1550–1812.* New York: Norton, 1968.

Keetley, Dawn. "Victim and Victimizer: Female Fiends and Unease over Marriage in Sensational Fiction." *American Quarterly* 51, no. 2 (1999): 344–84.

Kelley, Mary. "Designing a Past for the Present: Women Writing Women's History in Nineteenth-Century America." *Proceedings of the American Antiquarian Society* 105, part 2 (1995): 315–46.

———. "Introduction." In Catharine Maria Sedgwick, *Hope Leslie; or, Early Times in the Massachusetts.* New Brunswick, N.J.: Rutgers University Press, 1987.

———. *Private Woman, Public Stage: Literary Domesticity in Nineteenth-Century America.* New York: Oxford University Press, 1984.

———. "The Sentimentalists: The Promise and Betrayal of the Home." *Signs* 4, no. 3 (1979): 434–46.

Kelly, Catherine E. *In the New England Fashion: Reshaping Women's Lives in the Nineteenth Century.* Ithaca, N.Y.: Cornell University Press, 1999.

Kerber, Linda. *No Constitutional Right to Be Ladies: Women and the Obligations of Citizenship.* New York: Hill & Wang, 1998.

———. "Separate Spheres, Female Worlds, Woman's Place: The Rhetoric of Women's History." *Journal of American History* 75 (1988): 9–39.

———. *Women of the Republic: Intellect and Ideology in Revolutionary America.* New York: Norton, 1980.

Kessler-Harris, Alice. *Out to Work: A History of Wage-Earning Women in the United States.* New York: Oxford University Press, 1982.

LaBrew, Arthur R. *The Black Swan: Elizabeth T. Greenfield, Songstress: Biographical Study.* Detroit: n.p., 1969.

Lawes, Carolyn. *Women and Reform in a New England Community, 1815–1860.* Lexington: University of Kentucky Press, 2000.

Lebsock, Suzanne. *Free Women of Petersburg: Status and Culture in a Southern Town.* New York: W. W. Norton, 1985.

Leng, Charles W., and William T. Davis. *Staten Island and Its People, 1609–1929.* Vol. 1. New York: Lewis Historical Publishing Company, 1930.

Leonard, Elizabeth. *All The Daring of a Soldier: Women of the Civil War Armies.* New York: Norton, 1999.

———. "Civil War Nurse, Civil War Nursing: Rebecca Usher of Maine." *Civil War History* 41 (1995): 190–207.

———. *Yankee Women: Gender Battles and the Civil War.* New York: W. W. Norton, 1994.

Lerner, Gerda. *The Grimké Sisters from South Carolina: Pioneers for Woman's Rights and Abolition.* New York: Schocken, 1971.

———. "The Lady and the Mill Girl: Changes in the Status of Women in the Age of Jackson." *Midcontinent American Studies Journal* 10 (1969): 5–15.

Lewis, David Levering. *When Harlem Was in Vogue.* New York: Oxford University Press, 1979.

Lewis, Jan. "The Republican Wife." *William and Mary Quarterly* 44 (October 1987): 689–721.

Lindley, Susan Hill. *"You Have Stept Out of Your Place": A History of Women and Religion in America.* Louisville, Kentucky: Westminster John Knox Press, 1996.

McCall, Laura. "'The Reign of Brute Force Is Over': A Content Analysis of *Godey's Lady's Book*, 1830–1860." *Journal of the Early Republic* 9 (summer 1989): 217–36.

McDade, Thomas. *The Annals of Murder: A Bibliography of Books and Pamphlets on American Murders from Colonial Times to 1900.* Norman: University of Oklahoma Press, 1961.

———. "Lurid Literature of the Last Century: The Publications of E. E. Barclay." *Pennsylvania Magazine of History and Biography* 80 (1956): 452–64.

McFeely, William. *Frederick Douglass.* New York: Norton, 1991.

McLaurin, Melton. *Celia, a Slave.* Athens: University of Georgia Press, 1991.

McPherson, James. *Battle Cry of Freedom: The Civil War Era.* 1988. Reprint, New York: Ballantine, 1989.

———. *The Struggle for Black Equality: Abolitionists and the Negro in the Civil War and Reconstruction.* Princeton: Princeton University Press, 1964.

Marszalek, John F. *The Petticoat Affair: Manners, Mutiny, and Sex in Andrew Jackson's White House.* 1997. Reprint, Baton Rouge: Louisiana State University Press, 2000.

Matthews, Glenna. *The Rise of Public Woman: Woman's Power and Woman's Place in the United States, 1630–1970.* New York: Oxford University Press, 1992.

May, Henry. *The Enlightenment in America.* New York: Oxford University Press, 1976.

Meyer, Donald H. *The Instructed Conscience: The Shaping of the American National Ethic.* Philadelphia: University of Pennsylvania Press, 1972.

———. *The Life of the Mind in America.* New York: Harcourt, Brace & World, 1965.

———. *The New England Mind: From Colony to Province.* Cambridge, Mass.: Harvard University Press, 1953.

Mohr, James. *Abortion in America: The Origins and Evolution of National Policy, 1800–1900.* New York: Oxford University Press, 1978.

Morgan, Edmund. *American Slavery, American Freedom: The Ordeal of Colonial Virginia.* New York: Norton, 1975.

Navas, Deborah. *Murdered by His Wife: An Absorbing Tale of Crime and Punishment in Eighteenth-Century Massachusetts.* Amherst: University of Massachusetts Press, 1999.

Norton, Mary Beth. *Founding Mothers and Fathers: Gendered Power and the Forming of American Society.* New York: Alfred A. Knopf, 1996.

———, ed. *Major Problems in American Women's History.* Lexington, Mass.: Heath & Company, 1989.

Oates, Stephen B. *A Woman of Valor: Clara Barton and the Civil War.* New York: Free Press, 1994.

Painter, Nell Irvin. *Sojourner Truth: A Life, a Symbol.* New York: W. W. Norton, 1996.

Papashvily, Helen Waite. *All The Happy Endings: A Study of the Domestic Novel in America, the Women Who Wrote It, the Women Who Read It in the Nineteenth Century.* New York: Harper, 1956.

Parker, Allison. *Purifying America: Women, Cultural Reform, and Pro-Censorship Activism, 1873–1933.* Urbana: University of Illinois Press, 1997.

Pease, Jane H., and William H. Pease. *Ladies, Women, and Wenches: Choice and Constraint in Antebellum Charleston and Boston.* Chapel Hill: University of North Carolina Press, 1990.

Pease, William H., and Jane H. Pease. *Web of Progress: Private Values and Public Styles in*

Boston and Charleston, 1828–1843. New York: Oxford University Press, 1985.

Peiss, Kathy. *Cheap Amusements: Working Women and Leisure in Turn-of-the-Century New York*. Philadelphia: Temple University Press, 1986.

Poovey, Mary. *Uneven Developments: The Ideological Work of Gender in Mid-Victorian England*. Chicago: University of Chicago Press, 1988.

Potter, David. *The Impending Crisis, 1848–1861*. New York: Harper & Row, 1976.

Quarles, Benjamin. *Black Abolitionists*. New York: Da Capo, 1969.

———. *Frederick Douglass*. New York: Atheneum, 1968.

Rabble, George. *Civil Wars: Women and the Crisis of Southern Nationalism*. Urbana: University of Illinois Press, 1989.

Reynolds, David S. *Beneath the American Renaissance: The Subversive Imagination in the Age of Emerson and Melville*. Cambridge, Mass.: Harvard University Press, 1988.

———. *Faith in Fiction: The Emergence of Religious Literature in America*. Cambridge, Mass.: Harvard University Press, 1981.

———. "The Feminization Controversy: Sexual Stereotypes and the Paradoxes of Piety in Nineteenth-Century America." *New England Quarterly* 53, no. 1 (1980): 96–106.

Roberts, Brian E. *American Alchemy: The California Gold Rush and Middle-Class Culture*. Chapel Hill: University of North Carolina Press, 2000.

Rogin, Michael Paul. *Fathers and Children: Andrew Jackson and the Subjugation of the American Indian*. 1975. Reprint, New Brunswick, N.J.: Transaction Publishers, 1991.

Romero, Lora. *Home Fronts: Domesticity and Its Critics in the Antebellum United States*. Durham, N.C.: Duke University Press, 1997.

Rose, Anne C. *Victorian America and the Civil War*. New York: Cambridge University Press, 1992.

Rotundo, E. Anthony. *American Manhood: Transformations in Masculinity from the Revolution to the Modern Era*. New York: Basic Books, 1993.

Royster, Jacqueline Jones. *Traces of a Stream: Literacy and Social Change among African American Women*. Pittsburgh: University of Pittsburgh Press, 2000.

Ryan, Mary. *Cradle of the Middle Class: The Family in Oneida County, New York, 1790–1865*. New York: Cambridge University Press, 1981.

———. *Women in Public: Between Banners and Ballots, 1825–1880*. Baltimore: Johns Hopkins University Press, 1990.

Schultz, Jane. "The Inhospitable Hospital: Gender and Professionalism in Civil War Medicine." *Signs* 17, no. 2 (1992): 363–92.

Showalter, Elaine. "Introduction." In Louisa May Alcott, *Alternative Alcott*. New Brunswick, N.J.: Rutgers University Press, 1988.

Siegel, Adrienne. *The Image of the American City in Popular Literature, 1820–1870*. Port Washington, N.Y.: Kennikat Press, 1981.

Sizer, Lyde Cullen. "Acting Her Part: Northern Women Spies during the American Civil War." In *Divided Houses: Gender and the Civil War*, ed. Catherine Clinton and Nina Silber. New York: Oxford University Press, 1992.

———. "Narratives of Union Army Spies." In *Divided Houses: Gender and the Civil War*, ed. Catherine Clinton and Nina Silber. New York: Oxford University Press, 1992.

———. *The Political Work of Northern Women Writers and the Civil War, 1850–1872.* Chapel Hill: University of North Carolina Press, 2000.

Sklar, Kathryn Kish. *Catharine Beecher: A Study in American Domesticity.* New York: Norton, 1976.

———. *Florence Kelley and the Nation's Work: The Rise of Women's Political Culture, 1830–1900.* New Haven, Conn.: Yale University Press, 1995.

Slotkin, Richard. "Narratives of Negro Crime in New England, 1675–1800." *American Quarterly* 25 (1973): 3–31.

Smith, Henry Nash. *Virgin Land: The American West as Symbol and Myth.* Cambridge, Mass.: Harvard University Press, 1950.

Smith-Rosenberg, Carroll. "The Abortion Movement." In *Disorderly Conduct: Visions of Gender in Victorian America.* New York: Oxford University Press, 1985.

———. "The Beauty, the Beast, and the Militant Woman." Pp. 109–28 in *Disorderly Conduct: Visions of Gender in Victorian America,* by Carroll Smith-Rosenberg. New York: Oxford University Press, 1985.

Sotheby's Important Americana: Furniture and Folk Art, no. 1519, 18 January 1998.

Srebnick, Amy Gilman. *The Mysterious Death of Mary Rogers: Sex and Culture in Nineteenth-Century New York.* New York: Oxford University Press, 1995.

Stanley, Amy Dru, "Home Life and the Morality of the Market." In *The Market Revolution in America: Social, Political, and Religious Expressions, 1800–1880,* ed. Melvyn Stokes and Stephen Conway. Charlottesville: University Press of Virginia, 1996.

Stansell, Christine. *City of Women: Sex and Class in New York, 1789–1860.* Urbana: University of Illinois Press, 1982.

Steinberg, Ted. "Down to Earth: Nature, Agency, and Power in History." *American Historical Review* 107 (June 2002): 798–820.

Sterling, Dorothy. *Ahead of Her Time: Abby Kelley and the Politics of Anti-Slavery.* New York: Norton, 1991.

———, ed. *We Are Your Sisters: Black Women in the Nineteenth Century.* New York: W. W. Norton, 1984.

Stewart, James B. *Holy Warriors: The Abolitionists and American Slavery.* New York: Hill & Wang, 1976.

Stewart, Jeffrey C. "Introduction." In Sojourner Truth, *Narrative of Sojourner Truth,* ed. Henry Louis Gates Jr. New York: Oxford University Press, 1988.

Streitmatter, Rodger. *Raising Her Voice: African-American Women Journalists Who Changed History.* Lexington: University of Kentucky Press, 1994.

Tebbel, John. *A History of Book Publishing in the United States.* Vol. 1. New York: R. R. Bowker Co., 1972.

Tompkins, Jane. *Sensational Designs: The Cultural Work of American Fiction, 1790–1860.* New York: Oxford University Press, 1985.

Ulrich, Laurel Thatcher. *Good Wives: Image and Reality in the Lives of Women in Northern New England, 1650–1750.* New York: Oxford University Press, 1980.

———. *A Midwife's Tale: The Life of Martha Ballard, Based on Her Diary, 1785–1812.* New York: Knopf, 1990.

Varon, Elizabeth. *We Mean to Be Counted: White Women and Politics in Antebellum Virginia.* Chapel Hill: University of North Carolina Press, 1998.

Vicinus, Martha. *Independent Women: Work and Community for Single Women, 1850–1920.* Chicago: University of Chicago Press, 1985.

Vickery, Amanda. "Golden Age to Separate Spheres? A Review of the Categories and Chronology of English Women's History." *Historical Journal* 36, no. 2 (1993): 383–414.

Waterman, William Randall. *Frances Wright.* New York: Columbia University, 1924.

Watson, Harry. *Liberty and Power: The Politics of Jacksonian America.* New York: Noonday Press, 1990.

Weisenburger, Steven. *Modern Medea: A Family Story of Slavery and Child-Murder from the Old South.* New York: Hill & Wang, 1998.

Welter, Barbara. "The Cult of True Womanhood, 1820–1860." *American Quarterly* 16 (1966): 151–74.

White, Deborah Gray. *Ar'n't I a Woman? Female Slaves in the Plantation South.* New York: Norton, 1985.

Whites, LeeAnn. *The Civil War as a Crisis in Gender: Augusta, Georgia, 1860–1890.* Athens: University of Georgia Press, 1995.

Wilentz, Sean. *Chants Democratic: New York City and the Rise of the American Working Class.* New York: Oxford University Press, 1984.

Williams, Daniel E. "'Behold a Tragic Scene Strangely Turned into a Theater of Mercy': The Structure and Significance of Criminal Conversion Narratives in Early New England." *American Quarterly* 38, no. 5 (1986): 827–47.

———. "Introduction." In *Pillars of Salt: An Anthology of Early American Criminal Narratives*, ed. Daniel E. Williams. Madison, Wisconsin: Madison House, 1993.

———, ed. *Pillars of Salt: An Anthology of Early American Criminal Narratives.* Madison, Wisconsin: Madison House, 1993.

Williams, William Appleman. *The Contours of American History.* 1966. Reprint, New York: Norton, 1988.

Wilson, Dorothy Clarke. *Stranger and Traveler: The Story of Dorothea Dix, American Reformer.* Boston: Little, Brown & Co., 1975.

Wood, Ann Douglas. "The War within a War: Women Nurses in the Union Army." *Civil War History* 18 (September 1972): 197–212.

Yee, Shirley. *Black Women Abolitionists: A Study in Activism, 1828–1860.* Knoxville: University of Tennessee Press, 1992.

Yellin, Jean Fagan. *Women and Sisters: The Antislavery Feminists in American Culture.* New Haven, Conn.: Yale University Press, 1989.

Yellin, Jean Fagan, and John C. Van Horne, eds. *The Abolitionist Sisterhood: Women's Political Culture in Antebellum America.* Ithaca, N.Y.: Cornell University Press, 1994.

Young, Elizabeth. *Disarming the Nation: Women's Writing and the American Civil War.* Chicago: University of Chicago Press, 1999.

Index